THE SPY: BASEBALL '98

THE SPY:

BASEBALL '98

GARY GILLETTE AND STUART SHEA

TOTAL SPORTS

NEW YORK, NEW YORK

This book could not have been published without the efforts of many good people at Total Sports, especially John Thorn, Publisher, David Pietrusza, Editor-in-Chief, and Pete Palmer, baseball historian extraordinaire. Additional help above and beyond the call of duty was provided by David W. Smith of Retrosheet. Special thanks to Balliett & Fitzgerald, a splendid partner for editorial production, including editors Larry Burke and John Shostrom.

The book is dedicated to Vicki Gillette and Cecilia Garibay, multi-talented spouses who hit for average with plus power, good range, excellent speed, and outstanding judgment.

Published by Total Sports
445 Park Avenue, 19th Floor
New York, NY 10022

Distributed by Andrews McMeel:
Distribution Center, PO Box 419150
Kansas City, Missouri 64141

Design: Dan Miller Design, New York

Library of Congress Catalog Card Number: 98-84569

ISBN 0-9656949-5-x

Printed in the United States of America

TABLE OF CONTENTS

INTRODUCTION

Welcome to *The Spy: Baseball '98*, Total Sports's first baseball annual. We've put *The Spy* together with one guiding principle in mind: to start intelligent conversations among baseball fans about the game or their favorite team. We've tried our best to offer insights and information that isn't available in other places, hoping to enhance your enjoyment of the National Pastime.

GAME REPORTS

The opening section of the book contains four general essays, including updated information on Fall and Winter League performance for key players and prospects.

TEAM REPORTS

Each team chapter consists of four parts: an essay, sidebars, 1997 Scoreboard information, and 1998 Projections. The only exceptions to this format are for the two new expansion teams, who don't have full sidebar and Scoreboard pages because they didn't play in 1997.

The thirty team chapters are presented in alphabetical order by 1998 division.

SIDEBARS

Interspersed throughout each team essay are six sidebars discussing different aspects of that team's 1997 season. The seventh sidebar for each team is a listing of that team's top prospects as of Spring, 1998. Please note that these prospects were selected because they had a chance to play in the majors in 1998; other top prospects who are at least a year or more away from the big leagues are not shown.

SCOREBOARDS

The team statistics Scoreboards should shed some light on how and why each team finished where it did in '97. The abbreviated Scoreboard leading off each chapter includes various breakdowns of the team's 1997 record. The pre-season consensus line shows the average rank predicted for that team's 1997 finish by published sources.

A full Scoreboard page then follows each team essay and includes the categories listed below.

The **Team Batting/Baserunning** section shows key offensive breakdowns and puts them in the context of league performance. Each statistic is shown in raw form (total or average), its rank in the league, and its percentage above or below the league average. Runs per Game is R/G; Long Hits (LH) shows the combined total of doubles and triples. Production (PRO) is the sum of On-Base Average (OBA) and Slugging Average (SA).

The **Team Pitching/Fielding** section is organized in the same way as Batting/Baserunning section. Opposition Runs is OR; RA/G is Runs Allowed per Game; OOB is Opposition On-Base Average; OSA is Opposition Slugging Average;

The **Batting by Lineup Slot** and by **Defensive Position** are self-explanatory. These breakdowns clearly show each team's lineup strengths and weaknesses.

The final lines show each team's pitching staff performance broken down into starting and relief pitching. Quality Starts are QS; Innings per Start are IPS; Holds are HD; Blown Holds are BHD. Opponents' Production is OPR.

1998 PROJECTIONS

At the end of each team chapter you'll find *The Spy*'s player projections for 1998. Created by Pete Palmer, renowned baseball analyst and co-editor of *Total Baseball*, these take into account myriad important factors: age, career averages, recent performance, position, team, home ballpark, opportunity, and current injuries. If a player has seen little or no playing time in the majors, we also factored in his recent performance in the high minors.

Players were projected based on their teams as of January 5, 1998, and are shown with that team. Free agents as of January 5 are listed starting on page 248.

	Raw	Rank	+/- %		Raw	Rank		Raw	Rank	+/- %		Raw	Rank
	.84	8	-2	HR	176	7	R/G	5.39	3	+9	HR	220	2
	.332	12	-2	LH	300	10	OBA	.358	2	+5	LH	323	6
	.415	10	-3	BB	578	7	SA	.467	2	+9	BB	617	4
	.747	10	-3	SO	1164	13	PRO	.825	2	+7	SO	955	5

	Raw	Rank	+/- %		Raw	Rank		Raw	Rank	+/- %		Raw	Rank
OBA	.332	12	-2	LH	300	10	OBA	.358	2	+5	LH	3
SA	.415	10	-3	BB	578	7	SA	.467	2	+9	BB	6
PRO	.747	10	-3	SO	1164	13	PRO	.825	2	+7	SO	9

PITCHING/FIELDING

	Raw	Rank	+/- %		Raw	Rank		Raw	Rank	+/- %		Raw	Rank
	790	5	-1	BA	.266	5	OR	815	7	+2	BA	.276	10
/G	4.88	5	-1	HR	178	8	RA/G	5.06	7	+3	HR	181	9
B	.334	5	-2	LH	310	7	OOB	.347	11	+2	LH	304	6
A	.424	5	-1	BB	552	7	OSA	.434	10	+1	BB	575	9
	.758	5	-2	SO	982	9	PRO	.781	11	+1	SO	1,036	6

PITCHING/FIELDING

	Raw	Rank	+/- %		Raw	Rank		Raw	Rank	+/- %		Raw	Rank
OR	790	5	-1	BA	.266	5	OR	815	7	+2	BA	.27
RA/G	4.88	5	-1	HR	178	8	RA/G	5.06	7	+3	HR	18
OOB	.334	5	-2	LH	310	7	OOB	.347	11	+2	LH	30
OSA	.424	5	-1	BB	552	7	OSA	.434	10	+1	BB	5
PRO	.758	5	-2	SO	982	9	PRO	.781	11	+1	SO	1,0

BATTING BY LINE-UP SLOTS / BATTING BY LINEUP SLOTS

	R	HR	RBI	BA	OBA	SA
	114	4	45	.266	.331	.349
	110	25	90	.276	.371	.481
	99	27	119	.270	.332	.458
	107	32	116	.272	.369	.488
	96	27	94	.269	.353	.461
	82	31	109	.252	.326	.463
	60	15	65	.221	.307	.359
	69	13	57	.252	.312	.359
	47	2	48	.241	.272	.311

	R	HR	RBI	BA	OBA	SA
1	105	18	82	.263	.329	.413
2	107	9	66	.268	.319	.362
3	119	38	112	.292	.420	.539
4	103	34	107	.278	.353	.505
5	97	38	120	.319	.398	.567
6	87	31	107	.295	.350	.503
7	84	14	73	.285	.357	.426
8	80	22	77	.286	.349	.451
9	86	16	66	.294	.349	.450

BATTING BY LINE-UP SLOTS

	R	HR	RBI	BA	OBA	SA
1	114	4	45	.266	.331	.349
2	110	25	90	.276	.371	.481
3	99	27	119	.270	.332	.458
4	107	32	116	.272	.369	.488
5	96	27	94	.269	.353	.461
6	82	31	109	.252	.326	.463
7	60	15	65	.221	.307	.359
8	69	13	57	.252	.312	.359
9	47	2	48	.241	.272	.311

BATTING BY LINEUP SLOTS

	R	HR	RBI	BA	OBA
1	105	18	82	.263	.329
2	107	9	66	.268	.319
3	119	38	112	.292	.420
4	103	34	107	.278	.353
5	97	38	120	.319	.398
6	87	31	107	.295	.350
7	84	14	73	.285	.357
8	80	22	77	.286	.349
9	86	16	66	.294	.349

GAME REPORTS

TEAM PITCHING

	W-L	CG	QS
ROTATION	58-63	13	75
	60-53	4	70

	W-L	GR	SV	BSV	HD
BULLPEN	21-20	417	42	22	126
BULLPEN	26-22	428	39	15	123
BULLPEN	21-20	417	42	22	126
BULLPEN	26-22	428	39	

	R	HR	RBI	BA	OBA	SA
	56	10	53	.250	.302	.342
C	80	25	99	.317	.353	.517
C	56	10	53	.250	.302	.342
C	80	25	99	.317		

BATTING/BASERUNNING

	Raw	Rank	+/- %		Raw	Rank
	784	8	-2	BA	.258	13
G	4.84	8	-2	HR	176	7
A	.332	12	-2	LH	300	10
	.415	10	-3	BB	578	7
D	.747	10	-3	SO	1164	13

BATTING/BASERUNNING

	Raw	Rank	+/- %		Raw	Rank
R	868	3	+9	BA	.286	3
R/G	5.39	3	+9	HR	220	2
OBA	.358	2	+5	LH	323	6
SA	.467	2	+9	BB	617	4
PRO	.825	2	+7	SO	955	5

BATTING/BASERUNNING

	Raw	Rank	+/- %		Raw	Rank
R	784	8	-2	BA	.258	13
R/G	4.84	8	-2	HR	176	7
OBA	.332	12	-2	LH	300	10
SA	.415	10	-3	BB	578	7
PRO	.747	10	-3	SO	1164	13

BATTING/BASERUNNING

	Raw	Rank	+/- %		Raw	Rank
R	868	3	+9	BA	.2
R/G	5.39	3	+9	HR	2
OBA	.358	2	+5	LH	3
SA	.467	2	+9	BB	
PRO	.825	2	+7	SO	9

PITCHING/FIELDING

	Raw	Rank	+/- %		Raw	Rank		Raw	Rank	+/- %		Raw	Rank
	790	5	-1	BA	.266	5	OR	815	7	+2	BA	.276	10
/G	4.88	5	-1	HR	178	8	RA/G	5.06	7	+3	HR	181	9
B	.334	5	-2	LH	310	7	OOB	.347	11	+2	LH	304	6
A	.424	5	-1	BB	552	7	OSA	.434	10	+1	BB	575	9
D	.758	5	-2	SO	982	9	PRO	.781	11	+1	SO	1,036	6

PITCHING/FIELDING

	Raw	Rank	+/- %		Raw	Rank		Raw	Rank	+/- %		Raw	Rank
OR	790	5	-1	BA	.266	5	OR	815	7	+2	BA	.27
RA/G	4.88	5	-1	HR	178	8	RA/G	5.06	7	+3	HR	18
OOB	.334	5	-2	LH	310	7	OOB	.347	11	+2	LH	30
OSA	.424	5	-1	BB	552	7	OSA	.434	10	+1	BB	5
PRO	.758	5	-2	SO	982	9	PRO	.781	11	+1	SO	1,0

BATTING BY LINE-UP SLOTS

	R	HR	RBI	BA	OBA	SA
	114	4	45	.266	.331	.349
	110	25	90	.276	.371	.481
	99	27	119	.270	.332	.458
	107	32	116	.272	.369	.488
	96	27	94	.269	.353	.461
	82	31	109	.252	.326	.463
	60	15	65	.221	.307	.359
	69	13	57	.252	.312	.359
	47	2	48	.241	.272	.311

BATTING BY LINEUP SLOTS

	R	HR	RBI	BA	OBA	SA
1	105	18	82	.263	.329	.413
2	107	9	66	.268	.319	.362
3	119	38	112	.292	.420	.539
4	103	34	107	.278	.353	.505
5	97	38	120	.319	.398	.567
6	87	31	107	.295	.350	.503
7	84	14	73	.285	.357	.426
8	80	22	77	.286	.349	.451
9	86	16	66	.294	.349	.450

BATTING BY LINE-UP SLOTS

	R	HR	RBI	BA	OBA	SA
1	114	4	45	.266	.331	.349
2	110	25	90	.276	.371	.481
3	99	27	119	.270	.332	.458
4	107	32	116	.272	.369	.488
5	96	27	94	.269	.353	.461
6	82	31	109	.252	.326	.463
7	60	15	65	.221	.307	.359
8	69	13	57	.252	.312	.359
9	47	2	48	.241	.272	.311

BATTING BY LINEUP SLOTS

	R	HR	RBI	BA	OBA
1	105	18	82	.263	.329
2	107	9	66	.268	.319
3	119	38	112	.292	.420
4	103	34	107	.278	.353
5	97	38	120	.319	.398
6	87	31	107	.295	.350
7	84	14	73	.285	.357
8	80	22	77	.286	.349
9	86	16	66	.294	.349

TEAM PITCHING

	W-L	CG	QS	QS%	<6
ROTATION	58-63	13	75	46	36
ROTATION	60-53	4	70	43	31
ROTATION	58-63	13	75	46	36
ROTATION	60-53	4	70		

	W-L	GR	SV	BSV	HD
BULLPEN	21-20	417	42	22	126
BULLPEN	26-22	428	39	15	123
BULLPEN	21-20	417	42	22	126
BULLPEN	26-22	428	39	

	R	HR	RBI	BA	OBA	SA
	56	10	53	.250	.302	.342
C	80	25	99	.317		
C	56	10	53	.250	.302	.342
C	80	25	99	.317		

LOOKING
THE OTHER WAY

3

[FANS, as the umpire walks onto the field:]

Kill the umpire!

Kill the umpire!

Kill the umpire!

Kill the umpire!

Boil the Dirty Rat in Oil!

*Bounce a bottle off his head, leave him on the field
    for dead;*

*Burn the umpire, shoot the umpire, choke the umpire,
    hang the umpire;*

Kill the umpire!

[UMPIRE:]

Please folks, don't hold it against me.

I'm not an umpire because I want to be. It isn't that.

I've had a very unhappy childhood.

When I was a child it drove me wild,

When the other kids wouldn't let me play.

I resolved that there'd come a day,

In the not-so-distant future,

I'd have my revenge!

Well, I went to the devil and I sold him my soul,

And always in my mind was just one goal;

That one fine day I would slap the world's face,

For never having let me play second base.

I'd have my revenge!

Oh, I went to school where they taught me to call

A ball for a strike and a strike for ball.

I learned to be wrong nine times out of ten;

I've shattered my ties with all decent men.

So now I'm an umpire, glad of the chance,

Of singing the tune that will make them all dance.

I rant and I roar and I scream and I shout;

I stand at the plate and I call them all out!

Even DiMaggio himself!

I've had my revenge!

Revenge! Revenge!

Ha ha ha ha ha!!!

—"The Umpire's Song", from the 1940s'
    Brooklyn Baseball Cantata

LOOKING THE OTHER WAY

What follows is the strange-but-true tale of how the 1990s strike zone became disconnected from its definition. It is a tale which touches on what umpires call a strike, what the pitchers want, why the batters don't complain (too much), how the leagues are covertly complicit, and—most importantly—why the high strike has gone the way of afternoon baseball.

While the torrent of complaints about the strike zone is full of sound and fury, it most definitely signifies something very important. The strike zone—how it is defined in the rules, how it is defined on the field, and how it is perceived in the broadcast booth, in the press box, and in the stands—is at the very core of the game. Therefore, changes in the strike zone have very large ripple effects.

GET OFF THE UMPIRES' BACKS

Strange as it seems to say this—for it should be obvious—umpires are people, too. They react, both consciously and subconsciously, to pressure—and they have a hell of a lot more pressure on them in their jobs than most people do.

Major League Baseball, the media, the fans and, to a lesser extent, the players, have tried to blame this whole complex strike zone mess on the men in blue. Major league umpires are union men, represented by the Major League Umpires Association. However, it's pretty hard to blame an organization, so if you really want to point the finger, you need a specific bad guy to demonize. Therefore, MLB has made Umpires Association head Richie Phillips out to be the biggest bad actor in this long-running drama. Phillips has gamely risen to the bait, giving scores of interviews over the years in which he has loudly and longly castigated everyone—the owners, the league presidents, the television cameras, the players, the fans, even the hot dog vendors in the stands. (Okay, not the hot dog vendors, but certainly everyone else.)

Phillips's in-your-face defense of his men, plus the antagonistic relationships that exist between his union, the league offices, and the players' union, make it extremely difficult to effect positive change without name-calling, finger-pointing, or even legal action. The ugly Roberto Alomar spitting incident in 1996 showed just how deep the divisions are between the game's owners, players, and umpires. Who's to blame for the current sorry state of affairs? That's another difficult question, as the roots of the less-than-cordial relations between the umps, their employers, and the players date back to the nineteenth century. As The "Umpire's Song" shows, the men in blue have been favorite whipping boys for a long, long time.

Luckily, however, it's not necessary to figure out why fans have historically bellowed "Kill the umpire" with such great gusto in order to figure out why the strike zone has headed south in the past 15 years.

WRITTEN RULES VS. UNWRITTEN RULES

One of the reasons that union chief Phillips has failed to rouse much support for his troops is that he has never explained why the umps plainly haven't been calling balls and strikes as the rule book said they should. He's never been willing to admit that his men were under intense pressure to conform to a de facto system which was a distortion of the de jure strike zone.

Why? Because then he'd have to admit that the umps weren't enforcing the rules! Of course, the umpires don't enforce many of the other rules in the official rule book, either (we'll get to some examples shortly). Everyone knows it; no one cares. In fact, if the umpires took it upon themselves to enforce certain rules literally, the wailing and gnashing of teeth would be heard from coast to coast. So why should he be afraid to admit that the umps are now interpreting the strike zone in a different way than they used to?

Umpires, executives, managers, coaches, players, and fans all know that there is a whole set of unwritten rules. The game is sometimes the better, and sometimes the worse, for the unwritten rules and unspoken interpretations which prevail. As one would expect, these unwritten interpretations change over time, just as everything else in baseball changes over time.

Here are just a few examples of how the unwritten rules differ from the written code:

•Rule 8.02. Pitchers aren't supposed to throw intentionally at hitters.

While umpires can enforce this rule at any time, they typically only do so when a pitcher retaliates by throwing at an enemy batter after one of his own teammates has been hit. This has the paradoxical effect of letting the first offender

4

go unpunished, thus encouraging retaliation—even if the punishment unfairly falls on the avenging pitcher.

•Rule 6.03. Batters are supposed to stand with both feet inside the batter's box.

Hitters used to get around this by using their spikes to deliberately rub out parts of the chalk lines defining the batter's box. Now, however, this rule has become so widely flouted that grounds crews at almost every ballpark don't even lay down full-length inside or back chalk lines for the batter's box.

•Rule 2.00. Catchers aren't supposed to block home plate if they don't have the ball in their hands.

The current interpretation allows them to do so as long as a throw is on the way to the plate or even if an infielder has the ball and is about to throw it.

•Rule 7.08. Middle infielders are supposed to tag second base while they have the ball in their hand on the double-play pivot.

The wide latitude given has resulted in this colloquially being called the "neighborhood play"—because infielders are allowed to swipe the dirt in the neighborhood of second base and then throw to first. The standard justification is that these infielders would get injured by sliding runners if forced to comply with the rule.

•Rule 7.09. Runners aren't supposed to deliberately interfere with a fielder making the pivot at second.

In fact, a runner who doesn't try to take out the middle infielder with an aggressive slide or roll block on a double play is criticized by his teammates.

•Rule 8.04. Pitchers are supposed to deliver a pitch every 20 seconds if there is no one on base.

This rule is almost never enforced.

•Rule 8.02. Pitchers aren't supposed to "doctor" the ball.

While the frequency of spitballs and Vaseline balls has probably declined in recent years, scuffing the ball is still extremely common, but the guilty parties are almost never exposed or penalized. (Remember Mike Scott? Don Sutton? Rick Reuschel? Joe Niekro? Even Nolan Ryan was known to be scuffing the ball at the end of his career.) The operative unwritten rule is: "It ain't cheating if you don't get caught."

•Rule 6.06. Hitters aren't supposed to "cork" their bats.

While it's harder to tell how many hitters are cheating (as opposed to pitchers), some hitters drill out and illegally fill the center of the bat barrel with cork or other substances, supposedly to get extra power. Unlike scuffballing pitchers, however, the rare hitters found to be corking their bats are always severely punished. The bottom line is that if baseball really wanted to crack down on this sort of cheating, it could. But among the owners, players, and umps there is simply no desire to do so.

•Rule 4.03. First basemen aren't supposed to stand in foul territory when holding a runner on base.

It is technically a balk for any fielder except the catcher to be outside of fair territory—but you never see it called.

•Rule 3.09. Players aren't supposed to fraternize with members of the other team.

Yes, it's true, even if it is never enforced!

Now, it would surely be silly for Phillips to pretend that all of his union members are perfect and for him not to admit that they're reacting in an expectable way to circumstances. Furthermore, Phillips's bombast when responding to criticism doesn't play well on television. But he's not one whit different than the people in charge at 350 Park Avenue (the commissioner's office) or at 12 East 49th Street (the Players Association). If you listen to the owners, all of them are astute businesspeople and pillars of their communities who are being ruined by greedy players. If you listen to the players, all of them are .300 hitters or 20-game winners who give 110% all the time and are grateful for their adoring fans. And all their children are above average, too.

SECRETS AND LIES

One of the biggest reasons for this whole mess is that the leagues will not, and cannot, release their evaluations of individual umpires. Therefore, almost no one outside of the league offices and the umpires' union really has any idea how well any umpire is doing.

Selected television replays to the contrary, you can't tell how good an umpire is from watching a few games. Everyone has good days and bad days on their job; why should the men in blue be any exception? Where you're sitting in the ballpark or watching on TV, the camera angle you see on the replay, as well as several other factors (e.g., the distance of the camera from the play, the speed of the replay)

replay) can bias your judgment about close calls, where a fraction of an inch is all that separates ball from strike or safe from out.

Only systematic evaluation over many games can fairly determine whether an umpire is good at his job. The league office does that, but it can't divulge the results for obvious reasons. Imagine for a second that the league released evaluations of umpires. The players and the fans would never accept an arbiter's judgment on any close pitch or play if he wasn't among the best, leading to chaos on the field. The leagues have to keep all evaluative material confidential as a matter of necessity.

There are some valid criticisms of individual umpires, but generally speaking there are very few bad umpires. And it makes sense, too, when you think about it. There are less than six dozen major league umpires, making them the creme de la creme. If you picked teams from only the best six dozen players in the majors, you'd have teams composed of mostly All Stars. The same applies to the umps.

STRIKE ZONE(S)

One of the anachronisms of baseball in the 1990s is that each league still supervises its own crew of umpires. That historical anomaly is what led to the differing strike-zone interpretations that existed prior to the 1980s, with the NL universally acknowledged as a low-strike league and the AL known as a high-strike league (although in the '90s the two leagues' strike zones have basically been the same).

The definition of a strike has been altered many times in baseball history. Here are the definitions since 1950:

1950-1962: "The strike zone is that space over home plate that is between the batter's armpits and the top of his knees when he assumes his natural stance."

1963-1968: "The strike zone is that space over home plate that is between the top of the batter's shoulders and his knees when he assumes his natural stance. The umpire shall determine the strike zone according to the batter's usual stance when he swings at a pitch."

1969-1987: "The strike zone is that space over home plate that is between the batter's armpits and the top of his knees when he assumes his natural stance. The umpire shall determine the strike zone according to the batter's usual stance when he swings at a pitch."

1988-1996: "The strike zone is that area over home plate the upper limit of that is a horizontal line at the midpoint between the top of the shoulders and the top of the uniform pants, and the lower level is a line at the top of the knees. The strike zone shall be determined from the batter's stance as the batter is prepared to swing at a pitched ball."

In 1997 the lower level of the strike zone was extended to "a line at the hollow beneath the kneecap." This made only a marginal difference, because many umpires in both leagues were already calling those pitches strikes.

Traditionally, NL umpires wore inside-the-shirt chest protectors and called pitches while crouching over the catcher's "inside" shoulder (i.e., between the catcher and the hitter). AL umpires, however, wore outside-the-shirt "balloon" protectors until the 1970s. With this "mattress" hanging in front of them, AL umps stood directly behind the catcher and looked over his head, giving them an excellent view of high pitches but making it much harder to see low ones. As a result of these separate traditions, NL umps called more low strikes and let pitches high according to the rule book strike zone pass for balls.

This difference started to diminish in the 1970s when American League umpires were allowed to choose what kind of chest protector they wanted to wear. Most of them, except the most senior umps, went for the NL-style protector.

Just as in the Senior Circuit, these umps were then getting better looks at low pitches and no-so-good looks at high pitches, and their changed perspective resulted in changing calls on marginal pitches. By the mid-1980s all AL umpires were wearing the inside protector.

Over time, the two leagues' strike zones converged as the de facto strike zone moved permanently downward. This change also happened to coincide with another gradual trend, as most pitchers were abandoning the high fastball (for reasons other than the changing strike zone). After a while, pitchers didn't complain about the loss of the high strike, as more and more of them didn't have the "giddyup" on their fastballs to throw a pitch by good power hitters above the belt.

As more and more young pitchers started throwing the low fastball exclusively, the high fastball became rarer and rarer. And when a pitcher accidentally threw a pitch above the belt, he considered it a mistake and so didn't complain if the umpire called it a ball—assuming that the hitter didn't park it 400 feet away behind the nearest cloud.

At the nether end of the strike zone, it was a different story. Marginal pitches on the knees became extremely important to pitchers who were trying to keep the ball down. Therefore, if the umpire didn't call low strikes, he was in for an afternoon of arguments. (Yes, it's true that arguing balls and strikes is prohibited, but players and managers can, and most certainly do, make their feelings known when they are unhappy with the umpiring.) The net effect was to gradually but relentlessly reinforce a pattern in which borderline pitches at the knees became strikes, and pitches high above the belt became balls, regardless of what the rule book said.

Once the high pitch became rare, it was the hitters' complaints that told umpires that calling high strikes was wrong. Look at it this way: if a hitter expects a chest-high pitch to be a strike, but the ump calls it a ball, he's not going to complain. But if the hitter expects a chest-high pitch to be a ball, and the ump calls it a strike, he and his manager are going to protest the call—vigorously if it's strike three.

Fast-forward to the late 1980s. Overall offense is way up, and everyone (except the hitters) is bitchin' and moanin' about it. The leagues, who supervise the umpires, apparently don't want to do anything about it, despite public statements to the contrary. Then again, the league presidents don't have to stand behind home plate and get abused by irate hitters, pitchers, coaches, managers, and fans, either.

Finally, however, the umpires gave some help to the pitchers on their own. This wasn't a conspiracy in any way, shape, or form, it was merely the natural evolution of the trend toward a lower strike zone and more offense. With all but the very best pitchers continually trying to stay away from hitters' power (which, for most, is thigh-to-belt high and from the middle of the plate inside), and with ERAs going sky-high, pitchers were desperate to get the calls "on the black" (on the outside edge of the plate). And as hitters saw more and more pitches on the outside edge of the plate, and fewer up-and-in pitches, they became very comfortable standing close to the plate or striding into the pitch, where they could extend their arms and hit those outside pitches.

So the pitchers pressured the umps to call strikes on questionable pitches on the outside corner. And many of the umps obliged, since everyone from the owners to the media to the pitchers was braying incessantly about how horrible all these high-scoring games were.

Combine all of this, and some umps soon started giving a couple of inches on the outside edge of the plate to the pitchers. Remember the controversy at the 1993 World Series, when CBS used overhead-camera shots to show just how wide some of the called strikes really were? Phillips loudly protested, saying that the camera angles were very deceptive, but everyone could see what was going on.

It's important to note that the rule book states that it is a strike if any part of the ball passes through any part of the strike zone. That means that the outside edge of a regulation baseball (diameter: 2.9 inches) can be three inches from the plate on a strict-definition strike call. Combine that with a fastball tailing away as it crosses the plate, or with a sharply-breaking slider which snaps out of range, and see if your perspective changes when watching slow-mo replays of many supposedly "bad" calls.

The pitcher-friendly trend has continued since the late '80s, with most umpires now giving a couple of inches of leeway on the outside corner to pitchers. Some umps give 3 to 4 inches; a few give 5 to 6 inches of grace to pitchers with good control.

The effects of such latitude can be seen in Livan Hernandez's three-hit, 15-strikeout performance for Florida against Atlanta in Game 5 of the 1997 NLCS, in which home plate umpire Eric Gregg gave the pitchers 4 to 6 inches on the outside of the plate.

OF VETERAN PITCHERS AND VANISHING FASTBALLS

There is an apocryphal tale told in Detroit about Tigers great Al Kaline and his renowned batting eye. Variations of this story are also told about Ted Williams and other great hitters. Essentially, the story has a rookie catcher complaining to the home plate umpire about his ball/strike calls on Kaline—who, of course, is getting the benefit of the doubt on every close pitch. Finally, the ump leans over the catcher and says, "Son, Mr. Kaline will let you know when a pitch is a strike by swinging at it."

In a fair world, every player would be treated equally, and a wild rookie hurler would get exactly the same calls as a veteran with precise command. But that's not the way the world works in baseball, nor in any other sport, nor anywhere else for that matter. Get real: Does Michael Jordan get a couple of extra steps when he's headed for the hoop? Does Wayne Gretzky get protected from the other team's goons by hockey's zebras?

Veterans, especially veteran stars, have big reputations to uphold, and big egos to match their reputations. If they're struggling and they don't get a marginal call, do you think they're going to blame themselves? Of course not.

The prevalence of aging pitchers has thus become an unexpected factor that contributed to the pressure for low strikes. As all pitchers (except Nolan Ryan) age, they lose velocity but gain experience. If they're both smart and lucky, they're able to compensate for the loss in several ways: better breaking pitches, better changeups, better control, better ability to set up hitters.

But it's suicide to throw above the belt almost any other pitch except a hard fastball! So these veteran pitchers, even if they threw the high fastball earlier in their careers, have to keep their pitches low to succeed. (The only other common pitch that can be thrown above the belt and not necessarily get hammered is the 12-to-6 curveball. The overhand curve, the "rainbow curve" or the "drop" of bygone days, can be effectively thrown high, but that pitch isn't very common anymore.)

The classic high fastball is a "rising" four-seamer, gripped and thrown so that the rotating seams increase turbulence around the ball, giving it higher velocity and more lift. (Of course, it really doesn't rise; it just doesn't drop as much as expected.) When a pitcher wants to throw a low fastball, he uses a two-seam grip designed to keep the low pitch sinking away from the hitter's bat.

Whether a pitcher depends on his two-seam fastball, his sinker, his curve, his slider, his change-up, his split-finger fastball, his forkball, or his palm ball, he is taught to keep that pitch low. Even if a rebellious pitcher could stand the screaming of his pitching coach when he got the ball up, modern hitters would quickly tattoo his butt to the outfield fence.

Throw low strikes. Keep the ball down. This advice has become a veritable mantra of high school coaches, college coaches, professional pitching coaches, and professional managers. Unless you can consistently throw a plus-fastball (92-93 mph on the radar gun), you don't stand a chance if you get that pitch belt-high. Even at that velocity, a good hitter can turn that pitch around and hit a screaming line drive for a base hit or loft a long fly ball for a homer.

Now, when you get into the good fastball neighborhood (94-96 mph), you can live dangerously and succeed. You'll still watch more than a couple of your high hard ones get slammed downtown, but you'll also strike out a lot of overeager hitters who can't catch up to your heater. Former Tigers, Twins, and Blue Jays starter Jack Morris made a living doing this in the 1980s, as did many great power pitchers before him, but very few of today's pitchers can throw that hard.

How many major league pitchers possess good fastballs? Precious few, maybe a dozen at any given time, not counting the hard throwers in the minors or on the fringes of the majors who don't have good enough control to pitch regularly in the big leagues.

Working in tandem with aging pitchers, another unlikely trend that has contributed to the emphasis on low strikes is progress in orthopedic surgery. Years ago, a pitcher with a torn rotator cuff was finished, even if he went under the knife and attempted a comeback. Yet now pitchers undergo less-invasive (often arthroscopic) surgery with a far better prognosis and return to the mound. Sure, not all wounded pitchers can come back, but virtually none of those who do return to the mound ever regain their previous velocity if they were hard throwers.

Determined pitchers like Orel Hershiser can come back and pitch another thousand innings, constantly keeping the ball down. And umpires, being human, are more likely to ring up a hitter on a marginal pitch when the guy on the mound is a grizzled veteran with good control than when he's a callow rookie.

So veteran pitchers, comeback pitchers, breaking-ball pitchers, and almost all other pitchers depend on throwing strikes at the knees and pitches on the outside corner. Do you think it's any coincidence that the strike zone has moved down and to the outside?

THE BEST-LAID PLANS

Lest you think that the answer is simple—have the leagues order the umpires to enforce the rule book strike zone—a real-world example of just how quickly such simple "solutions" can go awry is easy to find.

In 1988, under pressure by NL president and future commissioner Bart Giamatti, both leagues decided to strictly enforce the balk rule. An intelligent man who was used to making tough decisions and giving controversial orders, Giamatti didn't listen to many baseball people who said that his strict-enforcement edict was well-intentioned but misguided.

Instead, Bart apparently listened to Whitey. Veteran St. Louis manager Whitey Herzog was furious during the 1987 World Series when AL pitchers didn't follow the NL interpretation of the balk rule, which called for a full, one-second stop in their motion with runners on base. The smugly superior NL (always ready to assert its moral rectitude when compared with its counterpart, which employs the hated DH) prevailed, with disastrous consequences.

Long before the end of May, the number of balks called had shattered the all-time mark for a full season. AL pitchers, usually worried more about home runs than stolen bases, had a lot more trouble adjusting; they were called for balks at almost twice the rate of their NL brethren. Fortunately, responding to constant criticism, the leagues finally relented and relaxed the balk rule interpretation around midseason. Everyone was happier; no one has since seriously suggested returning to such strict enforcement of balks.

Throughout this whole episode, the definition of a balk never changed. What changed was the official interpretation of when to call a balk. The dutiful men in blue did what they were told—and everybody hated it. The pitchers were furious, as they were called for balks seemingly every time they turned around.

The umpires hated it, because they were the ones on whom everyone else was venting. The fans hated it, as runners were advancing and scoring on invisible, imperceptible twitches instead of base hits. All this because of a tiny change in an unimportant rule, which wreaked unforeseen havoc.

If you've never read the Official Baseball Rules definition of a balk, consider yourself lucky. The language is so confusing and badly written that it could be the subject of a Jerry Seinfeld comedy routine. The balk rule (8.05) consists of more than 750 words. It has 13 subsections, several of which have their own subsections, plus a "Penalty" paragraph, plus two "Approved Ruling" paragraphs, one of which one has even more subsections!

BE CAREFUL WHAT YOU WISH FOR

The moral of this story? Theory is nice, but if it isn't grounded in a complete understanding of the way things work in the real world, it is useless—and possibly dangerous.

So, if something as simple as calling rule-book balks—which, after all, have but a minor impact on the play of the game when compared with something as integral as the strike zone—was so controversial, ponder for a minute how big an upheaval there would be if the men in blue really did what everyone says they want done.

"Calling a strike a strike" ain't as easy as it seems.

WE HAVE MET THE ENEMY, AND HE IS . . .

. . . human nature, which has reacted to the unintended effect of a change in umpiring equipment and the unexpected demise of the four-seam fastball. When looking at the bigger picture, the shifting strike zone in the past 15 years has been primarily caused by the inability of most big league pitchers to throw high fastballs or inside fastballs past most big league hitters anymore.

It's that simple—and that complex.

9

THE 10 WORST MANAGERS, 1987-97

10

In memory of the 1997 firings of Bob Boone (by Kansas City) and Ray Knight (by Cincinnati), herewith follows a list of the 10 worst managers in the past 10 years. Boone's and Knight's tenures may have been short and sour, but they weren't the only skippers to stink out the dugout. (More on their follies in K.C. and can Cincinnati be found in their respective team chapters.)

It's easy enough to rack up a bad won-lost record. It's something else, however, to manage a contender right down the drain, or to see the terrible club you managed win the year after you've gone. Or to be so bad in a truly memorable way that people use your tenure as an example of how not to manage a big league club.

There are no 0-6 "interim" managers here. The following list includes only those who either managed one full season or ended one season and started the next with the club. Many of these skippers stuck around for well more than one year. Which, in every case, was already far too long.

We've rated these managers from 1-10, with the absolute worst at No. 1.

1. Larry Bowa, San Diego Padres, 1987-88.

Following a long and successful playing career that ended in 1985, Bowa spent 1986 managing the Padres' Triple A club to an 80-62 record.

Hired to run the Padres for 1987, he inherited an aging team with a few good prospects. While some of the youngsters—John Kruk, 1988 Rookie of the Year Benito Santiago—played well, others, including Joey Cora, Stan Jefferson, and Jimmy Jones, failed to develop. Bowa's super-intense, in-your-face, "my way or the highway" micromanaging approach apparently instilled fear, not confidence, in his players. He had one relief ace, promising righty Lance McCullers, and rode him way too hard (78 games, 123 innings in '87; McCullers was never the same again). No other pitcher on Bowa's staff made more than 44 appearances in '87. The Padres finished last that year, at 65-97.

That winter, Bowa released an autobiography called *Bleep! Larry Bowa Manages*, in which he detailed his troubles with some of his players in painful and often embarrassing detail. How smart was that? Who would want to play for a manager who would rip his own players in a book?

After a 16-30 start in 1988, Bowa was canned by—and replaced by—San Diego GM Jack McKeon. Bowa's final mark with the Padres was 81-127. He has stayed in the game as a third base coach since then (with the Phillies and Angels), but Bowa is not likely to ever get another shot at running a big league team—even though he's been actively campaigning for one for the last decade.

In September 1996, just before the Phillies fired Jim Fregosi, the Philadelphia media was full of stories about how Bowa, who had starred as a player in Philly and was then the team's third base coach, supposedly had been promised Fregosi's job for 1997. These reports, widely believed to have been leaked by Bowa in a futile attempt at self-promotion, proved false, and he left the organization after Terry Francona was hired.

2. Chuck Tanner, Atlanta Braves, 1986-88.

After Eddie Haas failed to inspire the Braves in 1985, Tanner—a positive guy with a fairly good record before his Pirates unraveled in the early 1980s—came on board. The Braves were not good, but the depths to which they sank under Tanner was remarkable.

Tanner favored veterans, and he made liberal use of them. It seemed as if time had stopped for him back in 1980. With the Braves In '86, Tanner used his old (33 years old, to be exact) leadoff hitter from Pittsburgh, Omar Moreno. The ex-Buc was horrible, batting .234 in 118 games with a .276 on-base percentage. Tanner had only one player under age 28 in the starting lineup that season, and his bench boasted 37-year-old Chris Chambliss and 36-year-old Ted Simmons. The team's closer was 38-year-old Gene Garber. Atlanta finished last, at 72-89.

By 1987 Tanner had brought in some younger players (Dion James, Gerald Perry), but also had 37-year-old Ken Griffey, Sr., in left field, along with 42-year-old Graig Nettles and Simmons in reserve. His other subs were older former regulars found wanting, rather than promising players who could actually produce. The roles on his pitching staff changed every week; Tanner seemed unable to distinguish between who could help him and who could not. The '87 record: 69-92.

Finally, Tanner was fired the next May with the Braves at 12-27. He cleaned out his office to make room for ...

3. Russ Nixon, Atlanta Braves, 1988-90.

The hardscrabble Nixon was supposed to light a fire under the team that Chuck Tanner had lulled to sleep. It might have worked if Nixon had known what to do with what little talent the Braves actually had.

Nixon wasn't much better than Tanner in 1988, as the Braves finished 42-79 under him and hobbled home in last place at 54-106. Nixon, like Tanner, seemed unable to tell a good prospect from a bad one, giving Kevin Coffman as many starts as John Smoltz. Jeff Blauser, clearly a better player than incumbent shortstop Andres Thomas, was left in Triple A. Second baseman Ron Gant, a promising hitter, was moved to third base in spring 1989, a move that contributed mightily to the worst season of his career.

Those '89 Braves were one horrible club, with Thomas hitting .213 in 141 games and catcher Jody Davis batting an appalling .169. Superannuated 42-year-old Darrell Evans had 276 at bats, in which he hit .207. Paul Assenmacher was dropped from his co-closer role (in favor of Joe Boever) and was dealt to the Cubs in midseason for nothing.

The next season, Nixon still had Thomas at short and Blauser filling in off the bench. Gant had been moved again, this time to the outfield, where he stuck. But the new third baseman was Jim Presley, who hit .242 with 19 homers, 29 walks, and 130 strikeouts in 140 games. Nixon still had Boever closing, and Derek Lilliquist was in the starting rotation. Thirty-eight-year-old reserve catcher Ernie Whitt batted 180 times, while 25-year-old outfielder Geronimo Berroa got only four at bats and eventually a release from the organization. By June, the team was 25-40 and Nixon was impeached.

Bobby Cox came on board to manage the club. The next season, the Braves captured the NL West title.

4. Dallas Green, New York Mets, 1993-96.

They just don't play the game with grit and feeling any more, said old schoolmaster Dallas Green. When he was hired to salvage the train wreck that was the 1993 Mets, the former Phillies, Cubs, and Yankees manager stated that he was going to kick some butts and take some names.

11

So what happened during the tough guy's tenure? Plenty of comedy, a little tragedy, and very little winning. Green angered many when he "joked" that after a tough loss, he went home and beat up his wife. The inmates ran the asylum: center fielder Vince Coleman threw a firecracker into a crowd; third baseman Bobby Bonilla bitched and moaned about every little thing and threatened to beat up a sportswriter; John Franco spoke of physical reprisals against replacement players; Dwight Gooden was suspended (again) for drug use. The clubhouse exploded on Green's watch, and many articles and books were written about these historically horrible Mets.

Green's approach didn't work in '93, when the Mets were 46-78 for him after being 13-25 for Jeff Torborg. Dallas's best season with New York was '94, when he guided the Mets to a 55-58 mark during the strike season. The following year the Mets tied for a distant second at 69-75, 21 games out. The complete breakdown of Green's control was shown by his failure to intervene in a dispute between Bonilla and Mike Cubbage, New York's third base coach. Bobby Bo refused to obey Cubbage's baserunning signs, then lied about it, then ripped Cubbage in the media—all while Green sat on his hands.

The failures of the Mets' young players (especially their highly touted pitching prospects) noticeably frayed Green's nerves. Finally, in August 1996, with the Mets 59-72 and in fourth place, Green was dumped and returned to his Pennsylvania farm.

5. Terry Bevington, Chicago White Sox, 1995-97.

The White Sox fired manager Gene Lamont 31 games into the 1995 season (the team was 10-21) and tossed Terry Bevington, the club's third base coach, into the breach.

Just looking at Bevington's record, there was little reason to suspect he would do badly in Chicago. He had managed minor league clubs in the Brewers' organization to three straight first-place finishes from 1985 to '87, and had taken the White Sox's Triple A club to the top in 1988. He was familiar with Sox personnel, having coached for the big league club for six years.

Unfortunately for everyone concerned, Bevington never seemed comfortable with his players, the Chicago media, or the expectations of the fans. He almost immediately lost control of his players (and thus their respect). The more veteran free agents the club brought in, the worse Bevington managed. He did not handle the pitching staff well, failed to get sufficient production from his offensive talent, and established a reputation with the media as a paranoid, flinty control freak who could dissemble with the best of them. It was sad to see his players openly defy him, laugh at him, and question his judgment to the press.

The White Sox could have won the AL Central title in 1995 and 1996, but didn't. In 1997 the Sox completely collapsed, and Bevington paid with his job. This past winter he was hired to manage the Blue Jays' Triple A affiliate in Syracuse. Working in the minors, away from the media glare and the million-dollar egos, might be the best role for Bevington.

6. Bob Boone, Kansas City Royals, 1995-97.

Boone caught 2,225 games, which ranks second in major league history. All that time behind the dish gave Boone a fine baseball education, which he continued in the minors following his retirement. After guiding Tacoma to two fifth-place finishes in the Triple A Pacific Coast League in 1992 and '93, Boone was with the Reds in 1994 as a bench coach. He was then hired to manage the Royals in 1995 after the club had finished in third place the season before.

His initial Royals club finished second in the AL Central, but with a 70-74 mark. The next year, they were last at 75-86. Finally, in July 1997, Boone got the ax with his team 36-46 at the All-Star break.

As a manager in K.C., Boone couldn't commit to anything: a lineup, a pitching staff, a batting order, a plan for his young players. He fell in love with players who got hot for a few days. He shifted around good players to get his reclamation projects, like Craig Paquette and Doug Linton, more playing time. Having run Bob Hamelin out of town, Boone then complained that he lacked a power-hitting first baseman and installed Jose Offerman there instead. Plenty of talented Royals prospects failed to develop under Boone (e.g., Hamelin, Johnny Damon, Michael Tucker, Jon Nunnally, Chris Stynes).

While the organization didn't help Boone out—several poor trades were made, for example, the shipping out of Tucker, Nunnally, and Stynes—the fault here is largely that of the manager. While in Kansas City, Boone struck the press as a tireless self-promoter and earned the derisive nickname "The Genius." He frequently informed everyone within earshot of his intelligence, but the on-field results didn't match his high opinion of himself.

7. Ray Knight, Cincinnati Reds, 1996-97.

Following his retirement as a player after the 1988 season, Knight spent more than four years in the broadcast booth. In 1993 he was hired to be the Reds' bench coach, took over third base duties the next year and, in 1995, was named "assistant manager," as the Reds announced that he would replace then-manager Davey Johnson when Johnson's contract ended after the season, even though Johnson would go on to win a division title for his swan song.

Knight took over in 1996. The Reds finished 81-81, marred by on- and off-field problems. Some of these problems were created by Knight, who saw himself as indispensable and seemed to believe that his way was the only way. Many of his players had no respect for the skipper, and they said so openly.

In 1997 things were even worse. The Reds got off to a bad start, and Knight lost control of both himself and the team. Mercifully, he was given the boot on July 25, when he had a 43-56 mark. Like Larry Bowa, Terry Bevington and Bob Boone, Knight was another guy who simply took everything too hard. He may someday get another chance. If so, he needs to take to heart the he philosophy that there is always another game tomorrow.

8. Tom Runnells, Montreal Expos, 1991-92.

Runnells, a former utility infielder with the Reds, managed effectively in the Cincinnati system for two years. He joined the Expos organization in 1989, skippered their Triple A club to a first-place finish, and was brought to the big league club as third base coach.

Promoted to manager in mid-1991 to turn the Expos around, Runnells couldn't get the team out of last place (51-61). He was unlucky—several key players suffered injuries, including Andres Galarraga, Mike Fitzgerald, Mark Gardner, and Chris Nabholz—but he also did a poor job with lineup selection (going with Gil Reyes and his .217 average behind the plate while Nelson

Santovenia rode the bench) and the bullpen (using Barry Jones as his closer over Mel Rojas, Jeff Fassero and Scott Ruskin, all of whom had better stuff). The next spring, Runnells wanted to emphasize fundamentals for his club, and to drive his point home, he showed up for spring training in battle fatigues.

The gesture, meant as a joke, fell flat, and Runnells was roasted by the press. When the year started, Montreal had bullpen troubles, didn't score runs, and played uninspired ball. Despite the presence of several front-line players (Rojas, Larry Walker, Marquis Grissom, Moises Alou, Delino DeShields, Ken Hill, Dennis Martinez, John Wetteland), the Expos were the biggest underachievers in the game. On May 20, as Montreal blew a lead by allowing the Reds to score five runs in the seventh inning, fans at Olympic Stadium booed Runnells unmercifully and chanted for his ouster. Two days later, Runnells was canned with Montreal's record at 17-20.

Since then, Runnells's replacement, Felipe Alou, has brought the beggared Expos back to semi-respectability.

9. Nick Leyva, Philadelphia Phillies, 1989-91.

After six middling seasons managing in the Cardinals' minor league chain, Leyva was named Cardinals first base coach in 1984. He spent five seasons with the Redbirds before being hired by the Phillies to manage in 1989.

To be fair to Leyva, being hired to manage the '89 Phillies was a little like getting the job of kamikaze pilot. The '88 Phils had finished 65-96 and had very little talent to speak of. The farm system was completely unproductive, and the best players on the club were old (Mike Schmidt, Lance Parrish, Shane Rawley, Kent Tekulve) or injury-prone (Darren Daulton, Von Hayes, David Palmer, Steve Bedrosian). Or both (Schmidt, Parrish).

Leyva guided the Phils to a 67-96 finish in 1989. GM Lee Thomas made some good trades after that season, and the talent was substantially better in 1990 when the Phillies finished 77-85, tied for fourth place. Leyva still couldn't decide whom to play and where to play them, though, continuing to move pitchers from the bullpen to the rotation and back, and he got little production out of an offense that looked pretty good on paper.

April 1991 marked the end of the line for Leyva. After

passing over young Mickey Morandini at second base in favor of a veteran (washed-up Wally Backman), Leyva watched his team start the season 4-9. With the Phils in the cellar, he was fired on April 23 and replaced by Jim Fregosi. The team ultimately finished third in the NL East in 1991 and made it to the World Series two seasons later.

10. Phil Regan, Baltimore Orioles, 1995.

A successful big league pitcher, Regan was the Mariners' pitching coach from 1984 to '86, then served as a scout through 1993. Cleveland made him its pitching coach in 1994, and when the Tribe was successful that year, the team's luster rubbed off on Regan. He was hired to replace Orioles manager Johnny Oates and came to Baltimore with hopes and expectations of winning the AL East crown.

It didn't happen. A team that had finished second the season before, just 6.5 games out, ended up third, 71-73 and 15 games back, in 1995. Regan couldn't manage his offense or his pitching staff. He made offensive cipher Curtis Goodwin his leadoff hitter; he gave 36-year-old Kevin Bass 295 at bats; he couldn't decide who should play second or third base. The Orioles used a total of 23 pitchers as injuries, impatience, and poor performance made the ninth and tenth spots on the staff a revolving door. Following the embarrassingly poor season, Regan was relieved of his duties.

Davey Johnson came on board for 1996, and he had two successful seasons with the Orioles before being canned due to conflicts with strong-willed owner Peter Angelos.

14

THE WORST CONTRACTS OF ALL TIME

The breathtaking contract Matt Williams signed last winter with the Arizona Diamondbacks, a year after the record-breaking Albert Belle and Gary Sheffield contracts, raises once again the issue of megabuck, megarisk contracts. While the Arizona-Williams deal could work out well, there is a real chance that the five-year, $45 million contract that the Diamondbacks gave the 32-year-old third baseman could be one of those mistakes that goes down in baseball infamy.

All the ingredients for a disastrous contract are there with Williams, who is a real gentleman and who has been a fine player in the past. But neither of those positives make this deal a good long-term risk. Giving a $9-million-a-year contract to a player with an injury history who is past his prime is fraught with peril. The Diamondbacks are paying premium dollars for a player who has combined excellent power (30 homers) and high average (.280 or better) only once in his career (1993). While Williams has a gold glove, his lack of durability, speed, and a high on-base percentage makes him a substantial risk over the long term.

Of course, baseball, like life, is full of uncertainties. Not every player works out, not every contract is a smart move.

For a contract to be adjudged a serious mistake, it must be for a large amount of money for that time, must represent a clear overpayment from what the player probably would have gotten elsewhere, and must involve a serious decline in performance that could have been predicted when the contract was signed. Reasonable speculation about future performance is, of course, necessary when evaluating the deals signed this past off-season.

Many of our worst contracts of all time were so staggering that they limited the team's ability to replace that player or to make other moves. That's the dreaded double whammy: having an injured or underperforming player who is hurting the team on the field at the same time he's tying up salary money that could be spent to address other needs.

What all the worst contracts have in common is that the clubs responsible for the deals were, in large part, paying for what the player had previously done, with not enough thought as to what the player would do in the future. Chalk most of these contracts up to sharp agents who were able to exploit desperate or incompetent management. While gross overestimation of a player's ability was an integral part of all these deals, many were also driven by marketing concerns.

Baseball contracts today are generally guaranteed. The reason there weren't terrible contracts like these in the old days (i.e., before free agency) is that contracts then were almost always for one year only, so risk was minimal. Our list of the worst contracts of all time starts after 1980.

Questionable big-bucks deals began to explode dramatically in the early 1990s. This was partly due to the fact that the owners had been illegally colluding to hold down salaries in the late 1980s. It also had a lot to do with the huge television contracts Major League Baseball signed with CBS and ESPN for 1990-93, giving the owners much more money to madly spend on half-good players.

So let's get to the truly ugly stuff. The deals are listed in chronological order, because it's critical when evaluating these contracts to adjust dollar values over time— a $1 million annual salary in the early 1980s was a lot of money. Now it seems like petty cash in the super-inflated world of superstar salaries.

Each player is listed with the team that signed him and the year that the contract first took effect. The abbreviation M is used to show millions of dollars— and also to prevent gagging over all those zeros spent on so little.

If this litany of monetary misery doesn't cause you to reach for the antacids, rest assured that there are dozens of other deals that arguably could have been included. Without further ado, here's the roll call of some of the most egregious mad-money deals of the 1980s and 1990s:

Ken Griffey, Sr., New York Yankees, 1982.

Griffey was a good, solid player for a long time. In 1981, at age 31, he hit .311 for Cincinnati with two home runs; decent but not exactly All-Star production for an outfielder. That didn't stop the Yankees from offering him a six-year contract worth more than $6.2M, one of the largest deals in baseball at the time. While Griffey played well for the Yankees, hitting between .273 and .300 from 1982 to '86 (when he was dumped on the moribund Braves in exchange for Claudell Washington), he wasn't worth half of what he was paid.

George Foster, New York Mets, 1982. Like Ken Griffey, Sr., a part of the Big Red Machine, Foster was still a solid everyday player in 1981, though far below his pre-

vious level (he had led the NL in RBIs three times and homers twice in the 1970s). The Mets nonetheless inked Foster, 33, to a five-year contract that paid a total of nearly $9.5M. Foster had the second-highest salary in baseball in 1982, the first year of the deal, and batted a mighty .247 with 13 home runs. Things got only a little bit better for him in future seasons. By the time Foster's contract expired in 1986, he was already out of the game.

Julio Cruz, Chicago White Sox, 1984. The White Sox won the 1983 AL West. Cruz, acquired from Seattle in midseason, hit .251 for Chicago with 24 steals in 99 games and was viewed as a spark plug despite a spotty career record. The Sox, smelling the heady scent of success, gave a six-year, $8.6M contract to the 29-year-old "Juice." Cruz went on to bat .222, .197, and .215 in the next three years. His career, hastened to a close by bad knees, ended halfway through the contract.

Omar Moreno, New York Yankees, 1984. The Yankees often awarded huge sums of money to mediocre players because they could afford to repeat the same mistakes time after time; John Mayberry and Dyar Miller were good examples from this time period. But Omar Moreno? After getting the 32-year-old fly chaser in trade from the Astros the summer before (he batted .250 in 48 games for the Yanks), New York then signed him for five years, at $732,000 per year. Of course, Moreno played lousy, was dumped on Kansas City in 1985, and then spent 1986 hitting .234 for Chuck Tanner's Atlanta Braves. That was his last season in the majors, but Omar kept cashing paychecks through 1987.

Garry Templeton, San Diego Padres, 1986. Templeton had been a superstar-in-waiting with the St. Louis Cardinals in the late 1970s. However, his day had long passed by the mid-1980s. After being traded to San Diego for Ozzie Smith, Templeton spent nine uneventful years as the Padres' everyday shortstop, only once hitting higher than .263 and showing little power or speed. However, after the 1985 season—in which, at age 29, he made the All-Star team by hitting .282— Templeton inked a five-year contract worth $1.2M per

son. His performance declined sharply, as did the Padres' fortunes.

Juan Samuel, Philadelphia Phillies, 1989.

In 1987 Samuel had his best year (largely because he showed far more plate discipline than ever before), walking 60 times and hitting .272 with 37 doubles, 15 triples, and 28 homers. He said he wouldn't ever be that patient again, and the next season walked just 39 times and fell to .243 with 12 homers. The Phillies then signed the 29-year-old second baseman to a two-year deal for $2.9M. Samuel was so bad that he was traded in midseason to the Mets. He was so awful there that the Mets unloaded him on the Dodgers before the 1990 season, where he hit .242 with 13 homers.

Willie Hernandez, Detroit Tigers, 1989.

Hernandez won the 1984 AL Cy Young Award at age 30 with a splendid season as closer for the world champions. From that point on, he became increasingly less effective, and suffered a serious arm injury in 1987. But the Tigers, feeling they had few bullpen options, signed the 34-year-old to a five-year contract before the 1989 season. That $6.5M deal netted Detroit 32 appearances, 15 saves, and a 5.74 ERA. In the first year of the contract Hernandez suffered an elbow injury that ended his major league career.

Mark Davis, Kansas City Royals, 1990.

The hard-throwing lefty joined the Padres in 1987 and immediately became one of the NL's top relievers—largely due to a great performance in his home park. In 1988 his home ERA was 0.94; in 1989 it was 1.17. He won the NL Cy Young Award in '89, saving a league-best 40 games with a 1.85 ERA. The Royals, who already had a good closer in Jeff Montgomery, opened up their purse for Davis, inking him for four years at more than $3.3M per annum. Davis was miserable for K.C., posting ERAs of 5.11, 4.45 and 7.18 before being traded to Atlanta in mid-1992. Many baseball people feel that this is the worst contract ever.

Don Mattingly, New York Yankees, 1991.

One of the game's best players from 1984 to '87, Mattingly's production dropped sharply within three years due to serious back problems. In 1990 he batted .256 with five homers, but was signed to a new five-year, $20M deal anyway. Mattingly never got it back; although he batted between .288 and .304 in each of the next five seasons, he hit only 43 homers total. Sentiment, not smart evaluation of talent, made this deal happen.

Kelly Gruber, Toronto Blue Jays, 1991.

In 1990 Gruber, in his fourth year as a regular, exploded with an atypical 31-homer, 118-RBI season. Before the '91 season he signed a three-year contract for more than $11M. Of course, Gruber (who had his big year at age 28) immediately plummeted to .252 with 20 homers, missing time with a thumb problem, then fell to .229 with 11 homers. He was out of the majors a year later.

Teddy Higuera, Milwaukee Brewers, 1991.

An outstanding pitcher between 1985 and '90, Higuera began to experience shoulder troubles and other nagging injuries in the late '80s. However, the Brewers thought the 32-year-old lefthander could hold up and signed him for four years at $3.3M per. Higuera pitched only seven times in 1991 before tearing his rotator cuff. He did not pitch at all in '92, made eight appearances the next year, and tried 17 times in 1994 and barely got anyone out. The deal crippled the Brewers; dollars spent on Higuera were dollars they couldn't use to keep Paul Molitor in town.

Gary Gaetti, California Angels, 1991.

Gaetti, a star from 1986 to '88 with the Twins, began to decline sharply in 1989 and continued the next year. Nonetheless, California signed him for $11.4M over four years and watched him stink out the joint. Released by the Angels and signed by Kansas City in 1993, Gaetti made a surprising comeback.

Bobby Bonilla, New York Mets, 1992.

In Pittsburgh, Bonilla was a popular player who could hit for average and power and play adequate defense. In New York, he was extremely unpopular, turning into an arrogant, temperamental malcontent in a clubhouse full of others with similar problems. Five years and $29M got the Mets a whole lot of headaches until they dumped him on the Orioles in 1995. To be fair, much of the problem came

17

from the wildly exaggerated expectations engendered by his huge salary. Bonilla was unfairly beaten up by both the media and the fans when he proved to be a good, though far from great, player. Of course, that's what Bonilla was previously, so why did the Mets expect anything different?

Kevin McReynolds, Kansas City Royals, 1992.
The Royals traded Bret Saberhagen to the Mets for Gregg Jefferies and McReynolds, a 32-year-old left fielder, after the 1991 season. McReynolds was rewarded with a three-year contract at $3.4M per. McReynolds was dreadful in two years with K.C. and was dumped back on the Mets before retiring after the 1994 season.

Matt Young, Boston Red Sox, 1992. The six-foot, three-inch lefthander was 8-18 for the Mariners in 1991, fanning 176 but walking 107 in 225 innings while posting a 3.51 ERA. That was his first quality season since 1988. The Red Sox, desperate for pitching, signed the 32-year-old Young to a three-year contract for $6.4M. Young was almost unbelievably bad for Boston, going 3-10 in two years and pitching a lot of long relief; he was released before the last year of his contract. Cleveland tried Young for 22 games in '93 (1-6) and decided they could live without him.

Ruben Sierra, Oakland Athletics, 1993.
Sierra, once considered a potential superstar, signed a one-year, $5M contract with Texas for 1992. He hit .278 with 14 homers in 124 games before a trade to Oakland, for whom he hit .277 with three homers in 27 games. Even though Sierra was well on his way to becoming a classic, one-dimensional slugger by that time, the Athletics then agreed to a five-year, $29M contract and promptly watched his career go down the toilet. By the time Sierra's deal ended after 1997, he had been gladly dumped by Oakland and four other teams as well.

Cecil Fielder, Detroit Tigers, 1993. The Tigers' first-sacker hit 51 homers in 1990 and 44 in 1991, both league-leading totals. In 1992, turning 29, he dropped to 35 homers and a .244 average. However, the then-popular Fielder was able to command a five-year, $36M contract

from Detroit because new owner Mike Ilitch was afraid of fan backlash if Fielder went free-agent. What was so insane about the deal was that Fielder was making as much per year as Barry Bonds, the best player in the game. The portly Fielder's productivity predictably continued to drop as the years went on; by the time the contract ended in '97, Fielder was hanging on as a platoon DH. with the Yankees.

Andre Dawson, Boston Red Sox, 1993. After six seasons with the Chicago Cubs, the 38-year-old Dawson raked in a two-year deal from Boston for more than $9.3M. Why the Sox needed to pay the aged slugger that kind of money, when there were few other suitors interested, boggles the mind. Dawson did his best, hitting 29 homers in two seasons for the Carmines, but bad knees and a slowing bat limited his production.

Robby Thompson, San Francisco Giants, 1994.
At age 31, Thompson had his best offensive season in 1993, hitting 19 homers, driving in 65, and batting .312. All three were career highs. The Giants, concerned that the loss of Will Clark to Texas via free agency had already hurt the club, signed Thompson to a three-year deal with a club option for 1997, at more than $4M per season. Thompson spent the next three seasons hobbled by shoulder and back problems, playing 193 ineffective games as his career ground to a sad end.

Gregg Jefferies, Philadelphia Phillies, 1995.
Already burned on long-term deals for Lenny Dykstra and Darren Daulton (which at least made some sense, in as much as the team was rewarding its own top players and fan favorites), the Phillies went for the trifecta: a four-year, $20M deal with a 27-year-old first baseman. Jefferies, converted to left field, has been one of the game's biggest free-agent bombs due to his immediate and precipitous decline. Making the deal even more disastrous was that Jefferies essentially received power-hitter money when he was a high average-hitter, and that he was known to unpopular in the clubhouse. On the tight-knit and cliquish Phillies, it was like mixing gasoline with a spark.

18

Kevin Gross, **Texas Rangers, 1995.** A thoroughly average pitcher during his major league career, Gross had his best ERA seasons after moving into pitcher-friendly Dodger Stadium in 1991. The Rangers, needing a reliable starter, signed Gross, who was about to turn 34, to a two-year contract worth $6.2M. Gross posted ERAs of 5.54 and 5.22 for Texas, winning 20 while losing 23.

Ozzie Guillen, **Chicago White Sox, 1995.** Guillen, Chicago's shortstop for ten years, hit .288 in 100 games during the strike year of 1994. Jerry Reinsdorf awarded the 30-year-old with a new three-year deal for more than $4M per. The veteran infielder then batted .248, .263, and .245 with no speed, power, or on-base average while deteriorating defensively due to age and injury.

Bobby Bonilla, **Florida Marlins, 1997.** As was the case five years earlier, Bonilla's bat was just good enough to seduce a team into overpaying; this time, he received $22.4M for four years at age 34. Bobby Bo didn't have a bad year for the world champs, but a clear indication of how much Florida overpaid was the fact that no other team would touch his contract during Florida's post-Series fire sale.

Jamie Navarro, **Chicago White Sox, 1997.** After two good seasons with Milwaukee in 1991 and '92, Navarro signed a big two-year contract with them and proceeded to stink. Signed to a low-risk, two-year deal with the Cubs, Navarro got his game back in 1995 and '96, though he argued constantly with his manager and catcher. Departing for the generous White Sox, Navarro nailed down a four-year deal for $22.4M. In his first season for Chicago, Navarro went 9-14 with a 5.79 ERA, topping the AL in hits allowed, earned runs allowed, and wild pitches.

Albert Belle, **Chicago White Sox, 1997.** Much has been written about this contract already. What's really important is that while Belle is a good hitter, he has no defensive value, is a big negative with fans, and turned 31 last August. To pay $10-11M per season for a thirtysomething power hitter with a very dark side is outrageous. This is a good candidate for the worst deal ever, partly because of the money, which greatly inflated the game's salary structure, and partly because Belle will be under contract through 2001.

Steve Avery, **Boston Red Sox, 1997.** Coming off two straight mediocre seasons and having experienced a serious loss of velocity, Avery didn't merit much more than a Triple A deal. Luckily for the 27-year-old lefthander, the Red Sox were willing to drop a big bag of cash on his presumed comeback. Avery got more than $9.5M for two seasons, the second of which was guaranteed when he made 18 starts in 1997. His record last year: 6-7, 6.42 ERA.

Sammy Sosa, **Chicago Cubs, 1998.** The Cubs signed the popular Sosa to a $42M, four-year contract last summer. For a player with good home run power but declining speed and little else, this is a stunning amount of money. To his credit, Sosa plays hard every day, but he doesn't hit for average, is erratic in the outfield and on the bases, and rarely walks. Late in the season he was reamed out by his manager for concentrating more on personal goals—like trying to become a 30-30 guy—than on what could actually help win games. At age 29, Sosa will almost certainly play through the term of this contract, but his '97 batting average, on-base percentage, and slugging average were all his lowest since '92. Ominously, he hit .233 with a .264 on-base and .409 slugging away from Wrigley in 1997.

Finalists. The finalist for the worst deals can be divided by category. The worst deals, in terms of obvious overestimation of talent, were the Mark Davis, Kelly Gruber, Matt Young, and Gregg Jefferies signings. The grossest deals, in terms of huge dollars, were the Bobby Bonilla/Mets contract, the Cecil Fielder contract, and the Albert Belle contract. The stupidest deals, in terms of easily foreseeable risk, were the Teddy Higuera, Robby Thompson, and Steve Avery pacts.

All things considered, however, one deal stands out above the rest. Combining a healthy dose of all three mistakes—overestimation of talent, huge dollars, and foreseeable risk—the Ruben Sierra contract has to be considered the worst deal in recent history.

19

FALL AND WINTER LEAGUE
UPDATE

The fall and winter leagues in Arizona, Hawaii, and, most notably, Latin America, are where on-the-move youngsters cement their reputations, where fallen prospects can regain lost luster, and where even non prospects can suddenly become red hot. This is a team-by-team review of those players who made the biggest impressions—and those who fell flat—during fall and winter action.

AMERICAN LEAGUE

Anaheim: Outfielder Trent Durrington, a 22-year-old Australian native, hit .296 with 23 steals at Gold Coast in the Arizona Fall League. He also took 36 walks in 40 games. The Angels were also pleased at the AFL progress of lefthanded mound prospect Scott Schoenweiss, who was 3-2 with a 1.98 in six starts for Scottsdale. Righthander Brian Cooper, a one-year pro, was 3-4 with a 3.27 ERA at Honolulu of the Hawaiian League, and he struck out 61 and walked only eight in 52 innings.

Baltimore: Steve Montgomery, quickly becoming the organization's top mound hopeful, was 5-1 for Peoria of the AFL, compiling a 2.54 ERA in nine starts and fanning 46 in 39 innings. Hawaiian Leaguer Ryan Kohlmeier was 2-1 with eight saves in 23 relief appearances for Maui, allowing just 12 hits in 22.2 frames. Also for Maui, power prospect Calvin Pickering hit .301 with 10 homers in 52 games. The Virgin Islands native is just 21. Finally, outfielder Danny Clyburn batted .312 for Peoria with six homers in 24 games.

Boston: The Red Sox sent young righthanded pitcher Peter Munro to Phoenix this winter, and Munro started nine games. He finished 1-2, but allowed only 35 hits and 11 walks in his 42 innings, fanning 37.

Chicago: Magglio Ordonez played for Oriente in his native Venezuela this winter and hit .298 with eight homers and 40 RBIs in 55 games. He also walked nearly as often as he struck out and stole 12 bases. Another outfield prospect, Jeff Liefer, hit .370 for Nordeste in the Dominican Republic, clubbing six homers and 10 doubles in just 108 at bats.

Cleveland: Two of the organization's power-hitting infield prospects played for Mesa of the Arizona Fall League this year, and their results could not have been more different. While Sean Casey hit .396 with 34 RBIs in 38 games, Russ Branyan stumbled to a .232 mark with seven homers in 41 games, fanning 83 times in 164 at bats while walking just nine times.

Detroit: Catcher Rob Fick went to Hawaii this winter and batted .329 in 40 games, driving in 30 runs and slugging .500. Unsung outfielder Gabe Kapler, who has hit his way to prospect status, also played for Honolulu and batted .282 in 51 games. Lefthanded pitcher Sean Runyan, a Rule V pick from San Diego who could make the Tigers' opening day staff, pitched in 18 games for Sun Cities in the AFL, allowing just 19 hits and two walks in 23 innings while striking out 20.

Kansas City: Outfield hopeful Jeremy Giambi, brother of Oakland's Jason, hit .354 for the AFL's Grand Canyon club, with a .556 slugging average in 29 games. Catcher Mike Sweeney hit .301 for San Juan in the Puerto Rican League, with nine home runs in 176 at bats. Pitcher Jose Santiago compiled a 5-2 record, nine saves, and a 2.39 ERA in 31 relief appearances for San Juan. Finally, Jamie Walker, a lefthander converted to starting after spending last year as a Rule V pick with the Royals, was 5-1 with a 2.77 ERA at San Juan.

Minnesota: Twins third base prospect Corey Koskie, coming off a big year at Double A, followed with a fine performance at Sun Cities of the AFL, clubbing 10 homers in just 107 at bats while hitting .299. First baseman David Ortiz batted but .235 at Escogido of the Dominican Republic with only one home run in 45 contests.

New York: Outfielder Ricky Ledee showed few effects of a leg injury that sidelined him for much of 1997. At San Juan, he hit .315 with nine homers and 36 walks in 43 games.

Oakland: Catcher A.J. Hinch didn't hurt his chances to be the 1998 opening day catcher with a .277 average in a 25-game stint at Phoenix of the AFL. The former Stanford star completed a whirlwind '97 that saw him go from first-year pro to big league hopeful in just a few months. Shortstop Miguel Tejada did not fare so well at Aguilas in the Dominican, batting just .245 in 43 games with a .299 on-base percentage.

Seattle: Outfielder Raul Ibanez hit .360 for Santurce in Puerto Rico, knocking seven homers and driving in 26 runs in just 29 games. Pitchers Brett Hinchcliffe (3-1, 4.50 in nine starts for AFL's Peoria) and Edwin Hurtado (8-4, 2.77 in 15 games for Lara in Venezuela) could be helpful to the Mariners this season.

Tampa Bay: Cuban pitcher Rolando Arrojo pitched nine times (four starts) for Peoria of the AFL and was 5-0 with a 1.38 ERA in 39 innings. He struck out 39, walked eight, and allowed just 29 hits. Former Orioles righthander Esteban Yan worked in relief for Estrellas in the Dominican, appearing 17 times with a 3-2 record and four saves. He did not allow a homer in 41 innings.

Texas: Righthanded pitcher R.A. Dickey, the Rangers' first-round pick in 1996, was 3-0 in 16 games for Hilo in the Hawaii Winter League. He struck out 26 in 23.1 innings and allowed only 10 hits.

Toronto: Steve Sinclair, a lefthanded reliever, pitched this winter for Lara in Venezuela. He saved 15 games with a 2-1 record and a 2.10 ERA in 31 appearances, fanning 25 in 34 innings.

NATIONAL LEAGUE

Arizona: First baseman Travis Lee hit only .267 with two homers for Grand Canyon of the AFL, ending his big 1997 on a down note.

Atlanta: Glenn Williams, a 21-year-old Australian infielder whom the Braves will convert from shortstop to second base, hit .293 with 10 homers in 44 games this winter for Sydney in his native country. Williams has already played four pro seasons. First baseman Randall Simon hit .415 with four home runs for Escogido in the Dominican, showing improved discipline by fanning just three times in 23 games, though he only walked once.

Chicago: No player had a better winter league performance than the Cubs' utility infielder Jose Hernandez, who hit .323 with 20 homers in 61 games for Mayaguez in Puerto Rico. Righthanded relief-pitching prospect Justin Speier pitched 19 times for Mesa, going 2-4 with eight saves. He struck out 22, walked six, and allowed 22 hits in 23.2 innings.

Cincinnati: Aaron Boone, in contention for an infield job this spring in the Queen City, hit .297 with 5 homers in 35 games for Sun Cities in Arizona.

Colorado: Outfielder Derrick Gibson, considered the best overall athlete in the Colorado organization, batted

21

.250 with 30 RBIs for the AFL's Scottsdale club in 34 games, then went to Santurce in Puerto Rico and batted only .203 in 20 contests. Meanwhile, pitcher Steve Shoemaker had a tough fall at Scottsdale, finishing 1-5 with a 4.91 ERA in nine starts, but he did strike out 49 in 36.2 innings. Another mound prospect, lefty Mike Vavrek, was 3-2, 3.48 in seven starts for Maui.

Florida: Todd Dunwoody batted just .260 with two home runs in 51 games for Ponce in Puerto Rico; he walked only eight times and struck out 48. Mark Kotsay, another outfield prospect, hit .313 in 36 games for Peoria of the AFL. Future closer Oscar Henriquez was 3-1 with six saves in 20 appearances for Magallanes in Venezuela; starter Rafael Medina was 0-4 for Sun Cities in the AFL, but with a 2.09 ERA in nine games. He whiffed 44 in 38.2 innings. Lefthanded pitcher Jesus Sanchez, who came over from the Mets in the Al Leiter trade, made nine starts for Dominican League Nordeste team. He finished 3-3 with a 3.21 ERA, but did have some control troubles, walking 27 in 57 innings.

Houston: Righthanded reliever Jose Cabrera pitched in 21 games for Aguilas of the Dominican Winter League. He allowed just three runs in 19.2 innings and saved four games, walking just one and fanning 17. Scott Elarton, a future starter for Houston, pitched for Puerto Rico's Santurce club, posting a 2-4 record in nine starts despite a 2.53 ERA.

Los Angeles: The team's two best prospects, Adrian Beltre and Paul Konerko, played for Azucareros in the Dominican Republic. Neither did particularly well, Beltre batting .219 with one homer in 40 games and Konerko .254 with five homers in 36 contests.

Milwaukee: Lefty Mike Pasqualicchio, the Brewers' second-round pick in 1995 and one of the best prospects in the organization, pitched 12 games with a 2.61 ERA for the AFL's Sun Cities club. Pasqualicchio is working his way back up the ladder after a horrible 1997 season (1-10 at Class A) caused by an arm injury.

Montreal: First baseman Brad Fullmer hit .414 for Peoria in the AFL, cementing his position as the Expos' lat-

est phenom. He rapped 15 doubles and four homers in 31 games. Righty Shayne Bennett, an Australian native, pitched for Adelaide in his homeland over the winter. In 11 games, he was 5-3, 3.32 with 76 strikeouts and six walks in 62 innings.

New York: Catcher Vance Wilson, 25, didn't hurt his chances at getting a look in spring training by hitting .474 in 23 games for Grand Canyon of the Arizona Fall League. Wilson also smacked six homers and drove in 24 runs in his 78 at bats. He took just three walks in those 23 games, however.

Philadelphia: Tony Fiore, an unheralded pitcher who had a productive '97 at Double A and Triple A, followed up this winter with Arecibo in Puerto Rico, making 10 starts with a 4-3 record and a 3.43 ERA.

Pittsburgh: The AFL was no challenge for outfielder Chad Hermansen, a former No. 1 pick who hit .341 with eight homers in 45 games for Mesa. However, first baseman Ron Wright, playing for the same club, batted just .217, though he did club 11 homers. In 157 at bats, Wright struck out 67 times. In Hawaii, righthanded hurler Paul Ah Yat (a native) made 24 appearances for West Oahu and fashioned a 3-2 record with a 3.74 ERA. Ah Yat struck out 42 in 43.1 innings.

St. Louis: Righthanded prospect Manny Aybar was 4-1 with a 1.96 ERA in nine games for Licey in the Dominican Republic.

San Diego: Lefthanded starter Heath Murray, formerly San Diego's top pitching prospect, had a lost season in 1997 due to injuries and poor performance. However, his performance at Mayaguez (Puerto Rico) was encouraging. In seven starts, Murray compiled a 4-1 record and a 2.27 ERA in 39.1 innings.

San Francisco: Hard-throwing lefty Ricky Pickett pitched 30 games for Arecibo in Puerto Rico and saved six of them. His ERA was 1.35, but Pickett walked 26 and struck out 42 in 33.1 innings.

8	-2	HR	176	7		R/G	5.39	3	+9		HR	220	2
12	-2	LH	300	10		OBA	.358	2	+5		LH	323	6
10	-3	BB	578	7		SA	.467	2	+9		BB	617	4
10	-3	SO	1164	13		PRO	.825	2	+7		SO	955	5

OBA	.334	12	-2	LH	300	10		OBA	.358	2	+5	LH	323
SA	.415	10	-3	BB	578	7		SA	.467	2	+9	BB	617	4
PRO	.747	10	-3	SO	1164	13		PRO	.825	2	+7	SO	955	5

/FIELDING

Rank	+/- %		Raw	Rank
5	-1	BA	.266	5
5	-1	HR	178	8
5	-2	LH	310	7
5	-1	BB	552	7
5	-2	SO	982	9

PITCHING/FIELDING

	Raw	Rank	+/- %		Raw	Rank
OR	815	7	+2	BA	.276	10
RA/G	5.06	7	+3	HR	181	9
OOB	.347	11	+2	LH	304	6
OSA	.434	10	+1	BB	575	9
PRO	.781	11	+1	SO	1,036	6

PITCHING/FIELDING

	Raw	Rank	+/- %		Raw	Rank
OR	790	5	-1	BA	.266	5
RA/G	4.88	5	-1	HR	178	8
OOB	.334	5	-2	LH	310	7
OSA	.424	5	-1	BB	552	7
PRO	.758	5	-2	SO	982	9

PITCHING/FIELDING

	Raw	Rank	+/- %		Raw	Rank
OR	815	7	+2	BA	.276	10
RA/G	5.06	7	+3	HR	181	
OOB	.347	11	+2	LH	304	
OSA	.434	10	+1	BB	575	
PRO	.781	11	+1	SO	1,036	

BY LINE-UP SLOTS

HR	RBI	BA	OBA	SA
4	45	.266	.331	.349
25	90	.276	.371	.481
27	119	.270	.332	.458
32	116	.272	.369	.488
27	94	.269	.353	.461
31	109	.252	.326	.463
15	65	.221	.307	.359
13	57	.252	.312	.359
2	48	.241	.272	.311

BATTING BY LINEUP SLOTS

	R	HR	RBI	BA	OBA	SA
1	105	18	82	.263	.329	.413
2	107	9	66	.268	.319	.362
3	119	38	112	.292	.420	.539
4	103	34	107	.278	.353	.505
5	97	38	120	.319	.398	.567
6	87	31	107	.295	.350	.503
7	84	14	73	.285	.357	.426
8	80	22	77	.286	.349	.451
9	86	16	66	.294	.349	.450

BATTING BY LINE-UP SLOTS

	R	HR	RBI	BA	OBA	SA
1	114	4	45	.266	.331	.349
2	110	25	90	.275	.371	.481
3	99	27	119	.270	.332	.458
4	107	32	116	.272	.369	.488
5	96	27	94	.269	.353	.461
6	82	31	109	.252	.326	.463
7	60	15	65	.221	.307	.359
8	69	13	57	.252	.312	.359
9	47	2	48	.241	.272	.311

BATTING BY LINEUP SLOTS

	R	HR	RBI	BA	OBA	SA
1	105	18	82	.263	.329	.413
2	107	9	66	.268	.319	.362
3	119	38	112	.292	.420	.539
4	103	34	107	.278	.353	.505
5	97	38	120	.319	.398	.567
6	87	31	107	.295	.350	.503
7	84	14	73	.285	.357	.426
8	80	22	77	.286	.349	.451
9	86	16	66	.294	.349	.450

TEAM REPORTS

CHING

W-L	CG	QS	QS%	
58-63	13	75		

ITCHING

W-L	CG	QS	QS%	
60-53	4	70	43	

	W-L	GR	SV	BSV	HD
	21-20	417	42	22	126
BULLPEN	26-22	428	39	15	123
BULLPEN	21-20	417	42	22	126
BULLPEN	26-22	428	39	15	

	HR	RBI	BA	OBA	SA
	10	53	.250	.302	.342

	R	HR	RBI	BA	OBA	SA
C	80	25	99	.317	.352	.517

	R	HR	RBI	BA	OBA	SA
C	56	10	53	.250	.302	.342

	R	HR	RBI	BA	OBA	SA
C	80	25	99	.317	.352	

BASERUNNING

Rank	+/- %		Raw	Rank
8	-2	BA	.258	13
8	-2	HR	176	7
12	-2	LH	300	10
10	-3	BB	578	7
10	-3	SO	1164	13

BATTING/BASERUNNING

	Raw	Rank	+/- %		Raw	Rank
R	868	3	+9	BA	.286	3
R/G	5.39	3	+9	HR	220	2
OBA	.358	2	+5	LH	323	6
SA	.467	2	+9	BB	617	4
PRO	.825	2	+7	SO	955	5

BATTING/BASERUNNING

	Raw	Rank	+/- %		Raw	Rank
R	784	8	-2	BA	.258	13
R/G	4.84	8	-2	HR	176	7
OBA	.332	12	-2	LH	300	10
SA	.415	10	-3	BB	578	7
PRO	.747	10	-3	SO	1164	13

BATTING/BASERUNNING

	Raw	Rank	+/- %		Raw	Rank
R	868	3	+9	BA	.286	
R/G	5.39	3	+9	HR	220	2
OBA	.358	2	+5	LH	323	
SA	.467	2	+9	BB	617	4
PRO	.825	2	+7	SO	955	5

/FIELDING

Rank	+/- %		Raw	Rank
5	-1	BA	.266	5
5	-1	HR	178	8
5	-2	LH	310	7
5	-1	BB	552	7
5	-2	SO	982	9

PITCHING/FIELDING

	Raw	Rank	+/- %		Raw	Rank
OR	815	7	+2	BA	.276	10
RA/G	5.06	7	+3	HR	181	9
OOB	.347	11	+2	LH	304	6
OSA	.434	10	+1	BB	575	9
PRO	.781	11	+1	SO	1,036	6

PITCHING/FIELDING

	Raw	Rank	+/- %		Raw	Rank
OR	790	5	-1	BA	.266	5
RA/G	4.88	5	-1	HR	178	8
OOB	.334	5	-2	LH	310	7
OSA	.424	5	-1	BB	552	7
PRO	.758	5	-2	SO	982	9

PITCHING/FIELDING

	Raw	Rank	+/- %		Raw	Rank
OR	815	7	+2	BA	.276	10
RA/G	5.06	7	+3	HR	181	
OOB	.347	11	+2	LH	304	
OSA	.434	10	+1	BB	575	
PRO	.781	11	+1	SO	1,036	

BY LINE-UP SLOTS

HR	RBI	BA	OBA	SA
4	45	.266	.331	.349
25	90	.276	.371	.481
27	119	.270	.332	.458
32	116	.272	.369	.488
27	94	.269	.353	.461
31	109	.252	.326	.463
15	65	.221	.307	.359
13	57	.252	.312	.359
2	48	.241	.272	.311

BATTING BY LINEUP SLOTS

	R	HR	RBI	BA	OBA	SA
1	105	18	82	.263	.329	.413
2	107	9	66	.268	.319	.362
3	119	38	112	.292	.420	.539
4	103	34	107	.278	.353	.505
5	97	38	120	.319	.398	.567
6	87	31	107	.295	.350	.503
7	84	14	73	.285	.357	.426
8	80	22	77	.286	.349	.451
9	86	16	66	.294	.349	.450

BATTING BY LINE-UP SLOTS

	R	HR	RBI	BA	OBA	SA
1	114	4	45	.266	.331	.349
2	110	25	90	.276	.371	.481
3	99	27	119	.270	.332	.458
4	107	32	116	.272	.369	.488
5	96	27	94	.269	.353	.461
6	82	31	109	.252	.326	.463
7	60	15	65	.221	.307	.359
8	69	13	57	.252	.312	.359
9	47	2	48	.241	.272	.311

BATTING BY LINEUP SLOTS

	R	HR	RBI	BA	OBA	SA
1	105	18	82	.263	.329	.413
2	107	9	66	.268	.319	.362
3	119	38	112	.292	.420	.539
4	103	34	107	.278	.353	.505
5	97	38	120	.319	.398	.567
6	87	31	107	.295	.350	.503
7	84	14	73	.285	.357	.426
8	80	22	77	.286	.349	.451
9	86	16	66	.294	.349	.450

CHING

W-L	CG	QS	QS%	<6
58-63	13	75	46	36

TEAM PITCHING

	W-L	CG	QS	QS%	<6
ROTATION	60-53	4	70	43	31

TEAM PITCHING

	W-L	CG	QS	QS%	<6
ROTATION	58-63	13	75	46	36

TEAM PITCHING

	W-L	CG	QS	QS%	
ROTATION	60-53	4	70	43	

	W-L	GR	SV	BSV	HD
	21-20	417	42	22	126
BULLPEN	26-22	428	39	15	123
BULLPEN	21-20	417	42	22	126
BULLPEN	26-22	428	39	15	12

	HR	RBI	BA	OBA	SA
	10	53	.250	.302	.342

	R	HR	RBI	BA	OBA	SA
C	80	25	99	.317	.352	.517

	R	HR	RBI	BA	OBA	SA
C	56	10	53	.250	.302	.342

	R	HR	RBI	BA	OBA	SA
C	80	25	99	.317	.352	

BALTIMORE ORIOLES

MANAGEMENT

Manager	General Manager	Owner
Davey Johnson Career Record 985-727 .575	Pat Gillick	Peter Angelos

1997 RECORD

Won-Lost	Pct.	Division Finish/GB	Wild Card Finish/GB
98-64	.605	1 E	

Preseason Consensus Projection	2 (1.70)

1st Half	2nd Half	Home	Road	Intradivision	Interleague
51-27	47-37	46-35	52-29	25-23	8-7

Comebacks	Blowouts	Nailbiters
12-6	24-21	46-29

THE DEMISE OF DAVEY JOHNSON

The Orioles had the best record in the American League in 1997, but for the second straight year they couldn't turn an expensive team into a world champion. Their loss in the ALCS takes nothing away from their achievements, however, nor those of their since-departed manager, Davey Johnson. Baltimore had a superb regular season.

Johnson made the playoffs again in 1997 with a team that featured several offensive players having subpar seasons (at least by their own standards), including Rafael Palmeiro, Roberto Alomar, and Brady Anderson. How did Johnson do it? He fearlessly juggled, platooned, and shuffled his players—even the stars.

Surprisingly, Johnson hasn't been given adequate credit for managing—not just stewarding, but actually managing—the Orioles over the last two years. He skippered a team full of high-profile, high-salaried, high-ego players to

success, avoiding the dangers of battling these big egos by showing each player, directly or indirectly, that none of them was more important than the team—or, by extension, Johnson himself.

Having endured a hailstorm of criticism for moving Cal Ripken, a legend in his own time, to third base for a handful of games in 1996, Johnson went to the mat with his biggest star to effect the change on a full-time basis in 1997.

After Johnson discussed the matter with Ripken, the Orioles signed free agent Mike Bordick, a steady defensive shortstop, and moved Ripken to the hot corner in the off-season. As the year went on, complaints from the fans and the media ("You can't move Cal Ripken!") began to fade, and by September no one seemed to care much that Ripken wasn't playing shortstop anymore.

Baltimore had no full-time designated hitter in 1997. So

Johnson, understanding—as every great AL manager of the past quarter-century has—that the DH is a great way to platoon players and keep them in the lineup if they can't play the field, rotated whatever veterans he had in and out of the job. Harold Baines, Geronimo Berroa, and Pete Incaviglia logged DH duty, as well as Anderson and Eric Davis when they were unable to play defense due to injury. Jeffrey Hammonds also spent 25 games as DH. B.J. Surhoff and Chris Hoiles filled in on occasion, and Jeff Reboulet even appeared once.

Catcher Hoiles, a longtime regular due to a fine bat, has never been able to master the defensive side of the game. His inability to do so finally cost him a full-time job in 1997, and he ended up platooning with veteran Lenny Webster. Nary a word of complaint was heard, and Webster had his best overall season ever (.255, 7 homers, 37 RBIs).

In the Division Series, Johnson again did the unconventional thing, benching lefthanders Palmeiro and Alomar against Seattle's Randy Johnson in favor of Jerome Walton and Jeff Reboulet! The moves worked out well for the Orioles, which made the Orioles manager look good and also reminded every player on the team that the skipper was in charge.

However, Johnson did not manage well in the ALCS. A key reason for the Orioles' loss was a refusal to follow his own example. Davey's Baltimore clubs have been power-hitting teams that didn't rely much on the running game. In the ALCS, though, Johnson used the hit-and-run, sometimes to poor effect, despite not having the right personnel to do so. His curious, though occasional, use of the bunt came back to haunt him in the final ALCS game when, in the seventh inning of a scoreless tie with two on and none out, Alomar's sacrifice bunt attempt was turned into a rally-killing forceout.

This critical tactic deserves closer examination, because it was arguably the turning point of the game, the season and, eventually, Johnson's career in Baltimore.

Indians starter Charles Nagy had thrown more than 100 pitches. The two batters he had faced in the seventh, Bordick and Anderson, had smacked line-drive singles to the outfield. Either Nagy was tiring and getting the ball up, or the Birds had figured out what to do with his curves and sinkers.

TEAM MVP

None of the Orioles' position players had great seasons; Rafael Palmeiro hit just .254 despite his 38 homers; Roberto Alomar suffered through nagging injuries; Brady Anderson hit 32 fewer homers than he had the previous year. However, pitcher **Mike Mussina** had another outstanding campaign, even if he didn't get any Cy Young votes. He was 15-8, 3.20 in 33 starts, fanned 218 in 224.2 innings, and allowed opponents just a .282 on-base average.

BIGGEST SURPRISE

Righthanded starter **Scott Erickson** hit one of the high points in his up-and-down career. He won 16 games to co-lead the staff, losing just seven times and registering a very respectable 3.69 ERA. And although, over the course of a season, Erickson still has his wild games, overall he averaged only 2½ walks per nine innings. But the Birds couldn't have won the AL East without his stellar performance.

BIGGEST DISAPPOINTMENT

Most Orioles performed solidly in 1997, even .236-hitting shortstop Mike Bordick. One who didn't was young righthander **Rocky Coppinger**. After a 10-6 debut season in 1996, he sagged in five '97 appearances (1-1, 6.30) before being sent down to Triple A to improve not only his command but his attitude. He never resurfaced in Baltimore.

25

With Alomar at the plate, the bunt seemed like an obvious move. Third baseman Matt Williams went in to speak to Nagy about the play, and up in the TV booth, Fox analysts Tim McCarver and Bob Brenly were not only predicting the bunt, but also predicting that the Tribe would put on the rotation play. In fact, McCarver noted that Williams was probably telling Nagy to let Alomar bunt it to third, making the forceout at third base easier on the slow Bordick.

A proper question to ask, then, is, If McCarver knew what was up and had a logical defense for it, why did Johnson insist on the obvious? Especially since Alomar is one of the best hitters in baseball. Vintage Davey Johnson would have let Alomar have at least one cut at a tiring righthander whom he already touched for a hit earlier in the game.

Instead the Orioles took the textbook approach. Alomar's bunt was fielded cleanly by Williams, who made a smooth throw to Omar Vizquel to retire Bordick at third by two steps. Baltimore didn't get another hit until there were two out in the 11th inning, by which time it was too late.

Burn the book, Davey. You were always better without it anyway.

POSTSEASON POSTSCRIPT

Johnson, a very confident fellow, is clearly very impressed with his own abilities. He stated before the playoffs that the winner of the World Series had already been decided by fate. He then intimated during the ALCS with Cleveland that the Orioles' 3-1 deficit amounted to someone "messing with fate"—indicating that Johnson felt that the heavens and earth were united in their support for an Orioles world championship.

Of course, he was wrong, but if you feel the elements on your side, what's a little public scrap with the media about Ripken? Maybe that attitude is the secret of Johnson's success.

RX FOR THE O'S

The Orioles have played good-to-excellent ball the last two years with a veteran club. The team got older in 1997, shedding Greg Zaun (late in 1996), Jimmy Haynes, and Manny Alexander, among others, in favor of such players as Shawn Boskie, Scott Kamieniecki, Jimmy Key, Terry Mathews (late in 1996), Lenny Webster, Jeff Reboulet, Mike Bordick, Geronimo Berroa, and Harold Baines.

While Baines isn't a long-term acquisition, the point is clear: this is a veteran team not getting any younger. With Baltimore's farm system ranking as one of the least productive in the game in recent years, how will the big club stay in contention until the new influx of talent comes from the low levels of the minors?

The answer lies with the owner and with the fans. As long as more than 45,000 of them are willing to pay premium prices to pack Camden Yards every night, the team will have plenty of money to spend on free agents to cover for a lack of young talent. Owner Peter Angelos appears determined to give Orioles fans winning baseball, spending the millions it takes to do so, and so far he seems to trust GM Pat Gillick to make the necessary moves. The relationship between Angelos and Johnson, however, was worse than rough, as one would expect of any relationship between two successful, my-way-or-the-highway guys. New manager Ray Miller had been brought in by Angelos to be Johnson's pitching coach against Johnson's wishes.

With a winter off to recover from the aches and pains that bothered him all through 1997, Roberto Alomar should rebound in 1998. Assuming that Rafael Palmeiro and Brady Anderson remain productive, what does Baltimore most need to do to stay competitive? For starters:

•Sort out the rotation. The Orioles need one more solid starter. The team's no.5 men in 1997 included temporary solutions like Boskie, Rick Krivda, Rocky Coppinger (never one of Johnson's favorites), and Rule V lefty Mike Johnson. However, they also included youngsters Nerio Rodriguez and Esteban Yan (later lost in the expansion draft), both of whom have good stuff and a great deal of potential. Johnson didn't give young pitching the kind of opportunity in Baltimore that he had in his previous days with the New York Mets, a sign that he didn't think the baby Birds had that much potential.

It would not be prudent to expect good years from all four starters in 1998. While Mike Mussina is a star, Key turns 37 in April, and both Scott Erickson and Kamieniecki have had ups and downs in their careers.

Working in a viable young fourth or fifth starter would not only provide insurance but give the team more flexibility for the future. The Orioles, as they usually do, brought in a veteran option: Doug Drabek. Enough said.

That said, it may be time for Coppinger to receive another chance. Johnson sent Coppinger down last season, reportedly believing him to be extremely big-headed and difficult to teach. While Johnson was correct to assert his authority, Coppinger is still only 24 and is worth another shot.

•Come to terms with Cal Ripken's declining offensive productivity. In that Ripken was no longer a great defensive shortstop, the move to third fit the team's needs. However, Ripken ranks among the AL's lower half of third baseman offensively due to his slowing bat. Were it not for the Streak and his well-earned status as a demigod in Maryland, Ripken certainly wouldn't be playing every day and would most likely be on the verge of platoon status.

•Sort out the outfield. With Anderson set in center and B.J. Surhoff in left in 1998, and with Eric Davis returning, Joe Carter coming aboard, and Harold Baines set for another year at DH, the Birds need to figure out what to do with Jeffrey Hammonds. Hammonds had his best year in 1997, playing all three outfield spots, hitting for power (21 homers), and stealing bases (15). Perhaps left field is his future; Surhoff is not a top-notch offensive or defensive left fielder, despite his hustle and popularity.

ARMANDO BENITEZ: THE TIME IS NOW

The departure of Randy Myers to Toronto via free agency opens up the door for the Orioles to use younger pitchers in the closing role. Righthander Armando Benitez and lefthander Arthur Rhodes are the top candidates, though new manager Ray Miller has been talking about sharing roles in what used to be derisively called a bullpen-by-committee.

Both Benitez and Rhodes have the pure stuff to close. Benitez has the classic mid-90s fastball/hard slider combination, and the control problems that often come along with that arsenal (43 walks—but 106 strikeouts—in 73.1 innings). Rhodes (102 K's in 95.1 innings) throws harder than most lefthanders and also has an above-average slider, though he counts on a sharp, hard curve as his money pitch.

Rhodes bombed out as a starter earlier in his career, but

The Orioles didn't have a mighty struggle to win in 1997. The real moment of truth for the club was more personal and more inspiring even than a championship: the unexpected return of outfielder **Eric Davis** from colon cancer. He was disabled on May 31 and underwent surgery and chemotherapy, but Davis made an amazing recovery, came back to play on September 15, and even hit a home run in the American League Championship Series.

BEST DEAL

Inking veteran **Scott Kamieniecki** to take the fourth starter's spot worked out very well for the Orioles. Kammer was 10-6 in 30 starts, showing he could still throw hard as he pitched with better command than he had for much of the last few years. He's still easy to run on, but Kamieniecki filled a big hole for Baltimore.

WORST DEAL

Shawn Boskie, brought in to be the fifth starter, was 6-6 with a 6.43 ERA in 28 games (only nine of them starts). Boskie allowed 24 doubles and 14 homers in just 77 innings, further stretching the limits of his standing as a major league pitcher.

27

he has prospered over the last two seasons in middle relief, going a combined 19-4. The temptation is always to move a successful middle reliever into a more important role, but there are two good reasons not to convert Rhodes to a closer: First, he is very valuable in his current job, and second, Benitez has already been trained for the closer's job.

Benitez has spent the last two years as Myers' understudy, improving his control and picking up 13 saves in 15 chances. This is the right time for the Orioles to give the 25-year-old Benitez a chance to show his stuff when the game's on the line. He may not work out, in which case they can always try Rhodes in the ninth-inning role, but it's worth the risk to see if Benitez can handle the job full time.

MIKE BORDICK: GOOD ENOUGH

We're supposedly in an era of great stars at short, but only a few clubs sported good offensive shortstops in 1997: Atlanta, Boston, Cleveland, Kansas City, Montreal, the New York Yankees, and Seattle. A very generous padding of that list would include Chicago's and Pittsburgh's Shawon Dunston, Minnesota's Pat Meares, Florida's Edgar Renteria, and Milwaukee's Jose Valentin.

Of the short list, only three—Seattle's Alex Rodriguez, Boston's Nomar Garciapara, and Derek Jeter of the Yankees—are truly potential superstars, and two have won Rookie of the Year honors. Maybe Oakland's Miguel Tejada and Colorado's Neifi Perez will join the group next year.

TOP PROSPECTS
SPRING 1998

1. **Nerio Rodriguez, P.** A converted catcher, the 25-year-old righthander spent his first full season above Double A in 1997, making 27 starts in Triple A and six appearances in the bigs. He has displayed a good sinker and an improving slider, and he could wind up as a spot starter this year for the Orioles.

2. **Danny Clyburn, OF.** Clyburn, who turned 23 last April, hit .300 at Rochester with 20 home runs. He led the club in average, homers, and RBIs. The key to Clyburn's big season was improved patience at the plate; his 53 walks and 107 strikeouts don't look great on paper, but the combination is a great inmprovement over his past ratios. The Orioles could give Clyburn, a righthanded hitter, platoon duty in the outfield this season.

3. **Steve Montgomery, P.** A former Independent Leaguer, the soon-to-be-24-year-old righthander hooked on with the Orioles and was 10-5 with a 3.10 ERA at Double A Bowie last season. He has above-average stuff and is considered a candidate to start, probably in 1999 but possibly this year if other pitchers slump. Montgomery fanned 127 hitters in 136 innings at Bowie.

4. **Julio Moreno, P.** A reed-thin righthander from the Dominican Republic, Moreno made his first high-minor league experience count in 1997. He was 9-6 with a 3.83 ERA at Bowie, using three pitches with good—and still improving—control. The Orioles will probably not rush him to the majors this season due to his tendency to wear out near the end of the year.

5. **Johnny Isom, OF.** Isom was a 28th-round pick in 1995. Last season he had a big year at Bowie, smashing 20 homers and knocking in 91 runs. Isom had 121 strikeouts and walked just 44 times for Bowie, but he established himself as a power-hitting prospect. Since he has little speed and isn't a great outfielder, Isom will have to keep slugging to prove himself. He turns 25 in August.

6. **Brian Shouse, P.** Shouse is a lefthanded reliever who pitched six games for the Pirates back in 1993. He has enjoyed two solid seasons in the Rochester bullpen and is an odds-on favorite to capture a relief job for the Orioles in 1998. While Shouse doesn't throw hard, he does have a good breaking ball and is very stingy with walks.

7. **Tommy Davis, 1B.** After being outrighted off the team's 40-man roster, Davis had his best year in the minors. The righthanded hitter batted .304 with 15 homers for Rochester. A No. 1 pick in 1994 who turns 25 in May, Davis could still end up in some sort of part-time or platoon role with Rafael Palmeiro.

Probably not.

Every other shortstop in the majors ranges from below-average to execrable in offensive performance. At least ten or twelve teams are getting production from their shortstops that look like bad years for Tom Veryzer—and a lot of them are long in the tooth.

What's happening is another spike in the talent graph. In the early 1980s an outstanding crop of young shortstops, including Robin Yount, Alan Trammell, Cal Ripken, Dickie Thon, and Ozzie Smith, manned the fields. While all five were outstanding-to-great players, none of them had the potential that Rodriguez, Garciaparra, or Jeter have at their ages.

Rodriguez, Garciaparra, and Jeter all possess power, speed, baseball savvy, and defensive ability. Any one of them could be as good as any of the above-listed stars, three of whom—maybe four—will wind up in the Hall of Fame.

What does all of this have to do with the Orioles?

Well, Mike Bordick is 32, slow, and coming off several poor offensive seasons (he hit .264 with eight homers back in 1995, his last year over .240). He's one of the old guard, the shortstops who make their contributions in other ways: bunting, hitting, running and, most importantly, with steady, solid defense.

If you can't have a young phenom, you might as well have the best of the old guard, and Bordick is pretty good. Defensively in 1997 he had league-average range and made just 13 errors. By observation and statistical performance, he is a steady player.

The Orioles felt that they could live with Bordick's weak bat as long as he didn't make mistakes. And he didn't, which made his signing a plus for 1997. Bordick is under contract through 1999, by which time one of the young

stars in Seattle, Boston, or New York may have won an MVP award.

What Baltimore has decided, then, is that they can afford to have Bordick in the lineup for three years. To be able to make this strategy work, they'll have to continue to get good production from at least six other spots. That's no certainty, because these Orioles are getting old.

THE EX-CUB FACTOR

Much has been said, little of it seriously, about the so-called "Ex-Cub Factor," which holds that a team's chances of winning decrease in relation with the number of former Cubs it has.

The Yankees won the 1996 World Series despite employing two former Cubs during the season: catcher Joe Girardi and pitcher Dave Pavlas. This past season, New York upped it to three (Girardi, second baseman Rey Sanchez, and pitcher Willie Banks) and couldn't get past the Division Series.

Ex-Cubs populated the Orioles in 1997. In fact, Baltimore used four former Wrigley Field residents: Rafael Palmeiro, Jerome Walton, Shawn Boskie, and Randy Myers.

Cleveland, which won the American League, sported just one ex-Cub: reliever Paul Assenmacher, who did his best to uphold the tradition of his former team with a terrible Division and League Championship series before a solid World Series.

The world champion Marlins also had just one on their postseason roster: reserve infielder Alex Arias, who came to bat three times in October.

Maybe there is something to this after all.

29

BALTIMORE ORIOLES
1997 TEAM STATISTICS

BATTING/BASERUNNING

	Raw	Rank	+/- %		Raw	Rank	+/- %		Raw	Rank	+/- %
R	812	6	+2	BA	.268	9	-1	SB	63	14	-41
R/G	5.01	6	+2	HR	196	4	+11	CS	26	14	-50
OBA	.341	6	0	LH	286	14	-11	SB%	70.8	3	+6
SA	.429	6	0	BB	586	6	+3				
PRO	.770	6	0	SO	952	2	-9				

PITCHING/FIELDING

	Raw	Rank	+/- %		Raw	Rank	+/- %		Raw	Rank	+/- %
OR	681	1	-15	BA	.253	1	-7	OSB	149	13	+36
RA/G	4.20	1	-15	HR	164	3	-7	OCS	50	6	-6
OOB	.323	1	-5	LH	296	2	-8	OSB%	74.9	13	+13
OSA	.401	2	-7	BB	563	8	0	FA	.984	4	0
PRO	.724	2	-6	SO	1,139	4	+10	GDP	125	6	-4

30

BATTING BY LINEUP SLOTS

	R	HR	RBI	BA	OBA	SA
1	111	21	83	.297	.394	.482
2	105	16	81	.297	.360	.434
3	97	31	103	.254	.320	.441
4	92	25	92	.253	.334	.422
5	102	31	121	.304	.360	.520
6	89	27	93	.269	.344	.447
7	84	23	76	.244	.328	.402
8	70	15	76	.253	.331	.374
9	62	7	55	.235	.289	.314

BATTING BY DEFENSIVE POSITION

	R	HR	RBI	BA	OBA	SA
C	69	16	76	.251	.338	.376
1B	105	43	123	.262	.336	.512
2B	99	18	86	.309	.373	.455
3B	82	18	85	.273	.336	.407
SS	61	7	55	.239	.287	.319
LF	85	24	102	.274	.330	.456
CF	110	23	76	.281	.374	.469
RF	103	30	97	.276	.357	.479
DH	86	16	69	.251	.340	.382
PH	10	1	11	.220	.280	.308
P	0	0	0	.091	.231	.091

TEAM PITCHING

	W-L	CG	QS	QS%	<6	>6	IPS	IP	ERA	OPR
ROTATION	65-40	8	89	55	31	62	6.1	983.1	4.19	.740

	W-L	GR	SV	BSV	HD	BHD	IRS%	IP	ERA	OPR
BULLPEN	33-24	400	59	10	152	63	29	477.2	3.33	.689

BALTIMORE ORIOLES
1998 PROJECTIONS

BATTING

PLAYER	BA	G	AB	R	H	2B	3B	HR	RBI	BB	SO	SB	CS	SA	OBA
Alomar, Roberto	.313	135	511	86	160	30	4	17	72	57	51	15	4	.483	.382
Anderson, Brady	.275	148	575	100	158	36	7	25	78	78	101	20	10	.491	.362
Baines, Harold	.295	128	422	56	125	21	0	17	67	56	53	1	1	.467	.379
Bordick, Mike	.256	136	456	50	117	17	2	6	47	37	59	3	3	.344	.312
Carter, Joe	.245	123	483	63	119	25	3	20	80	33	83	7	2	.431	.294
Clyburn, Danny	.262	30	111	17	29	6	1	4	14	10	28	2	0	.437	.321
Davis, Eric	.276	59	201	36	55	10	0	10	33	26	59	9	3	.481	.358
Greene, Charlie	.231	8	23	3	5	1	0	1	3	1	6	0	0	.393	.265
Hammonds, Jeffrey	.255	121	410	68	105	19	3	20	54	34	78	13	2	.460	.312
Hoiles, Chris	.252	105	337	49	85	14	0	16	54	52	84	1	0	.435	.352
Laker, Tim	.241	11	40	6	10	1	0	1	5	5	9	0	0	.384	.320
Palmeiro, Rafael	.264	133	517	82	137	24	2	32	98	61	82	4	1	.503	.342
Reboulet, Jeff	.255	71	163	20	42	7	0	2	19	18	30	2	1	.341	.329
Ripken, Cal	.272	147	564	76	154	30	0	19	83	52	66	1	1	.425	.334
Rosario, Melvin	.254	12	42	7	11	3	0	1	6	3	12	0	0	.385	.298
Surhoff, B.J.	.286	140	509	75	146	28	4	17	82	45	62	2	1	.460	.344
Tarasco, Tony	.232	37	81	13	19	4	0	3	11	11	16	3	1	.400	.321
Walton, Jerome	.290	23	43	6	13	2	0	2	6	3	7	1	1	.484	.343
Webster, Lenny	.259	90	231	26	60	9	1	6	31	24	39	0	1	.381	.330

PITCHING

PITCHER	W	L	SV	ERA	G	GS	IP	H	HR	BB	SO
Benitez, Armando	4	6	15	3.26	81	0	83	57	8	51	116
Boskie, Shawn	5	4	0	5.34	18	10	71	83	14	23	46
Charlton, Norm	3	7	12	5.29	62	0	65	68	6	37	57
Coppinger, Rocky	5	2	0	5.14	12	11	63	63	11	35	57
Drabek, Doug	8	8	0	5.14	25	25	136	146	21	50	85
Erickson, Scott	13	8	0	4.31	29	29	190	203	15	56	104
Kamieniecki, Scott	10	7	0	4.41	30	29	173	176	20	73	103
Key, Jimmy	13	10	0	4.00	31	31	187	192	21	70	124
Krivda, Rick	4	4	0	4.21	12	12	77	75	8	21	52
Mathews, Terry	3	3	1	4.48	39	0	44	45	6	22	33
Mills, Alan	3	3	2	4.67	52	0	54	51	8	40	46
Mussina, Mike	15	9	0	3.85	32	32	215	205	26	55	192
Orosco, Jesse	6	3	0	2.95	84	0	64	42	7	37	61
Rhodes, Arthur	8	3	4	3.90	43	2	85	72	9	31	92
Rodriguez, Nerio	5	4	0	3.89	15	13	83	63	11	30	62
Stull, Everett	1	1	0	3.93	3	3	18	16	2	8	12

31

BOSTON RED SOX

MANAGEMENT

Manager	General Manager	Owner
Jimy Williams Career Record 359-325 .525	Dan Duquette	JRY Corp./John Harrington

1997 RECORD

Won-Lost	Pct.	Division Finish/GB		Wild Card Finish/GB	
78-84	.481	4 E	-20	6	-18

Preseason Consensus Projection	4 (3.65)

1st Half	2nd Half	Home	Road	Intradivision	Interleague
36-44	42-40	39-42	39-42	22-26	6-9

Comebacks	Blowouts	Nailbiters
12-13	29-29	33-37

DUQUETTE'S ROULETTE

After being traded from Montreal to Boston, Pedro Martinez signed the most lucrative deal in baseball history last winter, putting his John Hancock on a $75 million six-year contract. There is no arguing with Pedro's talent: he is certainly the top young pitcher in baseball, and arguably the best pitcher in baseball, period.

Unlike many stellar young hurlers, the wiry 26-year-old has probably not been overused; since 1993, his innings count has gone from 107 to 144.2 to 194.2 to 216.2 to last year's 241.1. Since Boston has plenty of experienced pitchers in its bullpen like Tom Gordon, Dennis Eckersley, and Butch Henry, Martinez will probably not have to throw 13 complete games again, as he did last season to pace the NL.

Martinez now heads up a wobbly Sox rotation. Other pitchers slated to start for Boston include veteran righthanders Tim Wakefield and Bret Saberhagen, lefthander Steve Avery, and rookies Robinson Checo and Brian Rose. The path is clear for Tom Gordon to return to the rotation should injuries, ineffectiveness, or the prevalent Sox bad karma infect any of the above-listed prospective starters. Certainly, counting on Saberhagen and Avery to enjoy effective and injury-free seasons is a gamble, and the team can afford to pile up talent to cut its risk.

Nonpitching acquisitions included Jim Leyritz and Damon Buford, who came over from Texas in exchange for righthanded starter Aaron Sele. The Red Sox may have been right in determining that Sele wasn't going to win for them, but what did they get in return?

Leyritz, a good hitter with celebrated pitch-calling skills and a mediocre arm, will fill the righthanded power reserve role formerly held by Mike Stanley and catch as well. Buford will be the team's newest slap-hitting backup outfielder, joining a recent lineage that includes Jesus Tavarez, Milt Cuyler, and Alex Cole.

Yet another player who could join that club is Darren Lewis, who was signed during the winter and was considered a front-runner for the club's left-field job. It remains highly unlikely that Lewis, a .247 career hitter with an extremely low .314 career slugging average, will end up as more than a reserve. If he plays every day, the BoSox will be hurting.

SECOND-GUESSING

If the Red Sox's 1997 season hadn't been such a debacle, it wouldn't be fair to spend a lot of time second-guessing their 1996-97 off-season changes. But Boston's season was a debacle, and second-guessing is the theme of this off-season. The Red Sox certainly did act with firmness and resolve in their dealings with Roger Clemens after the 1996 season. Also stupidity. As some writers wrote off the Rocket, Boston management, particularly general manager Dan Duquette, sniped about Clemens' "decline" and questioned his long-term value.

The Toronto Blue Jays, however, had few such reservations, choosing to pay Clemens $24.75 million for three years. It turned out to be the only truly good personnel move the Jays made in the entire 1996-97 off-season. How great was Clemens in 1997, and how much did the Red Sox miss him? Seattle's Randy Johnson had an amazing season, his best ever, and Clemens bested him in nearly every category, including wins, strikeouts, and ERA. While the Red Sox clearly had some valid questions about Clemens' future after his 10-13 record in 1996, they were wrong to write him off. Despite that mediocre won-lost mark, he could still pitch, having fanned 257 batters in 242.2 innings and posted a 3.63 mark in a year where the league mark was 4.99. None too shabby, to say the least.

A look at Clemens' career numbers indicates greatness as well. His career ERA in road games coming into 1997 was 2.92, an excellent mark for someone who had thrown nearly 1,400 career innings in foreign parks. Even more impressive, in a way, was his 3.19 ERA in Fenway, one of the toughest parks in the game for pitchers during most of Roger's career. Clemens is clearly the greatest pitcher of the last 25 years, and his 1997 season simply cements the

TEAM MVP

While first baseman Mo Vaughn had another superb season, there was no question as to who was the best and most important player on the Red Sox in 1997. Rookie shortstop **Nomar Garciaparra** won the AL Rookie of the Year Award with a spectacular offensive and defensive season.

BIGGEST SURPRISE

Rookie catcher **Scott Hatteberg** won the regular job from Mike Stanley and Bill Haselman with a good season. He played solid defense and as a bonus hit .277 with 10 homers.

BIGGEST DISAPPOINTMENT

The on-field performance of left fielder **Wilfredo Cordero** was average (.281, 18 homers, 122 strikeouts, .320 on-base percentage), but his off-field problems really hurt the team. Cordero was arrested for spousal abuse, and the organization didn't help matters by reacting too slowly. While some local fans and writers called for Cordero's head, amazingly, other prominent members of the local media defended him. The whole episode was more than ugly, and Cordero won't be back.

33

Rocket's place among the best of all time. Meanwhile, Boston gave more than $4 million to Steve Avery. What in the world were they thinking a year ago?

THIRD-GUESSING

When a team consists of 11 pitchers, 13 DHs and a short-stop, the chances are good that said team won't be able to catch the ball. The Red Sox led the AL with 135 errors, and their pitchers allowed 75 unearned runs, well above the league average. Of course, unearned runs only measure part of the damage bad fielding does; every catchable base hit which doesn't light up the "E" on the scoreboard still hurts the team and the pitching staff. Happily for Boston, which has rarely been accused in the recent past of having good chemistry in the clubhouse, this was a team effort. John Valentin, a good shortstop asked to rotate between second and third base, made 22 miscues. Jeff Frye, asked to play seven positions in 1997, made 12 more. Nomar Garciaparra, who could be a perennial Gold Glover in time, committed 21 errors, and first baseman Mo Vaughn kicked away 14. Scott Hatteberg finished second among AL catchers with 11 errors, despite playing just 106 games. Outfielders Darren Bragg and Troy O'Leary combined for 11, although Hub fans were thankfully spared the sight of O'Leary playing center field again.

Dan Duquette loves shuffling players back and forth from Triple A to the majors, and this has to take a huge toll on the team's chemistry and consistency. What young play-er doesn't start looking over his shoulder when the 23rd, 24th, and 25th men in the clubhouse get sent out every few days? Boston used 53 players in 1995, 55 in 1996, and 46 last season. The BoSox employed seven center fielders and 12 DHs in 1997 and suffered the consequences. Among the infielders only Garciaparra and Tim Naehring could be considered above-average defensive players; of the outfielders, Bragg has the top arm but is probably over-matched in center, and he's the best of the group.

It's not that Dan Duquette isn't smart or hasn't made some good trades; he is, and he has. Bragg was stolen from Seattle, John Wasdin came over for Jose Canseco last January, and Troy O'Leary was claimed on waivers from Milwaukee in 1995.

It's just that Duquette makes so many personnel moves

that it looks as if the Red Sox don't have a plan. One month it's, "Let's wait for the kids," and then the next thing it's Jose Canseco in right field, or Kevin Mitchell in left, or Shane Mack in center. Or Felix Jose. Or Tuffy Rhodes. A handful of 1995 at bats convinced Boston that Dwayne Hosey could be the team's center fielder in 1996, and we all know how well that turned out. Last season, the false hope was Rudy Pemberton, a 27-year-old rambler who never met a pitch he didn't think he could hit 400 feet. After batting .326 with 27 homers in 1996, his third straight season facing International League pitching, Pemberton batted .512 in 41 late-season at bats for Boston.

As a result the Carmines concluded that Pemberton was ready to be their regular right fielder. When he hit .238 with two homers in 27 games, Pemberton was buried and plowed over like the rest of the bodies in Boston's growing graveyard of mistakes.

WILFREDO CORDERO: OUT OF POSITION, OUT OF A JOB?

Another big Red Sox '97 memory was the Wilfredo Cordero ugliness. Everybody looked bad in this one: Cordero, who denied that he had a problem despite over-whelming evidence that he had beaten his wife; the MLBPA, who filed a grievance for him (don't these guys ever accept that players are sometimes guilty?); the Red Sox organization, which did not cover itself in glory with its half-hearted, too-little, too-late disciplinary action; and some pundits, who rationalized themselves into defending Cordero's actions as culturally misunderstood.

The Red Soxs' wavering about Cordero came, of course, after they screwed up his career. In 1996 Boston had moved him from shortstop to second base, where his leg was broken when he couldn't get out of the way of a slid-ing runner, and last season the team shifted him to left field. Cordero just isn't a good enough hitter to play left field every day; if he's going to help his team, he's got to do it while holding down an infield job. Players are not chess pieces that can be moved at a whim to suit a manager's or general manager's needs. When players are stretched past their capabilities, the team suffers. Boston has dealt with this harsh truth often in the last few years, often paying the price for having asked players to do things they can't do.

New skipper Jimy Williams seemed to bring some sanity to the clubhouse last season, but it came too late for Cordero, who once upon a time was a good young player. He may still be young, but his career is hanging by a thread.

NOMAR GARCIAPARA: COMPLETING THE PICTURE

The only thing that deserving AL Rookie of the Year Nomar Garciaparra apparently can't do is take a pitch. As a rookie, he was a resounding success in everything but drawing walks (just 22 in 153 games). He scored 122 runs (despite a barely above-par .342 on-base percentage) because he rapped out 84 extra-base hits and stole 22 bases, but the Red Sox would have been a better team with him hitting lower in the order. It will be interesting to see if the team uses someone else at the top this season. The candidates include just about everybody. Clearly, Nomar is primed to be a great player. Based on 1997 he has already demonstrated that he is a great player. Even if he suffers somewhat of a falloff in '98, as Alex Rodriguez did in '97, he must still be regarded as an incredibly gifted individual. He turns 25 in July, and with ten to twelve more years ahead of him, there are few limits to how good he can be. He may already be the best all-around shortstop in the major leagues, and he still has room to grow. Garciaparra doesn't have to acquire good plate discipline to continue his career at a stellar level. Only a few of the greatest players have put it all together, displaying no weaknesses. However, if he becomes a more selective hitter, he will see better pitches to hit and he will improve his already impressive power.

TOM GORDON: CLOSED OUT

Exactly how long the Red Sox could skate with Heathcliff Slocumb as their closer was answered last year. He was 0-5 in 49 games for Boston with an almost unbelievable a 5.79 ERA, walking 34 in 46.2 innings. Even so, it wasn't the worst performance by a pitcher who started the season as a closer. Norm Charlton was worse for the Mariners. But the only thing more incredible than Boston's reliance on Slocumb was that the Red Sox were able to get two middling prospects for him from a desperate Seattle. By the time Slocumb was gone, Tom Gordon was closing games

THE MOMENT OF TRUTH

By May 15 the Red Sox were already 9.5 games out and falling fast. There was never a pennant race for this team. One of the uglier games of the year came on May 10, when the Rangers and Red Sox were tied at five in the ninth with Heathcliff Slocumb on the mound. Texas' Juan Gonzalez hit a grand slam off Slocumb in a six-run ninth that gave the visitors an 11-5 win. It was one of Slocumb's five losses without a win for the Red Sox.

BEST DEAL

Getting rid of aging, troublesome DH Jose Canseco was a great move for Boston. It opened up a spot for a younger, cheaper, better player (Reggie Jefferson) and netted the Red Sox a valuable pitcher, John Wasdin, as well.

35

WORST DEAL

Signing Steve Avery last winter to a one-year contract with an option that kicked in at 18 starts was a move fraught with questions from the start. All the answers to those questions were negative; Avery (6-7) had a 6.42 ERA for Boston and allowed 15 homers in 96.2 innings, but he still insisted that he was throwing well. Manager Jimy Williams kept on using the left-hander, who will be back in 1998 as a result of making those 18 starts.

1. **Michael Coleman, OF.** Regarded by some as the best prospect in the Double A Eastern League, Coleman was promoted to Triple A late last season, when he played 28 games for Pawtucket. The 22-year-old got into eight games with Boston in September and made strong impressions with his talent and work ethic. He could be up for good in 1998.

2. **Brian Rose, P.** It is 90 percent certain that Rose, a 22-year-old righthander, will start 1998 in the Red Sox rotation. He was 17-5 at Pawtucket last season, pacing the minor leagues in victories and the International League with his 3.02 ERA. A tough battler with four solid pitches, Rose is stingy with walks but did allow 21 homers in 1997. The Red Sox will eagerly take that exchange.

3. **Arquimedez Pozo, 2B/3B.** It seems that Pozo has been around forever, but he won't be 25 until August and could still have a career if the Red Sox decide what to do with him. The righthanded-hitting infielder has proven all he can at Triple A and had a four-game trial in Boston (4 for 15, 3 RBIs). Glovework has been a concern at both second and third base, but if Pozo can't field, he at least merits a chance to platoon at DH with Reggie Jefferson.

4. **Robinson Checo, P.** A Dominican who came to Boston via Japan, the 26-year-old Checo began the season disabled with a sore right elbow. He made 21 minor league starts, compiling a 6-6 record at three levels, pitching his best ball at Triple A Pawtucket as he regained strength. Called to Boston in September, he pitched in five games, fanning 14 and walking three in 13.1 innings. Checo is expected to begin the season in the rotation, and sporting a fine fastball and sharp slider, he could dominate.

5. **Ron Mahay, P.** A former outfielder and replacement player, Mahay started over and has worked his way through the system as a left handed reliever. He was very effective at Double A and Triple A before a call-up in mid-July. For the Red Sox, he finished 3-0 in 28 games, fanning 22 in 25 innings and compiling a 2.52 ERA. While command is a question for Mahay, he has a better fastball than most lefthanders and should have a role with Boston again this year.

6. **Trot Nixon, OF.** Remember him? Nixon was the Red Sox's top pick in 1993 and is now considered over the hill by some baseball insiders. That would be premature judgement; Nixon turns 24 this year and has dealt with back injuries and adjustments to curveballs to fight his way up the ladder. Last season at Pawtucket, just his fourth pro campaign, Nixon's numbers, while not great, were at least encouraging to Boston management. He's still got a chance.

7. **Donnie Sadler, 2B/OF.** Just a year ago, Sadler was a top prospect. Now, after a 1997 season in which he hit just 11 homers with 121 strikeouts in 481 at bats at Triple A, the speedy Sadler has slid off the chart. He has too much talent to be written off; Sadler had hit well at every previous level, and probably slumped in part because the Red Sox haven't yet decided if he should be a shortstop, center fielder, or second baseman. Sadler will be 24 this summer.

8. **Peter Munro, P.** The Red Sox like the righthander because of his polish and command. However, Munro has a long injury history and hasn't yet harnessed his talent. Last season he was 7-10 with a 4.95 ERA at Trenton but did strike out 109 in 116 innings. Munro, who turns 23 this year, doesn't project to be ready until 1999 but could conceivably sneak in this year; Boston runs through an awful lot of pitchers in a season.

for Boston. He saved 11 in 13 chances and appeared to have the makeup for the job. However, on a team with only one dominant starter (Pedro Martinez), can the Red Sox really limit one of their best pitchers to 70 innings a season? Well, management sure seemed to think so, with hot starting pitching prospect Brian Rose on the way after a big season at Pawtucket. Gordon was being talked up as that exceptional kind of closer who could pitch two innings an appearance, negating the need for a top-grade setup man. However, the Red Sox never saw an old guy they didn't want, and they did the expected by jumping at 43-year-old free agent Dennis Eckersley. Boston signed him to a one-year deal and announced that Gordon would not be the closer. He will be used mostly in the setup role, occasionally spelling The Eck. By midseason or earlier, Gordon will probably be in the rotation or closing.

BRIAN ROSE: A KEEPER?

Two years ago, it was all set. The Red Sox potentially had three young righthanded pitching aces they hoped to count on for the next ten years: Jeff Suppan, Carl Pavano, and Brian Rose. Stuff happens, apparently. Suppan wasn't deemed good enough to protect in the expansion draft, and thus was taken by the Arizona Diamondbacks. Pavano was the ransom for acquiring Cy Young Award winner Pedro Martinez, and he will at least be able to start his major league career in Montreal with a minimum of pressure. This puts Boston's hopes on Rose, who at age 21 was 17-5 last season at Triple-A Pawtucket. Rose is indeed a fine prospect who led the minor leagues in wins in 1997

and moved ahead of Pavano in the eyes of management in 1997. Are the Red Sox right? Is Rose better? The numbers don't say he is. In 1997, Pavano was 11-6 with a 3.12 ERA, while Rose's 17-5 mark came with a 3.02 mark. The difference in won/lost records from the two, then, is probably due more to run support and luck than to Rose's talent. Pavano, who is just a month older than Rose, has a more consistent record of minor league success. Pavano also has a much higher strikeout rate in his minor league career than does Rose, and sports a control record nearly as good. Pitchers with high strikeout rates and low walk rates tend to be successful more often than not. Rose, who is not a power pitcher, does have a good sinker and fine control, and could be a good-to-excellent major leaguer. But his ceiling isn't as high as that of Pavano.

RICK TRLICEK: A TRUE JOURNEYMAN

Pitcher Rick Trlicek saw action in 18 games with Boston in 1997 before being dealt to the New York Mets. His career employers:

Year	Team(s)
1987-88	Philadelphia
1989	Atlanta
1990-92	Toronto
1993	Los Angeles
1994	Boston
1995	San Francisco, Cleveland
1996	Detroit, New York Mets
1997	Boston, New York Mets

37

1997 TEAM STATISTICS

BATTING/BASERUNNING

	Raw	Rank	+/- %		Raw	Rank	+/- %		Raw	Rank	+/- %
R	851	4	+7	BA	.291	1	+8	SB	68	13	-36
R/G	5.25	4	+7	HR	185	6	+5	CS	48	10	-7
OBA	.352	4	+4	LH	405	1	+26	SB%	58.6	14	-13
SA	.463	3	+8	BB	514	10	-10				
PRO	.815	3	+6	SO	1,044	7	0				

PITCHING/FIELDING

	Raw	Rank	+/- %		Raw	Rank	+/- %		Raw	Rank	+/- %
OR	857	12	+7	BA	.277	11	+2	OSB	171	14	+56
RA/G	5.29	12	+7	HR	149	2	-15	OCS	53	9	0
OOB	.351	13	+3	LH	360	12	+11	OSB%	76.3	14	+15
OSA	.424	6	-1	BB	611	13	+9	FA	.978	14	0
PRO	.776	9	+1	SO	987	8	4	GDP	145	12	+12

BATTING BY LINEUP SLOTS

	R	HR	RBI	BA	OBA	SA
1	129	31	108	.306	.342	.531
2	105	19	78	.270	.332	.427
3	115	34	108	.312	.406	.520
4	106	24	98	.305	.362	.486
5	93	25	100	.283	.347	.465
6	76	17	93	.302	.359	.466
7	82	13	75	.275	.334	.407
8	72	9	79	.291	.362	.423
9	73	13	71	.276	.322	.425

BATTING BY DEFENSIVE POSITION

	R	HR	RBI	BA	OBA	SA
C	74	16	74	.265	.332	.418
1B	112	40	114	.316	.420	.564
2B	94	9	82	.314	.363	.460
3B	90	20	87	.293	.362	.473
SS	126	30	100	.299	.336	.519
LF	94	21	93	.289	.331	.448
CF	67	12	72	.269	.335	.401
RF	74	14	78	.271	.331	.412
DH	94	21	97	.306	.358	.468
PH	17	5	21	.291	.361	.495
P	1	0	1	.167	.167	.167

TEAM PITCHING

	W-L	CG	QS	QS%	<6	>6	IPS	IP	ERA	OPR
ROTATION	50-53	7	69	43	46	52	5.6	909.1	4.95	.780

	W-L	GR	SV	BSV	HD	BHD	IRS%	IP	ERA	OPR
BULLPEN	28-31	417	40	26	112	86	40	542.1	4.70	.768

1998 PROJECTIONS

BATTING

PLAYER	BA	G	AB	R	H	2B	3B	HR	RBI	BB	SO	SB	CS	SA	OBA
Benjamin, Mike	.255	36	93	11	24	6	1	1	8	5	24	3	2	.372	.296
Bragg, Darren	.260	121	397	57	103	26	2	8	44	53	78	10	5	.393	.347
Buford, Damon	.240	98	257	40	62	13	0	7	29	25	61	14	7	.367	.307
Coleman, Michael	.258	59	224	31	58	10	4	8	29	20	66	8	0	.445	.319
Frye, Jeff	.299	80	274	41	82	21	1	2	31	24	33	11	4	.409	.355
Garciaparra, Nomar	.294	158	700	120	206	42	12	30	100	34	93	23	8	.519	.327
Hatteberg, Scott	.273	122	364	48	99	24	1	10	44	42	72	0	1	.424	.349
Hurst, Jimmy	.253	53	169	21	43	5	1	8	25	20	63	4	0	.431	.331
Jefferson, Reggie	.317	134	455	70	144	31	2	14	69	24	89	1	1	.487	.351
Lewis, Darren	.272	89	189	31	51	6	1	1	22	23	29	15	6	.340	.351
Leyritz, Jim	.268	105	330	44	89	11	0	9	52	47	74	2	1	.383	.360
McKeel, Walt	.232	12	42	5	10	3	0	1	5	5	8	0	0	.364	.317
Naehring, Tim	.286	89	323	50	92	18	1	11	47	44	48	1	1	.446	.373
O'Leary, Troy	.291	140	478	64	139	30	5	14	74	39	71	2	4	.460	.345
Pozo, Arquimedez	.234	39	146	19	34	6	0	7	23	11	27	1	0	.420	.290
Valentin, John	.294	143	572	95	168	40	4	18	77	63	64	10	6	.474	.365
Varitek, Jason	.223	18	63	9	14	3	0	3	8	7	17	0	0	.391	.297
Vaughn, Mo	.300	149	567	95	170	25	1	37	109	82	146	3	2	.541	.388

PITCHING

PITCHER	W	L	SV	ERA	G	GS	IP	H	HR	BB	SO
Avery, Steve	7	9	0	5.14	24	22	122	140	15	48	77
Checo, Robinson	5	4	0	3.06	15	12	76	57	8	20	66
Corsi, Jim	6	2	2	3.73	55	0	65	62	2	28	42
Eckersley, Dennis	1	6	31	4.19	66	0	62	64	9	9	52
Gordon, Tom	5	6	7	4.49	22	17	112	110	9	51	91
Henry, Butch	7	5	1	3.37	28	10	94	99	7	21	53
Hudson, Joe	1	1	0	4.33	16	0	21	24	1	10	9
Lacy, Kerry	1	0	0	5.20	16	0	21	26	3	10	9
Lowe, Derek	2	1	0	3.92	6	4	28	24	3	9	18
Mahay, Ron	11	1	2	2.78	45	17	39	30	6	18	33
Martinez, Pedro J.	17	11	0	2.81	36	36	263	199	20	81	302
Rose, Brian	6	6	0	4.34	17	17	118	137	15	34	61
Saberhagen, Bret	4	3	0	4.14	13	13	76	80	9	15	53
Wakefield, Tim	11	12	0	4.39	29	26	178	177	24	75	126
Wasdin, John	3	4	0	4.83	26	7	74	75	12	24	47

39

MANAGEMENT

Manager	General Manager	Owner
Joe Torre Career Record 1082-1139 .487	Bob Watson	George Steinbrenner

1997 RECORD

Won-Lost 96-66	Pct. .593	Division Finish/GB 2 E -2		Wild Card Finish/GB 1
Preseason Consensus Projection 1 (1.57)				
1st Half 2nd Half 46-33 50-33	**Home** 47-33	**Road** 49-33	**Intradivision** 29-19	**Interleague** 5-10
Comebacks 8-14	**Blowouts** 41-14	**Nailbiters** 36-35		

40

NO SUCH LUCK

Like lightning in that old saying, magic rarely seems to strike in the same place twice. It probably can't be any other way—otherwise the magic in magical events would be lost. The magical 1996 season in the Bronx, which ended in a world championship for Joe Torre and his lovable pinstriped crew, did not return in 1997.

The Yankees finished second in the AL in runs, second in ERA, and second in wins, just two victories behind the Orioles. However, a feeling lingered around the franchise all season that this was not to be the Yankees' year. From the Hideki Irabu fiasco to Darryl Strawberry's knees to Dwight Gooden's legal problems, as Mariano Duncan and Wade Boggs begged to be traded and Kenny Rogers sat and waited for a deal that didn't come until the fall, the defending world champs did not seem like a championship team.

Which is not to say that several Yankees did not perform in outstanding fashion. Bernie Williams and Paul O'Neill again had productive seasons at bat and in the field, while Tino Martinez and Derek Jeter were outstanding all-around players. Andy Pettitte and David Cone pitched excellent ball, and Mariano Rivera more than made up for the loss of Wetteland, posting 43 saves and a 1.88 ERA.

But the Yankees had problems with starting pitchers, infielders, and chemistry, that could not be addressed by the standard George Steinbrenner solution of hauling in veterans. That didn't stop the Yankees from trying. From far and wide came Chad Curtis, Mike Stanley, Pete Incaviglia, Mark Whiten, Rey Sanchez, Scott Pose, Joe Borowski, and even Willie Banks. Most of them made absolutely no difference.

At the end of the season the Yankees were left with only two starters that they really felt good about, an overworked bullpen, and a Division Series playoff loss to Cleveland.

Some of the trouble was of the club's own making. The Yankees did not act proactively to shore up their infield in the 1996-97 off-season and suffered for it. Duncan, a player of questionable value even when he hits .300, was still there but not hitting .300, as were Luis Sojo, Pat Kelly, and Andy Fox. Manager Joe Torre never could decide what to do with any of them until the club finally dumped Duncan and acquired Sanchez in August.

Third base was another problem. The Yankees spent two years juggling two players, Charlie Hayes and Wade Boggs, who hated platooning. Neither of them was good enough to play every day, but they didn't accept that.

New York was strong at nearly every other spot. First base, shortstop, left field, center field, and right field were positives, while DH and catcher were at least adequate. Defensively, the Yankees were strong everywhere when Curtis was in left and Sanchez manned second.

Getting Curtis off the scrap pile to play left field (in place of the oft-injured Tim Raines and the failed Whiten) was a good move. The '98 Yankees are probably a better team for letting go of veterans like Duncan, Boggs, Whiten, and Cecil Fielder, all of whom are old and highly salaried and bring either injury-proneness or excessive personal baggage along.

It's time to see if Jorge Posada, Ricky Ledee, Mike Figga, Shane Spencer, and Mike Lowell can play, instead of trading them to other teams. Of course it's unclear whether New York management has the patience.

Where the Yankees could really use an infusion of young talent is in the starting rotation. Cone and Pettitte were heroic, with Cone making a triumphant return from a career-threatening injury. However, the support staff wasn't supportive. Despite a good overall season, lefthander David Wells was his usual erratic self, and Dwight Gooden was not a quality fourth starter. Kenny Rogers was so bad that he couldn't even pitch long relief by August, and Ramiro Mendoza, despite his bulldog attitude, just couldn't pick up the slack. The Hideki Irabu venture was a failure all-around.

With Rivera getting off to a poor start and Jeff Nelson struggling for consistency, the bullpen lost some games that should have been won. However, Mike Stanton and Graeme Lloyd were good from the left side, and Brian

TEAM MVP

There are several candidates for this honor. Andy Pettitte had a terrific season, winning 18 with a 2.88 ERA. Mariano Rivera saved 43 games. Paul O'Neill had another outstanding year at the plate, and first baseman Tino Martinez hit .296 with 44 homers and 141 RBIs. However, the Yankees' best player is center fielder **Bernie Williams**. He plays a critical defensive position with skill and panache and hit .328 with 35 doubles, 21 homers, 15 stolen bases, and 100 RBIs last year to boot.

BIGGEST SURPRISE

Despite the departure of closer John Wetteland, the **New York bullpen** was fine in 1997. Mariano Rivera survived an early-season cold spell to save 43 games in 52 tries with a 1.88 ERA. Setup man Jeff Nelson had another big season, and southpaw Mike Stanton made a strong comeback, fanning 70 in 66.2 innings and allowing just three homers all year. Lefty Graeme Lloyd and righty Brian Boehringer also chipped in, pitching well in situational and long relief.

BIGGEST DISAPPOINTMENT

Lefthander **Kenny Rogers** got yet another trial at the starting rotation and bombed out once more. He made 22 starts but spent some of the year as the last man in the bullpen, becoming persona non grata late in the season. Final totals: 6-7, 5.65 ERA, and a trade to Oakland immediately following the season.

41

THE MOMENT OF
TRUTH

On **September 1**, the Yankees were 6.5 games behind the Orioles in the AL East title race. However, with three games in Philadelphia (the worst team in the NL) and then four at home against Baltimore, the Bombers still had a fighting chance. Disastrously for New York, the Phillies were up for the challenge, sweeping the three-game set 5-1, 5-0, and 5-4 while the O's were losing three in Florida. Then the Yankees went home and dropped three of four to the Orioles, ending any chance of closing the gap.

BEST DEAL

Picking up veteran outfielder **Chad Curtis** off the scrap heap was a big move for the Yankees. After hitting just .207 in 22 games before being released by the Indians, Curtis came to New York and filled in while erstwhile left fielders Mark Whiten, Tim Raines, and Darryl Strawberry all got into either legal or injury trouble. While Curtis isn't a star, he hit .291 with 12 homers and played good defense. That was enough to help the Yankees get into the playoffs.

WORST DEAL

The Yankees paid an awful lot of money and traded two key prospects (**Rafael Medina** and **Ruben Rivera**) to the Padres in order to obtain high-profile Japanese righthander **Hideki Irabu**, whose ERA for the Bombers (7.09 in 53.1 innings) was almost as fat as his ego. While Irabu still has the potential to be a terrific big league pitcher, he won't do it without some serious attitude adjustment.

Boehringer (who was lost in the expansion draft) filled in from the right side. One assumes that young Danny Rios and Borowski will compete for a job or two this coming year, as the Yankees need relief help.

WADING IN

Ending the 1997 season just 200 hits shy of 3,000 career safeties, Wade Boggs would be the first singles hitter to reach that vaunted plateau since Hall of Famer Rod Carew in 1985.

Boggs ranks as one of the best leadoff hitters in history because he has gotten on base well over 40 percent of the time. He has won five batting titles and led the league in on-base percentage six times. He has scored 100 runs seven times, twice leading the AL, despite having only doubles power and no speed.

Last year, though, was one of his worst seasons ever—perhaps the worst. Now with expansion Tampa Bay, the 40-year-old will almost certainly stick around long enough to get his 200 remaining hits and, thereby, punch his ticket to Cooperstown.

How good has he been? One thing that many critics say about Boggs is that he got a huge benefit from playing in Fenway Park for the first 11 years of his career. Certainly, his leading the league twice in doubles (1988-89) was a function of dumping routine fly balls off the Green Monster, right?

With the Red Sox between 1982 and 1992 Boggs batted .307 in road games, with 36 homers, 316 RBIs, and 965 hits. At Fenway, on the other hand, Wade batted .369 with 49 homers, 371 RBIs, and 1,133 hits. In 1985, the year he hit .368, his best-ever mark, Boggs batted .418 at Fenway and .326 on the road.

All things considered, Boggs was a very good player in Boston. He then went on to New York, where he spent five seasons and proved that he is an adaptable professional.

Despite entering 1993 with just a .276 career average at Yankee Stadium, the lowest of any city to that point in his career, he hit .314 in the Bronx that year as opposed to .291 on the road. Although his power numbers dipped severely upon going to New York and never recovered, he basically created his own chance to get 3,000 hits out of his ability to adapt. Bravo.

The question of just how good a player he is must be answered differently. When he was hitting for extra bases, getting on base 40-45 percent of the time, and playing good defense (he was underrated with the glove for years), Boggs was a very valuable player. Now that he is playing adequate defense but not hitting for power and getting on base 37 percent of the time, he is barely a platoon player.

The Yankees understood that and let him go after benching him in '96 and platooning him in '97. The Devil Rays will find that out in '98. What marketing value they will reap from having a 40-year-old hometown hero pursue his personal goal is unknown.

THE ICING?

As strong as the New York Yankees have been in the last few seasons, they have had a sore spot at second base. The team has also lacked a first-class leadoff hitter to supercharge the offense.

The early February deal bringing disgruntled All-Star second sacker Chuck Knoblauch over from the Minnesota Twins addressed both of those needs. Knoblauch is one of the best at his position, despite a subpar 1997, and won't turn 30 until July.

The Yankees gave up four young players for him: lefthanded pitcher Eric Milton, righthander Danny Mota, outfielder Brian Buchanan, and shortstop Cristian Guzman. Milton is the outstanding prospect, a pitcher who has blown away hitters at Class A and Double-A and may be in the majors later this season.

TOP PROSPECTS
SPRING 1998

1. **Ricky Ledee, OF.** Due to injuries, he had just 170 at bats in 1997, but he did hit .306 with 10 homers at Triple A Columbus in that span. Ledee, now 24, has genuine punch and is improving his knowledge of the strike zone. His speed and defensive ability are only average, but a lefthanded bat with power is always helpful in Yankee Stadium.

2. **Mike Lowell, 3B.** Just a 20th-round pick in 1995, Lowell has been in pro ball only three years, but has moved quickly. He began 1997 at Double A Norwich, hitting 15 homers with a .344 average, before moving up to Columbus, where he hit .276 with 15 more long balls. A contact hitter with good strike-zone judgment, the 24-year-old Lowell (a former shortstop and second baseman) is solid defensively and has a good chance to grow into a big league job soon.

3. **Mike Jerzembeck, P.** After missing most of the 1995 season due to a serious elbow injury, the righthander began to get his game together in 1996. Last year at Double A, Jerzembeck was 2-1 with a 1.71 ERA in eight starts (42 innings, 42 strikeouts) before advancing to Columbus. He was 7-5 for the Clippers in 20 starts, fanning 118 and walking 37 in 130 innings. This spring the 25-year-old Jerzembeck, who throws a heavy sinker with a good breaking ball and changeup, will fight for a spot in the New York bullpen.

4. **Gabby Martinez, SS.** Milwaukee's first-round draft pick in 1992 came over to the Yankees in the Pat Listach fiasco. Martinez has terrific defensive tools, and is starting to produce at the plate as well. He batted .321 at Double-A Norwich in 1997 with 21 steals. However, he is not a patient hitter and does not hit for power. If Martinez, 24, has a good season at Triple A, he could make himself attractive to several teams. He's not going to unseat Derek Jeter.

5. **Mike Figga, C.** The Yankees like Figga's power. However, he batted but .244 last year at Columbus with 12 homers. Worse yet, he had 18 walks and 104 strikeouts. His progress may have been hampered by a serious 1996 knee injury. Whatever the cause for his slump, Figga had better get it together quickly. He turns 28 this summer, and his catching skills aren't much to write home about.

43

1997 TEAM STATISTICS

BATTING/BASERUNNING

	Raw	Rank	+/- %			Raw	Rank	+/- %			Raw	Rank	+/- %
R	891	2	+12		BA	.287	2	+6		SB	99	9	-7
R/G	5.50	2	+12		HR	161	8	-9		CS	58	5	+12
OBA	.362	1	+6		LH	348	2	+8		SB%	63.1	13	-6
SA	.436	5	+2		BB	676	1	+19					
PRO	.798	4	+4		SO	954	4	-9					

PITCHING/FIELDING

	Raw	Rank	+/- %			Raw	Rank	+/- %			Raw	Rank	+/- %
OR	688	2	-14		BA	.260	2	-4		OSB	111	8	+1
RA/G	4.25	2	-14		HR	144	1	-18		OCS	47	3	11
OOB	.327	3	-4		LH	297	3	-8		OSB%	70.3	10	+6
OSA	.394	1	-8		BB	532	4	-5		FA	.983	6	0
PRO	.722	1	-6		SO	1,165	2	+13		GDP	133	8	+2

44

BATTING BY LINEUP SLOTS

	R	HR	RBI	BA	OBA	SA
1	134	11	81	.317	.392	.447
2	108	8	78	.271	.349	.374
3	144	28	129	.343	.430	.549
4	100	38	146	.283	.362	.525
5	87	28	119	.277	.355	.462
6	80	18	88	.272	.336	.433
7	92	16	75	.284	.370	.426
8	74	11	76	.288	.354	.408
9	72	3	54	.237	.296	.291

BATTING BY DEFENSIVE POSITION

	R	HR	RBI	BA	OBA	SA
C	67	7	75	.258	.326	.357
1B	100	46	150	.298	.382	.579
2B	79	5	61	.282	.331	.362
3B	88	14	76	.268	.348	.389
SS	118	10	71	.291	.369	.404
LF	105	12	69	.266	.353	.381
CF	123	25	124	.332	.405	.540
RF	101	24	125	.307	.381	.496
DH	87	17	87	.285	.360	.430
PH	8	1	8	.194	.324	.274
P	0	0	0	.000	.000	.000

TEAM PITCHING

	W-L	CG	QS	QS%	<6	>6	IPS	IP	ERA	OPR
ROTATION	72-42	11	84	52	23	77	6.3	1,017.1	4.12	.735

	W-L	GR	SV	BSV	HD	BHD	IRS%	IP	ERA	OPR
BULLPEN	24-24	368	51	25	117	60	29	450.1	3.22	.691

1998 PROJECTIONS

BATTING

PLAYER	BA	G	AB	R	H	2B	3B	HR	RBI	BB	SO	SB	CS	SA	OBA
Brosius, Scott	.241	115	420	61	101	20	1	14	48	39	88	8	3	.392	.306
Bush, Homer	.258	36	129	19	33	6	1	1	12	9	34	3	0	.343	.305
Cruz, Ivan	.240	16	54	7	13	4	0	3	10	7	12	0	0	.443	.324
Curtis, Chad	.267	102	341	56	91	19	1	12	43	43	57	12	7	.435	.350
Davis, Chili	.275	131	458	66	126	19	0	26	82	78	86	5	2	.486	.381
Figga, Mike	.247	11	40	5	10	1	0	1	6	2	13	0	0	.379	.279
Fox, Andy	.247	35	106	21	26	3	1	1	9	17	26	7	0	.342	.350
Girardi, Joe	.283	107	377	44	107	21	2	2	47	26	54	5	3	.367	.330
Jeter, Derek	.294	160	635	111	187	29	7	10	73	65	118	20	10	.409	.360
Martinez, Tino	.283	156	587	88	166	30	1	36	125	69	78	2	1	.521	.358
O'Neill, Paul	.302	150	554	87	167	38	1	20	105	81	84	5	4	.485	.391
Posada, Jorge	.246	87	265	40	65	17	0	8	34	42	49	1	2	.396	.349
Raines, Tim	.296	71	258	49	76	16	1	5	35	38	31	9	3	.429	.385
Sojo, Luis	.289	89	263	32	76	9	1	2	28	16	16	4	1	.360	.331
Sveum, Dale	.262	98	240	25	63	16	1	9	35	22	63	0	2	.446	.323
Williams, Bernie	.304	148	575	110	175	33	7	24	102	79	84	15	7	.508	.388
Lowell, Mike	.239	65	241	36	58	11	0	11	34	26	37	1	0	.415	.313

PITCHING

PITCHER	W	L	SV	ERA	G	GS	IP	H	HR	BB	SO
Alberro, Jose	2	2	0	3.93	8	6	37	34	3	12	18
Banks, Willie	3	3	0	3.52	14	9	59	56	6	17	40
Borowski, Joe	2	4	0	4.27	23	0	27	32	3	19	11
Cone, David	12	6	0	3.20	27	27	183	151	16	82	193
Holmes, Darren	9	3	1	3.78	65	4	102	105	11	36	86
Irabu, Hideki	12	8	0	6.41	28	20	118	145	33	42	123
Lloyd, Graeme	1	4	1	3.98	57	0	56	62	6	22	30
Mendoza, Ramiro	9	7	1	4.60	38	17	137	167	15	28	85
Nelson, Jeff	4	5	2	3.29	67	0	71	56	5	33	78
Pettitte, Andy	18	8	0	3.53	36	35	237	244	13	72	165
Rivera, Mariano	6	3	29	2.64	55	1	78	68	5	25	80
Rios, Danny	1	1	0	3.11	16	0	23	20	3	8	12
Stanton, Mike	5	2	4	3.30	71	0	71	64	6	32	64
Wells, David	13	9	0	4.41	28	28	192	207	23	43	128
Jerzembeck, Mike	3	2	0	3.54	9	9	56	51	5	18	44

45

TAMPA BAY DEVIL RAYS

MANAGEMENT

Manager	General Manager	Owner
Larry Rothschild (no record)	Chuck Lamar	Vincent Naimoli

QUICK FIXES

From the start Tampa management has stressed that it wanted its fans to have "realistic expectations" about competitiveness, that it was going to build the team slowly and carefully and not go for quick-fix solutions.

That plan, an admirable one that led to the ultimate success of the Kansas City Royals and Toronto Blue Jays, has already been borne out in the Devil Rays' minor league operations. They own outright four of the minor league affiliates that they will stock with players, allowing the club more control over the development process and over expenses. The Rays also spent generously for development by signing amateur free-agent pitchers Matt White and Bobby Seay during 1996. Both White and Seay were first-round picks of other teams who were set free after the drafting clubs failed to offer them valid contracts before a specified deadline.

But that strategy seemed to unravel during the November expansion draft. Right after the final pick of the draft, the quick fixes began.

Quick Fix No. 1 was the trade with Atlanta for Fred McGriff. The veteran will either play first base or serve as a designated hitter. The deal was a nice local-color/public-relations move, since McGriff was born in and still lives in Tampa.

Between 1988 and 1994 Crime Dog was one of the best offensive players in the game, combining the ability to hit for high average, draw close to 100 walks per season, and display tremendous home run power. But McGriff is now 34, not in tip-top physical condition, and clearly on the downside. He is no longer nearly as productive a hitter, nor is he as good in the field.

To make the trade for McGriff even less sensible, the Devils Rays had already selected three first basemen, plus two nonmobile outfielder/DH types (Bubba Trammell and Brooks Kieschnick), in the expansion draft. Then they went out and signed Paul Sorrento and Dave Martinez. While one of the drafted first sackers (Dmitri Young) was sent back to Cincinnati in a deal that netted Tampa career disappointment Mike Kelly, the Devil Rays still have draftees Steve Cox and Herb Perry around as well as Brooks and Bubba. Aren't there other needs to attend to?

Drafting shortstop Andy Sheets was an odd move; getting reliever Brian Boehringer was a better one. However, both were almost immediately sent to San Diego for catcher John Flaherty, who at least keeps the Devil Rays from having to start Mike Difelice. Flaherty is supposed to be good with young pitchers. Of course the Padres had their worst-ever ERA in 1997, and NL runners stole more bases off Flaherty than any other catcher. That's Quick Fix No. 2.

The Devil Rays chose starting pitchers almost exclusively in the draft, a good plan. They were apparently confident in the knowledge that they would almost immediately sign closer Roberto Hernandez to a long-term deal. Why, though, should a team that is trying to build for the future spend $22.5 million over four years on a big-name closer if it doesn't expect to contend for the first few years? The theory is that it is demoralizing to a young team to lose games in the final innings. Maybe, but Bryan Harvey's saving 45 games for the first-year Marlins didn't seem to do much for their young players, all of whom were long gone before the team bought a championship. Quick Fix No. 3: that money would be better spent investing in prime position players—Mike Lansing, for instance.

The Devil Rays apparently were very happy with their draft. They did pick up some good pitchers: Terrell Wade, Esteban Yan, Ramon Tatis, Jose Paniagua, Albie Lopez, Rick Gorecki, Tony Saunders, and Bryan Rekar all have major league arms, and some have already proven their abilities at the top level. Tampa, in fact, may have drafted better pitchers than did the Diamondbacks.

Unfortunately, everything else the club did was questionable. Several useless players were chosen with prime picks while good major league players languished unprotected on every club's roster. The best position player the Devil Rays picked up, Bob Abreu, was immediately traded for shortstop Kevin Stocker, who doesn't have much upside but should at least help solidify the infield for several years.

Some other Devil Ray picks were even more shaky. Miguel Cairo is going to be their regular second baseman? Quinton McCracken playing center field every day? (His lifetime road batting average is .256.) Ryan Karp? Dan Carlson? You get to pick a pitcher out of the Braves system and you take John LeRoy?

If part of this Tampa Bay "low expectations" policy was that the club wouldn't spend money on established regulars in the expansion draft, then why did the club acquire Stocker and McGriff, mediocre regulars who cost a lot of money? What is Paul Sorrento going to do at 32 after his career year? Signing Wade Boggs may provide the chance for him to get his 3,000th hit at home sometime in 1999, and Wilson Alvarez is the kind of solid starter a young team needs, but this collection of veterans isn't going to win, and most of them don't represent the future.

At least the newly refurbished Tropicana Field is supposed to look nice.

A DIP IN THE TALENT POOL

When Tampa Bay and Arizona built their rosters in the expansion draft, few names selected were recognizable to most baseball fans. That doesn't mean, however, that there was no talent out there.

Baseball America printed, in its December 8, 1997 issue, what it believed to be accurate versions of each club's initial, 15-player protected list. A quick look at those lists shows plenty of bona fide big league talent available for the asking. Most of the players exposed were considered undesirable due to large, multiyear contracts; others were coming off of injuries or poor performances.

The expansion clubs, especially Tampa Bay, chose to ignore these veterans and their big-league salaries in the draft, then make trades for veterans and sign veteran free agents. Whether this was a successful strategy will be revealed in the next two years.

Here is a 25-player roster selected from the players left unprotected in the first round. These are all players that the new clubs could have had.

• Pitchers: Juan Acevedo, Roger Bailey, Mark Gardner, Mark Guthrie, Mark Hutton, Mike Jackson, Mike James, Jose Mesa, Bill Taylor, Ron Villone, Steve Woodard.

• Catchers: Bill Haselman, Chris Hoiles.

• Infielders: Alex Arias, Carlos Baerga, Bobby Bonilla, Chris Gomez, Eric Karros, Tim Naehring, John Olerud.

• Outfielders: Jermaine Allensworth, Rich Becker, Darren Bragg, Henry Rodriguez, Ron Gant.

QUESTIONABLE TIMING

Being associated with a World Series winner is certainly good for one's career. Larry Rothschild, a pitching coach with no professional managerial experience—even if his Marlins did win the World Series—was named manager of the Devil Rays just two weeks before the expansion draft.

Is this any way to run an airline? This is bad organizational strategy. While the Diamondbacks made their manager, Buck Showalter, a part of the direction of the team almost immediately, hiring him in November 1995, Rothschild came in at the eleventh hour, and was unfamiliar with the setup of the club.

To be fair to the Devil Rays, it may be that the organization knew they wanted him but that Rothschild had to

47

wait until the end of the season. To be fair to Rothschild, it is possible that he will be a good manager; Larry Dierker didn't have managerial experience, and he did all right in his debut.

Somehow, though, this seems different. It's a brand-new club, a brand-new organization, yet management waits until two weeks before the expansion draft to hire the manager? Was he able to get up to speed with three years' worth of planning in two weeks?

BEYOND THUNDERDOME

The (former) Tampa Bay Thunderdome has been renamed, refurbished and turned into a big orange.

Renamed Tropicana Field, the stadium has been redone, adding good disabled access, more seats, new technology, more concession stands, more elevators and escalators, and play areas for children and their parents.

Devil Rays CEO Vincent Naimoli is credited with much of the design for the park, from the asymmetric dimensions to the Ebbets Field–like rotunda near the entrance. The field will be plastic, although for the first time since the 1970s, a turf park will have an entirely dirt infield.

Tampa will play in a park with a very short left field fence (312 feet) and a short right field porch (322 feet). The power alleys will be 371 feet away, while deepest left-center ranges 415 feet from home. Straightaway center is 407 feet. Expectations are that Tropicana Field will be a hitters' park, potentially an excellent one.

TOP PROSPECTS
SPRING 1998

1. **Esteban Yan, P.** Selected from Baltimore's roster in the expansion draft, Yan is a six-foot, four-inch righthander who spent 1997 at Triple A Rochester. He made 34 appearances (12 starts), and was 11-5 with a 3.10 ERA. Obviously the Orioles didn't think much of him, but Yan (who will be 24 in June) has added some velocity and now throws four pitches with command. He walked only 37 men in 119 innings last year, fanning 131.

2. **Rolando Arrojo, P.** A Cuban refugee who might be in his 30s but claims to be 28, Arrojo made 16 starts for Class A St. Petersburg in 1997. He was 5-6 with a 3.43 ERA, striking out 73 and walking 13 in 89 innings. While one would think he should pitch at Double or Triple A in 1998, the Devil Rays could elevate him all the way to the majors; Arrojo did finish 5-0 in the Arizona Fall League.

3. **Miguel Cairo, 2B.** Cairo, drafted from the Cubs, is a steady defensive player who could hit .280 in the majors. He has speed but lacks power and rarely walks, making his offensive game light. He paced the American Association with 40 stolen bases in 1997 but had a .314 on-base percentage and slugged just .381 in 135 games. With the Cubs he batted .241 in 29 at bats. Tampa says he will be their everyday second baseman this season.

4. **Rich Butler, OF.** Formerly a prize prospect with Toronto, Butler was left off the Jays' expansion protected list despite a .300, 24-homer, 20-steal season at Triple A Syracuse. The Jays had no place for Butler in their 1998 outfield, but it is still puzzling that they thought so little of him. He is only average defensively, and a bad shoulder (which kept him out of all but 10 games in 1996) is a question. Butler will be 25 on May Day.

5. **Jason Johnson, P.** After six years in the Pirates system he reached the majors, making three appearances for the Pirates. He was then chosen by the Devil Rays in the expansion draft. Johnson, a six-foot, six-inch righthander, started 17 games at Class A Lynchburg last season, going 8-4 with a 3.71 ERA. He then moved to Double A Carolina, where he finished 3-3, 4.08, before his trial with the Bucs. Johnson fanned 158 hitters and walked just 47 in 162.2 innings overall using an above-average fastball, a power curve, and a changeup.

1998 PROJECTIONS

BATTING

PLAYER	BA	G	AB	R	H	2B	3B	HR	RBI	BB	SO	SB	CS	SA	OBA
Boggs, Wade	.301	108	386	61	116	23	1	4	34	53	35	0	1	.396	.386
Butler, Rich	.244	93	358	51	87	17	5	12	47	33	85	9	0	.422	.307
Cairo, Miguel	.281	75	297	45	84	18	2	3	24	13	34	14	0	.384	.311
Difelice, Mike	.259	78	216	14	56	9	1	3	28	17	54	1	1	.355	.312
Flaherty, John	.287	123	416	40	119	23	1	11	52	27	61	3	3	.427	.331
Kelly, Mike	.256	122	226	40	58	19	2	8	30	19	55	11	2	.462	.313
Kieschnick, Brooks	.234	70	234	32	55	11	0	12	39	23	68	1	0	.438	.304
Ledesma, Aaron	.275	65	212	27	58	14	1	2	23	20	35	5	0	.374	.338
Martinez, Dave	.303	109	349	59	106	13	5	8	40	40	46	9	5	.437	.374
McCracken, Quinton	.265	138	307	56	81	11	2	2	33	35	61	24	9	.340	.340
McGriff, Fred	.276	135	509	69	141	24	1	21	86	58	97	4	1	.453	.350
Mendoza, Carlos	.310	44	144	21	45	6	1	0	7	10	20	6	0	.365	.355
Sorrento, Paul	.265	135	428	62	113	21	0	26	80	51	98	0	2	.499	.343
Stocker, Kevin	.269	151	507	56	137	25	5	4	45	55	100	11	5	.365	.341
Trammell, Bubba	.221	81	267	39	59	11	1	17	48	29	91	2	0	.463	.297

PITCHING

PITCHER	W	L	SV	ERA	G	GS	IP	H	HR	BB	SO
Alvarez, Wilson	11	10	0	4.00	30	30	191	179	18	88	156
Carlson, Dan	2	2	0	3.27	11	4	39	33	4	12	32
Eshelman, Vaughn	2	2	0	4.12	11	6	35	35	2	11	20
Hernandez, Roberto	7	4	36	2.72	72	0	79	70	6	39	85
Johnson, Jason	4	2	0	3.33	9	7	51	48	6	12	45
Leroy, John	1	1	0	3.55	7	3	23	20	4	9	16
Lopez, Albie	4	7	0	5.65	35	9	88	105	15	38	71
Mecir, Jim	0	4	0	5.33	34	0	49	52	7	19	40
Paniagua, Jose	5	5	0	4.45	15	13	77	85	7	27	39
Rekar, Bryan	4	6	0	4.48	17	16	88	94	12	23	58
Saunders, Tony	5	7	0	4.74	28	27	140	127	16	82	128
Springer, Dennis	7	8	0	4.94	26	23	153	150	27	57	69
Tatis, Ramon	1	1	0	5.05	48	0	48	55	11	24	28
Wade, Terrell	5	4	0	4.39	36	14	82	95	12	43	79
White, Rick	2	2	1	4.10	13	3	29	29	2	7	18
Yan, Esteban	6	5	0	3.64	28	10	94	87	11	30	82

49

TORONTO BLUE JAYS

MANAGEMENT

Manager	General Manager	Owner
Mel Queen Career Record 4-1 .800	Gord Ash	Inter-Brew S.A.

1997 RECORD

Won-Lost 76-86	Pct. .469	Division Finish/GB 5 E -22	Wild Card Finish/GB 8 -20
Preseason Consensus Projection 3 (2.74)			

1st Half 37-40	2nd Half 39-46	Home 42-39	Road 34-47	Intradivision 23-25	Interleague 4-11

Comebacks 8-13	Blowouts 15-20	Nailbiters 40-45

THE LESSONS OF THE PAST

The acrimonious end to the tenure of longtime Blue Jays manager Cito Gaston leaves Toronto with a bitter taste coming into 1998. Could it only have been four years ago that the Jays were coming off their second straight world championship, and selling out SkyDome every night?

That's all gone now. The 1997 Blue Jays were expensive and not much fun to watch as they stumbled to a 76-86 record. The club's 1997 media guide had a section previewing the team's big-name free-agent signings and trade acquisitions that was called, arrogantly enough, "A Return to Glory." Of the five new faces featured in the section, one was great (Roger Clemens), one got hurt (Orlando Merced), one performed as expected in a "B" role (Dan Plesac), and two were thoroughly disappointing (Benito Santiago and Carlos Garcia). The Jays-Pirates deal last win-

ter that sent several outstanding prospects, including pitchers Jose Silva and Jose Pett and infield dynamo Abraham Nunez to Pittsburgh for Plesac, Merced, and Garcia now looks to be one of the worst trades in the last 10 years. Ironically, it was also exactly the opposite of the kinds of deals that helped build the Jays into a perennial contender.

That deal was the latest in a series of moves designed to bring the Jays back to their earlier pinnacle of success. But Toronto seemed to have forgotten how they won in the first place. The really good players on the 1992 and '93 championship teams weren't the old guys, although Joe Carter and Paul Molitor helped put the team over the top. The stars of those clubs were the young players, like John Olerud, Roberto Alomar, Pat Hentgen, Juan Guzman, and Devon White. Most of them had been developed through the excellent Toronto scouting network and farm system.

The Jays didn't collapse due to a lack of talent from the

minor leagues. Here are the talented players in the Toronto chain who have made the majors since 1993: Carlos Delgado, Shawn Green, Alex Gonzalez, Darren Hall, Paul Spoljaric, Mike Timlin, Woody Williams, Domingo Cedeno, Jeff Ware, Tim Crabtree, Marty Janzen, Ed Hurtado, Paul Menhart, Tilson Brito, Felipe Crespo, Sandy Martinez, Shannon Stewart, Jose Silva, Chris Carpenter, and Kelvim Escobar. In addition, farm products like Randy Knorr and Ed Sprague were already in the majors as reserves by 1993.

With all this young talent available to plug gaps in the world champs as they aged, and with plenty of money available to sign or re-sign expensive veteran free agents, and with players like Alomar, Olerud, Hentgen, Carter, Guzman, and White in hand, how did the Jays fail?

There are three crucial positions in which Toronto management failed to show initiative, and fell back on inadequate veteran options.

•Second Base. The departure of Roberto Alomar to Baltimore via free agency following a rough 1995 season was a traumatic event from which the Jays have never recovered. Alomar, a true franchise player, certainly should not have been allowed to leave for nothing, and probably should have not been allowed to go at all. The failure of Carlos Garcia in 1997 is just the latest problem Toronto has experienced at the position since Alomar left.

Toronto didn't want for young options back in 1996. Gaston could have chosen between the defense and speed of young Miguel Cairo, the bat potential of Crespo (who had hit his way up the Toronto ladder), the overall ability of Brito (who played better defense than Crespo but doesn't hit quite as well), the defensive skill of young Tomas Perez, or Cedeno, a steady defensive player with the ability to produce a decent batting average.

But Gaston chose all of the above—that is to say, he failed to really decide on any of them. Cairo and Crespo got small, cold cups of coffee, Brito notched just 80 at bats, and Perez and Cedeno ended up splitting most of the playing time when they weren't playing shortstop, third base, or first base.

The acquisition of Garcia for 1997 was supposed to provide a solid veteran solution at the position. This is typical late-period Gaston thinking, which Toronto management

TEAM MVP

To win 21 games with a 2.05 ERA on a team that finished 76-86 is quite an achievement. **Roger Clemens**'s 1997 season more than justified the Jays' decision to sign him, and scuttled the notion that he was past his prime. At 35 there is no reason to expect that he will falter in the next few seasons.

BIGGEST SURPRISE

There were few pleasant surprises for the Blue Jays in 1997. Most of the players they dealt for to help them win suffered through awful seasons. One pitcher, however, was far more productive than expected: sinkerballing right-hander **Paul Quantrill** was 6-7 with an outstanding 1.94 ERA in 77 games. He walked only 17 men in 88 innings and was tagged for just five home runs.

BIGGEST DISAPPOINTMENT

There is competition in this category: catcher Benito Santiago was simply terrible, and third baseman Ed Sprague hit just .228 and struggled with a bad shoulder. Probably the biggest disappointment, however, was second baseman **Carlos Garcia**. Brought on board to clear up a perennial trouble spot, Garcia was poor in the field and hit only .220 in 99 games. He piled up an almost unreal .253 on-base percentage.

51

was only too happy to subscribe to: put young players in situations where they aren't likely to succeed and, when they don't succeed, go out and get a veteran.

While Garcia was having just about the worst year imaginable (for him) in 1997, the Jays were busy getting rid of as many of their young second basemen as they could. Cairo was waived to the Cubs while Brito was traded to the Athletics. Cedeno had already been shunted to the White Sox late in 1996. Perez hung around as a utility player while Crespo stayed in tne minors in 1997. Meanwhile, unproductive, shaky-gloved veteran malcontent Mariano Duncan was brought on board in September.

Duncan served as the perfect symbol of the overrated, underproductive 1997 Blue Jays. The disaster at second base was entirely of the Jays' making, and it as much as anything contributed to the club's miserable season and Gaston's eventual firing.

•Catcher. Things were almost as bad behind the plate. Randy Knorr, who at one time looked to be a promising power hitter, failed to develop. He was never an organizational favorite, and general manager Gord Ash even made unkind public comments about his play. Farm product Sandy Martinez showed outstanding defensive potential, but didn't hit. The Jays (again) decided on the veteran option, hauling in known attitude cases Charlie O'Brien for 1996 and Benito Santiago last year.

O'Brien, known for his defense, played well behind the plate in both seasons but hit terribly in 1997. Santiago was a complete disaster, both on the field and in the clubhouse. Once again the veteran approach backfired, as should have been expected. The adequate offensive season of O'Brien in 1996 has nothing to do with building a club for the long-term, but Toronto again got fooled into thinking it could win with veterans like O'Brien.

•Outfield. Another disaster. Veterans Otis Nixon and Orlando Merced were penciled into the 1997 equation, and both played almost every day until their eventual departures: Merced to shoulder surgery in August and Nixon via trade to Los Angeles late the same month. Neither helped the team.

It was almost as if the Jays had a death wish. When Nixon didn't play, 32-year-old Jacob Brumfield did, and hit about as well as one could expect (.207). Or if

Brumfield didn't play, Juan Samuel did. At one point, the Jays even hauled in perpetual disappointment Ruben Sierra in for a few weeks. Thank goodness it didn't get worse, as the Jays had Mike Aldrete, Ray Giannelli, Ryan Thompson, and Darrell Whitmore awaiting their turns at Triple A.

Finally, as the team continued to sink like an anchor in the AL East, some sense was made of the situation. Shawn Green, who had spent time in left field, right field, and, amazingly enough, as a designated hitter (allowing Joe Carter to patrol the outfield), had his best big league season yet with a good stretch drive. The Jays acquired power-hitting youngster Jose Cruz, Jr., from Seattle in midseason and watched him hit 14 home runs in 51 games. Last, 23-year-old center field prospect Stewart was given a job when Nixon departed, and he showed that he indeed is ready to contribute at the top of the order. That Stewart wasn't given a chance to do so back in 1995 or 1996 is attributable again to Gaston's and the organization's blind love of experienced players. It wasn't an accident that the Jays had Duncan and Samuel on the team in 1997.

Green and Cruz may not become superstars. In fact, there's no guarantee that either one has a long, productive career as a regular ahead of him. However, a team has to give its young players a chance if it's going to figure out who can play and who needs to be replaced. That's how the Jays did it the first time around, and Toronto fans can only hope that the serious damage done to the club in the last few years can be repaired quickly.

The news isn't all bad. Third baseman Sprague, a mediocre player even in his best year, 1996, may not be able to play in the field early in 1998 due to a torn-up shoulder that required surgery. That could give young Tom Evans, a multidimensional offensive player, the chance to claim a job. An outfield of Stewart, Cruz, and Green will certainly be much better than what was out there in 1997.

Finally, and perhaps most painfully for the organization and the fans, the popular Carter was shown the door. Carter has been in steady decline for several seasons, but 1997 was a new low. Some may be impressed by his 102 RBIs, but a designated hitter who hits .234 with 21 homers and 40 walks in 612 at bats is not just a below-average player, but a truly harmful one. Carter made 491 outs in

1997, a staggering total. Nonetheless, Gaston ran him out there every day, playing him 51 times in the outfield and 42 times at first base despite poor mobility in both the outfield and infield.

Gaston has always shown a clear preference for veterans. Although some of the organization's predilection for veterans could have come from GMs Pat Gillick and Ash, it is clear that given the choice between a youngster and a veteran, Gaston would go with the veteran almost every time. It's not clear how much Delgado's, Gonzalez's, and Green's careers have been hurt while Gaston looked at every Ruben Sierra, Dick Schofield, Candy Maldonado, and Jacob Brumfield to come his way, but one assumes Cito is disappointed that the managerial chair in Anaheim isn't currently available. He could really work his magic there with a wheelchair club and management team like the Angels.

JOSE CRUZ, JR.:
DON'T GET CARRIED AWAY

Isn't it strange that people made pitchers Mike Timlin and Paul Spoljaric into whipping boys for their roles in the Jose Cruz, Jr., trade? For all the crap the pundits piled on those two pitchers, one would have thought that Seattle had pitching to burn, that Timlin and Spoljaric were no good, and that Cruz is the second coming of Barry Bonds.

Cruz Minor has undeniable big league power. But before voting him into the hall of fame of bad Mariners trades, or even thinking about him as a future star, consider four things:

•He has below-average speed;

•He is a left fielder, and not a particularly good one;

•He finished the season with an on-base percentage of .315; and

•He struck out 117 times in 395 at bats.

Cruz, Jr., is a young player with a one-dimensional old player's skill: power. This season should tell whether Cruz can iron out his problems at the plate. He could go one of three ways: improve his hitting discipline and boost his performance, relapse and slide back to the minors, or stagnate; plenty of top Blue Jays hitting prospects have done that in the last few years.

THE MOMENT OF
TRUTH

On opening day at SkyDome, closer **Mike Timlin** began to punch his ticket out of town. With the Jays ahead 5-4 in the ninth, he allowed a first-pitch, game-tying pinch-homer to Chicago's **Paco Martin**. The Jays lost 6-5 in ten innings when **Alex Gonzalez**, trying to stop a single from going through the left side, inadvertently knocked the ball into short left field — just far enough so that nobody could field it. The winning run scored from first.

BEST DEAL

Getting **Jose Cruz, Jr.** from Seattle wasn't the steal people made it out to be, because the Jays had to give up two good pitchers in exchange. However, it did indicate that high-ranking people in the organization realized that getting young players was critical to rebuilding this team, and that the all-out veteran approach might not be the best way to win.

WORST DEAL

Dealing a handful of prospects, including real comers like **Jose Silva**, **Jose Pett**, and **Abraham Nunez**, to the Pirates last winter for **Dan Plesac**, **Carlos Garcia**, and **Orlando Merced** was intended to push the Jays over the top. It didn't, of course, and Toronto ended up wondering what to do with Garcia and Merced in a rebuilding scheme. They can never get those prospects back.

53

MONEY MATTERS

One year after opening the vault, what can the Blue Jays do to rebuild? Attendance at SkyDome was weak again in 1997. While the Jays still draw nearly 30,000 per game, that's a very big drop from the 50,000-plus sellouts of two years ago. Toronto still has expensive veterans under contract, though the club has divested itself of some older players and should have the savings to reinvest.

While 1998 should be viewed as a rebuilding year, it is unclear whether fans will buy it if the club's owners try to sell such an on-field strategy. Toronto has three top needs for 1998: a second baseman who can help out at the top of the order, a catcher with a bat, and a lefthanded starter who's good for a lot of innings would make their return to contention a lot more likely.

There were plenty of players in all three of these categories who were available last winter. Young second basemen in Detroit, Cleveland, and Milwaukee, just to name three, could have been a solution. There were also decent veteran options on the market.

At catcher, the team looks to be much improved. Sandy Martinez and Julio Mosquera didn't pan out, so the Jays went out and signed veterans Darrin Fletcher and Mike Stanley for 1998. Lefty-swinging Fletcher will platoon with Santiago; while Stanley won't spend much of his time behind the mask, he is an option if Santiago plays miserably or doesn't recover from his off-season auto accident.

Pitching-wise, the Jays can't count on righthanders Erik Hanson or Juan

TOP PROSPECTS
SPRING 1998

1. **Kelvim Escobar, P.** Escobar was signed in 1992 at age 16. Since then he has worked his way up the system as a starter and hit the jackpot in 1997. After recovering from elbow surgery over the winter, he pitched three games in the Florida State League. Escobar then made five starts at Double A Knoxville, going 2-1 with a 3.70 ERA. Promoted to Toronto on June 28, he became a reliever and won his first big league game the next day. He ended the season 3-2, 2.90 with 14 saves in 27 games for the Jays. This season Escobar, his 95-mph fastball, and his changeup could move back to starting due to the signing of Randy Myers.

2. **Carlos Almanzar, P.** Almanzar was signed as an outfielder by the Jays back in 1990. Converted to the mound, he has worked hard and emerged as a reliever in 1997. For Triple A Syracuse he pitched 32 games with a 5-1 record, three saves, a 1.41 ERA, 47 strikeouts and eight walks in 51 innings. He also pitched four times for the Jays. Almanzar has excellent command of an average-plus fastball and a plus changeup and could be the club's setup man this year.

3. **Tom Evans, 3B.** A third baseman with good glove skills and some power, Evans began 1997 disabled while recovering from right shoulder surgery. He spent 15 games at Class A getting his swing back, then went to Syracuse and hit .263 with 15 homers in 107 games. A promotion to Toronto followed, where Evans hit .289 in 12 games. But Evans tore up his left shoulder while with the Jays and underwent surgery in mid-September. He is 24 this summer and could take Ed Sprague's job in a year.

4. **Roy Halladay, P.** The Jays' first-round pick in 1995 was pushed beyond his limits last year and, predictably, did not respond. He began the season at Double A Knoxville with a 2-3 record and a 5.40 ERA in seven starts, but was promoted to Triple A anyway when Syracuse needed another starter. Halladay got waxed there, pitching 22 times with a 7-10 record and a 4.58 ERA. He fanned just 64, and walked 53, in 125.2 innings. The six-foot, six-inch righthander throws very hard and has a baffling knuckle-curve. It's just a matter of time before Halladay is in the Jays' rotation.

5. **Kevin Witt, 1B.** A former shortstop, Witt—the Jays' first-round pick in 1994—played both first and third base in 1997. He won't get to the bigs because of his glove, but rather for his pop. Witt hit .289 with 30 homers last year for Knoxville, leading the Southern League, and drove in an organization-leading 91 runs. Witt should be in the major leagues in some role within two years, assuming he can continue to improve at making contact.

Guzman to be healthy. If one of them recovers, it will be a bonus. However, even a recovery by both righties wouldn't address the biggest Toronto mound need: lefthanded starting pitching. A veteran lefthanded starter is almost a necessity for the Jays in 1998. Last year only four games were started by southpaws for the club: three by Omar Daal and one by Huck Flener.

The Jays' 1998 chances took a hit over the winter when Carlos Delgado injured his right shoulder diving for a ball while playing in Puerto Rico. Delgado, projected to work both at first base and DH, underwent surgery in January and may not play until June. Stanley will probably take Delgado's place in the lineup, and newly signed free agent Phil Plantier could also see some action because he, like Delgado, bats from the left side.

Rather than invest in a southpaw starter, the club decided to sign veteran lefthanded closer Randy Myers to a big contract in November. This move was made even though the Jays would probably have had a good bullpen in '98 with 22-year-old righty Kelvim Escobar as the closer. Now Escobar will probably be put in the rotation; he was a starter throughout his minor league career. The Jays will use Paul Quantrill, signed to a multiyear deal over the winter, to set up for Myers. Escobar could end up in that role, but it's not likely unless Quantrill flames out and Escobar doesn't work out as a starter.

TIM JOHNSON: THE RIGHT MAN FOR THE JOB

Considered an astute handler of young players, new Blue Jays manager Tim Johnson and his staff might be able to help Jose Cruz, Jr. (as well as Shawn Green, Carlos Delgado, and Alex Gonzalez) make that 10 percent improvement they all need to make to become good players. They've got the talent. Now they need some effective tutoring and mentoring.

Johnson spent 1997 managing the Cubs' Iowa affiliate in the Triple A American Association. After guiding a team thin in talent to a 74-69 mark, he was hired in December to succeed Cito Gaston. Before 1997 Johnson had spent four years in the majors as a bench coach: 1992-94 with

one of the best managers of recent times (Felipe Alou) and 1995-96 with one of the worst (Kevin Kennedy). Presumably, he learned valuable lessons from both.

Johnson has paid his dues and gained plenty of experience. After a seven-year big league career (1973-79) as an infielder with Milwaukee and Toronto, he spent 1980-86 working as a scout. His minor league managing career included successful stops in the Rookie-level Pioneer League, the Class A California League, the Triple A PCL, and several winter leagues.

As one can gather from his résumé, most of Johnson's experience is with young players. It is encouraging to see the Blue Jays putting an emphasis on young talent, because they have a very good record of developing players. As long as the organization can continue to scout and develop talent, Toronto should get back on its feet fairly quickly.

UPS AND DOWNS

With the Blue Jays' move from Exhibition Stadium to SkyDome in 1989, attendance rose sharply, from 32,039 to 42,199 per game. That attendance growth continued through 1993, with routine sellouts in the new stadium as the Jays won two World Series. Here are the yearly attendance figures show:

Year	Average	Increase
1989	42,199	31%
1990	47,966	14%
1991	49,202	3%
1992	49,732	1%
1993	50,098	1%

From the 1993 peak, attendance declined. The 1994 drop off was relatively small, but the fallout from the 1994-95 strike showed as attendance fell sharply.

Year	Average	Decline
1994	49,287	2%
1995	39,257	21%
1996	31,600	20%

Last season Toronto's average attendance rose 1 percent to 31,967. Not bad, but not what the Blue Jays expected after all of the club's off-season spending.

1997 TEAM STATISTICS

BATTING/BASERUNNING

	Raw	Rank	+/- %		Raw	Rank	+/- %		Raw	Rank	+/- %
R	654	14	-18	BA	.244	14	-10	SB	134	3	+26
R/G	4.04	14	-18	HR	147	12	-17	CS	50	9	-3
OBA	.310	14	-9	LH	316	8	-2	SB%	72.8	2	+9
SA	.389	14	-9	BB	487	14	-14				
PRO	.699	14	-9	SO	1,138	12	+9				

PITCHING/FIELDING

	Raw	Rank	+/- %		Raw	Rank	+/- %		Raw	Rank	+/- %
OR	694	3	-13	BA	.263	4	-3	OSB	77	3	-30
RA/G	4.28	3	-13	HR	167	4	-5	OCS	64	13	+21
OOB	.326	2	-4	LH	301	5	-7	OSB%	54.6	2	-18
OSA	.412	3	-4	BB	497	2	-11	FA	.984	3	0
PRO	.739	3	-4	SO	1,150	3	+11	GDP	117	2	-10

BATTING BY LINEUP SLOTS

	R	HR	RBI	BA	OBA	SA
1	93	2	60	.262	.341	.339
2	76	7	60	.232	.293	.324
3	71	26	106	.235	.306	.414
4	86	25	88	.243	.307	.444
5	87	21	74	.253	.334	.460
6	60	23	75	.247	.309	.407
7	59	16	69	.236	.285	.369
8	67	17	54	.235	.297	.380
9	55	10	41	.250	.309	.373

BATTING BY DEFENSIVE POSITION

	R	HR	RBI	BA	OBA	SA
C	54	17	69	.233	.292	.371
1B	82	27	100	.272	.345	.502
2B	58	3	40	.225	.265	.289
3B	75	17	56	.231	.309	.399
SS	54	12	45	.232	.293	.358
LF	80	27	85	.258	.308	.445
CF	91	2	62	.260	.343	.337
RF	79	15	65	.258	.332	.406
DH	71	26	97	.235	.300	.414
PH	8	1	8	.127	.200	.238
P	1	0	0	.118	.211	.176

TEAM PITCHING

	W-L	CG	QS	QS%	<6	>6	IPS	IP	ERA	OPR
ROTATION	57-62	19	86	53	23	85	6.5	1,054.0	3.99	.728

	W-L	GR	SV	BSV	HD	BHD	IRS%	IP	ERA	OPR
BULLPEN	19-24	336	34	21	122	60	32	388.2	3.77	.766

1998 PROJECTIONS

BATTING

PLAYER	BA	G	AB	R	H	2B	3B	HR	RBI	BB	SO	SB	CS	SA	OBA
Crespo, Felipe	.230	21	72	11	17	2	0	3	6	10	11	1	0	.382	.322
Cruz, Jose	.234	128	490	70	115	27	2	25	75	58	162	6	0	.450	.315
Delgado, Carlos	.256	155	527	75	135	37	3	28	92	62	137	0	2	.496	.334
Evans, Tom	.237	55	194	28	46	8	0	7	28	23	64	1	0	.386	.317
Fernandez, Tony	.275	113	393	55	108	20	2	8	45	32	44	7	6	.401	.329
Fletcher, Darrin	.269	109	345	40	93	20	1	14	54	22	35	1	1	.457	.312
Gonzalez, Alex	.247	139	479	58	118	27	3	13	49	43	118	15	7	.400	.308
Grebeck, Craig	.263	46	95	10	25	6	0	1	7	12	11	0	1	.343	.344
Green, Shawn	.282	139	440	57	124	27	4	15	53	34	91	10	2	.462	.334
Kelly, Pat	.244	77	162	30	39	8	1	2	16	18	49	8	2	.355	.319
Mosquera, Julio	.262	13	45	6	12	3	0	1	6	2	10	1	0	.372	.300
Perez, Robert	.282	44	101	11	28	5	0	2	9	2	14	1	0	.400	.299
Perez, Tomas	.256	40	134	15	34	6	1	0	11	18	36	1	0	.316	.344
Samuel, Juan	.261	30	72	12	19	3	2	3	12	7	21	3	1	.493	.329
Santiago, Benito	.260	91	318	38	83	13	0	15	48	23	72	1	0	.444	.311
Sprague, Ed	.239	116	427	59	102	25	3	17	55	44	92	0	0	.432	.310
Stanley, Mike	.275	122	365	62	100	23	0	18	65	56	70	1	1	.487	.372
Stewart, Shannon	.284	115	422	66	120	27	8	6	46	54	68	15	0	.426	.366

PITCHING

PITCHER	W	L	SV	ERA	G	GS	IP	H	HR	BB	SO
Almanzar, Carlos	4	2	3	3.16	38	0	54	45	4	10	43
Andujar, Luis	1	6	0	5.43	18	10	60	77	11	24	28
Carpenter, Chris	6	6	0	4.08	18	18	108	110	12	45	68
Clemens, Roger	17	10	0	2.94	36	36	263	227	14	89	284
Crabtree, Tim	3	3	4	4.72	46	0	53	65	6	20	39
Escobar, Kelvim	5	4	13	3.09	51	0	58	55	2	37	67
Flener, Huck	2	2	0	4.73	6	4	29	33	3	10	11
Guzman, Juan	6	9	0	4.38	22	22	123	110	18	51	104
Hanson, Erik	4	4	0	5.26	11	11	72	78	9	30	57
Hentgen, Pat	13	10	0	3.90	30	30	224	221	24	72	141
Myers, Randy	2	4	38	2.78	70	0	68	62	5	31	71
Person, Robert	3	6	0	5.11	17	13	81	76	12	35	64
Plesac, Dan	3	4	2	3.94	73	0	59	57	6	23	67
Quantrill, Paul	4	7	2	3.91	39	7	76	94	9	20	47
Robinson, Ken	2	1	0	2.98	15	0	21	12	2	10	21
Williams, Woody	7	11	0	4.37	29	24	158	163	24	56	103

57

CHICAGO WHITE SOX

MANAGEMENT

Manager	General Manager	Owner
Terry Bevington Career Record 222-214 .509	Ron Schueler	Jerry Reinsdorf

1997 RECORD

Won-Lost 80-81	Pct. .497	Division Finish/GB 2C -6	Wild Card Finish/GB 3 -15.5

Preseason Consensus Projection	2 (1.57)		

1st Half 2nd Half 40-39 40-42	Home Road 45-36 35-45	Intradivision Interleague 26-21 8-7

Comebacks 9-7	Blowouts 17-29	Nailbiters 36-34

WHITE SOX AND BLACK FANS

The White Sox and Chicago's black community have had an interesting but often difficult relationship. The Southside Sox clearly get more African-American fans to their games than do the Northside Cubs, even though both clubs' parks are in white neighborhoods closely surrounded by integrated communities.

While many believe that the entire South Side of Chicago is populated by African-Americans, this is not the case. Comiskey Park is located in Bridgeport, a white ethnic neighborhood, where the Mayors Daley grew up. Latino neighborhoods surround Comiskey to the immediate north and west, while African-American neighborhoods are located east and south of the park. It is, and has been for years, an uneasy alliance between cultures.

While the Cubs have made little outreach to the black community north of Wrigley Field, the White Sox in recent years have hosted promotions honoring the Negro Leagues, in particular the Chicago American Giants, the Negro Leagues' longest-running continuous franchise. Chicago had a long history as a black baseball capital. Comiskey Park often hosted the annual East-West Negro Leagues All-Star Game, the biggest event on the annual African-American baseball calendar for well over a decade. The East-West Game, and the great musical traditions of jazz and blues emanating from Chicago from the 1920s onward, helped to cement the city's place as a cultural center of Black America, a place that Chicago still holds.

Nonetheless, the Sox have spent most of their marketing dollars trying to attract middle-class and upper-middle-class white families to the ballpark. Trying to do that while your ballpark stands not far from gang- plagued, low-cost public housing isn't easy, but Sox marketing director Rob Gallas has a reputation as a man who can sell anything.

After the absolute desolation of the 1997 season and the ugly end to the Terry Bevington era, the Sox appear to be trying on a new hat by hiring a minority manager: the unheralded Jerry Manuel, who got the job over Davey Lopes, Chris Chambliss, and Cito Gaston, all of whom were mentioned as candidates. The Sox have previously had one African-American skipper; Larry Doby ran the team as an interim manager for 87 games in 1978 with little success, but that awful club could hardly be blamed on him.

Hiring a black manager may improve the club's ability to nurture and keep its black players. The failure to do so in the recent past has cost the team dearly, as a procession of good-to-excellent players has passed through the Sox's hands. Many have gone on to success with other teams. The list of African-American regulars the White Sox have lost in the past five years is pretty impressive: Harold Baines, Tony Phillips, Tim Raines, Ellis Burks, Lance Johnson, George Bell, Bo Jackson, Darrin Jackson, Julio Franco, Mike Devereaux, and Danny Tartabull. While Baines, Devereaux, and Phillips were traded, most left as free agents after the Sox declined to pay the price.

Baines, Phillips, and Raines have been effective since leaving the Sox. Burks had a fine 1993 season (.275, 17 homers, 74 RBIs) but his asking price was apparently too high. Ditto Franco (.319, 20, 98 in 1994). Johnson had been the Sox' starting center fielder for six seasons and was a favorite with fans and teammates.

Despite criticism, this is not necessarily racially motivated on the part of White Sox management. Owner Jerry Reinsdorf certainly showed in 1997 that he loved paring veteran salary of all colors from his team by dealing Baines and pitchers Roberto Hernandez, Danny Darwin, and Wilson Alvarez down the stretch. However, it is interesting to note that the Sox held on to fan favorites like Carlton Fisk, Ron Karkovice, Donn Pall, and even Ozzie Guillen for long periods after their productivity had declined, but they haven't felt the need to keep some of their black players around despite good performances.

In 1997 the Sox added Albert Belle, an African-American player who was counted on to be a superstar-quality hitter. It didn't happen. Belle came to Chicago with a five-year, $55 million-plus contract that made him The

TEAM MVP

It was **Frank Thomas**. He had a normal ho-hum Frank season, hitting .347 to win his first batting title. Big Frank also took 109 walks, hit 35 homers and knocked in 125 runs. He led the AL in on-base percentage and was second in slugging average. He's the best hitter in the world today.

BIGGEST SURPRISE

Jamie Navarro signed a four-year deal with the Sox last winter after two fine years with the crosstown Cubs. For his new South Side employers, however, Navarro was just terrible. Even with more than five runs of support per game, he managed just a 9-14 record because he had a 5.79 ERA. The 30-year-old Navarro, a combative and high-strung individual, likely has another comeback left in him, which he'd better start on immediately.

BIGGEST DISAPPOINTMENT

Robin Ventura's preseason injury shattered White Sox hopes. Substitute **Chris Snopek** was about as bad as one could be at third base in Ventura's absence (.218, 5 homers in 298 at bats, .263 on-base percentage 16 errors), and by the time Ventura returned in August, it was already too late.

59

Man, someone expected to join Frank Thomas in carrying the team. He had already clubbed 242 homers in his career, including 98 in the previous two seasons, and had led the AL in RBI three times. All he was last year, despite a late-season rush that led to 30 homers and 45 doubles, was an average power hitter. He led the AL by rapping into 28 double plays and hit .274, 37 points lower than his 1996 average. Belle would have been a good player at $3 or $4 million; at more than $10 million per season, he was a crushing disappointment. Although he could have better seasons in the future, it isn't likely that he'll make that huge paycheck just worthwhile to the Sox.

It is arguable whether Belle has any cachet within the African-American community, and he certainly didn't have the fan identification that a more classy individual like Baines or Raines did. Belle was quite popular with the passionate fans in Cleveland, but pounding 35-50 homers and driving in 100 runs year after year for a winning team will overshadow many other issues, regardless of who you are or where you play.

JERRY REINSDORF'S EXPLODING CIGAR

The Sox dealt Harold Baines, Roberto Hernandez, Wilson Alvarez and Danny Darwin in August because owner Jerry Reinsdorf decided to bail out on the '97 season with the White Sox still in the Central Division race. Later, Reinsdorf said he would have made the Alvarez-Hernandez deal even if the team were 3.5 games up in the standings, rather than 3.5 games back, as they were at the time, which shows how much Reinsdorf thinks about winning the pennant.

Reinsdorf didn't want to pay the money to sign Hernandez, one of baseball's best closers, or Alvarez, one of the game's better lefthanded starters. But it's not as if the Sox didn't know long before the trade that the two would be up for free agency after last season, so one must assume that Reinsdorf wouldn't sign Hernandez or Alvarez because he felt he got burned by the lucrative long-term deals the club had given righthanded starter Jamie Navarro and out-fielder Albert Belle less than one year earlier.

It is tempting to conclude that Reinsdorf, seeing that by late 1996 his hard-line stance would no longer carry the day with the owners when dealing with the fallout from the

1994-95 strike (which still wasn't permanently settled), decided to sign Belle to that ridiculously lucrative deal, knowing full well that he was raising the salary structure and widening the gap between rich and poor clubs. Why would he do that? Simply because he, Reinsdorf, has the money and the gall to do so. Whatever Reinsdorf's plan was, it all backfired horribly. Now White Sox fans will have to suffer through the aftereffects.

CRAWLING FROM THE WRECKAGE

Despite a terrible, rancorous 1997 season on the South Side, there were several positive developments that bode well for the club's future. Magglio Ordonez will enter 1998 as the team's everyday right fielder. Fan favorite Robin Ventura came back from a fractured right leg and a dislocated right ankle to hit and field well. Mike Cameron is close to becoming a top-flight center fielder. And manager Terry Bevington isn't around anymore.

Ordonez, who turns 24 in January, was never an organizational favorite. He wasn't even on the 40-man roster at the beginning of 1997, but he had his best professional season and hit himself all the way to the top rung. Ordonez captured the Triple A American Association batting title, hitting .329 with 14 homers and 90 RBIs. While he doesn't walk much and has not hit 20 homers in any season of his career, he is a good defensive rightfielder. That said, Ordonez may have his struggles in 1998. It's not likely that he'll get too many fastballs to hit if he continues to pop them like he did last season, and he's not very fast (one stolen base in 21 games with the Sox). However, he is young, has talent, and hustles. Ordonez is certainly a better option than was Lyle Mouton, who really disappointed in 1997 (.269, 5 homers, 23 RBIs in 88 games), or Dave Martinez, who was valuable due to his versatility and attitude but just didn't hit enough to be in the lineup every day.

Ventura, whose spring training injury was the single most destructive event of the disappointing Sox season, ran gingerly at times after his return but was productive at bat. A full healthy season at his regular level of performance will go a long way toward reconstructing the Sox's offense. Ventura's replacement was Chris Snopek, who had been impressive in both the minor leagues and in earlier trials with the White Sox. But given a job on a platter in 1997,

60

he was simply terrible at bat and merely average in the field. Snopek was sent down in midseason and didn't even get a callback in September.

If Bevington deserves credit for anything during his tenure as Sox manager, it may be for giving an everyday job to Mike Cameron. The Sox had a long-term free-agent albatross named Darren Lewis hanging around, but he was a disaster as a regular in 1996, so Bevington awarded the job to Cameron last season. The rookie didn't disappoint, displaying talent in every area, fielding his position extremely well, showing outstanding baserunning and basestealing skills, and hitting productively. But Cameron or no Cameron, Bevington's time in the Sox dugout was a disaster. He couldn't handle a pitching staff, didn't have the respect of most of his players, and failed to cultivate any relationships that could have made things easier for him. He often showed a paranoid streak and was unpleasant to the media throughout his tenure in Chicago. Many players and managers have learned that however richly they think the local media may deserve their scorn, it is ultimately counterproductive to be constantly at odds with the people who control what the fans read and see about the team.

General manager Ron Schueler, who has so far avoided being blamed for the Sox's failures in recent years, is ultimately responsible, of course. He not only chose Bevington as a fill-in when Gene Lamont was fired in June 1995, but also rehired him last winter. White Sox third base coach Doug Rader, considered by many to be Bevington's eventual successor, resigned a day before the end of the season. In an interview after the season ended, he essentially said that the organization was run by control freaks and populated by toadies and informants. "It seemed like the whole place revolved around silly games and politics," Rader told the *Chicago Tribune*. "You never know where it starts. I don't think it stops at Schu. I think it goes above that. We all get marching orders from somewhere."

You can read between the lines of what Rader was saying and conclude that Bevington apparently survived as long as he did by fitting much of that description. Rader and subsequently fired hitting coach Bill Buckner departed because they understandably had a hard time taking orders from such a manager.

All of this raises the question: can anyone with an inde-

THE MOMENT OF TRUTH

The Sox began poorly and never really got off the ground. Even the elements seemed to be working against them in 1997. A rescheduled game on **April 9** against the Blue Jays, under sunny skies with 34-degree temperatures, drew just 746 fans to Comiskey Park. The Sox got three hits and lost to Roger Clemens and the Blue Jays, 5-0. The local joke was that this was one of the season's biggest crowds.

BEST DEAL

The White Sox did not make any good trades in 1997.

WORST DEAL

The **Albert Belle** signing was a disaster on all fronts. While Belle hit .274 with 30 homers, this production was far below his norm and vastly inferior to what was expected of him. Jerry Reinsdorf's decision to pay Belle a $10 million-plus salary was a "screw you" to the rest of baseball, and apparently in the interest of fairness, Belle and the fates decided to screw Reinsdorf back.

pendent mind work for the White Sox? The club sometimes appears to be little more than a cash cow/tax write-off for Reinsdorf and his partner Eddie Einhorn. The universally scorned trade of last summer, combined with the inevitable unflattering comparisons to Reinsdorf's wildly successful Chicago Bulls franchise a few miles away, have cast a shadow over this team. Schueler has survived by accepting his marching orders and putting the blame on others. Locals often pine for the days when Tony LaRussa

61

TOP PROSPECTS
SPRING 1998

1. **<u>Magglio Ordonez, OF.</u>** Ordonez has been more suspect than prospect for most of his pro career, which began in 1992 after he signed as a non-drafted free agent. He simply hit his way up the ladder, and last season won the American Association batting crown (.329). He has a good arm and range in right field, some speed, and good work habits.

2. **<u>Mario Valdez, 1B.</u>** The White Sox see the smooth-swinging, 23-year-old first baseman as the man who will finally push Frank Thomas to full-time DH duty. Valdez, a good defensive player, has hit better than his 48th-round draft status would indicate, but the jury is out as to whether he will provide enough offense to play first base in the major leagues. Last year he hit 15 homers at Triple A Nashville in 282 at bats, taking 43 walks but also striking out 77 times. He could start the year with the White Sox; new manager Jerry Manuel is a fan of defensive-minded players.

3. **<u>Jeff Abbott, OF.</u>** A pure hitter, Abbott was the Sox's fourth-round pick in 1994. He entered 1997 with a .345 career minor league average, and lowered it even though he hit 327 at Nashville with 11 homers. The righthanded-hitting Abbott, who turns 25 in August, is likely to make the Sox this year and have a role in the majors for years, but regular duty may escape him. He lacks extra-base pop, doesn't run very well, and is only average in the field.

4. **<u>Scott Eyre, P.</u>** Eyre is a lefthander with better-than-average stuff and strikeout ability. He was 12-7 at Double A Birmingham in 1996, and last season returned there to go 13-5 before a promotion to Chicago. He made 11 starts for the Pale Hose, finishing 4-4 with a 5.04 ERA. If Eyre settles down and improves his command a bit more, he should settle in as a solid third or fourth starter.

5. **<u>Greg Norton, 3B.</u>** The versatile Norton, who can play both third and shortstop with skill, hit 26 homers at Nashville in 1997. That total, inflated by playing in a hitters' park, moved him above the other third basemen in the Sox system except, of course, incumbent big leaguer Robin Ventura. Norton is not going to be a power machine in the majors, but he can be useful because of his defensive skill and his bat.

6. **<u>Tom Fordham, P.</u>** A 56-32 minor league record makes Fordham attractive to the White Sox. A strong lefthander with okay velocity, he has had problems with command. He pitched seven games for the White Sox after an unimpressive 6-7, 4.74 record at Nashville. Fordham is likely to begin the year back in Triple A.

7. **<u>Robert Machado, C.</u>** The Sox love his defense, but not his work habits or attitude—thus the signings of veterans Chad Kreuter and Charlie O'Brien. Machado has a good arm and works pitchers well. He hit .269 with eight homers last year at Nashville, and Chicago would be ecstatic if he could duplicate that in the majors. Backup duty may beckon this season, but a more realistic big league timeline for Machado is 1999.

62

ran the club, but it's hard to imagine him or any other veteran manager putting up with the kind of U-turns, arrogant pronouncements, and front office shenanigans Reinsdorf presides over. New manager Jerry Manuel, a trainee of Jim Leyland and Felipe Alou, certainly knows how to deal with difficult financial and morale circumstances after spending six years as part of the damage-control squad in Montreal. The best thing about Manuel's hiring is that it gives the whole organization an opportunity to wipe the last three years off the map. Manuel is respected by baseball people and is a blank slate as a big league manager. For now, in Chicago, a fresh breeze and a blank slate look a lot better than what has preceded them. Manuel will need some luck and a lot of help from his players; in particular, Ray Durham, Albert Belle, and Jamie Navarro need to rebound in '98 to give the Sox a realistic chance of contending in the AL Central.

GIL-DING FOR '98

The White Sox finally said goodbye last fall to Ozzie Guillen, who had served as the team's everyday shortstop for the past 13 years. The 1998 starter is likely to be Benji Gil, brought over in an off-season deal from Texas for two scrub pitchers (Al Levine and Larry Thomas).

Gil had already bombed out in two extended trials with Texas. He is a fine defensive shortstop with the potential to get better. Since Guillen wasn't much of a stick, the gamble on the 25-year-old Gil, who has the ability to hit 15 homers a season, is a good one. However, Gil is a poor hitter because of his inability to resist swinging at bad pitches. Whether Gil can develop will be a test not only of his mettle but also of the White Sox coaching staff.

Frequent flyer Ruben Sierra will also be stopping over in the South Side of Chicago in 1998. He is now 32 and far removed from the promise of greatness that his early seasons showed. Can Sierra still help in a platoon role? He has not hit for power since 1994, and has not been a complete player (power, average, and good defense) since being traded from Texas to Oakland in 1992. The poor hitting conditions of Oakland Coliseum really hurt Sierra, and he has been in a free fall ever since.

Sierra is a much better hitter righthanded than left. If allowed to play a platoon role for a manager who can motivate him, he could help the White Sox—and Jerry Manuel is much respected for his people skills as well as his baseball acumen. Still, the Sox shouldn't push Magglio Ordonez out of the way just to find out what Sierra can do.

The midwinter signing of castoff righthander Jim Bullinger (7-12 and 5.56 ERA with the Expos in 1997) means the White Sox are making another attempt at turning dross into gold. They've failed to do the same for Doug Drabek, Dave Righetti, Kirk McCaskill, and others in recent seasons, and there is little reason to believe that they can gild the erratic Bullinger either.

The projected Sox rotation includes holdovers Jaime Navarro, James Baldwin, Scott Eyre, an apparently healed Jason Bere, and a fifth starter to come from a pool including Bullinger, Mike Sirotka, Carlos Castillo, or Keith Foulke. Navarro and Baldwin have plenty of talent and can expect to improve somewhat from their '97 performances, but the Sox will be lucky if Bere makes 25 starts and if anyone contributes as a fifth starter.

OLD FOLKS AT HOME

If the Sox were running a retirement home, they'd have plenty of catchers for the softball team. In the last three years Chicago has employed Tony Pena, Chad Kreuter, Pat Borders, Don Slaught, Mike LaValliere, and Barry Lyons behind the plate, as well as regular Ron Karkovice. For 1998 the Sox have added 36-year-old Charlie O'Brien and once again acquired Kreuter, who was traded in 1997 for Jorge Fabregas. In a move which shows the lack of long-range planning plaguing the team, Kreuter, 33, will now replace Fabregas, a younger and more talented player lost to Arizona in the expansion draft.

63

1997 TEAM STATISTICS

BATTING/BASERUNNING

	Raw	Rank	+/- %		Raw	Rank	+/- %		Raw	Rank	+/- %
R	779	9	-2	BA	.273	6	+1	SB	106	7	0
R/G	4.84	9	-2	HR	158	10	-11	CS	52	7	+1
OBA	.341	7	0	LH	288	13	-10	SB%	67.1	6	0
SA	.417	8	-3	BB	569	8	0				
PRO	.758	9	-1	SO	901	1	-14				

PITCHING/FIELDING

	Raw	Rank	+/- %		Raw	Rank	+/- %		Raw	Rank	+/- %
OR	833	10	+4	BA	.271	8	0	OSB	119	9	+8
RA/G	5.17	11	+5	HR	175	6	-1	OCS	52	7	-2
OOB	.340	6	0	LH	333	9	+3	OSB%	69.6	8	+5
OSA	.430	7	0	BB	575	9	+2	FA	.978	13	0
PRO	.770	6	0	SO	961	10	-7	GDP	102	1	-22

BATTING BY LINEUP SLOTS

	R	HR	RBI	BA	OBA	SA
1	112	11	42	.275	.346	.377
2	109	15	65	.286	.350	.403
3	121	36	129	.329	.435	.566
4	90	30	117	.273	.331	.487
5	81	14	82	.270	.345	.394
6	74	18	76	.250	.328	.391
7	72	15	93	.293	.344	.443
8	50	10	67	.226	.298	.324
9	70	9	69	.248	.277	.355

BATTING BY DEFENSIVE POSITION

	R	HR	RBI	BA	OBA	SA
C	50	14	75	.241	.290	.355
1B	96	30	119	.322	.425	.538
2B	109	11	55	.270	.331	.376
3B	69	11	71	.245	.311	.363
SS	70	5	66	.258	.288	.349
LF	91	30	116	.268	.322	.482
CF	88	17	78	.271	.356	.416
RF	102	18	62	.301	.372	.447
DH	90	20	85	.302	.394	.458
PH	7	2	13	.157	.211	.252
P	1	0	0	.125	.125	.125

TEAM PITCHING

	W-L	CG	QS	QS%	<6	>6	IPS	IP	ERA	OPR
ROTATION	57-64	6	76	47	26	64	6.0	965.1	4.97	.773

	W-L	GR	SV	BSV	HD	BHD	IRS%	IP	ERA	OPR
BULLPEN	23-17	389	52	18	119	82	36	457.0	4.25	.763

64

1998 PROJECTIONS

BATTING

PLAYER	BA	G	AB	R	H	2B	3B	HR	RBI	BB	SO	SB	CS	SA	OBA
Abbott, Jeff	.269	48	175	28	47	10	1	3	19	12	24	3	0	.392	.316
Belle, Albert	.279	150	583	95	162	41	1	35	117	63	88	5	2	.534	.349
Cameron, Mike	.253	146	446	72	113	21	3	16	63	64	124	26	3	.425	.346
Durham, Ray	.275	152	591	95	162	30	5	11	57	57	96	31	12	.396	.338
Gil, Benji	.233	113	332	36	77	15	2	6	35	20	114	1	3	.341	.276
Kreuter, Chad	.230	86	242	26	55	11	1	5	24	27	66	0	2	.344	.306
Machado, Robert	.250	21	72	9	18	4	0	2	7	3	18	1	0	.375	.278
Norton, Greg	.214	49	166	25	36	9	1	7	22	17	48	1	0	.405	.289
O'Brien, Charlie	.226	83	257	25	58	14	0	7	32	25	54	0	1	.363	.295
Ordonez, Magglio	.282	94	358	40	101	18	1	9	52	18	50	6	0	.414	.316
Snopek, Chris	.247	34	107	12	26	6	0	3	14	7	19	1	1	.373	.294
Thomas, Frank	.317	122	441	85	140	24	0	29	98	88	54	1	1	.572	.431
Valdez, Mario	.238	81	238	29	57	14	1	9	39	32	83	1	0	.416	.328
Ventura, Robin	.275	96	344	54	95	17	2	16	57	51	49	2	2	.472	.368

65

PITCHING

PITCHER	W	L	SV	ERA	G	GS	IP	H	HR	BB	SO
Baldwin, James	11	11	0	4.99	29	28	175	177	20	68	125
Bere, Jason	8	7	0	5.62	19	19	90	82	13	60	72
Bertotti, Mike	1	1	0	3.44	5	3	18	13	2	14	13
Castillo, Carlos	2	1	0	4.61	41	2	72	74	10	37	47
Castillo, Tony	3	3	5	4.23	48	0	57	62	6	19	36
Cruz, Nelson	2	1	0	3.32	9	4	32	29	5	7	21
Eyre, Scott	7	5	0	3.62	19	19	109	94	14	46	80
Fordham, Tom	4	3	0	3.35	11	8	54	44	5	22	34
Foulke, Keith	5	5	1	3.46	24	12	91	84	12	18	55
Karchner, Matt	5	2	18	3.70	60	0	66	65	7	36	43
Navarro, Jaime	9	9	0	4.78	27	27	173	199	18	55	117
Simas, Bill	4	5	3	4.38	62	0	66	72	7	38	61
Sirotka, Mike	6	4	0	3.78	16	14	88	102	12	18	59

CLEVELAND INDIANS

MANAGEMENT

Manager	General Manager	Owner
Mike Hargrove Career Record 535-453 .541	John Hart	Richard Jacobs

1997 RECORD

Won-Lost	Pct.	Division Finish/GB	Wild Card Finish/GB
86-75	.534	1 C	

Preseason Consensus Projection	1 (1.30)		

1st Half	2nd Half	Home	Road	Intradivision	Interleague
40-35	46-40	44-37	42-38	31-16	9-6

Comebacks	Blowouts	Nailbiters
11-8	28-26	32-29

CHANGE IS GOOD, PERSEVERANCE PAYS OFF

Following a disappointing '96 season, the Indians shed several marquee players in hopes of improving the team on the field and in the clubhouse. Outfielders Albert Belle and Kenny Lofton; pitchers Dennis Martinez, Julian Tavarez, and Alan Embree; and infielders Jeff Kent and Jose Vizcaino were traded away or let go as free agents. Newcomers Marquis Grissom, Matt Williams, Tony Fernandez, David Justice, and Mike Jackson replaced them on the roster and played critical parts in the club's '97 success.

In the early going the Indians were unproductive and disoriented, struggling just to say above .500. As late as June 4 the Tribe was 27-26, unable to put together a sustained stretch of good baseball. All season Cleveland scored runs with relative ease but had difficulty finding reliable starting pitching. The bullpen, searching for a replacement for legally troubled Jose Mesa, was bad as well, with Jackson, Paul Shuey, Paul Assenmacher, and Eric Plunk forced into different roles. Cleveland's middle relief was terrible and remained so all year.

When the season began Grissom was hitting leadoff for Cleveland. However, he had suffered a hamstring pull in spring training and got off to a very poor start. He scuffled to get up to .250 by midseason and wasn't providing the power or speed he had in previous years. But while Grissom struggled, fellow newbies Justice (16 homers, .383 average on June 1) and Williams (13 homers by June 1) were lighting up the scoreboard, and the Indians ranked at or near the top of the AL in runs throughout the year.

On the other hand, for much of the season the Tribe's rotation was paper-thin. Jack McDowell's elbow sent him to the sidelines for the year after just six starts. Orel Hershiser pitched poorly in the early going. While Charles Nagy was effective, youngsters Bart Colon and Albie Lopez couldn't get settled. Colon would spend the season bouncing back and forth between Triple A and Cleveland, but an elbow injury to Chad Ogea forced the Indians to run through Brian Anderson, Jason Jacome, Dave Weathers, Jeff Juden, and Terry Clark, among others, while trying to find healthy and reliable starters.

By July, Justice was disabled with a bad elbow and Williams was in a deep slump. However, Jim Thome—mastering the switch to first base necessitated by the acquisition of Williams—picked up the slack (22 homers by July 1). Right fielder Manny Ramirez hiked his average up to .339, and catcher Sandy Alomar, enjoying a career year, paced the AL at the All Star break with his stratospheric .375 mark.

In the All Star Game at the Jake, Alomar smashed a two-run, game-winning homer in a 3-1 AL victory. It was just one of many big hits Alomar would provide in '97. On May 25 he began a hitting streak that lasted 30 games, the second-longest in club history.

Justice returned from the sidelines after the break but didn't fully get back on track until late in the second half. Bolstered by improved performance from Hershiser and an injection of power pitching from hard-throwing rookie starter Jaret Wright (who arrived in July), Cleveland began to win at a steady .600 pace until early August.

The team then lost five in a row to fall back to 59-56, allowing the underachieving White Sox and the scrappy Brewers back into the race. Fundamental mistakes and poor pitching were costing the Indians games, and manager Mike Hargrove had to take stock of his team's needs.

Hargrove reinstated Mesa, who had run off a 12-game scoreless streak in setup work, to his old closer's job, with Jackson moving back to the setup role. This made the whole bullpen stronger and more effective. Wright solidified the rotation as the fourth starter, and Grissom was shifted down to the ninth spot in the batting order, with Omar Vizquel and Tony Fernandez moving to the top. The final piece of the rearranged puzzle was lefthander John

TEAM MVP

Jim Thome had the best offensive numbers of anyone on the club and worked hard at a new defensive position. Nobody heard a word from him about having to make room for Matt Williams, and he showed in the postseason why he's a lethal hitter. He probably shouldn't be platooned. Thome led the club in runs, home runs, RBI, walks, and slugging average and finished second to David Justice in on-base percentage.

BIGGEST SURPRISE

There are several good candidates. Tony Fernandez solidified the second base position, while a healthy David Justice put a lot of runs on the board. However, the best present the Indians got was an 8-3 rookie season from 21-year-old **Jaret Wright**, who stepped into a middling starting rotation and made a major impact during the regular season, not to mention his performance in the postseason.

BIGGEST DISAPPOINTMENT

The loss of **Jack McDowell** after just eight games (six starts) to elbow problems put a strain on the Indians' pitching staff that lasted all year. McDowell, a free agent who turns 33 this year, faces a cloudy future.

67

THE MOMENT OF
TRUTH

Cleveland swept the White Sox in a three-game set on September 5-7 at Jacobs Field, winning one close game and two easy ones to knock the Pale Hose out of the race and also put some distance between themselves and the Brewers, who were busy losing two of three against Boston. The Central Division race was never close after that.

Smiley, who was acquired from Cincinnati, though he was able to pitch just six times before breaking his pitching arm in a pregame warmup.

An early September three-game sweep of Chicago at Jacobs Field finished off the White Sox, while the over-achieving Brewers fumbled their chance with a late-season slide. The Indians thus pulled away from the competition to win the AL Central easily. Cleveland finished at 86-75 even though they never won more than six games in a row—and accomplished that feat only once, in May.

The August 31 acquisition of Bip Roberts (from Kansas City) gave Cleveland needed flexibility in the outfield and infield. Meanwhile, veterans such as Trenidad Hubbard, Kevin Mitchell, Julio Franco (released in early August after a prolonged slump), and Chad Curtis came and went, with youngster Brian Giles filling playing left field and veteran Kevin Seitzer providing bench strength.

The Indians' season was full of injuries, inconsistency, legal hassles and occasional clubhouse trouble, but the team was able to win a weak AL Central with its power-based attack. While Vizquel and Fernandez drew little attention, their ability to get on base and advance runners kept Cleveland's offense productive even when the power hitters slumped.

Defensively the Tribe was strong in the infield, with Gold Glove–caliber players at third and short. Grissom was well above-par in center, but Giles was just average in left and erratic right fielder Ramirez ranged from good to

nightmarish. Alomar remains one of the better overall receivers in the game.

The bench was slanted toward offense rather than defense. Seitzer is a good hitter, while catcher Pat Borders . Jeff Branson, acquired with Smiley, provides the true utility infielder the Indians did not have for most of the year.

By the end of the regular season, the starting pitching had worked itself out. Hershiser, Nagy, Wright, and Ogea were all healthy and throwing well, with Juden and Anderson available in long relief. Assenmacher and Jackson handled setup duty, with Plunk and lefty Alvin Morman in the middle. Mesa finished the season with 16 saves, 13 of them coming in the last few weeks.

EXTREME MAGNITUDE

Someone once said that the aim of a general manager should be to build a team of "extreme magnitude." I assume that he was thinking of a team like the 1997 Indians. They were not only solid at every regular position but at every spot on the bench as well. By the end of the year the Indians had Brian Giles or Bip Roberts, Marquis Grissom, and Manny Ramirez in the outfield, David Justice at DH, an infield of Matt Williams, Omar Vizquel, Tony Fernandez or Roberts, and Jim Thome, and Sandy Alomar behind the dish. A lineup without obvious weaknesses and plenty of strengths is a rare commodity in post-dynastic baseball.

Off the bench, late-season pickups like Roberts and Jeff Branson, who added flexibility, could be inserted as necessary at multiple positions. Kevin Seitzer, a pure hitter with the right attitude to come off the bench, and Pat Borders, were also available. Not a bad banana in the bunch, eh?

Many of those players are gone now, either traded for better players, allowed to walk as free agents, or released. What is clear from looking at the team's lineup and rotation is that over a very short period of time, the Cleveland brain trust has made numerous crucial decisions about the future of the team. GM John Hart has done a fine job of deciding who the keys to the team were—Vizquel, Thome, Ramirez, Mesa, Alomar—and keeping them. The Indians also showed, in the cases of Baerga, Murray, Belle, and others, that they knew when it was time to let go.

Despite the team's success, rumors repeatedly flared up

68

during the season that manager Mike Hargrove was in danger of being fired. First it was that he'd be fired if the Indians didn't make the playoffs; then he'd be fired if they didn't finish first; no, he'd be fired if the Indians didn't reach the World Series; oops, he'd be fired if his club didn't win the World Series.

If Hart had canned his manager in the off-season, he would have made a big mistake. Hargrove had kept a club full of big egos and big salaries competitive for a number of years and had been able to adjust to his talent. Nevertheless, Hart would only have been treating Hargrove as he did Ken Hill, Baerga, Belle, or any number of talented players he no longer needed or could afford: Nice to know you. Thanks for the memories, but we can get the job done without you.

If the essence of professional sports is a meritocracy based on performance, and the reality is sky-high salaries for veteran players, then you have to admire such ruthless efficiency.

THE LATEST COMINGS AND GOINGS

GM John Hart and the Indians displayed once again this off season a willingness to undergo massive change, making the following major moves:

•Center fielder Marquis Grissom and pitcher Jeff Juden were traded to Milwaukee for pitchers Ben McDonald, Mike Fetters, and Ron Villone. Fetters was then dealt to Oakland for pitcher Steve Karsay.

•Center fielder Kenny Lofton returned as a free agent for substantially less money than he had wanted one year earlier.

•Third baseman Matt Williams was shipped to the Arizona Diamondbacks for third baseman Travis Fryman, reliever Tom Martin, and cash. Fryman then inked a five-year deal with Cleveland.

•Veteran free agents Orel Hershiser, Bip Roberts, Jack McDowell, Tony Fernandez, and Kevin Seitzer (who retired) were let go.

After these moves the Tribe looks to have come out ahead both in terms of on-field talent—having traded older players for younger ones—and in terms of contracts. The signings of free-agent pitchers Dwight Gooden and Rheal Cormier and infielder Carlos Garcia provide further insurance that the Indians will field yet another strong club.

BEST DEAL

The trade of **Kenny Lofton** and **Alan Embree** to Atlanta for **Marquis Grissom** and **David Justice** worked out extremely well for Cleveland.

Even though Grissom had a bad start and ended the season batting ninth, he was much loved in the clubhouse, still played a fine center field, and did his bit on offense. Meanwhile, Lofton hit well for the Braves (.333) but without much power (5 homers); he also slumped on the bases (27 steals in 47 tries) and in the field (5 errors). Now the Indians hope Lofton will return to form back in Cleveland.

Justice had a stupendous year at bat for the Tribe while playing left field as well as serving as DH for 61 games. The Indians didn't really miss Embree that much with reliable lefty Paul Assenmacher around.

WORST DEAL

The August trade that brought **John Smiley** and **Jeff Branson** from Cincinnati for four prospects (**Damian Jackson**, **Danny Graves**, **Scott Winchester**, and **Jim Crowell**) didn't work out. Branson is just a mediocre utility player, while Smiley was hampered by shoulder problems (2-4, 5.54 ERA) before breaking his pitching arm while warming up in the bullpen at Kansas City on September 20. Smiley's injury, a spiral fracture of the left humerus, is expected to necessitate a long rehabilitation period.

The '98 lineup should include Sandy Alomar behind the plate; an infield of Jim Thome, Garcia or Enrique Wilson, Omar Vizquel and Fryman; an outfield of Brian Giles, Lofton, and Manny Ramirez; and DH David Justice. The rotation will include Charles Nagy, Chad Ogea, Jaret Wright, Gooden, and John Smiley or McDonald (when they return from injuries). Brian Anderson, Albie Lopez and Herbert Perry were lost in the expansion draft, but Karsay, Cormier, and Bartolo Colon are available to step in. The bullpen should include Jose Mesa, Villone, Martin, Eric Plunk, Paul Assenmacher, and Mike Jackson.

Change is good, when you're smart, tough, and unafraid of it.

ISN'T THE SAYING "BASEBALL IS 90 PERCENT PITCHING" REALLY 90 PERCENT BULL?

The Indians won the AL Central title despite turning over much of their lineup, struggling to find adequate starting pitching, and unloading several veterans during the season. Putting the lie to the maxim that teams can't win without a dominating starting rotation, Cleveland had the tenth-best ERA in the American League but finished 86-75 anyway because their offense scored 868 runs, second-most in the loop and just five fewer than the Yankees'.

Right from the start, it was as if the baseball gods didn't want the Indians' starting staff to have a smooth sail. Dennis Martinez was released before the season when his elbow problems

TOP PROSPECTS
SPRING 1998

1. **Sean Casey, 1B.** The 1995 second-round pick vaulted last season to the top of Cleveland's fine crop of power-hitting minor league first basemen. Casey, who turns 24 in July, started the season late due to ankle surgery but hit .368 for Double A Akron with 10 homers in 62 games before heading to Triple A Buffalo, where he batted .361 with five more homers in 20 contests. He then got a six-game look-see with Cleveland. A lefthanded hitter, he will be worked into the mix somewhere this season due to his tremendous offensive potential. First base is his only defensive position.

2. **Enrique Wilson, 2B.** He has been ready to play regularly in the majors for two years now, but Cleveland's overdependence on veteran infielders has kept Wilson (as well as the departed Damian Jackson) on the back burner. In his second full season at Buffalo, Wilson (now 24) batted .306 with 11 homers in 118 games, cutting his strikeouts from 78 to 41 in an almost equal number of at bats. He is a slick defensive player with good speed. This could be the year.

3. **Bruce Aven, OF.** An overachieving left fielder with power, grit, and a fair throwing arm, Aven batted .287 at Buffalo with 17 homers, 50 walks, and 10 steals. He also got into 13 games with the Indians. He turns 26 in April and is likely to stick this year as a righthanded-hitting reserve. Aven is probably not going to be a starter in the majors.

4. **Richie Sexson, 1B.** Sexson, who turned 23 this winter, led the American Association with 31 homers at Buffalo in 1997. He did this in just 115 games, proving to be a streaky player who sat out often because he just didn't hit. Sexson's weakness is overaggressive swinging; he fanned 87 times and had just 27 walks last season, hitting .260 with a poor .307 on-base percentage. However, his pop, age, and athleticism work in his favor. The Indians may ask him to play the outfield this year at Triple A.

5. **Russ Branyan, 3B.** Beginning the year in the Class A Carolina League, Branyan busted pitchers for 27 homers in just 297 at bats, hitting .290 with 52 walks. Promoted to Double A Akron, he then batted .234 with 12 more dingers in just 41 games. His 39 total homers led the minor leagues. Branyan, who turned 22 just before Christmas, had clubbed 40 homers in the South Atlantic League in 1996. The fact that he can play third base competently will grease his way to the majors, but his 150 strikeouts last year indicate that further improvement is needed.

finally proved unsolvable; Jack McDowell made just eight appearances before injury knocked him out; late-season acquisition John Smiley broke his arm after just six starts. Jeff Juden, an astonishing 11-5 with Montreal, came over in August and completely bombed, allowing 19 earned runs in 31 innings. Fill-ins Jason Jacome, Brian Anderson, and Terry Clark were little better.

The offense had to do the job to keep Cleveland in contention, and it did. But just how good was the offense, and how bad was the pitching? The truth is that the Indians had several outstanding offensive players and only a few quality pitchers.

Any lineup with Jim Thome, Matt Williams, David Justice, Manny Ramirez, and Sandy Alomar, Jr., will hit its share of home runs, and the outstanding plate discipline of Thome, Justice, Ramirez, and Brian Giles kept the table set for the entire lineup. Any club whose least productive hitters (Omar Vizquel, Marquis Grissom, and Tony Fernandez) are smart situational players with positives of their own is going to be a good club.

Mike Hargrove deserves a lot of credit for understanding the importance of "getting them on, getting them over, and getting them in." Although without Kenny Lofton the team lacked a true leadoff hitter in '97, Hargrove used what he had and arranged his talent so that his players' strengths could do the team the most good. When Grissom moved down to hit ninth after failing to improve his OBP, Vizquel led off and got on base enough that he scored 89 runs on the year. When the Tribe acquired Bip Roberts, Vizquel moved to the second spot and displayed his ability to bunt and move runners along.

For 1998 the Indians have to decide who is going to play second base and who will play left field. Both Roberts and Fernandez are free agents, and there are younger and cheaper players (e.g., Bruce Aven, Enrique Wilson) who would like their jobs. However, Roberts' speed and versatility could keep him in an Indians uniform.

The biggest need for '98 is to sort out the pitching staff. While the offense could carry the Indians most of the way, the starting pitching needs to be bolstered if they want to make it all the way. There is no legitimate rotation anchor on the staff now, even though Jaret Wright could fill that role in a couple of seasons.

Before the season Cleveland rejected a deal that would have brought Curt Schilling from Philadelphia for outfielder Brian Giles. It isn't likely that anyone will be offering Cleveland a 300-strikeout pitcher this spring, but there are still some good, healthy young arms in town.

One thing that Hargrove hasn't yet done is simply insert a farmhand like Albie Lopez or Bartolo Colon into the starting rotation for a full season and let them get the experience they need to become full-fledged major leaguers. The trade value of both young hurlers was thus limited (Lopez was lost in the expansion draft). Hargrove did use the 21-year-old Wright in critical situations, and that strategy paid off. Chad Ogea also proved that he is a big league starter, and he even might get a little bit better.

Short relief isn't really a problem. Jose Mesa, surmounting his legal problems, hit his stride by late summer. Mike Jackson and Paul Assenmacher set him up well, although Paul Shuey, Eric Plunk, and the designated situational southpaw (usually Alvin Morman) did not perform capably.

One can expect Shuey and Plunk to bounce back, as they're talented, throw hard, and mostly struggled due to unexpected lapses in control. However, having somebody in the pen who can come in from the right side and throw off-speed pitches, rather than relying on the fastball, might give the club even more strength. Unfortunately for the Indians such a pitcher (Danny Graves) was traded to the Reds for Jeff Branson late in the season.

Cleveland pitchers threw just four complete games in 1997, fewer than any other AL team save Oakland. Oddly, despite a bullpen featuring eight pitchers who worked at least 20 games in relief, the Indians' 39 saves ranked above just six other teams.

71

CLEVELAND INDIANS
1997 TEAM STATISTICS

BATTING/BASERUNNING

	Raw	Rank	+/-%		Raw	Rank	+/-%		Raw	Rank	+/-%
R	868	3	+9	BA	.286	3	+6	SB	118	6	+11
R/G	5.39	3	+9	HR	220	2	+24	CS	59	4	+14
OBA	.358	2	+5	LH	323	6	+1	SB%	66.7	7	-1
SA	.467	2	+9	BB	617	4	+8				
PRO	.825	2	+7	SO	955	5	-9				

PITCHING/FIELDING

	Raw	Rank	+/- %		Raw	Rank	+/- %		Raw	Rank	+/- %
OR	815	7	+2	BA	.276	10	+2	OSB	126	10	+15
RA/G	5.06	7	+3	HR	181	9	+3	OCS	54	10	+2
OOB	.347	11	+2	LH	304	6	-6	OSB%	70.0	9	+5
OSA	.434	10	+1	BB	575	9	+2	FA	.983	7	0
PRO	.781	11	+1	SO	1,036	6	0	GDP	134	9	+3

BATTING BY LINEUP SLOTS

	R	HR	RBI	BA	OBA	SA
1	105	18	82	.263	.329	.413
2	107	9	66	.268	.319	.362
3	119	38	112	.292	.420	.539
4	103	34	107	.278	.353	.505
5	97	38	120	.319	.398	.567
6	87	31	106	.295	.350	.503
7	84	14	73	.285	.357	.426
8	80	22	77	.286	.349	.451
9	86	16	66	.294	.349	.450

BATTING BY DEFENSIVE POSITION

	R	HR	RBI	BA	OBA	SA
C	80	25	99	.317	.352	.517
1B	118	42	110	.286	.411	.556
2B	90	16	68	.283	.337	.411
3B	92	33	111	.267	.313	.487
SS	93	5	51	.277	.342	.360
LF	104	31	105	.292	.388	.516
CF	86	16	74	.262	.322	.410
RF	103	28	97	.316	.407	.521
DH	88	22	84	.297	.369	.464
PH	4	2	12	.178	.265	.288
P	1	0	0	.056	.105	.056

TEAM PITCHING

	W-L	CG	QS	QS%	<6	>6	IPS	IP	ERA	OPR
ROTATION	60-53	4	70	43	31	59	5.9	955.0	4.90	.787

	W-L	GR	SV	BSV	HD	BHD	IRS%	IP	ERA	OPR
BULLPEN	26-22	428	39	15	123	84	32	470.2	4.38	.768

72

1998 PROJECTIONS

BATTING

PLAYER	BA	G	AB	R	H	2B	3B	HR	RBI	BB	SO	SB	CS	SA	OBA
Aven, Bruce	.268	74	252	38	67	15	2	9	42	27	69	4	0	.453	.339
Alomar, Sandy	.300	146	509	69	153	35	0	21	83	22	54	1	1	.491	.329
Borders, Pat	.284	42	122	11	35	5	1	3	11	6	23	0	2	.414	.318
Branson, Jeff	.240	90	195	21	47	9	1	5	21	20	46	1	1	.384	.311
Casey, Sean	.296	25	91	11	27	6	0	3	19	7	16	0	0	.478	.349
Diaz, Einar	.283	14	42	6	12	3	0	0	4	3	5	0	0	.382	.326
Fryman, Travis	.277	149	580	87	161	27	3	21	97	51	109	11	3	.442	.336
Giles, Brian	.272	140	393	66	107	19	3	17	65	63	50	13	3	.470	.373
Justice, Dave	.299	142	499	81	150	28	1	30	94	78	76	3	4	.537	.394
Lofton, Kenny	.316	138	570	105	181	25	7	8	56	61	80	46	19	.428	.383
Manto, Jeff	.215	16	51	7	11	2	0	3	8	6	15	0	0	.430	.302
Ramirez, Manny	.303	152	559	93	169	38	1	28	95	78	109	4	4	.526	.388
Sexson, Richie	.242	29	106	13	26	5	0	7	19	6	25	1	0	.485	.282
Thome, Jim	.280	157	526	108	147	26	2	37	102	118	140	2	2	.547	.412
Vizquel, Omar	.284	150	553	92	157	28	3	6	55	58	55	38	11	.381	.352
Wilson, Enrique	.280	88	333	52	93	12	1	7	26	27	37	5	0	.387	.335

PITCHING

PITCHER	W	L	SV	ERA	G	GS	IP	H	HR	BB	SO
Assenmacher, Paul	7	1	3	3.29	92	0	63	59	5	21	66
Batchelor, Rich	3	1	0	5.25	22	0	27	34	2	11	18
Colon, Bartolo	5	4	0	4.13	15	15	81	80	9	36	54
Gooden, Dwight	10	6	0	5.03	26	25	139	148	18	69	97
Jackson, Mike	2	4	11	3.42	66	0	68	57	6	26	66
Jacome, Jason	1	1	0	5.20	12	2	21	25	3	8	12
Karsay, Steve	3	8	0	4.90	18	18	103	119	14	34	69
Martin, Tom	5	4	2	2.41	62	0	63	65	2	28	40
McDonald, Ben	7	7	0	4.01	21	21	137	131	14	42	103
Mesa, Jose	3	5	29	2.83	66	0	76	76	6	27	66
Morman, Alvin	2	0	2	5.27	72	0	46	46	7	30	34
Nagy, Charles	14	8	0	4.16	30	30	195	212	22	64	136
Ogea, Chad	9	8	0	4.64	25	22	140	147	16	47	89
Plunk, Eric	4	3	2	3.83	50	0	63	54	8	32	66
Shuey, Paul	5	2	2	4.86	43	0	50	52	6	29	48
Smiley, John	8	9	0	4.45	19	19	115	125	15	29	89
Villone, Ron	1	1	1	3.76	55	0	57	55	7	39	51
Wright, Jaret	8	7	0	3.69	23	23	142	117	13	59	106

73

DETROIT TIGERS

MANAGEMENT

Manager	General Manager	Owner
Buddy Bell Career Record 132-192 .407	Randy Smith	Michael Ilitch

1997 RECORD

Won-Lost	Pct.	Division Finish/GB	Wild Card Finish/GB
79-83	.488	3 E -19	4 -17

Preseason Consensus Projection	5 (4.70)		

1st Half	2nd Half	Home	Road	Intradivision	Interleague
36-42	43-41	42-39	37-44	21-27	8-7

Comebacks	Blowouts	Nailbiters
8-9	24-25	41-38

MR. SMITH GOES TO MOTOWN

To move from horrid to respectable in one year is a mighty achievement, and the Detroit Tigers have much to be proud of. In some ways, the surprising success of the Tigers parallels that of the Pirates, another rebuilding club that was expected to lose last year 100 games but didn't. Only the fact that the Bucs played in the weak NL Central and the Tigers played in the much stronger AL East accounts for the relative lack of attention that Detroit's improvement received.

One of best things about the Tigers' quick return to respectability is that it came mostly with the use of young players. There were few Dave Hollinses or Darren Daultons leading the Detroit charge. Only Bob Hamelin, brought over in midseason to DH, was the kind of veteran has-been that many desperate teams turn to in their darkest hours.

In fact, the Tigers that contributed the least were some of the holdovers from '96—and don't think that GM Randy Smith didn't take notice. Travis Fryman, who continued his mediocrity as a power hitter (only 22 home runs), is no longer a top-tier third baseman. Slugger Mel Nieves lapsed from his 1996 performance, which wasn't that impressive, while prospect manque Phil Nevin didn't prove himself in his last chance. Veteran starter Felipe Lira was very, very bad. All four of those players have now been traded away.

The guys that did it for Detroit in '97, and will do it if the Tigers continue to improve, were their young, developing stars: Bobby Higginson, Tony Clark, Brian Hunter (who improved dramatically in his leadoff role), and—surprise!—Damion Easley, whose bulking up finally paid off in home runs. Pitchers Justin Thompson and Willie Blair had outstanding years, while unheralded Brian Moehler showed he could be a solid starter in the big leagues.

The improvement of the pitching staff was perhaps the biggest surprise of all. After using no-stuff or no-hope pitchers like Mike Christopher, John Farrell, Brian Williams, Scott Aldred, and Todd Van Poppel to fashion a wretched 6.38 staff ERA in 1996, the decisive Smith did some serious shuffling.

And did he ever do it right. The sudden infusion of talent into the Tigers' pitching staff was shocking. Four key pitchers came over in trades, while others were given jobs after coming up through the minors. While it wasn't that long ago that Detroit had a good pitching staff, it sure seemed like an eternity to Tigers' fans. By '96 they had begun to feel like Bill Murray's character in Groundhog Day, except that they were constantly waking up to another loud opposition homer instead of an alarm clock.

Not only does the new-look Detroit staff feature some pitchers with impressive stats, they also have good arms. Most of the guys that did the job in '97—Todd Jones, Doug Brocail, Thompson, Scott Sanders, Greg Keagle, and the now-departed Dan Miceli and Blair—aren't soft-tossing it up there. Even those who are still struggling, like Sanders and Keagle, are in better positions to develop than those who lack stuff.

That being said, the Tigers still need to do some tinkering. Their bench is slow and not very productive. They might need to find a short-term shortstop and give slick-fielding Rule V pick Deivi Cruz and his .263 on-base percentage some learning time at Double A or Triple A. The club also needs to figure out what to do behind the plate, and the starting pitching needs one more solid arm. Detroit has too many guys like Glenn Dishman, A.J. Sager, and Kevin Jarvis hanging around; expecting more Willie Blair–like surprises is not sound. Signing veteran Frank Castillo as a free agent in the off-season was an attempt to address that problem. Tiger Stadium could be good to Castillo, but only if he keeps the ball low and away from the many lefthanders who will be facing him. Castillo hasn't been able to do that for two seasons.

Ascending from the nadir is certainly impressive (and far preferable to the alternative), but reaching the zenith is never guaranteed by past improvement and lots of potential. The Tigers' owner and management need to make sure

TEAM MVP

First baseman Tony Clark had more homers and center fielder Brian Hunter had more stolen bases, but outfielder **Bobby Higginson** was the Tigers' best player in 1997. He led the club with a .299 batting average and a .379 on-base average, hit 27 homers, drove in 101 runs, and played excellent defense. Higginson split duty between left and right field, leading the major leagues with a phenomenal 20 outfield assists (nobody had garnered that many assists since 1991). Just a couple of years ago, many believed Higginson would never play regularly in the major leagues.

BIGGEST SURPRISE

Two Tigers contend for this distinction. Second baseman **Damion Easley** hit .264 with 22 homers and 28 steals, having his best season (by far) while staying healthy for the first time in ages. Meanwhile, starting pitcher **Willie Blair** went 16-8 for Detroit despite missing a month after being hit in the face by a line drive. Blair, 32 this season, never before had a year like 1997, but then again he never really had a chance to start every fourth day, either.

BIGGEST DISAPPOINTMENT

Outfielder **Mel Nieves** has had every chance to establish himself with the Tigers, but after a mediocre 1996, he fell back sharply in 1997. The big, strong switch-hitter fanned 157 times to finish second in the American League—despite having only 359 at bats! While he did clout 20 homers, Nieves's .228 average and his defensive problems didn't sit well with management, which dealt him to Cincinnati after the season.

75

that their foundation players—Thompson, Clark, Higginson, Jones, and Hunter—stay healthy, stay in Detroit, and develop into the kind of leaders that contending teams need.

It's amazing to say after the horror show that was 1996 in Tiger Stadium, but the core is here for Detroit to contend in a couple of years. The work Smith has done to turn this franchise around makes him the true Executive of the Year, and maybe of the decade, no matter who actually won the award.

AGE BIAS

While no one in baseball questions the phenomenon—except perhaps veteran ballplayers in danger of losing their jobs—modern baseball fans seem to discriminate blatantly in favor of youth. To be sure, fans have a right to root for whomever they want, and ballplayers of many different types, styles, and colors have basked in the adulation of the fans.

But isn't it more than a little curious that fans will mercilessly boo and heckle older players who are trying but not succeeding, while these same fans will cheer almost any aggregation of unproven youngsters? The 1997 Tigers and Pirates are perfect examples of this pattern.

Bluntly put, neither Detroit nor Pittsburgh played that well last year. Both teams finished with 79-83 records. In the AL East that was good for third place, 19 games off the pace; in the NL Central it was good for second place, five games back. Losing more than you win, even if luck allows you to contend in the weakest division in baseball, isn't that impressive. But the Pirates' crowds swelled to 1,657,022, their highest since 1992, while the Tigers' attendance grew to 1,365,157, their highest since 1993.

Of course, what made the '97 season special in both Motown and the Steel City was not their teams' final record, not their place in the standings, not even the way in which the teams played: it was the type of players who were on the field.

If either Detroit or Pittsburgh had kept their veteran teams largely intact, playing sub-.500 ball wouldn't have excited anyone. It was only the fact that most of the players on both clubs were young, and thereby not making a big salary, that made them special. It's sad to say, but unde-

niably true, that baseball fans' hatred of millionaire ballplayers has reached such intense levels that veteran teams are roundly despised unless they are winners.

What's the real difference between losing games with veterans and losing them with rookies? Oh, sure, people will tell you it has to do with the age or the future of those teams, and many are no doubt sincere. But you can't avoid the conclusion that fans basically hate a 32-year-old veteran making $3 million bucks if he's not a star, while they love a 23-year-old rook making $175,000 bucks, even if he's not one whit better than the vet.

The relevant difference is in the size of the paycheck, not in the performance nor in the result. That says a hell of a lot about the level of fan anger and resentment in the game today.

LET'S MAKE A DEAL

Youthful Randy Smith took over as Tigers GM in November 1995, inheriting a dead-end club that had finished the season 60-84, in fourth place in the AL East. At the end of the season, this was the club's makeup:

C	John Flaherty
1B	Cecil Fielder
2B	Lou Whitaker
SS	Chris Gomez
3B	Travis Fryman
LF	Danny Bautista
CF	Chad Curtis
RF	Bobby Higginson
DH	Kirk Gibson
SP	Felipe Lira, Sean Bergman, Mike Moore, Jose Lima, Brian Bohanon
RP	John Doherty, Dwayne Henry

Every one of those players save Higginson is now gone. Gibson, Moore, and Whitaker retired, while all the others have been released or traded, often for younger players with far more potential.

Smith has been an incredibly busy executive, constantly wheeling and dealing to change the structure of the team. This past winter's deals show that few, if any, Tigers are safe, especially if they slump or get too expensive.

While Smith is clearly fearless about trading to improve

the team, there is no consistent pattern. He has cleared out deadwood in exchange for youngsters, but has also dealt talented youngsters (even former No. 1 draft picks) to get established players he thinks can help the club.

The only real pattern one can glean from Smith's machinations is that he likes to make trades (often big ones) with the people he knows: either the team that his father, Tal, runs (Houston), or the team where he himself used to run (San Diego). He has, since taking over, made seven deals with San Diego and three with the Astros; those ten trades involved a total of 41 players.

His best deals have been those in which he simply judged talent better. He stole second baseman Damion Easley, whose career was dead in the water, from Anaheim for going-nowhere first-rounder Greg Gohr, acquired hard-throwing Roberto Duran from Toronto for Anton French, and picked the Astros' pockets for Brian Hunter and Todd Jones for a bunch of guys that might work out in Houston.

Over this past off-season, the Tigers dumped DH Bob Hamelin, outfielder Mel Nieves, catcher Matt Walbeck, and third baseman Travis Fryman, replacing them with infielder-outfielder-DH Bip Roberts, left fielder Luis Gonzalez, catcher Joe Oliver, and third baseman Joe Randa.

Roberts offers the club flexibility and speed, two things they didn't have much of last season. Hamelin performed well, but designated hitters aren't hard to find; Walbeck wasn't going to hit; and it is doubtful Nieves will ever conquer his strikeout problems and become a good everyday player.

The Fryman deal with Arizona (netting Randa, third base prospect Gabe Alvarez, and pitching prospect Matt Drews, who had been drafted off Detroit's roster) made the Tigers younger and cheaper. Fryman is a good player, but hardly worth the millions he's getting from Cleveland. Detroit also signed the popular Higginson and Easley to long-term deals last winter, moves which show the fans the Tigers are interested in building a team for the long haul.

Detroit looks like a much better club after the switches. The deal sending Mike Myers, the indifferent situational lefty, to Milwaukee for promising righthander Bryce Florie (yet another former Padre) also looks good. Finally, snagging outfielder Trey Beamon and starter-reliever Tim Worrell from San Diego for Donne Wall, Miceli, and infield prospect Ryan Balfe gives the Tigers more bench

THE MOMENT OF TRUTH

Detroit struggled for most of the year to get to the .500 mark, often winning three in a row and then losing three or four straight. However, a strong streak in which the club won 23 of 35 contests put them at a lofty (for the Tigers, anyway) 79-78 on September 23. That day's win, a 6-0 shutout of the Red Sox by second-year man **Greg Keagle** and two relievers, was the Tigers' last of the year. They lost their last five and finished the season at 79-83.

BEST DEAL

The Tigers have made several good trades in the last few seasons. In December 1996 they acquired pitcher **Willie Blair** and catcher **Brian Johnson** from San Diego for pitchers **Joey Eischen** and **Cam Smith**, both of whom are already gone from the Padres organization. It's a wonder that San Diego GM Kevin Towers even wants to trade with Tigers GM (and former Padres GM) Randy Smith anymore.

WORST DEAL

Not all of Randy Smith's trades have been winners, of course. The deal bringing **Jody Reed** over from the Padres in exchange for outfielder **Mike Darr** and pitcher **Matt Skrmetta** didn't work out; Reed was never a factor and was released in September, while the 21-year-old Darr batted .344 with 104 runs at Class A Rancho Cucamonga to become a prospect, and Skrmetta moved quickly through the Padres system as a reliever.

78

1. **Juan Encarnacion, OF.** The soon-to-be-23-year-old Encarnacion, a righthanded-hitting right fielder, broke out at Double A Jacksonville last season by hitting .323 with 26 home runs and 17 stolen bases. While Jacksonville is a very good hitters' park, Encarnacion has truly matured as a hitter, cutting his strikeouts and increasing his walks. He got into 11 games with the Tigers in September and is likely to begin 1998 at Triple A. Encarnacion is considered by the organization to be their best position-playing prospect.

2. **Seth Greisinger, P.** Greisinger was the club's first-round pick in 1996 and began his career last season at Jacksonville. The Tigers are pushing the 22-year-old righthander because they believe he is mature enough to handle the pace. He is known for pitching smarts and command rather than for stuff. Although he began last season poorly, Greisinger got the hang of the league and finished 10-6 with a 5.20 ERA, fanning 105 and walking 53 in 159.1 innings. He will most likely advance this year to Triple A with hopes of reaching Detroit by 1999.

3. **Mike Drumright, P.** Perhaps promoted to Triple A too quickly last spring after five good starts at Double A, the hard-throwing righthander was 5-10 with a 5.06 ERA at Toledo, fanning 115 hitters and walking 91 in 133 innings. Command of both his fastball and his curve was a problem. Another season at Toledo is in the cards. Drumright was the club's first-round draft pick in 1995 and is still the best mound prospect in the organization.

4. **Roberto Duran, P.** A lefthander who throws in the mid-90s, Duran was stolen from the Blue Jays for itinerant minor leaguer Anton French. Duran was 4-2 with 16 saves last season at Double A with a 2.37 ERA and struck out—yes, this is correct—95 men in 60.2 innings. He did walk 39 men in that same span and threw 11 wild pitches, but that kind of performance at Jacksonville is impressive. The Tigers brought him up for 13 games last summer (he allowed nine runs in 10.2 innings and walked 15 men, none intentionally) but will likely send him to Toledo this year for more work. He turns 25 in March.

5. **Frank Catalanotto, 2B.** A scrappy, productive player, Catalanotto has now had two straight good seasons in the high minors and has earned his chance at big league duty. He turns 24 in April. Catalanotto hit .300 with 16 homers at Toledo in 1997 and .308 in 13 games for the Tigers. His defense is solid though not flashy, and he runs well. A tenth-round draftee in 1992, Catalanotto is a classic overachiever who just needs a break.

6. **Eddie Gaillard, P.** The righthander, who turned 27 in August, saved 28 games at Toledo to lead the International League and earn a 16-game trial with the big club. Gaillard doesn't have much of a fastball but has pitched effectively at every level since becoming a reliever in 1994. He could wind up a middleman or setup pitcher this season for Detroit.

7. **Jesse Ibarra, 1B.** Acquired from the Giants in December 1996 for infielder Mark Lewis, Ibarra turned 25 last summer and clouted 25 homers at hitting-friendly Jacksonville. Ibarra has little chance to be a big league regular but might work his way into a platoon situation since he can switch-hit. Ibarra, likely to head to Triple A this spring, has 86 homers in four professional seasons.

8. **Marino Santana, P.** A former Seattle farmhand signed last winter by Detroit, Santana (who turns 26 in May) went to Double A for the first time and was 4-1, 3.28 as a middle reliever, fanning 98 men in just 74 innings. While control has been a problem for the righthander—he walked 43 and fired 13 wild pitches last season—Santana's arm makes him something of a prospect.

and bullpen strength. Worrell had a very poor '97. However, he still has good stuff and could be helpful as a starter or setup reliever in 1998. Florie could also start; he has a fine curve and has improved his command of the pitch. The situational southpaw role could be filled by either of two rookies: Roberto Duran or Sean Runyan.

It is unlikely that Smith can keep up this torrid pace. He has already achieved many of his objectives in a short time, making the Tigers younger, cheaper, and more talented. Smith could cut his trading and simply concentrate on fine-tuning while letting his young team continue to grow.

The Tigers have returned from the dead to the cusp of contention, and a very large portion of the credit for that transformation should go to Randy Smith. Current Cincinnati manager and former San Diego general manager Jack McKeon was dubbed "Trader Jack" in the 1980s for his love of the deal. It's time for McKeon to pass that appellation on to Smith, who should henceforth be known as "Trader Randy."

BLUE-COLLAR HERO

Philadelphia native Bobby Higginson was a star at hometown Temple University before being selected by the Tigers in the 12th round of the 1992 draft. In his first two pro seasons he hit better than .290 at Class A and Double A but combined for just five homers.

However, the Tigers liked the outfielder's grit, arm, and bat potential, and after a .275, 23-home-run breakout at Triple A in 1994, Higginson made the majors. His 1995 rookie season, in which he batted .224 with 14 homers, wasn't a success, but Detroit stayed with the young outfielder and reaped big dividends in '96.

Higginson hit .320 in 130 games with 35 doubles, 26 homers, and 65 walks. He followed that up last year by batting .299 with 30 doubles, 27 homers, and 70 walks.

Perhaps most important, he ironed out his previous problems against lefthanded pitchers. Higginson has stated in interviews many times that he hates being platooned.

On the greensward, Higginson's throwing arm is something else. Bobby winds up and releases with a smooth, powerful delivery. Whereas before his throws were cannon-like with mediocre aim, he now has improved his accuracy. In 1997 he threw out 20 baserunners, a total no outfielder had reached since Joe Orsulak six years before.

In 1998 Higginson turns 28. He is in the prime of his career and is the team's best player. More power to him and to the Tigers for sticking with him. It's really too bad for the Phillies that they didn't sign him. They must not have known about Higginson; after all, Temple is in north Philly, while the Vet is in south Philly.

BLUE-COLLAR TEAM

In honor of Bobby Higginson, then, our choices for the 1997 Blue-Collar Team:

MGR	Dusty Baker, Felipe Alou, or Lou Piniella
1B	Kevin Seitzer, Jeff Conine
2B	Jeff Frye, Mark Lemke
SS	Greg Gagne, Mark Grudzielanek
3B	Ken Caminiti, Jeff Cirillo
LF	Rusty Greer, Bobby Higginson
CF	Steve Finley, Marquis Grissom
RF	Orlando Merced, Geronimo Berroa
C	Joe Girardi, Lenny Webster
DH	Reggie Jefferson
UT	Archi Cianfrocco, Jose Hernandez, Luis Sojo, F.P. Santangelo
SP	Rick Reed, Kirk Rueter, Roger Bailey, Armando Reynoso, Mark Gardner
RP	Jeff Montgomery, Jeff Brantley, Doug Jones, Ramiro Mendoza, Dennis Cook

79

1997 TEAM STATISTICS

BATTING/BASERUNNING

	Raw	Rank	+/- %			Raw	Rank	+/- %			Raw	Rank	+/- %
R	784	8	-2		BA	.258	13	-5		SB	161	1	+51
R/G	4.84	8	-2		HR	176	7	-1		CS	72	1	+39
OBA	.332	12	-2		LH	300	10	-7		SB%	69.1	4	+3
SA	.415	10	-3		BB	578	7	+2					
PRO	.747	10	-3		SO	1,164	13	+11					

PITCHING/FIELDING

	Raw	Rank	+/- %			Raw	Rank	+/- %			Raw	Rank	+/- %
OR	790	5	-1		BA	.266	5	-2		OSB	130	11	+18
RA/G	4.88	5	-1		HR	178	8	+1		OCS	48	4	-9
OOB	.334	5	-2		LH	310	7	-4		OSB%	73.0	11	+10
OSA	.424	5	-1		BB	552	7	-2		FA	.985	1	0
PRO	.758	5	-2		SO	982	9	-5		GDP	124	5	-5

BATTING BY LINEUP SLOTS

	R	HR	RBI	BA	OBA	SA
1	114	4	45	.266	.331	.349
2	110	25	90	.276	.371	.481
3	99	27	119	.270	.332	.458
4	107	32	116	.272	.369	.488
5	96	27	94	.269	.353	.461
6	82	31	109	.252	.326	.463
7	60	15	65	.221	.307	.359
8	69	13	57	.252	.312	.359
9	47	2	48	.241	.272	.311

BATTING BY DEFENSIVE POSITION

	R	HR	RBI	BA	OBA	SA
C	56	10	53	.250	.302	.342
1B	106	33	118	.274	.372	.497
2B	95	21	76	.263	.360	.439
3B	96	23	106	.270	.325	.439
SS	50	3	45	.239	.271	.314
LF	88	24	96	.246	.323	.426
CF	114	5	46	.266	.332	.353
RF	87	32	106	.266	.353	.497
DH	81	23	87	.252	.341	.439
PH	12	4	18	.226	.309	.361
P	1	0	0	.154	.154	.308

TEAM PITCHING

	W-L	CG	QS	QS%	<6	>6	IPS	IP	ERA	OPR
ROTATION	58-63	13	75	46	36	59	5.9	958.0	4.46	.757

	W-L	GR	SV	BSV	HD	BHD	IRS%	IP	ERA	OPR
BULLPEN	21-20	417	42	22	126	95	42	487.2	4.76	.760

1998 PROJECTIONS

BATTING

PLAYER	BA	G	AB	R	H	2B	3B	HR	RBI	BB	SO	SB	CS	SA	OBA
Bartee, Kimera	.261	16	54	9	14	1	1	0	4	7	20	3	0	.351	.344
Beamon, Trey	.274	35	102	15	28	5	1	1	12	11	24	3	0	.379	.346
Casanova, Raul	.250	93	284	26	71	10	1	6	25	25	49	1	1	.354	.311
Catalanotto, Frank	.235	57	206	23	48	11	1	5	22	15	41	3	0	.371	.287
Clark, Tony	.263	157	577	96	152	25	2	33	110	77	153	1	2	.484	.350
Cruz, Deivi	.254	154	457	38	116	29	0	2	45	16	61	3	6	.331	.279
Easley, Damion	.256	150	496	82	127	31	3	18	65	60	92	22	11	.440	.336
Encarnacion, Juan	.238	40	149	20	35	7	1	6	20	10	33	4	0	.418	.284
Gonzalez, Luis	.271	132	466	69	126	28	3	11	66	61	55	8	6	.414	.355
Higginson, Bobby	.284	152	544	89	154	31	4	26	92	72	88	10	6	.498	.367
Hunter, Brian Lee	.282	148	599	101	169	28	5	4	43	50	111	61	15	.368	.337
Oliver, Joe	.257	118	362	34	93	15	0	14	49	29	65	1	2	.413	.311
Randa, Joe	.291	136	451	54	131	27	7	7	59	39	66	7	3	.428	.348
Ripken, Billy	.273	44	119	12	32	6	1	2	14	6	19	0	1	.377	.305
Roberts, Bip	.298	111	410	56	122	21	2	3	46	27	58	18	5	.381	.341

81

PITCHING

PITCHER	W	L	SV	ERA	G	GS	IP	H	HR	BB	SO
Brocail, Doug	3	4	1	3.84	43	4	66	67	9	28	46
Castillo, Frank	9	10	0	4.01	28	27	155	158	20	45	109
Duran, Roberto	4	2	2	2.23	46	0	53	30	1	34	65
Florie, Bryce	4	4	0	4.25	54	7	95	91	7	54	78
Gaillard, Eddie	2	2	2	3.53	40	0	41	33	5	16	31
Jones, Todd	5	4	32	3.58	68	0	75	71	4	40	71
Keagle, Greg	5	5	0	4.26	16	16	91	88	8	36	66
Martinez, Pedro A.	2	3	0	4.91	15	4	37	37	5	20	14
Moehler, Brian	11	12	0	4.66	31	31	174	196	22	62	94
Pugh, Tim	1	1	0	4.38	4	4	23	22	3	6	16
Sager, A.J.	2	3	1	4.53	20	2	50	52	6	15	32
Sanders, Scott	7	9	1	4.85	38	16	121	118	20	48	114
Thompson, Justin	13	13	0	3.43	33	33	223	200	21	74	153
Worrell, Tim	5	8	1	4.71	60	11	117	124	14	51	92
Runyan, Sean	4	3	0	3.52	36	1	56	61	4	31	39

KANSAS CITY ROYALS

MANAGEMENT

Manager	General Manager	Owner
Tony Muser Career Record 31-48 .392	Herk Robinson	Greater Kansas City Community Foundation

1997 RECORD

Won-Lost	Pct.		Division Finish/GB		Wild Card Finish/GB	
67-94	.416		5 C	-19	10	-28.5

Preseason Consensus Projection		5 (3.91)

1st Half	2nd Half	Home	Road	Intradivision	Interleague
36-41	31-53	33-47	34-47	17-30	6-9

Comebacks	Blowouts	Nailbiters
8-14	20-23	34-45

A ROYAL MESS

The 1997 season was utterly disastrous for the Kansas City Royals. The manager was fired; the club finished in last place, 19 games out; and the team's owners shopped the franchise in a half-hearted way. The big plan for '97 of adding veteran power failed miserably despite their production, so the Royals are now left with a skeletal lineup, few good youngsters, a very thin pitching staff, and a level of fan interest bordering on the catatonic.

Before the '97 season the Royals, deficient in the power department in the recent past, acquired veteran sluggers Chili Davis and Jeff King (along with shortstop Jay Bell, who had moderate power). They then picked up Dean Palmer during the season. With these big bats added to a speed-heavy lineup, K.C. expected the runs to roll in.

It didn't happen. The Royals finished 12th among AL teams in runs (ahead of just Milwaukee and Toronto)

despite a collective 74 homers from Davis, King, and Bell, and nine more from Palmer in 187 at bats.

What killed the Royals offense? Everything. Despite the veteran punch, Kansas City hit more homers than only three other clubs, getting no power from their outfielders or their catchers. The Royals' slugging percentage ranked 12th in the AL. Their .264 batting average was seven points below the league average, and they took just 561 walks, ninth in the AL. Their .333 on-base percentage ranked a lowly 11th.

To top it all off, the hitters left more runners on base than seven AL teams, despite not having many runners on in the first place. Kansas City did steal 130 bases for the year, which placed fourth in the league and again showed that overemphasis on the running game produces little offense.

The outfield for the 1997 Royals was a bloody mess, with almost all the wounds self-inflicted. It all started late in spring training when K.C. dumped Michael Tucker for Jermaine Dye, a trade that defied reason then and defines reason now. Manager Bob Boone obviously felt Tucker wasn't good enough to play for Kansas City. As things turned out, Tucker was plenty good enough to play for the defending NL champion Braves, while Dye wasn't good enough to play for anybody in '97, and might not ever be.

Until being fired, Boone continued his campaign to destroy whatever talent Johnny Damon might have had by continuing to juggle Damon between left, center, and right fields and using him at nearly every lineup spot. That Damon still hit .275 was a miracle.

The other outfielders either played average-to-good ball and were traded (Bip Roberts, Tom Goodwin) or were terrible disappointments (Dye and Joe Vitiello). Dye showed decent bat speed but had a propensity to chase terrible pitches, hitting .236 with seven homers. Vitiello, coming off knee surgery, batted only .238. Yamil Benitez, another youngster acquired via trade from Montreal, never met a pitch he didn't like. He batted .267 with eight homers, but walked just 10 times in more than 200 plate appearances. If he were really good, wouldn't Expos skipper Felipe Alou have found a way to use him?

Kansas City compounded its misery with another questionable deal on July 15, packing off outfielder Jon Nunnally and infielder-outfielder Chris Stynes to Cincinnati for relievers Hector Carrasco and Scott Service. Carrasco, the key to the trade for Kansas City, was terrible in Royals garb after having been mediocre and full of complaints while with the Reds.

Nunnally and Stynes, passed over in favor of others in Kansas City, hit very well for Cincinnati. While neither is going to be a star, they certainly can play baseball and are worth a lot more than two middle relievers, neither of whom is on the Royals' roster any longer. It was a very poor trade, putting a Band-aid on the Royals' awful bullpen problems while giving away decent talent.

Behind the plate, veteran repatriate Mike Macfarlane had a bad season that a late rush couldn't save, while young Mike Sweeney did not hit up to expectations. However, Sweeney threw very well and showed above-average mobility. He deserves a chance to grow into the job, and will apparently be mentored by Macfarlane in 1998.

TEAM MVP

Jay Bell had his best-ever season at the plate in 1997, hitting .291 with 21 homers, 92 RBIs, and 71 walks, and he played his usual steady shortstop. That made him the most valuable player this horrid club had.

BIGGEST SURPRISE

Kansas City had few positive surprises in 1997 and many negative ones. Perhaps the best unexpected thing to happen to the Royals last season was that two second base candidates emerged—**Jed Hansen** (.309 in 34 games) and **Shane Halter** (.276 in 74 games). It's likely that the 25-year-old Hansen will get first chance at the position in 1998, while Halter will fill a utility role.

83

BIGGEST DISAPPOINTMENT

Lefthanded pitcher **Jose Rosado**, the Royals' only All Star, went to the midsummer classic with a 7-4 record and a 3.39 ERA. From that point on he was 2-8, lasting six or more innings in only seven of his last 15 starts and piling up a 6.75 ERA. Some said that he was going through growing pains, but others felt that the American League was finally catching up to the youngster, who has never experienced failure as a professional and must adjust.

PITCHING IN TO THE DISASTER

As rotten as the offense was, the starting pitching was even worse. Kevin Appier, who has clearly lost some velocity, continued to adjust in '97, finishing 9-13 despite a good 3.40 ERA. AL hitters are now waiting Appier out and no longer will chase after the pitches he can't throw for strikes.

The rest of the mound corps was just bad. Jose Rosado, who was simply miserable after the All-Star break, sagged to a 9-12 mark and a 4.69 ERA, while Tim Belcher's 5.02 ERA belied his 13-12 record. Rookies Glen Rusch (6-9, 5.50) and Jim Pittsley (5-8, 5.46) gave little encouragement for the future. Things got so bad that castoff Ricky Bones wound up in the starting rotation and performed at his usual level (4-7, 5.97).

The injury to Chris Haney certainly left the Royals' rotation short one pitcher, but Haney has never won more games than he's lost in a season anyway. This group was bad before the season started and worse when it ended.

Worse than the rotation was the bullpen. Longtime closer Jeff Montgomery stumbled through his shoulder rehabilitation, only finding his groove late in the season. A rotator cuff injury kept prospect Jaime Bluma out all year, leaving the bullpen even thinner. To hammer the last nail into the coffin, Hipolito Pichardo's sore shoulder sent him to the disabled list and then to Triple A at midseason.

As a result Kansas City had to bring the humpties in. Mike Williams, Larry Casian, Mike Perez, and (almost unbelievably) Mitch Williams, the original "Wild Thing," trudged in from the Kansas City bullpen as the year dragged on. Royals pitchers recorded just 29 saves, one fewer than the Twins and the lowest figure in the major leagues.

The bullpen's terrible performance, as well as bad fundamental play and an inability to score runs, finally cost Boone his job at the All Star break with the club's record at 36-46. Tony Muser, at the time the Cubs' hitting coach and highly respected around baseball, was brought in to replace Boone.

Shortly after taking the reins, Muser straightened some things out. He made Damon the club's regular center fielder, precipitating the Tom Goodwin trade. The Royals also released third baseman Craig Paquette, a terrible player who was one of Boone's pet projects, almost immediately, and gave the job to Dean Palmer (acquired for Goodwin).

The club didn't immediately improve. Boone left on an eight-game losing skid, which stretched to 12 before the Royals finally won. Muser's record as manager was worse than Boone's (31-48), but it would have been hard to do anything with the team he inherited.

WHAT MIGHT HAVE BEEN

Perhaps the biggest failure of Bob Boone's tenure in Kansas City was his inability to develop outfielders Michael Tucker and Johnny Damon. Both were good homegrown prospects with plenty of natural ability.

Damon, drafted in 1992 at age 18, was a .300 hitter at both Class A and Double A. He came up to Kansas City in late 1995 and played 47 games, all in center field. The next season Boone played Damon 89 times in center and 63 in right, starting him in every single spot in the batting order at least once! He led off 25 times but spent 74 games batting either sixth, seventh, or eighth.

How in the world is a young player supposed to learn how to do his job in the majors when that job keeps changing every day?

By the time Boone was fired last July, Damon had spent 39 games in left field, 10 in center, and 38 in right. When Tom Goodwin was traded two weeks after Tony Muser took over from Boone, Damon became the everyday center fielder. His career still ahead of him at age 24, Damon could still develop into one of the AL's best players.

Tucker, picked just before Damon in the first round of the 1992 draft, also made his K.C. debut in 1995. He began the season as the Royals' left fielder after a fine performance at Triple A in 1994 but slumped to .207 with no home runs in 31 games before being sent down. Recalled in August, Tucker batted .305 with four homers in 31 games.

Tucker then spent a dizzying 1996 hitting .260 in 108 games with 12 homers. Twice he was disabled, first with a broken wrist and near the end of the season with a broken finger. When he could play, Tucker was seen in right field (73 games), left field (28 games), and even at first base early in the season (9 games).

The deal that sent Tucker and Keith Lockhart to Atlanta in spring training 1997 netted the Royals lefthanded reliever Jamie Walker—a Rule V pick who stayed with Kansas City all year—and outfielder Jermaine Dye, who is three

84

years younger than Tucker but has little chance of surpassing him as a player. While Tucker went to a division championship team and played good baseball with a clearly defined role, Dye struggled with big league breaking balls (.284 on-base, .369 slugging) and ended up back at Triple A.

WHAT NEXT?

So what can the Royals do? Among the veterans, Jeff King is signed. Jay Bell and Chili Davis left via free agency for greener pastures, while Dean Palmer hit just .256 on the season with 23 homers. He was re-signed by K.C. in the off-season.

The organization doesn't have much in the pipeline to help out. If the Royals do decide on younger players, they could turn to either Jed Hansen or Shane Halter at second. Hansen, 25, is the better prospect; the 28-year-old Halter projects as a utility player. Mata Martinez, a spectacular fielder, could move in at shortstop, but he won't hit much. The Royals' off-season moves didn't really solve any of the club's many problems, but at least addressed some of them.

Kansas City was short on runs last season, so the team added three veterans with hitting credentials. Orlando Miller, plucked from the waiver wire, has some power and can play a fair major league shortstop, assuming he is recovered from the back problems that plagued him in 1997. Another veteran acquisition, Jeff Conine (originally a Royals prospect, taken in the 1992 expansion draft by Florida), will vie for a spot in left field but could also end up platooning at DH with yet another off-season pickup, free agent Hal Morris.

While these veterans aren't stars, each could provide some production until the next group of prospects (Mark Quinn, Carlos Mendez, Carlos Febles) arrives in 1999 or 2000. The Royals' off-season acquisitions began to drift into self-parody, however, with the January signings of Lee Smith and Terry Pendleton. The two former stars are now burnt out and will almost certainly disappoint if they see much action.

But hope springs eternal, and Kansas City GM Herk Robinson must be one hopeful fellow. In the pasture, outfielder Rod Myers, expected to contend for an everyday job, broke a wrist in spring training in '97 and got only 101 at bats for Kansas City. He has a good shot at regular

THE MOMENT OF TRUTH

With a 36-38 record on **June 28**, the Royals were three games back in the AL Central race. That night the club lost 5-3 to Milwaukee and didn't win again until **July 14**, dropping 12 games in a row. Perhaps the worst of those losses came on June 30 in Chicago, where the Royals led 7-3 in the bottom of the eighth before the Cubs scored five runs against the bullpen to pull out an 8-7 win. Less than a week later, Royals' manager Bob Boone was fired.

BEST DEAL

While it didn't turn their season around, the Royals did beef up their lineup with the July 26 acquisition of third baseman **Dean Palmer** from Texas. Palmer hit .278 with nine homers in 49 games for K.C. and was certainly better than Craig Paquette, who had played the position before the trade. The player Kansas City dealt to the Rangers, **Tom Goodwin**, is really best suited to a reserve role.

WORST DEAL

This club made some bad trades in 1997, but the worst came on July 15. Needing something—anything—to prop up their miserable, injury-plagued bullpen, the Royals traded **Jon Nunnally** and **Chris Stynes** to Cincinnati for erratic, hard-throwing **Hector Carrasco**. While Nunnally and Stynes hit the cover off the ball for the Reds, Carrasco was 1-6 with a 5.45 ERA for the Royals and was later selected by Arizona in the expansion draft.

85

duty in 1998, but he won't solve the problem by himself.

Triple A Omaha's best hitters in 1997 were outfielder Yamil Benitez (.295, 21 homers, 24 walks, 82 strike-outs), first baseman Larry Sutton (a 27-year-old Bob Hamelin wannabe), and journeyman Pork Chop Pough. Not an encouraging picture.

One of the biggest problems during Bob Boone's tenure was his "play 'em all, play 'em everywhere" philosophy. Because of that, Kansas City ended up making good prospects into mediocre players who could perform in a mediocre fashion at several positions. In 1997 Halter played six spots and David Howard five; both also served as DH. Bip Roberts played three positions. Boone seemed to feel the big leagues were an audition stage, giving Jose Offerman a full-time job at second after trying to make him a first baseman the season before.

Boone's use of players all over the field wasn't new. In 1995, his first season running the Royals, he used Edgar Caceres at all four infield spots and Howard at three infield and two outfield positions. In '95 Boone used 51 players total; he had 13 pitchers start games and used 22 different players at DH.

In 1996 Howard, Kevin Young, and Craig Paquette each played five positions, Chris Stynes appeared at four, and Offerman played at least 35 games at three different spots. Offerman and Michael Tucker played first base, Paquette played shortstop, and Joe Randa spent 15 games at second base. Another 17 Royals were DHs.

TOP PROSPECTS
SPRING 1998

1. **Mata Martinez, SS.** Martinez is a thin switch hitter who turns 24 this May. He shows outstanding defensive skills but hasn't hit much. In 1997 at Triple A Omaha, Martinez batted .254 with two homers in 112 games. He did steal 21 bases but took only 29 walks. Martinez has not won the organization over with his attitude and is not faring well from the right side of the plate. Nevertheless, he could start the season with Kansas City anyway.

2. **Enrique Calero, P.** "Kiko," a 23-year-old 27th-round draft pick in 1996, spent last season at Double A Wichita and was 11-9 with a 4.44 ERA. The polished righthander throws mostly sinkers and sliders, occasionally mixing in a changeup. In '97 he fanned 100 and walked 44 in 127.2 innings. The Royals think he could be in the majors later this season.

3. **Jeremy Giambi, OF.** The brother of Athletics slugger Jason is a better outfielder than his sibling and the same type of pure left-handed hitter. The 23-year-old Jeremy was a sixth-round pick in 1996. He hit .336 in 31 games at Class A Lansing before a promotion to Wichita, where he batted .321 in 74 games with 11 homers, 52 RBIs, and 44 walks. Expect Giambi in the majors by next spring.

4. **Mark Quinn, OF.** After batting .308 with 16 homers and 71 RBIs in just 87 games at Class A Wilmington in 1997, Quinn earned a promotion and batted .375 in 24 games for Wichita. A patient hitter with a high on-base percentage, Quinn has sneaked up on the organization; he was an 11th-round pick in 1995 and turns 24 in May. Although he is injury-prone and a mediocre left fielder, Quinn is now on the fast track due to his bat.

5. **Carlos Mendez, 1B.** Mendez is a notorious bad-ball righthanded contact hitter who had 19 walks in 129 games in '97 at Wichita, but he hit .329 with 12 homers and 90 RBIs and played above-average first base. After six seasons in Class A, he turns 24 in June and could be a platoon player soon, in Kansas City.

6. **Jose Santiago, P.** Santiago pitched for two Class A teams, Wichita, and K.C. in '97. He has a live right arm as well as a live temper, which he showed last year when he threw a baseball at a verbally abusive fan. The 23-year-old has been a reliever his entire four-year pro career and could begin this season closing at Omaha.

7. **Larry Sutton, 1B.** Sutton, a lefty swinger, batted .300 last year at Triple A with 19 homers, 72 RBIs, and 61 walks in just 106 games. However, he turns 28 this May. Sutton could fill in as a platoon first baseman with Jeff King or be a reserve, because he can hit.

The pitching staff needs some serious help. Tim Belcher and Kevin Appier can eat plenty of innings, but neither pitched like a staff ace in 1997. Appier is talented and experienced however, and will obviously enter the year as the top gun.

Jose Rosado, who had the usual troubles that lefthanded finesse pitchers experience when adjusting to the league the second time around, is a big question mark. He is still just 23 and has decent stuff, but must do something about the control problems he occasionally suffered in '97.

Pittsley, who still appears to be recovering from serious elbow surgery performed in 1995, could get another shot due to his fine minor league performances in 1993 and '94. However, it's questionable whether he will ever really be back. Rusch will probably get another shot because he's lefthanded and is young enough (23) to improve.

The bullpen will be different in 1998. Montgomery will be back, but an entirely different middle relief corps is projected. Hipolito Pichardo will be given a shot at the starting rotation. If Jaime Bluma can return from injury (which is not certain), the pen would be that much stronger.

While it's no guarantee of success, new manager Muser must avoid the biggest mistake of his predecessor. He must have the courage to take risks with young players, based on his experience and the expertise of his staff. This means evaluating his players before leaving Florida, coming up with a plan, and giving that plan time to work.

Those were three things Boone could never do.

JOSE OFFERMAN: DH IN WAITING?

The Royals, like the Dodgers before them, decided that Jose Offerman was not capable of playing shortstop for them. After a brief experiment at first base in 1996, Offerman spent last season as Kansas City's everyday second baseman.

While he continued to hit well (.297, though his on-base percentage slipped to .359), Offerman did not impress at second base. He made just nine errors during the season, but his range was far below par. There is almost no chance that Offerman will complete the quadrangle by moving to third base in '98. If Muser decides to use Jed Hansen at second, where would that leave Offerman, who is signed through 1998?

Since Offerman didn't wind up with one of the expansion clubs, could he be the Royals' DH? Chili Davis, the DH in '97, is history and, with the departure of Tom Goodwin and Bip Roberts, Kansas City lacks a top-of-the-order speed guy.

This is something Offerman can't do. He could be a decent leadoff hitter if he did one thing: stop trying to steal bases. This ability deserted him very early in his career. Counting 1997's horrid 9-for-19 performance on the basepaths, he has a very poor 61 percent career stolen base rate. However, the Royals' team speed was gutted by the trades of Roberts and Goodwin, so putting Offerman at the top of the order will be tempting.

Offerman is not a bad player; he just isn't a good one. He could DH if his on-base average were higher or if he had more power. Unfortunately, he isn't a great hitter, and his inability to hit well enough to be a DH or to play any defensive position well makes his future uncertain.

87

1997 TEAM STATISTICS

BATTING/BASERUNNING

	Raw	Rank	+/- %		Raw	Rank	+/- %		Raw	Rank	+/- %
R	747	12	-6	BA	.264	10	-2	SB	130	4	+22
R/G	4.64	12	-6	HR	158	10	-11	CS	66	3	+28
OBA	.333	10	-2	LH	291	12	-9	SB%	66.3	9	-1
SA	.407	12	-5	BB	561	9	-1				
PRO	.740	12	-4	SO	1,061	8	+2				

PITCHING/FIELDING

	Raw	Rank	+/- %		Raw	Rank	+/- %		Raw	Rank	+/- %
OR	820	8	+3	BA	.274	9	+1	OSB	72	2	-34
RA/G	5.09	9	+3	HR	186	10	+6	OCS	42	1	-21
OOB	.340	7	0	LH	288	1	-11	OSB%	63.2	5	-5
OSA	.430	8	0	BB	531	3	-5	FA	.985	2	0
PRO	.770	7	0	SO	961	10	-7	GDP	140	10	+8

88

BATTING BY LINEUP SLOTS

	R	HR	RBI	BA	OBA	SA
1	95	3	61	.297	.351	.391
2	94	8	60	.256	.327	.348
3	97	24	96	.292	.367	.459
4	97	32	118	.255	.353	.469
5	75	25	101	.270	.352	.446
6	74	25	78	.239	.300	.425
7	72	13	60	.225	.291	.327
8	69	14	75	.275	.324	.391
9	74	14	62	.262	.327	.408

BATTING BY DEFENSIVE POSITION

	R	HR	RBI	BA	OBA	SA
C	69	17	69	.232	.301	.372
1B	88	29	112	.241	.339	.441
2B	83	4	68	.302	.363	.403
3B	63	16	73	.249	.293	.398
SS	89	21	96	.286	.367	.442
LF	75	9	57	.284	.332	.374
CF	93	8	46	.258	.313	.350
RF	74	17	73	.263	.320	.419
DH	88	34	106	.277	.377	.502
PH	14	3	13	.213	.327	.323
P	0	0	0	.053	.053	.105

TEAM PITCHING

	W-L	CG	QS	QS%	<6	>6	IPS	IP	ERA	OPR
ROTATION	47-61	11	73	45	28	72	6.2	1,002.0	4.81	.775

	W-L	GR	SV	BSV	HD	BHD	IRS%	IP	ERA	OPR
BULLPEN	20-33	393	29	21	137	74	43	441.0	4.47	.759

1998 PROJECTIONS

BATTING

PLAYER	BA	G	AB	R	H	2B	3B	HR	RBI	BB	SO	SB	CS	SA	OBA
Conine, Jeff	.274	140	440	57	121	19	1	20	74	57	91	1	1	.457	.358
Damon, Johnny	.280	149	505	72	142	17	8	8	53	41	72	20	9	.389	.334
Dye, Jermaine	.259	107	351	37	91	19	0	12	36	19	76	2	2	.416	.298
Fasano, Sal	.202	21	65	10	13	3	0	4	8	7	24	0	0	.412	.275
Halter, Shane	.276	76	127	17	35	5	1	2	10	10	29	4	3	.368	.329
Hansen, Jed	.252	77	246	26	62	12	2	6	28	22	66	5	0	.390	.312
King, Jeff	.247	145	522	79	129	29	2	25	103	75	86	14	3	.457	.342
Long, Ryan	.252	11	41	5	10	3	0	2	5	2	12	0	0	.444	.283
Macfarlane, Mike	.248	79	256	36	63	15	1	11	36	23	46	1	2	.438	.311
Martinez, Felix	.272	38	129	18	35	6	1	0	12	10	33	5	0	.342	.326
Miller, Orlando	.266	79	236	26	63	15	2	7	27	10	57	2	3	.432	.297
Morris, Hal	.292	104	372	52	109	23	2	6	47	30	52	4	2	.419	.345
Myers, Rod	.263	81	256	36	68	21	0	6	28	40	58	11	1	.409	.363
Offerman, Jose	.296	111	427	63	126	22	6	3	37	50	68	11	9	.397	.370
Palmer, Dean	.266	145	544	80	145	29	1	28	91	48	133	2	1	.476	.325
Stewart, Andy	.264	13	43	5	11	2	0	1	4	2	7	0	0	.347	.303
Sutton, Larry	.241	40	134	17	32	7	0	5	19	16	25	0	0	.404	.323
Sweeney, Mike	.259	97	284	37	74	12	0	9	38	24	40	3	3	.391	.316
Vitiello, Joe	.244	34	93	9	23	5	0	3	14	11	25	1	0	.406	.324

PITCHING

PITCHER	W	L	SV	ERA	G	GS	IP	H	HR	BB	SO
Appier, Kevin	10	11	0	3.75	29	29	197	181	18	68	174
Belcher, Tim	11	10	0	4.60	26	26	176	195	23	59	91
Bevil, Brian	2	2	1	5.63	21	1	24	21	2	12	18
Bones, Ricky	5	8	0	5.46	23	13	92	110	14	36	40
Delamaza, Roland	2	2	0	4.10	9	4	31	33	4	13	16
Haney, Chris	3	6	0	4.49	16	13	86	100	9	21	45
McDill, Allen	1	1	0	4.32	9	1	19	18	2	7	12
Montgomery, Jeff	2	4	23	3.88	50	0	58	54	10	18	44
Olson, Gregg	3	1	1	5.05	33	0	36	38	3	21	25
Pichardo, Hipolito	7	9	2	4.70	85	0	98	103	10	44	64
Pittsley, Jim	5	8	0	5.28	22	22	116	123	17	54	54
Rosado, Jose	9	10	0	4.45	28	28	178	181	20	60	112
Rusch, Glendon	4	6	0	5.34	20	18	113	136	19	34	77
Walker, Jamie	3	3	0	5.24	48	0	41	44	5	19	23
Whisenant, Matt	2	0	0	4.59	64	0	49	43	0	41	46

89

MINNESOTA TWINS

MANAGEMENT

Manager	General Manager	Owner
Tom Kelly Career Record 853-885 .491	Terry Ryan	Carl Pohlad

1997 RECORD

Won-Lost	Pct.	Division Finish/GB		Wild Card Finish/GB	
68-94	.420	4 C	-18.5	9	-28

Preseason Consensus Projection	3 (3.74)

1st Half	2nd Half	Home	Road	Intradivision	Interleague
35-44	33-50	35-46	33-48	22-26	7-8

Comebacks	Blowouts	Nailbiters
3-7	20-31	32-37

90

GIVE THE KIDS A CHANCE

Since Minnesota won the 1991 World Series the club has fallen about as far as it could. From the heights of a well-deserved world championship, the Twins have tumbled to the embarrassment of finishing among the also-rans in front of small crowds while rumors of their leaving town swirled around them. Add to that the ugly statewide bickering about using public money for a new stadium and you can safely say that the Twins haven't covered themselves in glory in the last six years.

One amazing thing is that Twins GM Andy MacPhail was able to get out of town and head to the Chicago Cubs without receiving his share of the blame for this state of events. Twice—after the club's 1987 title and after the 1991 title—he dismantled a victorious veteran team and reassembled it. The second time around, it didn't work. An underachieving farm system and the terribly unlucky career-ending ailment to Kirby Puckett just put the icing on the cake.

There were a few bright spots for the 1997 Twins: pitcher Brad Radke had a remarkable stretch of 12 straight wins that lifted him to a 20-victory season; second baseman Chuck Knoblauch again demonstrated why he's one of the best at his position; and 41-year-old homeboy Paul Molitor hit .309 and drove in 89 runs.

Aside from that, it was slim pickings for Minnesota fans, who had to make do with relatively small-time achievements of bargain-bin pickups like Ron Coomer, Greg Colbrunn, Bob Tewksbury, Greg Swindell, and Roberto Kelly, while big-time free agent Terry Steinbach had a disappointing first season after his homecoming (.248, 12 homers, 54 RBIs).

Homegrown players such as Rich Becker, Matt Lawton, Marty Cordova, Scott Stahoviak, LaTroy

Travis Miller, Mike Trombley, Frankie Rodriguez, and Todd Walker all performed below expectations, and by the end of the season, manager Tom Kelly was fed up with most of them.

When the Twins won their two World Series, the surprising performances of fill-ins such as Dan Gladden, Les Straker, Juan Berenguer, Mike Pagliarulo, Brian Harper, among others, gave extra depth to a team with very strong front-line talent. Coomer was just as good in '97 as Pagliarulo was in '91, but there were no Pucketts, Gaettis, or Hrbeks in the lineup to carry this team. Radke's excellent season elevates him into the role of staff ace, but the problem is that there's nobody to help him. Current shortstop Pat Meares may be close to Greg Gagne in talent, but Gagne was never one of Minnesota's best players in its glory years. Sad to say, Meares is one of the current Twins' best players.

So what should the Twins do? What choices do they have? They should ahve kept Knoblauch. He is a franchise-quality player, even if he did slump somewhat last year (.291, 9 homers, 58 RBIs).

The Twins' brain trust needs to sort through the team's young talents and give them a chance to play. Using veterans Eric Anthony, Darrin Jackson, and Roberto Kelly in the outfield did nothing but take away at bats that others needed in order to develop. The best bets the Twins had to grow into good big league players were their young outfielders: Cordova, Lawton, and Becker (who was dealt to the Mets in the off-season for outfielder Alex Ochoa). Signing Otis Nixon for 1998 does nothing to help this team rebuild.

As part of this audition process the team needs to turn the starting rotation in a new direction. Hawkins and Rich Robertson have proven that they are not capable of winning for this franchise, and it's time to give some of the others a chance. Radke and Tewksbury give Minnesota two strong-armed starters, and there are a few candidates in the minors (Dan Serafini, Shane Bowers, Travis Miller, and maybe Jason Bell) who deserve an extended tryout to see if they've got the stuff to be starters in the big leagues.

With crane-like lefthander Robertson finally wearing out his welcome and earning his release, the club picked 38-year-old righthander Mike Morgan off the free-agent

TEAM MVP

Righthanded pitcher **Brad Radke** was 20-10, which meant that he accounted for nearly 30 percent of the Twins' victories. He cut his homers allowed from 40 in 1996 to 28 last season while pitching seven more innings. At one point Radke won 12 straight starts, allowing two or fewer runs in 11 of them.

BIGGEST SURPRISE

Veteran southpaw **Greg Swindell** resuscitated his career in middle relief, finishing 7-4 in 65 games, walking just 25 in 115.2 innings and finishing the season with a fine 3.58 ERA. Aside from Radke's big year, that was about as pleasant as things got for the 1997 Twins.

BIGGEST DISAPPOINTMENT

Young third baseman **Todd Walker** hit just .237 with three homers in 52 games, failing to claim the job despite many chances. Just as harmful to the team was **Marty Cordova**'s lingering foot injury, which hampered him both at bat and in the field. He finished with a .246 average and just 15 homers in 103 games.

91

pile to gobble up some innings. The Twins are putting a lot of faith in this "tutelage" thing, having veterans Morgan and Tewksbury around for educational reasons as much as for their on-field performance.

Lastly, Minnesota would be better off spending what money it has for veterans on getting one quality player rather than three or four players like Darrin Jackson. You can always find someone at Triple A to imitate Darrin Jackson; the money spent on signing Nixon and Jackson last winter could have have been better spent elsewhere.

ALL THE WRONG MOVES

The Twins led the way, but they weren't alone. Some of the most ill-fated managerial gambits of the 1997 season were:

1. The Twins' attempt to convert failed closer Dave Stevens into a starter. He allowed 23 runs in 23 innings for Minnesota before finally being released.
2. Scott Aldred "earning" 15 starts with the Twins. His record in those games: 2-10, 8.00 ERA.
3. The White Sox' use of rookie finesse pitcher Keith Foulke, who had never posted a save in his life before joining the team, as a closer.
4. Terry Clark, a 36-year-old itinerant arm, starting four games for the Indians and five more for the Rangers. His 1997 totals: 1-7, 6.00 ERA.
5. Vince Coleman making the Tigers' roster. He was 1 for 14 before being released.
6. The Reds and Blue Jays giving Ruben Sierra another chance. In 138 at bats he hit .232 with three home runs. (After the season the White Sox signed him.)
7. Bob Boone's attachment to Craig Paquette as his regular third baseman in K.C. Paquette managed a .230 average in 77 games, with eight home runs and 57 strikeouts.
8. Kansas City's reliance on Ricky Bones for 11 starts after he had bombed out with the Reds. In those starts, Bones compiled a 6.95 ERA. (He signed a minor league deal this winter with—guess who?—the Twins.)
9. Kansas City giving Mitch Williams seven games to show what he could do. In those seven games he allowed 11 hits and seven walks in 6.2 innings. Good

night, Mitch.
10. Thirty-six-year-old Mark Davis returning to the majors as Milwaukee's situational lefthander.
11. Thirty-four-year-old Scott Bailes returning to the majors as Texas' situational lefthander.
12. Thirty-five-year-old Greg Cadaret returning to the majors as Anaheim's situational lefthander.
13. Lou Piniella using Brent Gates, a mediocre second baseman, 32 times at third. He hit .238.
14. The Cubs' use of Brant Brown, a career first baseman, as their left fielder.
15. Dave Swartzbaugh, sometimes a decent Triple A pitcher, getting two early-season starts for the Cubs.
16. The desperate, marketing-driven promotion of Pete Rose, Jr., to the Reds.
17. Tony Pena's late-season acquisition by Houston. He closed out his career in 1997 with a .174 batting average, his third sub-.200 mark in five years.
18. Doug Strange getting 327 at bats for the Expos. That he clubbed 12 homers wasn't the point.
19. Montreal bringing back old war-horse Lee Smith: 25 games, 21.2 innings, 5.82 ERA.
20. The Phillies' giving overmatched Wendell Magee (.200 in 38 games) their starting center field job.
21. The Cardinals and Padres swapping Danny Jackson for Fernando Valenzuela. It was like trading pieces of stale toast.
22. Doug Creek getting three starts for the Giants. Twenty-six men reached base in his 13 innings.
23. The Phillies signing the three Marks: Portugal, Leiter, and Parent. Enough said.
24. The Athletics reuniting the Bash Brothers by bring back Jose Canseco, who celebrated his return with a .235 average and 23 home runs.
25. The Brewers giving Pete Harnisch, whose last good year was 1993, another chance.

A few desperate gambles did work out, of course:
1. The New York Mets converting Brian Bohanon into a starter. He was 6-4 with a 3.33 ERA in the role.
2. Kevin Young playing first base for the Pirates, hitting .300 with 18 homers.
3. Dale Sveum playing everywhere for the Bucs and serv-

ing as one of the club's best all-around producers.

4. The Phillies letting Darren Daulton take over in right field, where he batted .264 with 11 homers before a trade to Florida.

5. The Marlins moving Bobby Bonilla back to the hot corner. Result: a happy and productive Bonilla.

6. The Astros giving Chuck Carr the center field job late in the season. He really wasn't bad, hitting .276 with line-drive power.

PAUL MOLITOR: HEADING TO THE HALL?

While there may not be much else to look forward to for Twins fans, there is some comfort in the fact that Paul Molitor will be back with the club in 1998. He is a genuine fan favorite and a very smart player, one who could well become a manager when he finally decides to hang it up.

The Hall of Fame will eventually page Molitor, chiefly because he has 3,178 career hits, as well as 495 stolen bases and 230 home runs. The 3,000-hit milestone has become an automatic qualifier for the Hall of Fame, just as 300 wins has become for pitchers—even if your name is Don Sutton, in which case you still have to wait your turn.

Maybe, however, the 3,000-hit standard should be rethought. The use of aging players as designated hitters has created a cushion allowing elderly American Leaguers to stretch out their careers and pile up offensive totals not possible with the requirement of playing the field every day.

Exactly 20 hitters have reached 3,000 hits (not counting Cap Anson, whose totals have been corrected downward to 2,995). Of those 20, fully half have done so since the designated hitter was instituted in 1973. That's not a coincidence. Those ten are (ranked in order of career hits):

Pete Rose	4,256
Carl Yastrzemski	3,419
Eddie Murray	3,255
Paul Molitor	3,178
George Brett	3,154
Robin Yount	3,142
Dave Winfield	3,110
Rod Carew	3,053
Lou Brock	3,023
Al Kaline	3,007

THE MOMENT OF TRUTH

The Twins were still tied for first place as late as April 24, but the slide began in earnest shortly after. The club finished under .500 in every month, and the Twins were at their worst in August (8-20). In the midst of a nine-game losing streak, they were shut out 11-0 by the Yankees on August 11 to end a 2-6 homestand. That's the way it was.

BEST DEAL

The Twins dumped several veterans down the stretch, including **Greg Myers**, **Greg Colbrunn**, and **Roberto Kelly**. In the best of those trades, the Twins got outfielder **Marc Lewis** from Atlanta in exchange for Colbrunn. Lewis, who turns 23 in May, has some power and good speed.

WORST DEAL

Veteran catcher **Terry Steinbach** was signed for two years to add some pop as well as to marshal a young pitching staff to maturity. At season's end, Steinbach had a .248 average, 12 homers, and mixed reviews for his work with the mound corps. He's still a decent player, but Steinbach needs a big comeback in 1998 if Minnesota hopes to improve.

93

1. **Dan Serafini, P.** The Twins' first-round draft choice in 1992 has taken several years to develop, but now appears ready to be a starter in the majors. Serafini was impressive at Triple A Salt Lake last season before a six-game trial with the Twins. The 24-year-old southpaw has three above-average pitches, including a strong overhand curve, and has improved his control.

2. **David Ortiz, 1B.** Formerly known as David Arias, the 22-year-old, 6-4, 238-pound lefthanded hitter was acquired from the Mariners in August 1996. He played at four levels in 1997. Ortiz hit .331 at Class A Fort Myers in 1997 with 13 homers, then .322 at Double A New Britain with 14 more long balls. After two weeks at Salt Lake City he joined the Twins in September and batted .327 in 49 at bats. While Ortiz is full of promise, he is also a very aggressive swinger, fanning 19 times and walking twice with the Twins. He could start this year in a platoon role with Minnesota or end up back at Triple A for a while.

3. **Travis Miller, P.** The lefthanded Miller was a sandwich pick in 1994 and has moved up fast. He was 10-6 last season at Salt Lake City, posting a 4.73 ERA that led the team's full-time starters. Miller, 25, was a star pitcher at Kent State University before turning pro, and is polished. He has nothing special in his repertoire, but does throw sinkers and sliders effectively.

4. **Corey Koskie, 3B.** Koskie, a 26th-round draft choice in 1994, turns 25 in June but is viewed as a good prospect. He hit .286 at New Britain last season, smacking 23 homers and drawing 90 walks. Koskie can play third base in the major leagues and might get a chance to do that later this year if Todd Walker continues to struggle.

5. **Shane Bowers, P.** The 6-5 righthander, a 21st-round pick in 1993, was a combined 13-4 with New Britain and Salt Lake before (and after) a five-game promotion to Minnesota. He doesn't win with velocity, but rather with good movement on all of his pitches. The Twins have plenty of mound prospects, so Bowers will have to continue his winning ways back at Triple A this spring.

6. **Jason Bell, P.** The righthander was 11-9 with a 3.39 ERA at Double A last year. He fanned 142 men in 164.2 innings despite having only an average fastball. His ability to pitch, rather than just throw, is one of the reasons the Twins like him. A curveball pitcher with good control, Bell was a second-round draft pick in 1995 and should continue to move quickly toward the major leagues in 1998.

7. **Fred Rath, P.** A non-drafted free agent signed in 1995, the righthander hasn't started a game in his pro career. Last season at New Britain he saved 12 games with a 2.68 ERA before a 10-game stint for Salt Lake City, where he allowed just two runs in 11 innings and saved three more. His best pitch is a hard sinking fastball that produces ground balls consistently. Despite the lack of a strong second pitch, Rath could end up in the Twins' bullpen later this season.

8. **Marc Lewis, OF.** Brought over from the Braves as the player to be named later in last summer's deal that sent Greg Colbrunn to Atlanta, the righthanded Lewis hit .273 with 17 homers and 21 steals at Double A Greenville at age 22. However, Lewis also walked just 25 times, continuing a career-long trend of overaggressive swinging that is likely to hurt him as he progresses upward.

9. **Chris Latham, OF.** A speedy outfielder acquired in trade from the Dodgers organization, the almost-25-year-old switch hitter got into 15 games for the Twins last year after a .309, 8-homer season at Salt Lake. Latham continues to have a problem understanding the strike zone, and unless he tightens his swing he will strike out too often to play in the majors. Latham has stolen 215 bases in his seven-year minor league career.

Many of them were primarily American League players. Eight of them played in the junior circuit, and six of them never played a game in the NL. Most of these eight availed themselves freely of the DH:

Rod Carew, a second baseman and later a first baseman, played 68 career games as a DH.

Robin Yount, a shortstop and later a center fielder, played 138 games as a DH.

Al Kaline, a right fielder, played 146 games as a DH.

Carl Yastrzemski, a left fielder and later first a baseman, played 411 games as a DH.

Dave Winfield, a right fielder, played 419 games as a DH.

George Brett, a third baseman and later a first baseman, played 506 games as a DH.

Eddie Murray, a first baseman, played 573 games as a DH.

Paul Molitor, a second, third, and first baseman, has played 1,059 games as a DH so far. That's 300 more games than he has played at any defensive position; a full 40 percent of his career has been spent as a designated hitter.

Without detracting from the accomplishments of these players, it's reasonable to assume that some of these players wouldn't have been able to stick around long enough to collect 3,000 hits without the DH rule. This would certainly seem to be the case for the injury-prone Molitor, whose career has probably been lengthened considerably by being able to avoid playing the field.

While Yount, Kaline, and Carew, all of whom were good enough late in their careers to play defensive positions for contending teams, got to 3,000 without much help from the DH rule, most of the others can't say the same.

Plenty of veterans have been working their way onto the all-time lists for base hits, homers, and runs batted in with what amounts to a half-free pass. Harold Baines now has 2,561 hits; he could get 3,000 with three more full seasons. Is he a Hall of Famer? Should getting 3,000 hits make him one?

What about Chili Davis, a full-time DH since 1991? He has 2,222 hits right now, and although he's 38, Davis is still productive. In fact, he's had a pretty impressive career, with 328 homers, 1,285 RBI, and more than 1,100 walks in 17 seasons. With three more 130-hit seasons, he'll be over 2,500. That's Hall of Fame territory. Here's a sobering thought: late in 1998, Chili is likely to enter the top 100 in all-time hits.

Is Harold Baines or Chili Davis your idea of an immortal? If not, what does that say about Paul Molitor?

95

1997 TEAM STATISTICS

BATTING/BASERUNNING

	Raw	Rank	+/- %		Raw	Rank	+/- %		Raw	Rank	+/- %
R	772	10	-3	BA	.270	8	0	SB	151	2	+42
R/G	4.77	10	-3	HR	132	14	-25	CS	52	7	+1
OBA	.333	11	-2	LH	345	3	+7	SB%	74.4	1	+11
SA	.409	11	-4	BB	495	12	-13				
PRO	.741	11	-3	SO	1,121	11	+7				

PITCHING/FIELDING

	Raw	Rank	+/- %		Raw	Rank	+/- %		Raw	Rank	+/- %
OR	861	13	+8	BA	.283	12	+4	OSB	85	4	-23
RA/G	5.31	13	+8	HR	187	11	+6	OCS	46	2	-13
OOB	.342	8	0	LH	371	13	+15	OSB%	64.9	6	-2
OSA	.454	13	+6	BB	495	1	12	FA	.983	5	0
PRO	.796	13	+3	SO	908	14	12	GDP	143	11	+10

96

BATTING BY LINEUP SLOTS

	R	HR	RBI	BA	OBA	SA
1	124	10	62	.291	.383	.409
2	90	14	89	.258	.337	.394
3	83	11	101	.302	.348	.437
4	94	19	92	.251	.291	.416
5	80	14	81	.262	.331	.383
6	75	20	81	.261	.312	.414
7	83	22	92	.273	.340	.445
8	69	11	57	.259	.314	.387
9	74	11	75	.273	.330	.390

BATTING BY DEFENSIVE POSITION

	R	HR	RBI	BA	OBA	SA
C	88	19	91	.260	.311	.419
1B	79	17	70	.261	.320	.407
2B	119	9	61	.293	.386	.410
3B	72	13	89	.287	.321	.412
SS	74	11	75	.278	.323	.410
LF	78	18	77	.250	.318	.415
CF	79	15	71	.249	.329	.378
RF	94	17	75	.273	.356	.434
DH	69	11	104	.290	.333	.418
PH	15	2	17	.250	.316	.350
P	0	0	1	.111	.111	.111

TEAM PITCHING

	W-L	CG	QS	QS%	<6	>6	IPS	IP	ERA	OPR
ROTATION	50-76	10	61	38	51	50	5.6	906.0	5.42	.832

	W-L	GR	SV	BSV	HD	BHD	IRS%	IP	ERA	OPR
BULLPEN	18-18	390	30	19	116	73	36	528.0	4.33	.731

1998 PROJECTIONS

BATTING

PLAYER	BA	G	AB	R	H	2B	3B	HR	RBI	BB	SO	SB	CS	SA	OBA
Coomer, Ron	.296	131	442	56	131	25	2	14	73	22	71	4	2	.453	.329
Cordova, Marty	.272	112	424	61	115	25	3	16	67	38	89	8	3	.461	.332
Gates, Brent	.266	48	147	18	39	9	1	2	19	14	23	1	1	.375	.328
Hocking, Denny	.258	70	158	20	41	8	2	1	16	11	33	2	3	.360	.308
Hunter, Torii	.268	12	43	6	12	2	0	1	6	5	10	1	0	.390	.343
Knoblauch, Chuck	.300	151	587	117	176	29	11	10	61	84	80	53	12	.434	.388
Latham, Chris	.283	42	162	25	46	7	1	2	18	18	45	5	0	.385	.354
Lawton, Matt	.251	138	447	70	112	25	3	13	62	68	73	7	5	.404	.349
Meares, Pat	.277	144	478	68	133	25	4	10	65	19	90	9	7	.410	.305
Molitor, Paul	.307	132	533	67	164	32	5	10	84	46	64	12	4	.439	.362
Nixon, Otis	.300	132	532	88	160	18	3	1	42	68	75	56	13	.350	.379
Ochoa, Alex	.280	83	205	29	57	14	2	3	22	15	27	2	3	.400	.330
Ortiz, David	.270	91	340	47	92	22	1	16	62	21	126	1	0	.483	.313
Stahoviak, Scott	.255	84	253	35	65	17	1	8	32	28	68	4	2	.428	.330
Steinbach, Terry	.263	122	438	60	115	26	1	18	66	36	99	3	1	.449	.318
Valentin, Javier	.263	20	74	9	19	4	0	2	10	6	15	1	0	.386	.319
Walker, Todd	.268	92	323	49	87	16	1	8	41	34	64	5	0	.402	.338

PITCHING

PITCHER	W	L	SV	ERA	G	GS	IP	H	HR	BB	SO
Aguilera, Rick	5	4	25	4.47	42	4	68	69	11	20	62
Bowers, Shane	3	3	0	4.38	11	10	57	61	8	18	36
Guardado, Eddie	2	6	3	4.68	74	1	63	60	10	27	65
Hawkins, Latroy	4	5	0	4.90	16	15	81	98	10	27	42
Miller, Travis	4	4	0	4.73	15	12	78	84	7	34	42
Morgan, Mike	7	11	0	4.63	28	27	150	157	14	47	90
Naulty, Dan	2	2	2	4.81	47	0	52	44	10	24	45
Radke, Brad	15	11	0	4.31	32	31	211	214	30	47	140
Ritchie, Todd	2	2	0	4.44	33	0	59	69	9	22	34
Rodriguez, Frank	5	7	1	4.85	30	15	119	124	12	49	59
Serafini, Dan	5	5	0	4.46	17	14	89	93	9	33	55
Tewksbury, Bob	7	10	0	4.37	26	25	156	183	11	30	86
Trombley, Mike	3	3	3	4.39	46	3	70	67	6	27	60

97

ANAHEIM ANGELS

MANAGEMENT

Manager	General Manager	Owner
Terry Collins Career Record 308-275 .528	Bill Bavasi	Gene Autry/Disney

1997 RECORD

Won-Lost	Pct.	Division Finish/GB		Wild Card Finish/GB	
84-78	.519	2 W	-6	2	-12

Preseason Consensus Projection	3 (3.13)				

1st Half	2nd Half	Home	Road	Intradivision	Interleague
41-39	43-39	46-36	38-42	25-11	4-12

Comebacks	Blowouts	Nailbiters			
17-14	19-16	41-40			

THE OLD GET OLDER

Once again in 1997 the Anaheim (formerly California, née Los Angeles) Angels couldn't do it for the Ol' Cowboy, even though they tried as hard as they could to bring in as many of Gene Autry's contemporaries as possible.

Anaheim began last season with several of baseball's oldest players on their roster, and added more as the season progressed. However, the Angels didn't have enough gas in the tank for a run at Seattle late in the year. They settled for second place, a bit of a disappointment but certainly an improvement over their last-place finish of '96.

Anaheim's 14-game improvement last year (from 70-92 to 84-78) came as a result of improvement on both offense and defense. The '96 Angels finished next-to-last in the AL in both runs scored and ERA. Last season they improved to fifth in ERA and fourth in runs.

At the start of the season the new-look Angels planned on changes at several positions: Darin Erstad at first, Dave Hollins at third, Jim Leyritz behind the plate, Eddie Murray at DH, and Allen Watson, Jason Dickson, Mark Gubicza, and possibly Steve Ontiveros or Todd Van Poppel in the starting rotation. Kevin Bass and Bernardo Brito were in camp as well, showing that the Angels had swept the streets looking for former big leaguers.

The list of changes grew larger in spring training when second baseman Randy Velarde suffered an elbow injury that would sideline him all season except for one pinch-running appearance. Luis Alicea took over at second base.

The sum of Anaheim's preseason moves was potential disaster. Erstad, a speedy young outfielder, at first? Hollins, a defensive nightmare, at third? Alicea playing second every day? Gubicza? Van Poppel? Bass? Murray? Ontivereros?

Most of those things did go predictably wrong, but the

Angels played well anyway. Gubicza, brought over in a head-scratcher of a trade from Kansas City (the Angels gave up dependable DH Chili Davis), made two awful starts before being sidelined for the year due to shoulder troubles that required surgery. Hollins made 29 errors and showed very poor range. Alicea was maddeningly inconsistent in the field and lost his job late in the year. Ontiveros never pitched for the Angels, spending the whole year on the DL for the umpteenth time.

Murray hit so badly (.219) that the Angels decided to make DH a revolving door. The 41-year-old veteran was disabled for much of the season with a slight but convenient injury, which got him off the active roster. He was finally waived late in the year and signed with the Dodgers.

Erstad had a promising year at the plate, spending much of the season in the leadoff spot and showing multidimensional offensive skills. His speed was indeed wasted at first, though, while Garret Anderson, Jim Edmonds, and Tim Salmon patrolled the outfield.

Anderson had yet another mediocre season disguised by a good batting average. He hit .303 and drove in 92 runs (who wouldn't knock in a lot of runs batting behind Salmon, Edmonds, and Hollins?) and threw out 14 baserunners. Unfortunately, he showed little power, didn't walk, didn't run much, and played a mediocre left field. To top it all off, his attitude is said to be somewhere between "okay" and "sullen."

The Angels have been trying to trade Anderson, but they obviously want too much in return and haven't been able to consummate a deal. Now, they are discussing trading Jim Edmonds to make room for Darin Erstad in the outfield! Moving Erstad to the outfield is a no-brainer, as is letting Anderson hit an empty .300 for someone else.

Edmonds and Salmon had terrific years, providing power and average against both righthanded and lefthanded pitching. Salmon nailed 15 baserunners, although he made 11 errors, and Edmonds once again demonstrated fantastic range and made more than a season's worth of great catches.

Despite Hollins' defensive problems, he really helped Anaheim. Not only did he show some power and stay in the lineup on a regular basis, he also took 62 walks and led the team by scoring 101 runs. He's likely to play first base

TEAM MVP

Despite his wife's having being diagnosed with cancer, right fielder **Tim Salmon** had another MVP-caliber season in 1997. While other Angels had surprisingly good years at the plate and in the field (Dave Hollins, Jim Edmonds), Salmon's top-rank performance (.296, 33 homers, 125 RBIs, 95 walks) came as no surprise at all. Perhaps that is the biggest indication that Tim Salmon is the Angels.

BIGGEST SURPRISE

Third baseman **Dave Hollins** was able to stay healthy for almost an entire season and, despite some defensive problems, had a big year. Batting .288, stealing 16 bases, and taking 62 walks, he scored more than 100 runs for the third time in his career. The intense Hollins also hit 16 homers and drove in 85 runs. Some said that his biggest contribution to the Angels was giving a kick in the ass to a team that sorely needed one.

BIGGEST DISAPPOINTMENT

Injuries took a piece out of two critical players' seasons. Utilityman **Randy Velarde** hurt his elbow in spring training and appeared in only one game (as a pinch runner). Closer **Troy Percival**'s bad back took away some of his effectiveness. Lefthanded starter **Mark Langston** had served three stints on the disabled list in 1996 with knee problems, and last season made only nine starts (2-4, 5.85) due to elbow injuries.

99

THE MOMENT OF
TRUTH

Anaheim had been red-hot since early July, winning 26 games in a 37-game stretch and moving from 5.5 games down to a half-game up on Seattle on August 15. But the next night the Angels' season began to unravel. They lost to Baltimore, 10-9, blowing an 8-3 lead by surrendering seven runs in a nightmarish bottom of the sixth. That evening the Mariners blew out the White Sox and took over first place for good. Within a week, both **Todd Greene** and **Chuck Finley** were lost for the year with injuries as the Angels lost six of seven.

BEST DEAL

Despite snorts of derision from some (us included), the Angels' decisions to sign **Hollins** and **Luis Alicea** turned out to be good moves, especially when Velarde came up lame and help was needed in the infield. Hollins hit well, while Alicea (despite not being best-suited to everyday duty) was a decent fill-in at second. Neither player was particularly expensive.

WORST DEAL

Getting **Tony Phillips** from the White Sox seemed like a good idea. The Angels needed a leadoff hitter, and Phillips has been one of the best for several years. However, he didn't produce up to his usual standard, was bad at every position he played, and—to make things far worse—was arrested in July on cocaine charges. The legal controversy forced the disastrous **Rickey Henderson** deal, and although Phillips came back to hit well down the stretch, there was no way the Angels would even think of taking a chance on him for 1998. He remains unsigned at press time.

in 1998, a much better spot for him. Meanwhile, shortstop Gary DiSarcina (.246) had another miserable offensive season and made only the routine plays.

The Angels ended up bringing over Tony Phillips in a trade from the White Sox, and the 38-year-old firebrand performed slightly below his usual level. He played some second base (not well) and some left field, but his legal and personal problems caused the team plenty of friction and forced the Angels to acquire another 38-year-old, Rickey Henderson, who hit only .183 in 32 games.

In May when the Angels dealt disappointing catcher Jorge Fabregas and reliever Chuck McElroy to the White Sox to get Phillips, they split the catching between Todd Greene, Leyritz, and Chad Kreuter (also acquired in the deal). When Greene began to display some power, the Angels shipped Leyritz, a productive offensive player, to Texas for starter Ken Hill.

When Greene suffered a broken right hand that eventually required surgery, it forced the Angels to go with the 33-year-old Kreuter as their everyday catcher down the stretch. Kreuter hit .234 in 218 at bats. Things were bad enough that Anaheim had to call on Triple A catchers Angelo Encarnacion and Chris Turner.

Meanwhile, the pitching was both better and worse than expected. Better because Watson had somewhat of a comeback year, going 12-12, and the rookie Dickson impressed, going 13-9. Knuckleballer Dennis Springer didn't fool many people, and stalwart southpaws Chuck Finley and Mark Langston suffered injuries that took big chunks out of their seasons. Langston signed a minor league deal with San Diego after the season. Springer was taken by Tampa Bay in the November expansion draft.

TROY PERCIVAL: A WANTED MAN

Closer Troy Percival's back problems posed a huge problem for the bullpen, forcing Mike James into a short relief role, which he couldn't handle, and putting pressure on everyone else.

To illustrate this point, note that lefthanders Mike Holtz and Chuck McElroy and righties Pep Harris, Rich DeLucia, and Shigetoshi Hasegawa blew, between them, 22 of 28 save chances. Anaheim led the American League

100

with 32 blown saves—more than even Seattle.

The Angels need a healthy Percival, and they need him badly. He was reasonably effective in 1997, fanning well over a hitter per inning, but was far from the dominating closer that the club has to have. His supporting cast was stretched past its capability.

SLIM PICKINGS

What's in the Angels' future? Although they allowed many of their older recent acquisitions to depart, they don't have much in the upper levels of the farm system to help out. One good pitching prospect, Matt Perisho, was dealt to Texas for third baseman Mike Bell.

The Angels were reportedly still trying to deal an outfielder (Jim Edmonds or Garret Anderson) for starting pitching or a third baseman. Of course, they had a third base prospect in George Arias, but never wanted to give him a shot. (He went to San Diego in the Henderson trade.) Perhaps that unwillingness to give youngsters a chance is why the club is consistently rifling through the Chad Kreuters and Kevin Grosses of baseball's bargain basement.

The acquisition of Matt Walbeck at least gives the club a decent backup catcher who can step in should Todd Greene fail. Meanwhile, 34-year-old DH Cecil Fielder signed a one-year deal and will try to recapture his lost form (insert joke here).

For every one of those veteran acquisitions that works out well for Anaheim, five more flop. In short, that's the recent history of the Angels.

TOP PROSPECTS
SPRING 1998

1. **Mike Bovee, P.** After being traded from Kansas City last year in the Chili Davis deal, Bovee had a fine 1997 season at Double A and Triple A. Beginning the year at Double A Midland, Bovee was 8-2 with a 4.24 ERA in 20 games, 13 of them starts. Promoted to Triple A Vancouver, Bovee went 4-3 with a 3.44 ERA in 12 starts. On September 6 he was then promoted to the majors, where he pitched three times. The 24-year-old righthander has only average velocity but a decent breaking ball and good command.

2. **Jarrod Washburn, P.** Washburn is that big league rarity: a left-handed power pitcher. He was 15-12 with a 4.80 ERA last year at Midland, a good place to hit, before making one good start at Vancouver. A second-round pick in 1995, Washburn has four pitches including a low-90s fastball. He fanned 152 batters in 194 innings last year and could end up in Anaheim this summer.

3. **Scott Schoeneweis, P.** Schoeneweis had just his second pro season in 1997. A third-round 1996 draftee out of Duke University, the 24-year-old southpaw spent the year in the starting rotation for Midland, where he was 7-5 with a 5.94 ERA, fanning 94 and walking 39 in 113 innings. Injuries and serious illness have stalked him so far, but Schoeneweis is a polished prospect with three solid pitches. He could be in the majors as soon as this summer.

4. **Geoff Edsell, P.** Edsell, a 200-pound righthander, has been in the Angels organization for five years. His 1997 season was spent at Vancouver, where he finished second in the league with 14 wins and led in innings, complete games—and walks. He has only a decent repertoire and can't afford poor control. Edsell is viewed as a possible fourth or fifth starter in the majors.

5. **Jason Herrick, OF.** The best position player that the Angels have in the high minors, Herrick hit .252 with 27 doubles and 20 homers last season at Midland. Admittedly, that's a good park and league in which to hit, but Herrick has succeeded at every stop so far. All the ancillary points are against him right now, though: Herrick turns 25 in July, is injury prone, doesn't play great defense, and has poor strike-zone judgement. He'll have to keep hitting.

101

1997 TEAM STATISTICS

BATTING/BASERUNNING

	Raw	Rank	+/-%		Raw	Rank	+/-%		Raw	Rank	+/-%
R	829	5	+4	BA	.272	7	+1	SB	126	5	+18
R/G	5.12	5	+4	HR	161	8	-9	CS	72	1	+39
OBA	.346	5	+2	LH	304	9	-5	SB%	63.6	12	-5
SA	.416	9	-3	BB	617	4	+8				
PRO	.762	7	-1	SO	953	3	-9				

PITCHING/FIELDING

	Raw	Rank	+/-%		Raw	Rank	+/-%		Raw	Rank	+/-%
OR	794	6	-1	BA	.269	7	-1	OSB	101	6	-8
RA/G	4.90	6	-1	HR	202	14	+15	OCS	63	12	+19
OOB	.343	10	+1	LH	313	8	-3	OSB%	61.6	4	-7
OSA	.437	11	+2	BB	605	12	+8	FA	.980	11	0
PRO	.780	10	+1	SO	1,050	5	+2	GDP	117	2	10

BATTING BY LINEUP SLOTS

	R	HR	RBI	BA	OBA	SA
1	107	11	73	.243	.346	.349
2	122	15	74	.281	.371	.432
3	113	23	106	.293	.363	.463
4	114	34	112	.279	.378	.500
5	90	23	121	.299	.366	.465
6	86	20	98	.291	.338	.441
7	74	21	81	.261	.329	.400
8	65	10	56	.244	.319	.358
9	58	4	54	.254	.288	.332

BATTING BY DEFENSIVE POSITION

	R	HR	RBI	BA	OBA	SA
C	82	23	85	.268	.334	.425
1B	122	23	96	.295	.354	.467
2B	83	7	58	.266	.374	.390
3B	103	19	100	.280	.359	.432
SS	54	4	48	.248	.281	.324
LF	92	12	90	.294	.351	.408
CF	99	25	95	.275	.353	.453
RF	99	33	131	.291	.389	.502
DH	78	15	62	.237	.319	.359
PH	9	0	8	.211	.296	.282
P	1	0	2	.056	.056	.111

TEAM PITCHING

	W-L	CG	QS	QS%	<6	>6	IPS	IP	ERA	OPR
ROTATION	53-51	9	76	47	31	52	6.0	965.1	5.01	.808

	W-L	GR	SV	BSV	HD	BHD	IRS%	IP	ERA	OPR
BULLPEN	31-27	400	39	27	145	67	31	489.1	3.55	.722

ANAHEIM ANGELS
1998 PROJECTIONS

BATTING

PLAYER	BA	G	AB	R	H	2B	3B	HR	RBI	BB	SO	SB	CS	SA	OBA
Anderson, Garret	.303	143	569	73	172	32	2	10	83	27	73	8	5	.419	.334
DiSarcina, Gary	.272	144	518	60	141	30	3	4	50	20	32	6	6	.368	.299
Edmonds, Jim	.284	139	530	89	150	29	2	29	84	57	97	4	5	.511	.353
Eenhoorn, Robert	.264	19	70	10	18	4	1	2	8	3	11	0	0	.413	.297
Encarnacion, Angelo	.268	22	68	7	18	4	0	1	7	4	10	1	0	.353	.305
Erstad, Darin	.292	149	572	102	167	32	4	16	76	53	88	22	9	.448	.352
Fielder, Cecil	.255	106	392	50	100	15	0	21	71	57	93	0	0	.451	.350
Greene, Todd	.242	104	410	58	99	21	0	26	77	21	71	5	0	.485	.279
Hollins, Dave	.274	149	547	96	150	28	1	16	80	73	118	12	5	.417	.359
Nevin, Phil	.246	68	192	24	47	11	1	8	27	19	54	1	1	.432	.315
Palmeiro, Orlando	.248	55	97	13	24	3	1	0	7	12	10	1	1	.308	.329
Salmon, Tim	.285	156	582	93	166	28	2	32	114	91	129	7	8	.503	.381
Scarsone, Steve	.209	24	69	10	14	2	0	2	8	11	27	1	0	.349	.316
Walbeck, Matt	.275	76	243	31	67	10	0	3	25	17	41	4	3	.349	.321

PITCHING

PITCHER	W	L	SV	ERA	G	GS	IP	H	HR	BB	SO
Bovee, Mike	3	3	0	3.97	9	6	48	53	4	12	28
Chavez, Anthony	2	2	1	3.58	24	1	30	30	2	10	20
DeLucia, Rich	5	5	2	4.29	48	0	59	50	7	32	56
Dickson, Jason	11	9	0	4.36	31	30	192	224	30	55	106
Finley, Chuck	12	9	0	4.31	25	25	165	159	19	68	154
Harris, Pep	4	3	0	3.92	46	1	67	69	6	33	45
Hasegawa, Shigetoshi	2	5	0	4.07	37	5	86	88	11	34	61
Hill, Ken	9	9	0	4.33	26	25	162	168	15	73	97
Holtz, Mike	5	7	2	3.36	94	0	67	59	8	30	65
James, Mike	5	5	7	3.96	62	0	70	69	5	34	59
May, Darrell	2	2	0	4.15	12	4	37	33	4	15	24
Olivares, Omar	6	8	0	5.10	26	24	139	151	15	65	78
Percival, Troy	4	5	30	3.04	65	0	68	46	7	29	93
Watson, Allen	9	10	0	4.79	30	29	173	185	30	64	117
Williams, Shad	1	1	0	4.29	9	2	21	22	3	10	9

OAKLAND ATHLETICS

MANAGEMENT

Manager	General Manager	Owner
Art Howe Career Record 535-599 .472	Billy Beane	Steve Schott/Ken Hofman

1997 RECORD

Won-Lost	Pct.		Division Finish/GB		Wild Card Finish/GB	
65-97	.401		4 W	-25	11	-31

Preseason Consensus Projection		4 (3.52)			

1st Half	2nd Half	Home	Road	Intradivision	Interleague
34-49	31-48	35-46	30-51	11-25	7-9

Comebacks	Blowouts	Nailbiters
14-9	14-31	34-40

104

LOW EBB IN THE EAST BAY

When the bad news spills off the page and the good news is basically that a 28-year-old DH hit 27 home runs, you know it's been a dark year. That's the way it was in Oakland in 1997. It was a season in which an old hero, Jose Canseco, came back (though not successfully) and two current heroes, Mark McGwire and Geronimo Berroa, were traded because the club couldn't afford them anymore.

The exploits of Matt Stairs aside, the Athletics finished at 65-97, the worst record in Major League Baseball. However, with some more retooling, continued development, and a little luck, last season should be the low ebb and the team's fortunes should improve.

On the field, the Athletics were a lot of sound and fury, signifying nothing, with their bats last season pounding out 197 homers to finish third in the AL. However, they finished 11th in the loop in runs, due to three factors: a .260 batting average (12th), 1,181 strikeouts (the most in the league and a franchise record), and 1,221 runners left on base (the second-highest total in the AL).

Oakland had a bunch of guys who swung from the heels and sometimes delivered, but they also had no speed on the bases and poor situational hitting. Finishing second in the league in walks should have resulted in more crooked numbers on the scoreboard; instead, it resulted in more LOBs.

The infielders really stunk out the joint; Tony Batista hit .202; Scott Brosius hit .203. Both are now gone. Mark Bellhorn batted .228, and Scott Spiezio, considered one of the best young players on the team, hit .243 with 14 homers in 147 games. Veterans Rafael Bournigal and Dave Magadan had to step in, and were at least adequate.

The outfield, meanwhile, was a revolving door. Seven players started 40 or more games in the outfield, but none started as many as 80. The defensive ability of most of them (Berroa, Canseco, Stairs, Jason Giambi) was best left unspoken, while none of the center fielders (Damon Mashore, Ernie Young, Jason McDonald) could win manager Art Howe's favor.

To make things worse, the A's pitchers were terrible. Oakland's 5.48 team ERA was the worst in baseball (almost a quarter-run higher than Colorado's!) and the highest of any Athletics team in nearly 50 years. The A's allowed 10 or more runs in a game 19 times in '97; their leading winner was middle reliever Aaron Small, who finished the season at 9-5. Oakland didn't have a 10-game winner in 1996, either.

Oakland was just the fifth team ever to have fewer than 30 wins total from its starting pitchers. The other clubs? The 1962 Mets, the 1919 Athletics, the 1996 Tigers, and the 1928 Phillies. That's lousy company. Athletics pitchers led the AL in most negative categories, and had only one shutout, which tied the league record. Art Howe went to his bullpen 480 times last year, which broke the American League mark by a huge margin of 54!

Oakland's 1997 pitching staff just didn't belong in the major leagues, except for Small, Buddy Groom, Billy Taylor, Ariel Prieto, Jimmy Haynes, and Steve Karsay (traded to Cleveland in December for Mike Fetters). It was so bad that Oakland almost didn't have a starting rotation last season. Karsay led the team with just 24 starts, with nine pitchers in double figures in that category. Most of the starters weren't really viable; Mike Mohler was given 10 starts because the A's had nobody else from the left side. Willie Adams was unbelievably rotten, and Dave Telgheder and Mike Oquist pitched about as well as they were capable of (which means badly). Karsay was run on like crazy (17 of 18 runners stole successfully on him), and Prieto had some very good periods but walked more than five per game. Brad Rigby was 1-7, while Mohler ended up 1-10.

RISING TIDE

The Athletics made several important moves in the last half of the '97 season and in the off-season to improve their chances for 1998. These should result in a greatly improved pitching staff and a lot more production from the outfield.

TEAM MVP

Two potential MVPs for this team were traded in midseason: Mark McGwire and Geronimo Berroa. Of the players left, the best day-in, day-out hitter was **Jason Giambi**, who batted .293 with 41 doubles and 20 homers. **Matt Stairs** was excellent (.298, 27 homers in 352 at bats) in a platoon role.

BIGGEST SURPRISE

There were few happy surprises for the 65-97 Athletics. **Stairs**' fine season came for a team that had few other options, but at least the beefy veteran got to show that he can indeed play. Stairs now has 38 home runs in 615 major league at bats.

BIGGEST DISAPPOINTMENT

The non-development of young pitchers such as Mike Mohler, Willie Adams, and Don Wengert caused problems for the Athletics, but perhaps the biggest disappointment to the Athletics in 1997 was the poor play of infielders **Tony Batista** and **Scott Brosius**, both of whom were barely above .200. Batista was lost in the expansion draft, and Brosius was dumped to the Yankees after the season.

105

Trading Geronimo Berroa to Baltimore for 25-year-old Jimmy Haynes was a very good deal. Berroa is productive, but when an excellent mound prospect like Haynes is available for an aging outfielder-DH without defensive value, dealing for him is a no-brainer. After coming to the A's in August, Haynes fashioned a 4.42 ERA in 13 starts. That's more than a whole run below Oakland's team ERA. Haynes was, in 1996, the Orioles' top pitching prospect. He struggled, lost manager Davey Johnson's confidence, and never got another shot in Crabtown. Haynes has the potential to be an ace.

Promoting top prospects Ben Grieve and Miguel Tejada was also a big step in the rebuilding process. Grieve, son of former Rangers GM Tom Grieve, blasted through Double A and rushed through Triple A before a dazzling 24-game late-season trial with the Athletics (see Top Prospects). Grieve has a good chance to be the savior of this franchise, and many feel he is a future MVP.

Tejada, a five-tool shortstop who turns 22 in May, could take the over the starting job for good in spring training even though he was overmatched in his debut season, fanning 22 times and walking just twice in 26 games in Oakland. Even if he can't do the job right away, it won't be long until he can.

By acquiring several hard-throwing relief pitchers the Athletics have almost completely revamped their bullpen. T.J. Mathews, Doug Bochtler, and Mike Fetters will be big improvements over their '97 counterparts. While the A's had to give up Mark McGwire, Don Wengert, and Steve Karsay to do so, those were reasonable deals, considering that McGwire had to be dealt for financial reasons and the other two pitchers didn't help in 1997.

Mathews and incumbent closer Billy Taylor should form a very strong late-inning duo from the right side: Mathews has closer stuff, and Taylor is effective if not brilliant. Aaron Small and Buddy Groom (despite his 5.15 ERA) have good arms and should also help.

What the Oakland brain trust has to do is make a plan and stick with it; let the kids pitch without panicking and dragging in no-hopers like Carlos Reyes, Dave Telgheder, and Richie Lewis. At least there was some point to letting Karsay or Prieto get his head bashed in last year; the same can't be said for using Steve Wojciechowski.

However, there were two pitchers who might have helped but never got the chance. Steve Montgomery, who came over from St. Louis in the Dennis Eckersley trade, was effective in 1996 for the Athletics' Triple A club in Edmonton, though hit hard there in 1997. Yet he got just 20 innings with Oakland before being waived to Cleveland in August. Meanwhile, hard-throwing righty John Johnstone passed through the organization's hands briefly in midseason, but the Athletics decided that they didn't want to take the time to try to iron out his control problems (he finished the season with the Giants, and has signed with them for '98).

A better team might have jettisoned these pitchers without much thought, but why would the Athletics dump guys who have good arms while bringing up Gary Haught, Dane Johnson, and Richie Lewis for a look? Did the Athletics (who used 49 players) just become shellshocked?

While hope doesn't by itself make a good team, it's preferable to being a bad team with no hope. If Tejada is ready to take over at shortstop, if Grieve does what he's capable of doing, and if Mathews, Haynes, and a couple of the other young pitchers can come through, the Athletics should be far more competitive in 1998 and could establish the foundation for a good club after that.

RICKEY, CANDY & THE GAMBLER

For a rebuilding team, the Athletics picked up quite a few veterans in the off-season. The major additions were Rickey Henderson, Tom Candiotti, and Kenny Rogers, but Oakland also re-signed Dave Magadan, inked Shane Mack and Mike Blowers, and traded for Kurt Abbott.

Mack is penciled in to play center field. Magadan, Blowers, and Mark Bellhorn will fight for playing time at third base, while utility infielder-outfielder Abbott can play shortstop if Miguel Tejada isn't ready or Rafael Bournigal is judged overripe.

Henderson signed a one-year deal in January. This will be the 39-year-old's fourth tour of duty with Oakland. He will play regularly in left field, allowing Matt Stairs to DH and Jason Giambi to remain at first base. With Mack set in center and Grieve in right, the A's will have a far better defensive outfield than in '97, which will make their pitching that much better.

Henderson's arrival also means that Ernie Young will be traded if Oakland can find any takers and that gifted 26-year-old Jason McDonald is now likely to end up back in Triple A or sitting on the bench. He is potentially a fine offensive and defensive center fielder.

The Athletics' starting pitching in 1997 should also be substantially better this season, due to some promising youngsters, and two experienced innings-eaters: knuckle-baller Tom Candiotti and lefthander Kenny Rogers. Candiotti, 40, was 10-7 with a 3.60 ERA for Los Angeles last year. He is still a durable and reliable arm who can take the pressure off some of the youngsters as well as teach them a lot about survival in the big leagues. Rogers' acquisition is intriguing. He was terrible with the Yanks but still appears to have decent stuff. Since New York essentially agreed to pay half his salary to unload him, he is a low-risk pickup. Last season righthanded batters had a tough time connecting for home runs in Oakland, which should be good news for Rogers.

NOW AND THEN

Ben Grieve's 27-game trial with Oakland at the end of 1997 was impressive, to say the least. The 21-year-old outfielder hit .312 with three homers and 24 RBIs in 108 at bats.

In 1985 Jose Canseco was a 21-year-old outfielder who came up for a 29-game trial with Oakland, hitting .302 with five homers and 13 RBIs in 96 at bats.

The regard with which the current Oakland management holds Grieve appears to be even greater than the hosannas inspired by Canseco back in the mid-'80s. This is somewhat odd; Canseco had both more speed and raw power than Grieve does now, even though he struck out far more often and did not hit for as high an average as Grieve has. Arm strength is a draw, while Grieve is the better defensive outfielder.

Although Canseco's career is rated as a terrible disappointment in most quarters, he was an excellent hitter for several seasons. In his years in Oakland, Canseco hit 114 homers at home, but 140 on the road. Now that his career has dissolved into an ugly mass of injuries, personal problems, and bad contracts, Canseco is almost a joke in baseball.

Will Grieve be considered a disappointment if, at age 33, he has led the AL twice in home runs and has 351 career

THE MOMENT OF
TRUTH

Oakland actually got off to a 7-4 start, but that early optimism quickly faded under a barrage of fireworks from opposing bats. Perhaps the most representative game the Athletics played in 1997 came on **May 28**, when they scored 10 runs against the Angels. But the thin Athletics bullpen allowed four runs in the seventh and five more in the ninth, leading to a 14-10 Anaheim victory.

BEST DEAL

Anytime a last-place team can trade a left fielder/DH and receive a good pitching prospect in return, it's a good deal. The Athletics parted with popular and productive **Geronimo Berroa** on June 27, sending him to the Orioles for righthanded hurler **Jimmy Haynes**, who had lost the confidence of the Baltimore organization. Pitchers such as Haynes are exactly the type of players the Athletics must build around. In his 13 starts after the trade, he posted the lowest ERA (4.42) of any Oakland starter.

107

WORST DEAL

The Athletics acquired **Jose Canseco** last winter for pitcher **John Wasdin**. Failed "Bash Brothers" marketing campaigns aside ("Be There When It Happens Again!"), the aging, moody, and fragile Canseco was a failure. He hit some home runs, struck out a lot, and batted .235, doing nothing to help the team win in the present or improve for the future.

round-trippers (like Canseco)? Even for the brightest prospects, nothing is certain. Good luck to Grieve, even if it looks at this point as if he doesn't need it.

BASH BROTHERS REUNION A BIG BUST

When the Athletics reacquired prodigal son Jose Canseco from the Red Sox last winter, it was the genesis of the club's 1997 "Return of the Bash Brothers" marketing push. That campaign lasted only a couple of months, until the club decided that Mark McGwire was going to have to be traded before he left as a free agent. For most of the late spring and summer, rumors swirled that McGwire would be dealt. He finally went to St. Louis after hitting 34 homers for the Athletics, on his way to 58 overall. So Oakland was left with Canseco, who had another boring, one-dimensional, unspectacular season. So much for the marketing campaign.

The Athletics really were in a tough spot with McGwire. He missed tremendous amounts of time in both 1993 and 1994 (playing in only 74 games combined in two years), plus more than a month in 1995. Turning 34 on October 1, 1997, McGwire looked like he had spent some of his best years on the disabled list. It would have been very difficult to commit to a contract of the required magnitude for a player with such a serious injury history.

All along, GM Sandy Alderson said that McGwire's trade wouldn't just be a salary dump, that talent would have to come back in exchange. If that's so,

TOP PROSPECTS
SPRING 1998

1. **Ben Grieve, OF.** Grieve, 22 in May, will begin the season as the Athletics' everyday right fielder. The 1994 first-round draft pick started 1997 at Double A, where he hit .328 with 24 homers, 108 RBIs, and 100 runs in just 100 games. In Triple A he batted .426 with seven homers in 27 contests. Finally, brought to Oakland, he batted .312 with 24 RBIs in 24 games. Grieve is going to be a star.

2. **Miguel Tejada, SS.** Some feel that Tejada, a sparkling defensive shortstop with speed and outstanding offensive potential, is ready to play in the majors right now. The soon-to-be-22-year-old righthanded hitter batted .275 with 22 homers last season for Double A Huntsville, but on promotion to the big leagues hit .202 in 99 at bats, fanning 22 times and walking twice. If he doesn't start the season with the Athletics, he'll probably come up soon.

3. **A.J. Hinch, C.** Drafted in the third round in 1996, the righthanded-hitting Hinch made a solid pro debut last year at Class A Modesto by hitting .309 with 20 homers in just 95 games. He also won raves for his defense. The Athletics promoted him to Triple A, where Hinch batted .376 in 39 games. A patient hitter with a strong arm, Hinch, who turns 24 in May, could be Oakland's everyday catcher this season. He starred at Stanford, spurning two other teams' draft picks in order to finish his degree.

4. **Jeff D'Amico, P.** Unrelated to the Brewers pitcher, this D'Amico—a righthander—spent three years in the A's system as a shortstop before converting to the mound in 1996. He's been on the rise since. D'Amico began 1997 by going 7-3 with a 3.80 ERA and 89 strikeouts in 97 innings at Modesto. Promoted to Triple A Edmonton, D'Amico struggled in 10 appearances, going 1-2 with an 8.22 ERA, in 30.2 innings. He is likely to take his fastball, slider, and change to Double A this spring.

5. **Tim Kubinski, P.** The unheralded lefthander, who sports the usual decent southpaw arsenal, pitched 47 times with a 4-4 record, 4.50 ERA (good for the PCL), and seven saves last year in Triple A. He also made 11 appearances for the Athletics. Kubinski has been very effective in four of his five pro seasons and has some chance to assume the lefty setup role this year for Oakland.

6. **Todd Weinberg, P.** A lefthanded reliever with a hard curve, average-plus fastball and a goofy attitude, Weinberg saved 20 games in 38 appearances at Class A Visalia before moving to Double A Birmingham. There he appeared 20 times with three saves and a 2.33 ERA. He hurt his elbow pitching in the Arizona Fall League, so his progress could be stalled.

why wait so long to deal? After his outstanding 1996 season, when he hit 52 homers, McGwire's market value shot up dramatically. It's reasonable to speculate that Oakland management could have gotten far more in trade for him before the '97 season than what it did during the season (T.J. Mathews, Eric Ludwick, and Blake Stein).

Of course, even having McGwire healthy and hitting homers at near-record rates in 1997 didn't help the Athletics win, and a major rebuilding was inevitable. Despite finishing second in the AL in walks and third in home runs, the A's ended up 11th in runs. They had too many old, slow power hitters (McGwire, Canseco, Matt Stairs, Scott Brosius, and Geronimo Berroa) and not much else. Jason McDonald, who played only 78 games, led the Athletics with just 13 stolen bases. Even their young regulars Jason Giambi and Scott Spiezio have old players' skills (can hit for power and will take walks, but don't have speed and aren't good defensively). How many of those guys do you want to have in one lineup?

Over the winter, former superstar Canseco was arrested and charged with physical abuse of his second wife. He pleaded no contest, and received a sentence of probation and counseling, so he will apparently be free to continue his career this spring if anyone wants him. Not so long ago many believed that the powerful outfielder was the most complete offensive player in the American League. He led the AL in homers in 1988 and 1991, stole bases often and effectively, hit for a decent average, and drew plenty of walks.

Now he's nothing but a wandering 33-year-old DH looking for another last chance. He hasn't been healthy since 1994 and has had only two good seasons since 1991. Some of Canseco's decline was predictable. He lost his speed , and his musclebound build may have caused some of his many injuries. Chronic back problems, which surfaced early in his career, were partly responsible for his up-and-down performance. However, Canseco's decline in 1992, when he was traded from Oakland to Texas (for fellow problem slugger Ruben Sierra), is more difficult to explain; he was 28 and should have been in his prime. Moving from Oakland, annually the best pitchers' park in the league, to Texas should have improved his hitting (in 1991 he hit 28 of his 44 homers on the road), but it didn't.

By now he's past the point of being considered a championship-quality player. Canseco was disabled twice last season, for 45 games, with back problems. He batted .235 with 23 homers and 122 strikeouts. That package isn't attractive for a club looking for a free agent with a bat to bolster the middle of its lineup, especially considering that Jose is an attitude case with no defensive value.

ANNIVERSARY WALTZ?

The 1967 season was the Athletics' last in Kansas City. The team finished 62-99, drawing but 726,639 fans to Memorial Stadium. The team's best offensive player was 21-year-old center fielder Rick Monday, who led the team with 14 home runs and 58 RBIs and batted .251. The left fielder, Mike Hershberger, batted .254 with one home run. Righthander Lew Krausse finished 7-17. Ramon Webster, the team's first baseman, hit .256 with 11 homers.

The seeds of the great Athletics teams of the 1970s were already there, however: Bert Campaneris, Dick Green, Catfish Hunter, Paul Lindblad, and Blue Moon Odom were already playing major roles, and on the bench future stars Reggie Jackson, Joe Rudi, Sal Bando, and Dave Duncan were busy soaking up lessons on how not to play.

By 1969 the relocated Oakland A's were a second-place team. Jackson hit 47 homers and drove in 118 runs while leading the league in slugging, at .608; Bando hit .281 with 31 homers and 113 RBIs. Odom won 15 games, while Green batted .275 with 23 homers. A 1970 second-place finish was followed by an AL West title in 1971, starting a five-year run at the top of the division, that included consecutive world championships from 1972 to '74.

Last season the Athletics finished 65-97 but drew 1,261,219 fans to Oakland Coliseum. (Attendance disasters aren't nearly as bad as they used to be.) In 30 years, will we be talking about the early days of Jason Giambi, Jimmy Haynes, Scott Spiezio, T.J. Mathews, Miguel Tejada, and Ben Grieve? The raw talent might be there.

109

1997 TEAM STATISTICS

BATTING/BASERUNNING

	Raw	Rank	+/- %		Raw	Rank	+/- %		Raw	Rank	+/- %
R	764	11	-4	BA	.260	12	-4	SB	71	12	-33
R/G	4.72	11	-4	HR	197	3	+11	CS	36	13	-30
OBA	.339	8	0	LH	297	11	-7	SB%	66.4	8	-1
SA	.423	7	-1	BB	642	2	+13				
PRO	.762	8	-1	SO	1,181	14	+13				

PITCHING/FIELDING

	Raw	Rank	+/- %		Raw	Rank	+/- %		Raw	Rank	+/- %
OR	946	14	+18	BA	.301	14	+11	OSB	131	12	+19
RA/G	5.84	14	+18	HR	197	13	+12	OCS	48	4	-9
OOB	.372	14	+9	LH	384	14	+19	OSB%	73.2	12	+10
OSA	.476	14	+11	BB	642	14	+14	FA	.980	8	0
PRO	.848	14	+10	SO	953	12	-8	GDP	147	14	+13

110

BATTING BY LINEUP SLOTS

	R	HR	RBI	BA	OBA	SA
1	115	10	35	.235	.334	.339
2	99	12	85	.263	.341	.378
3	103	34	129	.296	.386	.515
4	78	43	116	.246	.337	.507
5	90	34	97	.275	.366	.508
6	58	15	67	.250	.325	.386
7	71	16	59	.243	.303	.360
8	84	18	63	.280	.342	.444
9	66	15	63	.248	.310	.371

BATTING BY DEFENSIVE POSITION

	R	HR	RBI	BA	OBA	SA
C	62	12	48	.268	.339	.383
1B	80	42	113	.279	.368	.550
2B	70	15	69	.247	.305	.384
3B	81	15	54	.228	.306	.354
SS	62	10	54	.233	.289	.336
LF	85	22	76	.260	.338	.433
CF	102	13	43	.242	.338	.363
RF	101	41	127	.274	.365	.518
DH	83	24	102	.284	.372	.474
PH	22	3	32	.349	.447	.428
P	0	0	0	.071	.071	.071

TEAM PITCHING

	W-L	CG	QS	QS%	<6	>6	IPS	IP	ERA	OPR
ROTATION	29-73	2	50	31	52	25	5.3	858.2	5.94	.869

	W-L	GR	SV	BSV	HD	BHD	IRS%	IP	ERA	OPR
BULLPEN	36-24	480	38	23	154	89	35	586.2	4.82	.818

1998 PROJECTIONS

BATTING

PLAYER	BA	G	AB	R	H	2B	3B	HR	RBI	BB	SO	SB	CS	SA	OBA
Abbott, Kurt	.275	101	294	40	81	19	4	9	36	21	83	3	2	.457	.323
Bellhorn, Mark	.233	72	244	39	57	12	2	8	29	42	82	5	0	.391	.346
Berryhill, Damon	.259	64	161	17	42	9	0	3	22	18	33	0	0	.373	.335
Blowers, Mike	.273	78	223	29	61	10	0	8	34	29	55	0	0	.425	.356
Bournigal, Rafael	.277	85	242	30	67	11	1	1	22	17	19	2	2	.344	.325
Giambi, Jason	.283	149	548	74	155	40	1	20	82	57	93	0	1	.472	.351
Grieve, Ben	.252	99	379	69	96	22	1	17	78	52	92	3	0	.450	.342
Lesher, Brian	.247	59	206	32	51	9	2	8	29	23	53	5	0	.421	.322
Mack, Shane	.306	55	175	25	53	11	1	5	27	15	29	3	1	.478	.361
Magadan, Dave	.292	93	209	28	61	10	1	2	24	38	30	1	1	.381	.401
McDonald, Jason	.231	95	313	64	72	13	5	4	24	59	78	19	0	.346	.352
Molina, Izzy	.238	48	146	17	35	6	2	4	18	6	23	1	0	.401	.270
Spiezio, Scott	.253	148	541	62	137	29	4	15	69	46	78	9	3	.407	.313
Stairs, Matt	.281	143	365	59	102	18	1	26	70	47	59	3	2	.545	.363
Tejada, Miguel	.242	59	228	33	55	8	2	9	37	19	54	4	0	.412	.300
Voigt, Jack	.242	59	164	22	40	12	1	5	24	24	47	2	0	.413	.338
Williams, George	.259	103	265	38	69	12	1	4	28	48	62	0	1	.362	.373
Young, Ernie	.254	69	204	31	52	8	0	8	31	28	68	2	0	.407	.345

PITCHING

PITCHER	W	L	SV	ERA	G	GS	IP	H	HR	BB	SO
Bochtler, Doug	3	5	4	4.50	56	0	62	53	4	46	55
Candiotti, Tom	9	9	0	4.48	37	23	155	167	22	49	99
Fetters, Mike	2	5	15	3.66	56	0	66	66	4	32	59
Groom, Buddy	2	2	1	4.88	51	1	50	57	6	20	35
Haynes, Jimmy	8	7	0	3.82	21	21	123	115	12	62	100
Kubinski, Tim	2	2	1	3.82	21	0	33	25	3	14	19
Mathews, T.J.	6	5	7	3.17	54	0	65	61	7	27	62
Mohler, Mike	2	6	2	4.59	49	5	69	73	7	37	47
Oquist, Mike	5	5	0	4.36	17	16	99	102	11	36	57
Prieto, Ariel	7	9	0	4.74	25	24	139	159	15	72	94
Rigby, Brad	6	7	0	4.80	22	22	122	145	18	37	53
Rogers, Kenny	8	5	0	4.98	25	21	135	142	16	58	75
Small, Aaron	7	4	4	4.70	52	1	75	85	5	34	45
Taylor, Billy	4	4	20	4.09	67	0	70	66	4	33	68
Telgheder, Dave	4	7	0	5.29	22	20	105	130	16	34	57

111

SEATTLE MARINERS

MANAGEMENT

Manager	General Manager	Owner
Lou Piniella Career Record 864-781 .525	Woody Woodward	Baseball Club of Seattle

1997 RECORD

Won-Lost	Pct.	Division Finish/GB	Wild Card Finish/GB
90-72	.556	1-W	

Preseason Consensus Projection	1 (1.04)		

1st Half	2nd Half	Home	Road	Intradivision	Interleague
47-34	43-38	45-36	45-36	21-15	7-9

Comebacks	Blowouts	Nailbiters
7-15	29-19	35-36

112

NO RELIEF IN SIGHT

Relief pitching has been a problem for the Mariners for almost their entire franchise history. They traded their first quality closer, Enrique Romo, after he saved 16 games in 1977 and 10 in '78, and they've rarely had good relief pitching since. In 1997 Seattle felt compelled to deal at midseason for struggling closers Mike Timlin from Toronto and Heathcliff Slocumb from Boston after their own options, Norm Charlton and Bobby Ayala, had failed.

The signing of situational lefty reliever Tony Fossas was another indication of Seattle's desperation. Fossas, 40, was hit harder in '97 than he had been in years, though he was reasonably effective against lefthanded hitters.

Want evidence of the team's historically poor relief pitching? Charlton, who has been with the Mariners for just two-and-a-half years, already stands second on the club's

all-time saves list, ranking behind the already-forgotten Mike Schooler and directly ahead of Bill Caudill, Ayala, and—believe it or not—Shane Rawley.

Charlton's sudden collapse in 1997 almost destroyed the club's season, but it did give Seattle a chance to contemplate the future and plan for it. Actually, it forced them to do so. But they did it poorly.

It's not that the trading of prospects Jose Cruz, Jr., and Jason Varitek were such bad things. It's that the Mariners continued their habit of trading for other teams' veteran rejects (e.g., Slocumb and Timlin) while opening up a big hole in left field and not really solving the bullpen problem. The ex-Blue Jay Timlin isn't bad, but it's lefthander Paul Spoljaric, also acquired in the Cruz deal, who may be the one pitcher who helps the Mariners the most in the long term.

Spoljaric is Seattle's answer why general manager Woody

Woodward didn't trade Cruz to the Phillies, who were dangling strong-armed closer Ricky Bottalico in front of the Mariners. Many people, both in Philly and elsewhere around the game, couldn't believe that Woodward had turned down Bottalico to get Timlin. In the City of Brotherly Love, it was believed that a lack of brotherly love between Woodward and the Phils, dating back to his abrupt dismissal in the middle of the 1988 season, was the real reason.

PLUGGING HOLES

Despite outstanding offensive contributions from Ken Griffey, Jr., Edgar Martinez, Alex Rodriguez, and Jay Buhner, the Mariners just haven't been able to produce enough offense to glide by with their poor pitching. Perhaps the chief reason for this has been a consistent, and almost stubborn, reliance in recent years on patchwork solutions at two critical offensive positions: left field and third base.

The Mariners' late-season acquisition of Roberto Kelly to play left field continued their long history of a revolving door at the position. Kelly played 28 regular-season games for Seattle and started in left during the playoffs, but four other players had seen at least 30 games worth of action at the position for the '97 M's.

For 1998 the Mariners say they will throw the position up for grabs between Rob Ducey, Raul Ibanez, Shane Monahan, and Rich Amaral. Same old line, different channel. Don't be surprised if David Segui ends up in left field at some point; he used to be an awfully good defensive outfielder.

Fixtures Griffey and Buhner have been in the same outfield since mid-1990. Since then, the club's left fielders who have appeared in at least 30 games are:

1990	Jeff Leonard, Greg Briley, and Henry Cotto
1991	Briley, Cotto, and Tracy Jones
1992	Kevin Mitchell and Cotto
1993	Mike Felder (89 games)
1994	Eric Anthony (62 games, strike year)
1995	Rich Amaral, Vince Coleman, and Darren Bragg
1996	Amaral, Bragg, and Mark Whiten
1997	Jose Cruz, Jr., Rob Ducey, Amaral, and Lee Tinsley

TEAM MVP

With respect to the outstanding performances of pitchers Randy Johnson, Jeff Fassero, and Jamie Moyer, the 1997 Mariners couldn't have gotten anywhere without a healthy and happy **Ken Griffey, Jr.** Despite being intentionally walked 23 times—the highest total in the American League—Griffey drove in 147 runs, even though the Mariners' first two hitters were only slightly above average at getting on base. Junior had 93 extra-base hits and played his usual high-caliber center field.

BIGGEST SURPRISE

Randy Johnson's return from the back problems that held him to just five wins in 1996 was an almost incalculably huge boost to the club. He had what was in some ways his best season, allowing two or fewer runs in 20 of his 29 starts and pitching at least six innings in all but one of them.

BIGGEST DISAPPOINTMENT

The entire bullpen could qualify for this award, but **Norm Charlton**'s complete free fall forced the Mariners into trades they would rather not have made. Charlton pitched well enough in April, but by mid-May he had begun a precipitous descent that finally cost him his job by midsummer. His last save came on July 14 while the Mariners sifted through several others in an attempt to find a reliable closer.

113

Not to be forgotten in this parade are other part-time left fielders like Shane Turner, John Moses, Dave Cochrane, Chris Widger, Pete O'Brien, Quinn Mack, Alonzo Powell, Dann Howitt, Alex Diaz, Marc Newfield, Greg Litton, Keith Mitchell, Doug Strange, Luis Sojo, Brian Hunter, Warren Newson, and even Mackey Sasser (26 games in 1993).

The above-listed solutions have, in toto, worked out as could have been expected—which is to say, badly. When you give little or no thought to who to play in left field, a relatively undemanding defensive position that has to produce offense, you can go a long way toward neutralizing the rest of the outfield's productivity—no matter how spectacular.

Oddly enough, Bragg has shown he is a capable major league hitter with an outstanding arm, and he has played well in Boston after leaving the Pacific Northwest. But manager Lou Piniella didn't seem to like him very much and jettisoned him. Use the revolving door recklessly enough, and something will eventually get caught inside.

Meanwhile, these are the third basemen Seattle has used for at least 30 games since moving Edgar Martinez to DH in 1993:

1993	Mike Blowers
1994	Martinez and Blowers
1995	Blowers and Doug Strange
1996	Russ Davis, Strange, and Luis Sojo
1997	Davis and Brent Gates

While injuries played a part in some of this merry-go-round, it is certainly easy to conclude that the Mariners have not placed a high priority on getting a quality major league third baseman. Davis still has to prove that he is that player, Blowers never was that player (despite the team's faith in him), and other fill-ins like Gates, Sojo, Dave Hollins, Andy Sheets, et al. are just poor imitations.

RANDY JOHNSON: SOUTHPAW SUPREME

What's left to say about Randy Johnson? After suffering what many felt were career-threatening back problems that limited him to just 14 starts in 1996, Johnson came back to have his greatest season ever last year. The really Big Unit won 20 games for the first time (20-4), posted a career-best 2.28 ERA (also 2.28 better than the league average) and notched 291 strikeouts in just 213 innings. He finished second to Cy Young Award winner Roger Clemens (292) in K's, but the Rocket pitched 51 more innings than the Unit.

Johnson did all this despite suffering from tendinitis in his pitching hand that caused him to miss four starts in August. While he may not have deserved the 1997 Cy Young—Clemens had a season even greater than Johnson's—Johnson's contribution to the success of the Mariners in the last few years is greater than that of any other player but Ken Griffey, Jr. How many more seasons like this will Johnson need to have to put himself in the Hall of Fame, with his Sandy Koufax–like peak?

To properly illustrate the issue, let's look at Koufax's peak. From 1962 to '66, his greatest seasons, Koufax

- three times led his league in wins,
- twice led his league in winning percentage,
- twice led his league in complete games,
- three times led his league in shutouts,
- twice led his league in innings pitched,
- three times led his league in strikeouts, and
- all five times led his league in ERA.

Randy Johnson, like Koufax, had a rough patch early in his career vis-a-vis control. Thrice (1990-92) he led the AL in walks. However, beginning in 1993, he steadily refined his game to become the great pitcher he is. From 1993 to '97, Johnson's greatest seasons, he

- twice led his league in winning percentage,
- once led his league in ERA,
- once led his league in complete games,
- once led his league in shutouts,
- three times led his league in strikeouts, and
- once led his league in ERA.

There doesn't really seem to be much of a comparison, does there? However, there is one critical thing to remember: Koufax pitched in Dodger Stadium while Johnson has toiled in the Kingdome, a very good hitters' park until recent seasons.

While it may seem unfair to pick 1993-97 as Johnson's peak (he could ascend to greater heights), because he pitched only 14 times in '96 and 30 in '97 due to injuries, remember that Koufax threw only 28 times in 1962 and 28 in 1964 because of injuries. In addition, Koufax pitched in pain constantly during the last few seasons of his career. Today it is doubtful that any pitcher would be allowed to risk the club's investment by pitching in pain constantly.

Overall, Johnson simply hasn't dominated his league the way Koufax did in the mid-'60s. However, Koufax had the winds of time and place behind him; those same winds have been blowing into Johnson's face. Maybe Johnson isn't Koufax; that doesn't remove him from his pinnacle as one of the three best pitchers in baseball.

KEN GRIFFEY, JR.: SIMPLY THE BEST

Now that he's been healthy the last two years, baseball fans the world over have gotten a good look at exactly how good Ken Griffey, Jr., really is. He is now the best all-around player in the game and starts the season at age 28.

San Francisco's Barry Bonds had been the best player in baseball for a long time. He should have won four straight MVP awards, but the BBWAA chickened out in 1991 and gave the trophy to Terry Pendleton. The 33-year-old Bonds is still the top all-around player in the National League, and the only serious contender other than Griffey to be called the best in baseball.

However, much of Bonds's tremendous statistical value now comes from his incredibly high totals of bases on balls. While Bonds's ability to work the walk is a great thing for the Giants, Griffey now produces more power and a higher average. Griffey does give up points in on-base percentage, which is very important.

Bonds is a better offensive player than Griffey—not by much, but better. However, Griffey's defensive play rates as a significant advantage over Bonds's. That's not because Bonds isn't a great left fielder, because he is, but because a great center fielder is much more important than a great left fielder. Right now Junior is the man. And he's five years younger than Barry.

What is Griffey's peak? Is this it, or can he be even better? Most players have their peak seasons at ages 27 and 28. Griffey began to really add power in 1993, at age 23, vaulting from 27 homers to 45 and then leading the AL with 40 dingers in 1994, when he was on a pace to threaten Roger

THE MOMENT OF TRUTH

On **August 20** the Mariners were tied for first with Anaheim but had dropped three in a row. That night Randy Johnson took the hill and, with the help of three relievers, tossed a 1-0 gem at the Indians in front of 32,546 at the Kingdome. Heathcliff Slocumb got the save and Edgar Martinez's fourth-inning homer off starter and loser Charles Nagy was all scoring the Mariners needed. Meanwhile, the Angels lost a doubleheader to the Yankees and fell 1.5 games back of Seattle. Anaheim would never see the top again.

BEST DEAL

Acquiring **Jeff Fassero** from the Expos in October 1996 gave the club a top-flight starter in exchange for catcher **Chris Widger**— whose path was blocked by Dan Wilson—and rookie righthander **Matt Wagner**, who missed all of 1997 due to injury. The durable and very competitive Fassero (16-9, 3.61, 234.1 innings) was simply outstanding.

WORST DEAL

Some might nominate the July 31 deal sending **Jose Cruz, Jr.**, to Toronto as the worst, even though the Mariners got a very promising hard-throwing lefthander in return (**Paul Spoljaric**). If Cruz turns out to be the star people expect—which is by no means guaranteed—then Woodward will never live down this trade. The same day the Mariners dealt promising but underachieving pitcher **Scott Sanders** to Detroit in exchange for **Omar Olivares** and **Felipe Lira**. Both pitched very poorly for the Mariners. Not really a good day for GM Woody Woodward.

115

Maris's record if not for the strike. He ratcheted it up again in 1997, leading the league by smashing 56 over the fence.

Griffey has benefited from his home park over his career, hitting .315 with 155 homers at the Kingdome and .291 with 139 clouts on the road (in 165 more at bats). However, these are not huge differences, and in 1997 Junior hit 29 of his 56 homers in away games.

As for the argument that diluted pitching is responsible for home run feats like those of Griffey, note that last year Junior hit two home runs off David Cone, two off Roger Clemens, two off Joey Hamilton, two off Tom Candiotti, one off Jason Dickson, one off Mike Mussina, one off Arthur Rhodes, one off Jimmy Key, one off Brad Radke, and one off Pat Hentgen.

As for an argument that his homers didn't mean much in the end, note that 21 of them put the Mariners ahead in the game. Twenty-eight of them went at least 400 feet, with nine traveling more than 440 feet. He had a big year, and he had it loudly.

JAMIE MOYER: THE DESTROYER

Over the last two seasons, Jamie Moyer is 30-8.

Left for dead at age 29 in 1991 after an 0-5 season in St. Louis, Moyer went back to the minor leagues and reestablished himself, posting a 25-22 record in three years for the Orioles before signing with the Red Sox in 1996.

He was 7-1 for Boston before a trade to Seattle, where he fit right in with a 6-2 record. Last year he had even more fun, finishing 17-5 for the Mariners.

TOP PROSPECTS
SPRING 1998

1. **Shane Monahan, OF.** Seattle is high on Monahan, a fiery, scrappy player with speed who is a bit short on offensive production. A second-round draftee in 1995, he batted .302 in 107 games with 12 homers at Double A Memphis, then .294 in 21 games for Triple A Tacoma. However, Monahan also whiffed 132 times last season and had a mediocre on-base percentage because he rarely walked. He's Lou Piniella's kind of player, though, and might end up with the left field job in 1998.

2. **Raul Ibanez, OF.** The Mariners can't decide what to do with Ibanez, but they know he can hit. Last season at Tacoma he batted .304 with 30 doubles and 15 homers. Ibanez has provided offense in every season of his six-year pro career, but he turns 26 in June and still doesn't have a position. Left field is now considered the current option, but the team keeps coming up with obstacles to put in his way.

3. **Giomar Guevara, SS.** The one reason Guevara, who batted .263 at Memphis and .244 at Tacoma last year, has moved up the chain is his defense, which is simply outstanding. That alone could win the 25-year-old a utility job this season in Seattle. There is no reason to believe that he will ever hit, but Guevara has some speed, will take a walk, and can bunt.

4. **Greg Wooten, P.** A star college pitcher at Portland State, the righthander was a third-round 1995 draft pick. He spent last season at Memphis, making 26 starts with an 11-10 record and a 4.47 ERA. Wooten throws four pitches and is intelligent—but has nothing near 90 mph and had stretches when he was hammered around the Southern League.

5. **Ryan Franklin, P.** Last season was the slim righthander's fifth in the Seattle system, and his best. Using a fine breaking ball as his out pitch, Franklin was 4-2 in 11 games (8 starts) for Memphis, garnering 49 strikeouts and walking just 14 in 59 innings. Promoted to Tacoma, Franklin was 5-5 with a 4.18 ERA—good numbers for a starter in the Pacific Coast League. He has moved into the prospect category.

6. **Brett Hinchcliffe, P.** Drafted fairly low (16th round) because he does not throw especially hard, the righthander has spent six years in Seattle's system. Last year was his chance at Double A, and Hinchcliffe was 10-10 with a 4.45 ERA for a 67-72 club. He made 24 starts and completed five of them, a total that led Mariners minor leaguers. Hinchcliffe, a battler who doesn't issue many walks, will move to Triple A this year.

What Moyer has done is simply refine his control. Pitching early in his career in Wrigley Field, he was terrified of giving up homers and walked the ballpark (leading to three-run homers). Now he is extremely stingy with walks, still gives up homers, but ends up with ERAs close to or better than the league average. His stuff is certainly suspect, but Moyer gets ground balls, makes hitters work their way on base, and throws strikes.

Moyer has also benefited from pitching in the Kingdome—believe it or not. He was 12-2 in home games in 1997. He is far more effective these days against righthanded batters because he throws a lot of breaking pitches and cut fastballs, and the left field wall in Seattle is farther away than the right field wall. In other words, Moyer is effective against the people he has to be effective against in the place he must be effective against them. Against some lefthanded hitters, he suffers.

He can keep pitching well as long as he's healthy. After living through pitching for Don Zimmer and having to re-gear in mid-career, Moyer is better now than ever.

DON'T LET THE DOOR HIT YOU ON THE WAY OUT

Seattle signed lefthanded starting pitcher Greg Hibbard to a four-year free-agent contract in 1994. He went 1-5 for the Mariners that year before undergoing surgery to repair a partially torn rotator cuff. He never came off the disabled list, spending his third full year on the sidelines in 1997. Hibbard is now a free agent who should enjoy his retirement.

Lee Tinsley spent his first big league season with Seattle, then was waived to Boston, then was dealt to Philadelphia. He then was traded back to Boston and finally shipped back to Seattle, where he spent 1997. After the season, he was cut loose, of course, presumably so he could look for a job in Philadelphia. All this wheeling and dealing over a guy with a .241 lifetime average, little power, and an average throwing arm. Sheesh.

117

1997 TEAM STATISTICS

BATTING/BASERUNNING

	Raw	Rank	+/- %		Raw	Rank	+/- %		Raw	Rank	+/- %
R	925	1	+16	BA	.280	4	+4	SB	89	10	-16
R/G	5.71	1	+16	HR	264	1	+49	CS	40	11	-23
OBA	.355	3	+4	LH	333	5	+4	SB%	69.0	5	+3
SA	.485	1	+13	BB	626	3	+10				
PRO	.839	1	+9	SO	1,110	9	+6				

PITCHING/FIELDING

	Raw	Rank	+/- %		Raw	Rank	+/- %		Raw	Rank	+/- %
OR	833	10	+4	BA	.267	6	-2	OSB	99	5	-10
RA/G	5.14	10	+4	HR	192	12	+9	OCS	66	14	+25
OOB	.342	9	+1	LH	334	10	+3	OSB%	60.0	3	-10
OSA	.433	9	+1	BB	598	11	+7	FA	.979	12	0
PRO	.775	8	+1	SO	1,207	1	+17	GDP	117	2	-10

BATTING BY LINEUP SLOTS

	R	HR	RBI	BA	OBA	SA
1	122	12	66	.294	.349	.417
2	111	26	93	.281	.335	.472
3	132	59	152	.299	.379	.638
4	118	30	115	.332	.457	.552
5	111	36	104	.263	.366	.493
6	96	41	117	.266	.347	.511
7	79	23	88	.263	.325	.437
8	83	26	90	.283	.331	.484
9	73	11	65	.240	.291	.353

BATTING BY DEFENSIVE POSITION

	R	HR	RBI	BA	OBA	SA
C	72	16	81	.271	.327	.408
1B	91	38	99	.289	.367	.529
2B	115	13	68	.299	.352	.431
3B	75	23	81	.257	.303	.440
SS	113	25	92	.289	.339	.474
LF	84	24	78	.268	.316	.454
CF	125	54	146	.304	.378	.634
RF	110	41	110	.245	.378	.500
DH	107	26	113	.315	.440	.518
PH	18	4	22	.214	.297	.381
P	1	0	2	.188	.235	.188

TEAM PITCHING

	W-L	CG	QS	QS%	<6	>6	IPS	IP	ERA	OPR
ROTATION	66-46	9	83	51	30	63	6.1	985.2	4.47	.751

	W-L	GR	SV	BSV	HD	BHD	IRS%	IP	ERA	OPR
BULLPEN	24-26	392	38	27	93	80	39	462.0	5.47	.824

118

1998 PROJECTIONS

BATTING

PLAYER	BA	G	AB	R	H	2B	3B	HR	RBI	BB	SO	SB	CS	SA	OBA
Amaral, Rich	.290	62	149	30	43	5	1	1	15	14	26	11	4	.359	.352
Buhner, Jay	.245	152	542	100	133	21	1	40	116	98	158	0	0	.510	.361
Cora, Joey	.295	150	564	98	166	37	4	9	51	48	44	7	6	.422	.350
Davis, Russ	.265	134	457	63	121	30	1	19	65	33	114	6	2	.462	.315
Ducey, Rob	.277	75	153	24	42	14	2	5	11	9	30	3	3	.491	.315
Griffey, Ken	.283	161	621	124	176	30	2	53	140	80	115	15	3	.592	.365
Guevara, Giomar	.260	15	48	7	13	2	1	1	5	3	12	1	0	.350	.307
Huson, Jeff	.258	61	111	13	29	3	0	0	11	7	14	3	1	.287	.299
Ibanez, Raul	.262	44	167	28	44	10	2	5	28	11	35	2	0	.427	.306
Listach, Pat	.245	40	123	18	30	4	1	0	11	13	24	8	2	.300	.319
Martinez, Edgar	.311	157	555	110	173	42	1	27	106	118	84	3	3	.538	.432
Marzano, John	.278	22	52	4	14	2	0	1	5	4	9	0	0	.361	.333
Rodriguez, Alex	.304	155	636	115	194	45	3	28	100	47	108	25	5	.516	.352
Rohrmeier, Dan	.226	15	55	8	12	4	0	3	11	4	11	0	0	.458	.281
Segui, David	.286	140	509	78	146	27	2	18	70	60	66	2	2	.452	.361
Wilkins, Rick	.225	64	189	23	43	6	0	6	27	28	62	0	1	.360	.324
Wilson, Dan	.277	142	496	60	137	28	1	15	75	37	77	5	2	.430	.328
Monahan, Shane	.259	51	192	23	50	10	2	5	30	12	57	5	0	.411	.303

PITCHING

PITCHER	W	L	SV	ERA	G	GS	IP	H	HR	BB	SO
Ayala, Bobby	7	4	7	4.36	53	0	70	68	10	30	68
Carmona, Rafael	1	1	0	2.39	12	2	23	16	3	11	18
Cloude, Ken	7	6	0	3.09	19	19	111	89	12	38	85
Fassero, Jeff	14	10	0	3.82	31	31	205	205	18	69	176
Fossas, Tony	2	6	1	3.49	82	0	59	65	8	28	49
Hurtado, Edwin	2	2	0	3.94	6	4	30	30	3	10	18
Johnson, Randy	17	3	0	2.71	29	27	196	145	17	72	269
Lira, Felipe	6	10	0	5.26	26	20	120	129	18	48	75
McCarthy, Greg	1	1	0	4.87	34	0	28	24	3	14	31
Moyer, Jamie	13	5	0	4.04	28	24	158	162	20	39	90
Slocumb, Heathcliff	2	7	28	4.34	68	0	70	72	4	45	65
Spoljaric, Paul	1	4	1	4.01	68	0	85	74	7	46	84
Timlin, Mike	4	4	12	3.50	54	0	59	55	6	18	42
Wells, Bob	4	2	1	5.19	28	4	59	67	10	19	42

119

TEXAS RANGERS

MANAGEMENT

Manager	General Manager	Owner
Johnny Oates Career Record 532-497 .517	Doug Melvin	J. Thomas Schieffer/ Edward W. Rose

1997 RECORD

Won-Lost	Pct.	Division Finish/GB		Wild Card Finish/GB	
77-85	.475	3 W	-13	7	-19

Preseason Consensus Projection		2 (1.87)			

1st Half	2nd Half	Home	Road	Intradivision	Interleague
39-40	38-45	39-42	38-43	15-21	10-6

Comebacks	Blowouts	Nailbiters
12-8	21-24	35-40

120

GOOD NEWS, BAD NEWS

The Texas Rangers have been a case study in mediocrity in recent years. They have had some good players, some bad players, and a helluva lot of mediocre players. Their farm system is very dry, and the organization's long-term prospects are gray—the color of their history in Texas. On the positive side, they have a new owner who inherits a new park and a fan base that is larger than ever before.

Dallas businessman Tom Hicks purchased an 80 percent interest in the Rangers in January. The sale must be approved by the other owners, but no problems are expected. Hicks came to prominence in the leveraged buyout business, founding the firm of Hicks, Muse, Tate & Funst in 1989. The firm has now moved heavily into entertainment, purchasing radio and television stations as well as movie theaters. Hicks also owns the Dallas Stars NHL hockey team.

Hicks inherits a team that largely stood pat over the winter. The biggest change in the lineup will be the return of Kevin Elster at shortstop. Otherwise, only reserve catcher Bill Haselman, reserve infielder Luis Alicea, and reserve outfielder Roberto Kelly were added.

Haselman came over in a deal with Boston that cost Jim Leyritz but also netted pitcher Aaron Sele (13-12, 5.38), the biggest addition to the pitching staff. While the Rangers finished 1997 with a staff ERA of 4.69, seventh in the AL, the starting corps was especially shaky with an ERA of 5.11, ranking a lowly 12th.

Despite the rotation's performance, its three top members (John Burkett, Bobby Witt, and Darren Oliver) are all back for 1998, as are Roger Pavlik and Rick Helling. Excepting his 22-7 season in '93, Burkett is basically a .500 pitcher, sporting records of 6-8, 14-14, 11-12, and 9-12 the last four years. He has average stuff and above-average command but is no staff ace. Witt isn't any better; his 12-12, 4.82 log in '97 is representative. Pavlik is erratic and is coming off an elbow injury.

Oliver, the only southpaw in the rotation, is the best of the group, even though he still has control troubles. Helling, who returned to Texas in a midseason trade from Florida, isn't likely to land in the rotation unless another righthander is hurt.

Sele hasn't regained his velocity after 1995 shoulder problems and was extremely inconsistent with his command last year. The big righthander finished second in the league with 15 hit batsmen while walking 80 in just 177 innings. Lefthanders have always given him serious problems. What Sele looks like is another Rangers .500 pitcher who will take the ball without excelling. It's not easy for a team to win without an ace to anchor the rotation, and the Rangers don't have one.

The bullpen received unexpected help last year from the left side from retreads Scott Bailes and Eric Gunderson; neither should be counted on in '98. Closer John Wetteland was effective, saving 31 games and winning seven while holding opponents to a .182 average. From the right side, he had help from bulldog Danny Patterson (10-6). However, veteran righties Matt Whiteside and Xavier Hernandez were very disappointing. The Rangers did nothing in the off-season to beef up the pen except trade for young lefty Matt Perisho of Anaheim and not-so-young lefty Larry Thomas.

COMING UP SHORT

The Rangers went from being the 1996 AL West champions to a third-place club, finishing eight games under .500 and reminding nobody of a contender. How did this happen? Several key positions were utter disasters for Texas in 1997:

•Shortstop. Kevin Elster, coming off his career year for Texas in 1996, went to Pittsburgh for a much higher salary than the Rangers wanted to pay, so perennial prospect Benji Gil got his "last chance" at the job. He played good defense, but just didn't hit a lick. Gil's inability to work the strike zone is killing his career, and all the Rangers' wishing and hoping didn't change that simple fact. The team was able to dump him on the White Sox over the winter, where

TEAM MVP

Juan Gonzalez is a great power hitter. Last season, despite nagging injuries, he smashed 42 homers and drove in 131 runs. However, the Rangers' best overall player in 1997 was left fielder **Rusty Greer**, who batted .321 with 26 homers, 87 RBIs, 83 walks, and 112 runs. He finished seventh in the AL in batting and eighth in on-base percentage, leading Texas by wide margins in both categories. While Greer isn't a great defensive player, he has a strong arm and always hustles. He takes special advantage (.370, 18 homers last year) of his home field.

BIGGEST SURPRISE

Longtime minor leaguer **Lee Stevens** got into 137 games for the Rangers last year due to injuries to first baseman Will Clark and the retirement of DH Mickey Tettleton. He didn't blow his chance, batting .300 with 21 homers. While the 30-year-old Stevens isn't a long-term solution, he proved in 1997 that he learned from his vast minor league experience.

BIGGEST DISAPPOINTMENT

Texas had plenty of disappointments in 1997—second baseman Mark McLemore's hand injury, third baseman Dean Palmer's decline, the inability of the starting pitchers to get hitters out consistently—but perhaps the most crushing failure was that of shortstop **Benji Gil**, who in his "last chance" to claim an everyday job batted .224 in 110 games. While his defense continues to impress, Gil is just not a hitter. Unfortunately, Texas management tried to "wish" Gil's problems with the strike zone out of existence, and that approach almost never works.

another team can wish and hope he learns how to hit.

•Center field. Darryl Hamilton, the center fielder who had one of the best years of his career in 1996 with Texas, was allowed to go to the Giants as a free agent. His bargain replacement, Damon Buford, couldn't do the job. He batted .224 in 122 games and lost his place in the lineup to Tom Goodwin, acquired from Kansas City in midseason. Goodwin hit .237 in 53 games for the Rangers.

•Second base. Mark McLemore tore a ligament in his right hand during the season opener against Milwaukee and was either injured or playing at half capacity most of the year. Mac also had knee troubles that necessitated surgery in September. He was expected to jump-start the Rangers' lineup, but managed but a .338 on-base percentage and seven stolen bases in 12 tries.

•Starting pitching. Nobody stepped up to do the job in 1997. Veterans John Burkett and Bobby Witt were on the low side of average, while Ken Hill was terrible before being unloaded on Anaheim. Overrated Roger Pavlik missed most of the season because he had to undergo elbow surgery. The only above-average starter was left-hander Darren Oliver, who was 13-12 with a 4.20 ERA. While Rick Helling was tolerable in eight starts after coming over in an August 13 trade, the other fill-in starters were worse than awful (Terry Clark: 6.75 ERA; Julio Santana: 7.36 ERA; Tanyon Sturtze: 8.87 ERA).

It's not that the Rangers brain trust expected all of the above-named disappointments to be All Stars in 1997. However, Texas needed—and would have settled for—just average production from most of these spots. With players like Pudge Rodriguez, Rusty Greer, Juan Gonzalez, John Wetteland, and even Lee Stevens and Danny Patterson around, the Rangers had the front-line talent. They only needed to be mediocre at the other positions to contend.

The Rangers can no longer use the excuse that they don't have the resources to compete with the big boys. Since the debut of The Ballpark in Arlington, they have the financial muscle to sign and keep the players they need. Furthermore, they've been competing in the AL West, which has been a historically weak division for most of their history.

Not spending a lot of money on Elster, who could easily have been a flash in the pan, can be justified. Having

enough faith in Gil to give him another chance at short can be argued. Letting Hamilton (who is not a great player by any description) go when you intend to play Buford (who is not even a big league regular of any description) is the way you watch your pennant hopes wash downstream.

The 1996 Rangers, who won the AL West title with a 90-72 record, were a good club, but one which couldn't afford to make many mistakes if it wanted to repeat in 1997. In a tacit admission of one of its biggest mistakes of a year ago, Texas signed free agent Elster in the off-season to play shortstop for 1998. This was after Elster spent most of '97 on the DL with Pittsburgh.

TROUBLE DOWN ON THE FARM

Texas's recent minor league troubles have been well-documented. The system is extremely thin at all levels, due to an embarrassing set of amateur drafts in the late 1980s and 1990s. The franchise's first-round picks from 1988 to 1996 were Monty Fariss, Donald Harris, Dan Smith, Benji Gil, Rick Helling, Mike Bell, Kevin Brown (the catcher), Jonathan Johnson, and R.A. Dickey.

Despite this, however, the Rangers managed to lose two good infield prospects in the expansion draft and trade another. How could this happen?

Texas left shortstop Hanley Frias and second baseman Edwin Diaz unprotected in the draft, and both were eagerly snapped up by the Arizona Diamondbacks. Frias, 24, batted .264 with 35 steals at Triple A Oklahoma City and played a solid shortstop. The 22-year-old Diaz batted just .105 in 76 at bats at Triple A and .275 with 15 homers at Double A Tulsa. He has problems with the strike zone, but he has outstanding tools.

Why the Rangers thought they could spare these two is a puzzle. They have little depth at any position in the minors, and will be paying heavily for utility infielders in 1998. Frias could do that job now for the major league minimum.

In addition to losing Frias and Diaz, Texas also traded third baseman Mike Bell to the Angels for pitcher Matt Perisho. Bell, just 23, split the season between Double A and Triple A and was considered to be one of the jewels of their farm system a year ago. Apparently the Rangers think that Fernando Tatis is good enough that they won't need Bell.

122

RUSTY GREER: MAN OF THE PEOPLE

Rusty Greer was Texas' 10th-round pick in the 1990 draft. The best players the Rangers drafted ahead of him were pitchers Dan Smith, Terry Burrows, and Steve Dreyer, plus shortstop Jon Shave. Not a star in the group.

Already 21 years old when drafted, Greer was considered an average "tools" guy and didn't blast his way through the minors. He spent more than two full seasons at Double A Tulsa. However, then Rangers manager Kevin Kennedy, who rarely got credit for doing anything right during his tenure in Texas, saw something in Greer that many of the scouts didn't. On May 16, 1994, Rusty was brought up from Triple A Oklahoma City, and he hasn't looked back since.

After hitting .314 that season to pace all AL rookies, Greer batted .271 in 1995, largely a consolidation year for him, before a .332, 100-RBI season in 1996 and an even better overall campaign in 1997.

Greer hustles as much as anyone in baseball and plays defense well in both left field and right field. He can even play center if need be, simply because he works so hard and learns quickly. He's a multidimensional offensive player (.392 career on-base percentage, .500 career slugging average), a smart baserunner, and one of the better-liked players on his team. Of course, Greer is happy to play in The Ballpark in Arlington (18 homers there with a .370 average last season), and local fans are happy to watch him play as well.

Given the general image of major league ballplayers as smug, self-satisfied, ungrateful millionaires, it's always a pleasure to see hustling, complete players make it in the majors—especially when they exceed everyone's expectations. Rusty Greer, and players like him, mean more to baseball fans than just their numbers.

While divinely gifted stars like Ken Griffey, Jr., Frank Thomas, Mo Vaughn, Jeff Bagwell, Roger Clemens, and the like have the respect and adoration of baseball fans due to their hard work, determination, hustle, and talent, many fans love even more to watch gritty, overachieving players like Greer succeed.

Fan favorites in many cities often fit the profile of the hustling, sometimes diminutive, sometimes pugnacious

THE MOMENT OF TRUTH

On **June 18** Texas was 36-31, one game out of first place in the AL West. That night at Colorado the Rangers squandered a 7-2 early lead and a 9-6 bottom-of-the-ninth advantage as **John Wetteland** blew a three-run lead and a save opportunity for the second night in a row. The Rockies came back to win in the ninth, 10-9, when Wetteland delivered a bases-loaded walk, starting the Rangers on a seven-game losing streak that dropped them from one game out to six games out. They were never close to contending again.

BEST DEAL

The Rangers' 1997 trades didn't make much of a difference either way. However, some of their free-agent signings provided them with helpful, inexpensive players. Infielder **Domingo Cedeno**, who for some reason isn't regarded highly despite some obvious skills, signed a Triple A deal in January. He ended up playing 113 games for the Rangers, hitting .282 and playing good defense at both shortstop and second base.

WORST DEAL

Possibly the worst deal the Rangers made was a non-deal. The decision to allow 1996's center fielder, **Darryl Hamilton**, to leave the club via free agency thrust **Damon Buford** into the regular job. Buford couldn't handle it, batting .224 in 122 games and garnering mediocre defensive reviews. He was so bad that the Rangers were forced to get **Tom Goodwin**, who is far from a championship quality regular, from the Royals in late July in exchange for **Dean Palmer**.

123

"street player." Think of recent fan faves like F.P. Santangelo and David Segui in Montreal, Joey Cora in Seattle, Jeff Frye in Boston, Lenny Dykstra in Philadelphia, Lance Johnson in New York and Chicago, Dave Hollins in Anaheim, and Bobby Higginson in Detroit. Al Newman was that kind of player in the 1980s; so were Mickey Hatcher, Pat Sheridan, Craig Lefferts, and Wayne Tolleson. Even mild-mannered but iron-willed stars Orel Hershiser and Greg Maddux have some of the "street player" in them.

Why are players like this so popular, even if they're not as valuable to their teams as the big stars? Something that may look incredibly easy for Roberto Alomar may look harder for Jeff Frye, and if they both make the same play, some folks will think that Frye hustled more—just because his extra work and effort were more noticeable.

The truth, of course, is that Alomar hustles just as much but also has more natural talent, and he probably makes better use of his talent than most other players. Nevertheless, this appearance makes Frye's extra effort a lightning rod for public support.

Players such as Greer, Frye, and Walt Weiss, also give hope to those folks who, at some point in their lives, have been passed by for someone more gifted or more attractive. Those people can use the examples of Greer and his brethren and keep plugging, hopeful that if they just keep on hustling, their ships will eventually come in. As Rusty made it, so can the rest of us.

TOP PROSPECTS
SPRING 1998

1. **Matt Perisho, P.** Brought over from Anaheim in a postseason trade for infielder David Bell, the lefthander is expected to fight for a bullpen job in 1998. Perisho, a third-round pick in 1993, throws four solid pitches but has trouble with command. He walked 26 in 73 innings for Double A Midland (5-2, 2.96), 29 more in 52 frames for Triple A Vancouver (4-4, 5.33), and then 28 in 45 innings for the Angels (0-2, 6.00). Perisho turns 23 in June and has a decent future.

2. **Kevin Brown, C.** Brown hit .241 last year at Oklahoma City with 19 homers. Those aren't great numbers, but for Brown, a good defender, they might be enough to make him a backup in Texas. However, the second-round pick was once considered a possible regular, and his poor 1997 average damaged his career. Brown turns 25 in April and might be headed back to Triple A.

3. **Eric Moody, P.** The dearth of pitching prospects in the Texas organization is good news for the versatile 27-year-old righthander, who has risen through the system as a starter and reliever. Last season at Triple A he pitched 35 times (10 starts), and threw 112 innings. Moody throws sinkers and sliders with good velocity and rarely allows walks. However, he did give up 17 homers in 1997, including four in just 19 innings during a late-season trial with the Rangers.

4. **Jonathan Johnson, P.** The Rangers were hoping the righthander could advance all the way to the majors in 1997. No such luck. Johnson was 1-8 with a 7.29 ERA in 13 games for Oklahoma City before earning a demotion to Double A Tulsa. While there, he was 5-4 with a 3.52 ERA in 10 starts. The Rangers and their 1995 No. 1 pick will try again this spring. Johnson, whose best pitch is a darting curveball, will get every shot to start.

5. **Andrew Vessel, OF.** A promising outfielder with tools, Vessel spent four years at Class A before reaching Tulsa last season. Just 23 this spring, he batted .261 there with 35 doubles and 12 homers. He is playing better defense, taking more walks, and striking out less than he had previously, but has not yet learned how to use his speed on the bases.

6. **Warren Morris, 2B.** The scrappy infielder, whose game-winning homer gave LSU the 1996 NCAA title, began his pro career last season in the Florida State League. After batting .306 with 12 homers in 128 games, Morris was promoted to Oklahoma City for eight games (.219, one homer). He is likely to spend the year at Double A Tulsa and could have an everyday major league job by 1999 if he continues to shine at bat.

124

Another huge reason is that these so-called lunchpail players often appeal to the "lunchpail" mentality of a great number of sports fans, especially baseball fans. Working-class fans can't usually afford the premium ticket prices commanded by NFL, NBA, and NHL teams in the 1990s, but they can easily afford baseball tickets. Baseball, for all the undeserved criticism it takes annually about ticket-price inflation, remains by far the cheapest major spectator sport. While many in the media cry crocodile tears about how much it costs the oft-cited "family of four" to go to the ballgame, they rarely—if ever—write about how much it costs a family of four to go to a pro football or basketball game. With good reason: the vast majority of families can't afford to attend other pro sports.

LOOK BACK IN ANGER

Last year marked the Rangers' 25th anniversary in Texas since moving from Washington, D.C., where they had been known as the Senators (albeit the second edition). The nation's capital has a pro basketball team, a pro hockey team, and a wildly popular pro football team, but still no baseball franchise. Just another reason why baseball has slipped behind football in popularity and is in danger of being passed by basketball as well.

125

1997 TEAM STATISTICS

BATTING/BASERUNNING

	Raw	Rank	+/- %		Raw	Rank	+/- %		Raw	Rank	+/- %
R	807	7	+1	BA	.274	5	+1	SB	72	11	-32
R/G	4.98	7	+1	HR	187	5	+6	CS	37	12	-28
OBA	.334	9	-2	LH	338	4	+5	SB%	66.1	10	-2
SA	.438	4	+2	BB	500	11	-12				
PRO	.771	5	0	SO	1,116	10	+7				

PITCHING/FIELDING

	Raw	Rank	+/- %		Raw	Rank	+/- %		Raw	Rank	+/- %
OR	823	9	+3	BA	.283	13	+4	OSB	60	1	-45
RA/G	5.08	8	+3	HR	169	5	-4	OCS	56	11	+6
OOB	.347	12	+2	LH	338	11	+5	OSB%	51.7	1	-22
OSA	.439	12	+2	BB	541	5	-4	FA	.980	9	0
PRO	.786	12	+2	SO	925	13	10	GDP	130	7	0

126

BATTING BY LINEUP SLOTS

	R	HR	RBI	BA	OBA	SA
1	102	8	54	.248	.327	.353
2	111	21	87	.308	.347	.469
3	115	28	92	.322	.402	.534
4	109	46	147	.289	.340	.553
5	88	23	91	.310	.376	.488
6	76	25	95	.244	.296	.417
7	75	18	77	.253	.324	.416
8	70	8	66	.235	.286	.334
9	61	10	64	.245	.291	.357

BATTING BY DEFENSIVE POSITION

	R	HR	RBI	BA	OBA	SA
C	106	21	84	.307	.357	.475
1B	88	26	95	.328	.395	.527
2B	84	4	57	.272	.332	.372
3B	81	23	90	.253	.300	.419
SS	51	6	49	.235	.274	.313
LF	113	27	90	.306	.388	.515
CF	94	11	61	.239	.308	.357
RF	82	29	107	.267	.321	.464
DH	79	36	109	.253	.313	.492
PH	15	6	33	.241	.314	.423
P	4	1	5	.368	.400	.632

TEAM PITCHING

	W-L	CG	QS	QS%	<6	>6	IPS	IP	ERA	OPR
ROTATION	49-66	8	66	41	34	56	5.9	959.0	5.11	.823

	W-L	GR	SV	BSV	HD	BHD	IRS%	IP	ERA	OPR
BULLPEN	28-19	382	33	24	124	74	36	470.2	3.88	.706

TEXAS RANGERS
1998 PROJECTIONS

BATTING

PLAYER	BA	G	AB	R	H	2B	3B	HR	RBI	BB	SO	SB	CS	SA	OBA
Alicea, Luis	.262	99	301	46	79	16	4	4	31	50	52	14	6	.382	.367
Cedeno, Domingo	.282	85	278	39	78	14	4	3	26	19	60	3	2	.390	.327
Clark, Will	.299	122	445	67	133	28	1	13	66	59	64	0	0	.455	.381
Cooper, Scott	.251	43	121	12	30	6	1	3	14	14	26	0	1	.376	.330
Diaz, Alex	.267	24	93	12	25	5	1	3	11	7	14	3	0	.430	.318
Elster, Kevin	.246	88	287	39	70	17	2	13	54	35	79	2	2	.453	.328
Gonzalez, Juan	.289	132	527	82	152	26	3	41	126	34	93	1	0	.582	.332
Goodwin, Tom	.280	115	433	70	121	17	4	2	30	34	69	45	14	.349	.333
Greer, Rusty	.306	160	603	103	184	40	4	23	90	76	87	8	3	.499	.383
Haselman, Bill	.259	55	165	20	43	10	0	6	23	14	36	1	2	.425	.316
Kelly, Roberto	.304	106	369	53	112	23	2	10	56	23	63	11	5	.457	.344
McLemore, Mark	.274	104	389	59	107	18	2	2	32	53	58	13	7	.353	.361
Newson, Warren	.234	66	145	21	34	8	1	7	19	26	47	3	0	.439	.351
Rodriguez, Ivan	.303	147	592	95	179	36	3	19	76	34	72	5	2	.469	.341
Simms, Mike	.240	58	107	12	26	7	0	5	20	8	26	1	1	.442	.295
Stevens, Lee	.282	147	452	56	127	25	3	20	74	27	90	1	3	.482	.323
Tatis, Fernando	.244	92	342	48	84	16	0	15	42	29	77	8	0	.422	.303

PITCHING

PITCHER	W	L	SV	ERA	G	GS	IP	H	HR	BB	SO
Bailes, Scott	2	1	0	4.69	49	0	52	56	6	28	36
Brandenburg, Mark	2	3	0	4.68	36	0	50	56	5	19	42
Burkett, John	8	10	0	4.49	27	27	166	195	16	36	118
Gunderson, Eric	2	2	1	4.11	61	0	48	47	6	17	29
Helling, Rick	5	8	0	4.48	36	15	118	98	16	59	91
Hernandez, Xavier	2	3	2	4.42	44	0	55	56	7	21	49
Levine, Alan	2	2	0	6.30	24	0	27	33	4	14	21
Moody, Eric	1	1	0	4.18	8	2	24	28	3	5	13
Oliver, Darren	13	9	0	4.39	31	29	180	193	24	78	103
Patterson, Danny	8	6	1	3.45	52	0	68	71	3	23	65
Pavlik, Roger	8	6	0	4.72	21	21	120	121	15	55	80
Perisho, Matt	5	5	0	4.38	16	15	94	103	7	45	67
Santana, Julio	2	3	0	6.17	16	8	57	74	8	25	35
Sele, Aaron	10	10	0	5.15	29	29	154	172	19	67	114
Wetteland, John	5	3	39	2.66	71	0	74	56	8	25	75
Whiteside, Matt	4	2	0	4.94	44	1	76	87	7	26	47
Witt, Bobby	10	10	0	4.76	28	27	174	200	25	68	116

ATLANTA BRAVES

MANAGEMENT

Manager	General Manager	Owner
Bobby Cox Career Record 1312-1089 .546	John Schuerholz	Ted Turner

1997 RECORD

Won-Lost	Pct.	Division Finish/GB	Wild Card Finish/GB
101-61	.623	1 E	

Preseason Consensus Projection	1 (1.09)

1st Half	2nd Half	Home	Road	Intradivision	Interleague
52-29	49-32	50-31	51-30	29-19	8-7

Comebacks	Blowouts	Nailbiters
7-10	32-9	49-34

128

RETOOLING A WINNER

Having made the postseason in every year since 1991 in which there was a postseason (in 1994 they were leading the wild-card race when a players' strike ended the season), the Braves have a legitimate claim to dynasty status. If not for three tough World Series losses—they've won only once in the '90s—no one would question their dynastic record.

The Braves are still formidable, but several of their key players are getting up there in years, and management faced some tough off-season decisions at several spots. Atlanta opted to promote from within and sign a couple of free agents. Infielders Mark Lemke and Jeff Blauser and outfielder Kenny Lofton (all of whom were let go as free agents) and first baseman Fred McGriff (who was traded to Tampa Bay in November), have been replaced, respectively, by Tony Graffanino, Walt Weiss, Andruw Jones, and Andres Galarraga.

Graffanino should be able to handle the second base job and ultimately prove to be an upgrade from Lemke. It's not as if Lemke did anything in 1997 any worse than he had before. He's always been a steady defensive second baseman and a .250 hitter with good bat control but little other offensive talent. Except for a .294 average in the strike-shortened 1994 season, Lemke has batted .255 or under in each of his eight years with the Braves. He's not an unknown quantity.

The primary reasons that Lemke won't be back are money and youth. The Braves believe the 25-year-old Graffanino (8 homers in 186 big league at bats last year) can outproduce the 32-year-old Lemke at the plate and come close to his performance in the field—and he'll cost less than 10 percent of the $2 million that Lemke made in '97. Those are pretty good reasons.

The Braves' budgeting might still have been headed out the window, though, due to the availability of disgruntled Twins second sacker Chuck Knoblauch. The 29-year-old standout wanted out of Minnesota, and his club was happy to oblige—but wanted fair value in return. In the Braves' case, "fair" seemed to mean "Denny Neagle."

Knoblauch is a much better player than the talented Graffanino, but he was also several million bucks more expensive. Rich clubs like the Braves can afford to take on those kinds of salaries. However, a Knoblauch trade not only would have added to Atlanta's already-fat payroll, or caused some salary dumping, it would (like the Galarraga signing) have told good prospects in their farm system that they are unlikely to get their chance with the Braves.

Weiss was brought in to anchor the infield defense; Atlanta places a premium on steady D and doing the little things right. He'll probably bat low in the order because drawing walks has been his sole offensive contribution of late. Weiss isn't being paid for his bat, but his .235 average away from Coors last year isn't a good sign.

The 20-year-old Jones is still developing as an offensive player, but Galarraga's production will dip sharply now that he won't be playing his home games in Coors Field. Turner Field is not a power hitters' park, which made McGriff's decline look a bit worse than it was last year (he hit just .265 with 8 dingers in 78 home games, compared with .289 and 14 in 74 games on the road). But the 34-year-old Crime Dog has been slipping for a couple of years.

Watch what a change of 4,000 feet in altitude does to Galarraga's numbers, inflated for five years by playing half his games at 5,280 feet. Unlike Vinny Castilla, the Big Cat wasn't a power-hitting apparition created by Colorado's home field, but he's nonetheless going to the bank with several extra millions thanks to his former home. Since 1993 Galarraga has hit 69 points lower on the road (.281, versus .350 at home), with 28 fewer homers away from home and a dip of 70 points in on-base percentage and 132 points in slugging average.

The Braves would have liked to have moved sluggish slugger Ryan Klesko (.261, 24 homers, 130 strikeouts) to first base, but they decided that it was more important to land the Big Cat. Galarraga will be 39 when his contract is up after the 2000 season, and it's unlikely that he'll be

TEAM MVP

Third baseman **Chipper Jones** does everything well. He plays a solid, if not especially rangy third base, runs the bases efficiently, and hits, hits, hits. He led the 1997 Braves in games, runs, hits, RBIs, doubles, and walks, and chipped in 21 homers to boot. Jones is durable, smooth, and talented, just the kind of player every championship team depends on.

BIGGEST SURPRISE

Shortstop **Jeff Blauser** played 151 games and hit .308 with 31 doubles, 17 homers, 70 walks, and 20 times hit by pitch. His .405 on-base average was second only to Kenny Lofton's on the club, while his .482 slugging average ranked third. The big surprises were: 1) Blauser's hitting so well and 2) his staying healthy all season. He had missed substantial chunks of action due to injuries in each of the three previous years.

BIGGEST DISAPPOINTMENT

The Braves didn't have too many things go wrong for them until the NLCS, but one player who didn't have a happy year was pitcher **Terrell Wade**. The beefy southpaw began the season in the starting rotation but went to the sidelines in June with a torn muscle in his left elbow after just 12 appearances. Wade was claimed in the expansion draft by the Tampa Bay Devil Rays.

129

THE MOMENT OF TRUTH

After losing the first two games of the season in Houston, the Braves trailed the Astros 2-0 in the seventh in the season's third game on April 3. In the top of the seventh **Fred McGriff** homered to bring the visitors within one. In the eighth Atlanta pushed two more runs across against **Darryl Kile** to eke out a 3-2 win. **Tom Glavine** got the victory with **Mark Wohlers** picking up the first of his 33 saves. The Braves reached first place 10 days later and never relinquished it.

BEST DEAL

Right fielder **Michael Tucker** and useful utilityman **Keith Lockhart** came over from Kansas City in exchange for outfielder **Jermaine Dye** and lefthanded reliever **Jamie Walker**, neither of whom were in Atlanta's plans. While both Dye and Walker struggled last season, Lockhart hit .279 in multipurpose use and Tucker batted .283 with 14 home runs.

WORST DEAL

Trading outfielders **Marquis Grissom** and **Dave Justice** to the Indians for outfielder **Kenny Lofton** and lefthanded reliever **Alan Embree** may have cleared up budget concerns for Atlanta, but it weakened the club. The Braves' outfield options were sorely limited after the trade, which put pressure on **Ryan Klesko** and **Andruw Jones** that neither one handled all that well.

worth the $24.75 million the Braves are paying him.

A big reason why the Braves signed Galarraga and Weiss is that they think the defensive abilities of the two veterans is critical to the success of their pitching staff. Another is that none of the organization's young upper-level position players are first-rate prospects. But there is some talent in the Braves' system, even though there are now few jobs available for them (see Top Prospects).

FORTIFYING THE BULLPEN

Braves manager Bobby Cox created a rumble when he shipped out three veteran members of his bullpen last July 12. Slumping Joe Borowski (later waived), Paul Byrd, and Brad Clontz were demoted to Triple A, and rookies Mike Cather, Chad Fox, and Kevin Millwood took their place.

Millwood made eight starts for the Braves and was good enough to win a spot on Atlanta's expansion-draft protection list. Between Double A, Triple A, and the majors Millwood posted a 15-8 record and pitched well down the stretch.

Fox and Cather pitched for the Braves two days after being recalled, quickly winning raves from Cox for their poise even though neither has above-average stuff. Fox appeared 30 times for Atlanta, faring well in a middle relief role (3.29 ERA, 28 strikeouts in 27.1 innings); he was dealt to Milwaukee in December for outfielder Gerald Williams. Cather, who moved into a setup role almost immediately, had a 2.39 ERA in 35 games for the Braves.

Atlanta also brought up another rookie, former Northern Leaguer Kerry Ligtenberg, and used him 15 times in August and September (19 K's in 15 innings). Finally, John LeRoy, a hard-throwing righty, came up in late September and won a game in relief in his only appearance. (LeRoy went to Tampa Bay in the expansion draft.) Earlier in the season the Braves had given rookie Chris Brock six starts before deciding he wasn't suitable (5.58 ERA).

With all these young pitchers playing key roles for a division-winning club, it raises the question of just how important veteran pitching is when filling out a staff that boasts a strong closer and a very successful starting corps. None of the rookie hurlers Atlanta brought up was a highly rated prospect, but almost all of them were effective.

Cox and general manager John Schuerholz deserve a lot of credit for sticking their necks out and taking a chance on their youth. This is the mark of a solid, well-run organization.

FORGETTING THE BULLPEN

Unfortunately for the Braves, Cox all but ignored those young pitchers in the postseason, instead staying with his veteran starters even when they had lost their stuff. As a result the Braves lost the NLCS to Florida.

Atlanta's bullpen corps for the NLCS included Ligtenberg, Cather, Embree, Clontz, and Wohlers, but the entire bullpen pitched just 7.2 innings in the six games.

In Game 3 Cox left John Smoltz in to allow four runs on three doubles and three walks (two intentional) in the sixth inning as the Marlins came back for a 5-2 victory. Where was the bullpen?

In Game 6 Tom Glavine gave up four runs in the first before settling down. In the sixth, with the Braves trailing 4-3, the Marlins scored three runs to salt the game away as Glavine allowed four hits and two walks. While only two of the hits got out of the infield, Glavine wasn't getting hitters out. But Cox chose not to go to another pitcher. Result: a Braves loss.

While the Braves may have used this approach for much of the regular season, there's no sense in sticking to something when it doesn't work. Cox was outmanaged in the NLCS by the Marlins' Jim Leyland, who knew how and when to go to his bullpen.

TOP PROSPECTS
SPRING 1998

1. **Kevin Millwood, P.** He spent four years in Class A, but in 1997 he rose all the way to the majors. He pitched decently at Double A Greenville before a hot streak at Triple A Richmond and a call to Atlanta. He has never been highly rated due to the lack of an outstanding fastball, but Millwood showed in his 12 games for the Braves that he has what it takes to pitch at the top. He hasn't quite gotten over the hump yet but should be the Braves' fifth starter this season as long as he continues to show good command.

2. **Randall Simon, 1B.** The lefty-swinging Curaçao native spent 1997 at Triple A Richmond at age 22. Simon batted .308 there with 45 doubles and 17 homers. However, he drew just 17 walks all season in nearly 550 plate appearances. A good defensive first baseman, Simon played in 13 games for the Braves, collecting 6 hits in 14 at bats. He's probably not in Atlanta's short-term plans because the club signed Andres Galarraga this fall.

3. **Damon Hollins, OF.** The almost-24-year-old recovered from injury problems that cut short his 1996 season. Hollins hit .265 with 31 doubles and 20 homers at Richmond, reaching full-season career bests in walks (45) and fewest strikeouts (84). The Braves don't have a regular spot for Hollins, but platoon duty (he bats righthanded) could be in the cards. He has some speed and plays good defense.

4. **Kerry Ligtenberg, P.** Signed out of the independent Prairie League in 1996, Ligtenberg was spectacular at Double A (3-1, 2.04, 16 saves) and then fanned 35 and walked just two in 25 innings at Richmond before an August call-up to Atlanta. A soft-tossing righthander in the Greg McMichael mold, Ligtenberg pitched well in 15 games for the Braves and will almost certainly have a major league job coming out of spring training.

5. **Mike Cather, P.** Released from the Rangers' organization in 1995, he went to the Northern League and signed with the Braves in 1996. He pitched well enough last season to earn a ticket to the majors, where he was quite effective in short relief. Cather, who survives on a good sinking fastball and the ability to change speeds, could help out in the middle again this season.

6. **Chris Brock, P.** He was a combined 12-19 in 1995 and '96 at Richmond. Just a 12th-round draft choice, Brock pitched well last spring as a starter at Richmond and on June 10 was promoted into Atlanta's starting rotation when Terrell Wade got hurt. While Brock, who has three average pitches, was not overly impressive in his six starts, he could well end up in the majors again this year.

131

ATLANTA BRAVES
1997 TEAM STATISTICS

BATTING/BASERUNNING

	Raw	Rank	+/- %		Raw	Rank	+/- %		Raw	Rank	+/- %
R	791	3	+6	BA	.270	3	+3	SB	108	11	-17
R/G	4.88	3	+6	HR	174	2	+13	CS	58	9	-3
OBA	.343	4	+3	LH	305	8	-3	SB%	65.1	11	-4
SA	.426	2	+4	BB	597	5	+8				
PRO	.769	2	+3	SO	1,160	12	+6				

PITCHING/FIELDING

	Raw	Rank	+/- %		Raw	Rank	+/- %		Raw	Rank	+/- %
OR	581	1	-22	BA	.241	2	-8	OSB	124	8	-2
RA/G	3.59	1	-22	HR	111	1	-28	OCS	54	4	-8
OOB	.301	1	-10	LH	259	1	-17	OSB%	69.7	9	+3
OSA	.354	1	-13	BB	450	1	-19	FA	.982	4	0
PRO	.654	1	-12	SO	1,196	3	+8	GDP	113	6	-5

132

BATTING BY LINEUP SLOTS

	R	HR	RBI	BA	OBA	SA
1	119	12	72	.312	.394	.430
2	109	21	80	.272	.346	.442
3	101	20	118	.303	.375	.478
4	87	25	110	.277	.352	.440
5	93	33	108	.269	.340	.494
6	73	26	87	.248	.328	.443
7	73	17	61	.239	.296	.364
8	85	16	71	.291	.364	.455
9	51	4	48	.197	.274	.254

BATTING BY DEFENSIVE POSITION

	R	HR	RBI	BA	OBA	SA
C	74	30	90	.272	.330	.482
1B	81	24	109	.270	.347	.433
2B	70	12	52	.262	.327	.380
3B	104	22	116	.293	.367	.474
SS	95	18	70	.297	.389	.460
LF	88	27	95	.268	.332	.470
CF	118	15	81	.313	.396	.448
RF	93	19	76	.265	.335	.424
DH	3	1	9	.231	.250	.410
PH	24	5	32	.188	.285	.305
P	24	1	25	.168	.237	.195

TEAM PITCHING

	W-L	CG	QS	QS%	<6	>6	IPS	IP	ERA	OPR
ROTATION	75-37	21	114	70	17	98	6.8	1,096.2	3.05	.644

	W-L	GR	SV	BSV	HD	BHD	IRS%	IP	ERA	OPR
BULLPEN	26-24	374	37	16	124	70	33	369.0	3.56	.685

1998 PROJECTIONS

BATTING

PLAYER	BA	G	AB	R	H	2B	3B	HR	RBI	BB	SO	SB	CS	SA	OBA
Bautista, Danny	.244	50	100	14	24	3	1	3	10	7	26	2	1	.397	.293
Galarraga, Andres	.269	146	571	96	154	28	3	34	114	39	133	15	6	.507	.316
Graffanino, Tony	.248	136	246	43	61	11	2	9	25	33	62	7	5	.419	.337
Jones, Andruw	.233	161	431	64	100	21	1	20	74	58	117	21	11	.424	.323
Jones, Chipper	.286	158	598	101	171	35	3	23	106	78	89	16	4	.473	.369
Klesko, Ryan	.267	139	458	68	122	22	5	25	81	52	116	5	4	.502	.342
Lockhart, Keith	.285	78	178	25	51	11	2	4	28	13	17	3	1	.442	.333
Lopez, Javier	.286	147	502	59	144	26	2	25	76	38	91	1	3	.497	.337
Perez, Eddie	.243	45	113	13	27	4	0	4	12	6	20	0	1	.381	.283
Simon, Randall	.263	43	157	16	41	12	0	3	26	5	27	0	0	.401	.285
Tucker, Michael	.274	150	517	82	142	27	6	15	63	49	118	13	7	.437	.337
Weiss, Walt	.249	136	441	59	110	19	3	4	36	69	64	8	2	.337	.351
Williams, Gerald	.265	110	350	49	93	22	2	7	31	16	60	14	7	.401	.297

PITCHING

PITCHER	W	L	SV	ERA	G	GS	IP	H	HR	BB	SO
Brock, Chris	5	5	0	4.52	15	14	84	79	6	42	47
Byrd, Paul	2	2	0	4.68	28	2	42	39	5	20	31
Cather, Mike	4	3	1	3.50	44	0	64	54	3	25	43
Clontz, Brad	4	1	1	4.34	48	0	48	49	4	18	36
Embree, Alan	4	2	0	3.84	76	0	61	53	5	32	60
Glavine, Tom	14	8	0	3.24	33	33	228	206	16	80	153
Ligtenberg, Kerry	5	3	3	2.32	50	0	62	38	7	15	67
Maddux, Greg	18	6	0	2.54	34	34	241	217	10	25	183
Millwood, Kevin	7	6	0	3.11	22	19	122	102	8	41	88
Neagle, Denny	17	7	0	3.38	33	33	226	220	21	50	162
Smoltz, John	14	9	0	3.27	29	29	207	186	17	54	205
Wohlers, Mark	4	6	34	3.30	72	0	71	63	5	32	94
Edmondson, Brian	4	2	1	3.31	27	0	54	55	4	31	42

133

FLORIDA MARLINS

MANAGEMENT

Manager	General Manager	Owner
Jim Leyland Career Record 943-933 .503	Dave Dombrowski	H. Wayne Huizenga

1997 RECORD

Won-Lost	Pct.	Division Finish/GB		Wild Card Finish/GB
92-70	.568	2 E	-9	1

Preseason Consensus Projection	2 (1.83)

1st Half	2nd Half	Home	Road	Intradivision	Interleague
48-32	44-38	52-29	40-41	25-23	12-3

Comebacks	Blowouts	Nailbiters
18-11	25-16	48-37

134

ON THE TOP OF THE WORLD — BUT NOT FOR LONG

The batter chipped the two-out pitch up the middle. As he headed to first, everyone on the field began to move, some toward the middle of the diamond, one man spinning toward home. The ground ball squirted between the scrambling middle infielders, and the winning run raced across the plate.

Lithe Edgar Renteria did in the eleventh inning what all the muscular sluggers in both lineups couldn't do—drive home the winning run as the Florida Marlins defeated the Cleveland Indians 3-2 in Game 7 of the 1997 World Series.

It happens every day in baseball, but when such an exciting play ends a thrilling game and wins the World Series in front of a stadium full of screaming fans, the joyful smile of the batter and the quickly rising tide of communal joy etch themselves instantly into memory.

In a Series marred by much unjustified criticism of both teams, Cleveland and Florida played a classic game of "good old country hardball" in Miami on October 26. A procession of hard-throwing pitchers dominated the hitters throughout the game, so it was entirely fitting that the game-winning hit came on a bouncer up the middle rather than a blast into the seats.

The Marlins won the world championship in only their fifth year of existence, the fastest of any expansion franchise. The teal team was also the first wild-card club to advance to the Series since Major League Baseball instituted its new playoff system in 1995.

Both teams in the Series were eminently likable, giving the postgame scene both heartwarming and heartrending aspects. Florida manager Jim Leyland, after 34 years in professional baseball, was so ecstatic at winning the world championship that he did a lap around the field after the game, the last leg while holding a Marlins pennant aloft. Leyland, universally regarded as one of the best managers of recent times, had led several Pittsburgh teams to the brink of the Series, but had never made it to the Fall Classic.

Cleveland, the underdog in the series, gamely fought till the bitter end, extending the eventual champions to the last out of the eleventh inning of the seventh game. The overachieving Indians were able to surmount every obstacle in their way in 1997 except the Marlins, who, in the end, simply outlasted their opponents from the north. Defying predictions of pundits and oddsmakers, the Indians perfectly fit the cliché of a team that "didn't deserve to lose."

TEAL-BLUE LIGHT SPECIALS

The bargain shoppers were out in full force this winter at Wayne Huizenga's Wholesale House of Players as the Marlins' salary purge divested the team of much of its major league talent base. The only positive aspect of the disgraceful fire sale held by the world champs immediately after the World Series is that the talent-rich Florida system will get even richer.

Many of the minor leaguers the team acquired in trade for its veterans are real prospects and should show up in Marlins teal-and-black togs in the future. Of course, they might end up playing in front of manager Jim Leyland and 50,000 empty seats.

Fortunately for the team's remaining fans, Florida GM Dave Dombrowski did far better in most of these deals than anyone could have expected, since these trades were publicly mandated by ownership. The Marlins' big off-season deals (through December) were enough to take your breath away:

•Kurt Abbott traded to Oakland for Eric Ludwick.

•Moises Alou traded to Houston for Manny Barrios, Oscar Henriquez, and a player to be named.

•Kevin Brown traded to San Diego for Derrek Lee and Rafael Medina.

•Jeff Conine traded to Kansas City for Blaine Mull.

TEAM MVP

Nobody in the Marlins' lineup, or even on the pitching staff, had a superstar season. Almost everyone chipped in their fair share to the team's success. In a way, catcher **Charles Johnson** was the most valuable player Florida had. He not only did not make an error or allow a passed ball all season, he threw out 50 of 112 men (44.6 percent) trying to steal, second in the NL. Johnson has already won accolades for his fine pitcher-handling skills. At bat, CJ enjoyed his best big league season despite a typically slow start.

BIGGEST SURPRISE

Rookie second baseman **Craig Counsell** came over in trade from Colorado on July 27, just after his big league debut. He immediately stepped in as the Marlins' regular second baseman and showed a pesky bat and very strong defensive skills. While he may not have a long tenure as an everyday player, the scrappy 27-year-old Counsell hit and fielded his way toward future employment.

BIGGEST DISAPPOINTMENT

Second baseman **Luis Castillo** hit so badly that he was sent down on July 28. **Devon White** had a mediocre, injury-plagued season. However, the biggest disappointments were **Gary Sheffield** and **Jeff Conine**, neither of whom could duplicate their usual performances. Sheffield struggled partially because most moundsmen simply would not give him quality pitches to hit, but he just did not hit up to standard. Conine had an excellent April, but sagged in May and only occasionally got his stroke back. By August he was platooning at first base.

135

•Dennis Cook traded to the Mets for Fletcher Bates and Scott Comer.

•Kurt Miller traded to the Cubs for a player to be named.

•Robb Nen traded to San Francisco for Joe Fontenot, Mike Villano, and Mick Pageler.

•Ed Vosberg traded to San Diego for Chris Clark.

•Devon White traded to Arizona for Jesus Martinez.

In dumping five major league pitchers, two infielders, and two outfielders, Florida received in return eleven pitchers, one first baseman, and one outfielder, most complete unknowns to the fans. An assessment of the young talent (six are on the Top Prospects page):

Manny Barrios: For Triple A New Orleans in 1997 Barrios finished 4-8 with a 3.27 ERA in 57 games. The 23-year-old righthander has no special pitches but is durable and has fanned more than a hitter per inning as a professional.

Fletcher Bates (see Top Prospects).

Chris Clark: Brought over from San Diego, Clark is a 23-year-old righthander who has very good stuff but is very raw. Last season at Class A Clinton he struck out 91 in 89 innings, but also walked 46. A long-range prospect.

Scott Comer: In '97 Comer was 7-1 with a 1.74 ERA in 14 starts, leading the New York–Penn League with 98 strikeouts. A 20-year-old lefthander, Comer has dominated two low-level Class A leagues and could jump to Double A this season. He was a 10th-round draft pick in 1996.

Joe Fontenot: The Giants' first-round pick in 1995, the 21-year-old righthander throws three strong pitches with good velocity. He was 10-11, 5.53 at Double A last season, and may spend another year at that level. Fontenot is considered a potential No. 2 starter.

Oscar Henriquez (see Top Prospects).

Derrek Lee (see Top Prospects).

Eric Ludwick (see Top Prospects).

Jesus Martinez: Brother of Ramon and Pedro, this Martinez is a hard-throwing lefthander with poor command. Last season at Triple A Albuquerque, Martinez was 7-1 but had a 6.21 ERA, striking out 80 while walking 52 in 84 innings. Although he has played professionally for seven years, Martinez does not turn 24 until mid-March.

Rafael Medina (see Top Prospects).

Blaine Mull: Mull, a 1994 sixth-round draft pick, is a finesse righthander. He lacks any outstanding pitches but was effective in Class A. Promoted to Double A Wichita last season, he went 1-2 with a 6.65 ERA in eight starts.

Mick Pageler: At Class A Bakersfield, Pageler saved 29 games, fanning 68 in 65 frames. A 15th-round pick in the 1995 draft, Pageler is far from the majors.

Mike Villano (see Top Prospects).

While none of these 13 players is a can't-miss prospect, almost all of them have a chance at making the majors. Henriquez, Comer, Lee, Fontenot, Villano, Medina, and even Martinez are potential impact players. Considering Dombrowski had a gun to his head when making these deals, he did very well indeed.

CHANGING OF THE GUARD

The Marlins farm system has churned out a good number of sound major league players recently. In fact, the system is so productive that even the young regulars on the parent club have to be worried about losing their jobs to someone even younger.

In the last couple of seasons, homegrown prospects like Edgar Renteria, Luis Castillo, Charles Johnson, Billy McMillon, and Ralph Milliard have gotten chances at everyday jobs, while hopefuls such as Felix Heredia, Rob Stanifer, Livan Hernandez, and Tony Saunders have taken the hill.

Not all of those players have worked out, but some of them are exceptional. Renteria, Hernandez, and Johnson will be regulars for years, and possibly perennial All-Stars.

There are more on the way. Outfielders Mark Kotsay and Todd Dunwoody and shortstop Alex Gonzalez are the top prospects in the organization. Second baseman Lionel Hastings, catcher John Roskos, and pitchers Brian Meadows and Dan Chergey can all play ball, but are a bit farther down the chain. Kotsay and Dunwoody will get shots at regular duty this season, the former in left field and the latter in center.

Renteria, already a stellar defender and a helpful offensive player, doesn't turn 23 until August. The 22-year-old Gonzalez, on the other hand, is a hot prospect both afield and at bat in terms of tools, but is very unpolished. Last season at Double A Portland, Gonzalez made 37 errors, many of them on bad throws; hit .254 with only 27 walks; and stole just four bases in 11 tries. Of course, Gonzalez also smacked 19 homers and made a full recovery from the shoulder problems that sidelined him for most of 1996. Eventually the Marlins may shift Renteria to third when Gonzalez is ready.

Kotsay, a 1996 first-round pick, is a well-rounded offensive player: he batted .305 with 20 homers, 75 walks, and 17 steals at Portland in 1997 and even won a short promotion to Florida. Dunwoody has terrific pop (23 homers in 401 at bats last year at Triple A Charlotte) and good speed and can play center field in the majors, but he has terrible problems with breaking pitches. He fanned 129 times last season.

After the trade of closer Robb Nen, it appears that the Marlins will promote Jay Powell (originally an Orioles prospect) from a setup role to closer in '98. Powell, a 26-year-old hard thrower, has been a closer for exactly one of his five professional seasons (5-4 with 24 saves and a 1.87 ERA at Double A Portland in 1995).

While all of these top prospects may not pan out, the Marlins are well-positioned to feed a steady stream of talent from their system to the major for the next few years. Everyone in baseball seems to agree that their organization is overflowing with prospects, as multiple players from the Florida farm system were snatched up in the expansion and Rule V drafts.

NOW INTRODUCING...

After the smoke had cleared from the trading floor, the Marlins were left with a very unsettled pitching staff but a relatively set lineup. While the Fish badly wanted to move the multimillion-dollar contracts of Sheffield, Bonilla, and Leiter, there were no takers, so all three veterans will probably be around for the ceremonial hoisting of the world championship flag at Pro Player Stadium in April.

The rotation starters, after Al Leiter and Series MVP Livan Hernandez, will be chosen from a group of young, inexperienced, but talented hurlers. The prime contenders are Heredia (who will probably be converted to starting), Ludwick, Barrios, and Medina. Prospect Andy Larkin, who pitched badly at Triple A last year after missing most of 1995 and 1996 due to an elbow injury, probably won't be

THE MOMENT OF
TRUTH

In a season where the Marlins won several games on key late-inning home runs, the September 3 contest against Baltimore was one of the most dramatic. In front of a crowd of 35,988 at Pro Player Stadium and a national TV audience on ESPN, the Orioles came back from an early 2-0 deficit to grab a 6-3 lead in the fifth inning. In the last of the sixth Florida scored three runs to tie the game. The score stayed 6-6 until **Gary Sheffield**'s ninth-inning home run off Shawn Boskie gave the Marlins a 7-6 win. On the night, Sheffield had three hits and threw out two Baltimore baserunners.

BEST DEAL

Owner Wayne Huizenga made a lot of high-profile signings in the off-season, and almost all of them paid off handsomely—at least in the short term. The best move was bringing in **Moises Alou**, a quality hitter and outfielder who turned out to be the club's top offensive player in 1997. But he was dealt to Houston after the season in Florida's fire sale.

WORST DEAL

On March 26 the Marlins acquired outfielder **Cliff Floyd** from Montreal but had to deal pitcher **Dustin Hermanson** to do it. While Floyd is a great physical talent with power some compare to that of the all-time greats, he hasn't ever turned that potential into production. He's 26 and may get a chance at regular duty, but has hit just .245 with 12 homers in 567 at bats against righthanders in his career—very poor for a lefthanded batter. Hermanson is an immensely talented pitcher who could be a quality starter for years.

137

1. **Mark Kotsay, OF.** The first player from the 1996 draft to make the majors, Kotsay was the Marlins first-round selection and fully merited the choice. In his first pro campaign Kotsay hit .306 with 20 homers, 75 walks, and 17 steals at Double A Portland. He could be a regular for the Marlins as early as this year.

2. **Derrek Lee, 1B.** The 22-year-old righthanded-hitter had a productive 1997 at Triple A Las Vegas, but he hit only 13 homers after clouting 34 the season before at Memphis. Lee raised his batting average 45 points, and also cut his strikeouts and walked 60 times, but was then sent to Florida in the Kevin Brown trade. Lee isn't especially good at first base, his only position.

3. **Oscar Henriquez, P.** Brought over from Houston in the Moises Alou deal, the 24-year-old Henriquez is a hot prospect due to his 95-mph fastball. If he can improve on a second pitch, Henriquez will be a big league closer. In 1996 he saved 15 for Kissimmee in the Class A Florida State League; last season he nailed down 12 saves at Triple A New Orleans and whiffed 80 hitters in 74 innings.

4. **Todd Dunwoody, OF.** A 22-year-old center fielder with a strong arm and big league power, Dunwoody may begin the 1998 season playing every day for the Marlins despite his not handling the strike zone in the minor leagues. At Triple A Charlotte in 1997 he hit 23 homers, but fanned 129 times in 401 at bats and batted .262.

5. **Rafael Medina, P.** Traded from the Yankees to the Padres last summer for Hideki Irabu, Medina came to the Marlins in the Kevin Brown trade. Medina, 23, is a righthander with a mid-90s fastball, who is expected to enter the Marlins' rotation sometime in the next year. He'll have to improve his control to do so.

6. **Alex Gonzalez, SS.** Called by some a better defensive shortstop than Edgar Renteria—which is really saying something—Gonzalez turned 21 in February. He is a raw offensive player, hitting 19 homers at Portland last season but with a .254 average and only 27 walks. He could be in the majors sometime later this season.

7. **Eric Ludwick, P.** Acquired from Oakland over the winter for Kurt Abbott, Ludwick will be looked at for rotation duty this spring in Florida. The 26-year-old righthander, a breaking-ball pitcher with good command and control, has been with four organizations but never gotten a fair shake in the majors.

8. **Rob Stanifer, P.** Last year in 22 games for Triple A Charlotte, the four-year pro had a 4-0 record and four saves despite a 4.88 ERA. Since he does not throw very hard, Stanifer will probably be a situational or long reliever for Florida this season. Nonetheless, the Marlins have kept him on their 40-man roster for two years.

9. **Kevin Millar, 1B.** A bit too old (25) for Double A, Millar had a spectacular 1997 at Portland. His .342 average and 131 RBIs led the Eastern League, and he hit 32 home runs and took 66 walks. There may not be room for him in Florida, but he could be a quality hitter on somebody's club in 1998.

10. **Mike Villano, P.** Converted from catcher in 1995. Villano was used as a reliever in Class A and Double A, but made 11 starts at Triple A Phoenix after a mid-1997 promotion. He has three strong pitches and just needs a little more experience. He was 5-3 at Phoenix with a 4.15 ERA—a very good mark for that ballpark. Villano, 26, heads to Florida with a chance to stick in the bullpen.

11. **Fletcher Bates, OF.** At Class A St. Lucie he batted .300 with 41 extra-base hits in 253 at bats. Promoted to Double A Binghamton, Bates hit .257 with 13 homers. Bates, doesn't have great speed or defensive skills, so he'll have to hit his way up.

138

ready until midseason or later. Highly regarded prospect Henriquez could emerge from spring training as the closer, but he will more likely set up for Powell.

Assuming Bonilla's rehabilitation from wrist surgery doesn't carry over into the regular season, the Fish will start holdovers Counsell, Renteria, Bonilla and Sheffield at second, short, third, and right. Dunwoody should end up starting in center, with Kotsay flanking him in left. First base will be held down by Derrek Lee or Cliff Floyd, the two of whom may well end up platooning. Veteran reserve Jim Eisenreich will probably be dealt during spring training.

THE DYSFUNCTIONAL FAMILY

The Marlins were able to win the NL wild-card berth despite scoring just 740 runs, which ranked eighth in the league. Florida plays in one of the better pitchers' parks in the league, but that alone does not address the team's offensive dysfunction. Several players contributed to the team's slump at the plate:

• Gary Sheffield. A late-season rush brought his final totals to .250, 21, 71, far below what was expected of him. Sheffield walked 121 times, which added tremendously to the offense as well as to Bonilla's RBI total, but a third-place hitter earning as much as he does ($6.1 million last year) has to do a whole lot more.

• Jeff Conine. While he had never been a great hitter, Conine had always been steady and productive. In '97 he had by far the worst season of his career, leaving the Marlins searching for an answer. Darren Daulton, brought over midseason from Philadelphia, did not entirely fill the first-base gap.

• Luis Castillo. When the diminutive young infielder came up in '96 to play second base for Florida, it was immediately clear that his was one of the slower and weaker bats to surface in the majors in recent memory. While a

shortage of power is not in itself fatal, Castillo has to work so hard to meet the ball that he gets nothing on his swings. Although he takes a few walks and fields his position very well, he isn't ready to hit major league pitching and is not yet a good basestealer. When Castillo, still just 22, failed in the leadoff spot, the Marlins were stuck with . . .

• Devon White. It is has been clear for several years that White is not even an average major league leadoff hitter. However, the Marlins were forced to find a new top-of-the-order guy after Castillo washed out. Leyland chose White, even though many others might have been better (Jim Eisenreich, John Cangelosi, Craig Counsell, even Edgar Renteria). Although White walked more than usual, he was bothered for much of the season by injuries and hit just .245.

White continued to lead off during the postseason, even with the lefthanded-hitting Counsell in the lineup. White had his usual miserable performance during the playoffs and Series, not getting on in front of Sheffield and virtually ensuring that the club's top power threat would be walked at least once per game.

THE FUNCTIONAL FAMILY

The Marlins were full of human-interest stories last season. Their top outfield reserve, Jim Eisenreich, had come back strong from early-career problems with Tourette's syndrome. Outfielder-infielder Cliff Floyd had returned from a broken arm suffered in a horrific on-field collision. Florida called up a relief pitcher, Antonio Alfonseca, who has six fingers on each hand and six toes on each foot. Pitcher Mark Hutton became the first Australian to start a major league game. Outfielder Russ Morman is the active leader in career minor league homers. And new first baseman Darren Daulton played the entire season on battle-scarred knees that had endured 10 operations in his career.

139

FLORIDA MARLINS
1997 TEAM STATISTICS

BATTING/BASERUNNING

	Raw	Rank	+/- %		Raw	Rank	+/- %		Raw	Rank	+/- %
R	740	8	-1	BA	.259	9	-1	SB	115	10	-11
R/G	4.57	8	-1	HR	136	10	-12	CS	58	9	-3
OBA	.346	2	+4	LH	300	11	-4	SB%	66.5	9	-2
SA	.395	12	-4	BB	686	1	+25				
PRO	.741	7	0	SO	1,074	5	-2				

PITCHING/FIELDING

	Raw	Rank	+/- %		Raw	Rank	+/- %		Raw	Rank	+/- %
OR	669	4	-10	BA	.250	3	-4	OSB	95	2	-25
RA/G	4.13	4	-10	HR	131	3	-16	OCS	70	12	+19
OOB	.334	8	0	LH	281	5	-10	OSB%	57.6	1	-15
OSA	.384	4	-6	BB	639	14	+15	FA	.981	7	0
PRO	.718	6	-3	SO	1,188	4	+7	GDP	128	9	+8

140

BATTING BY LINEUP SLOTS

	R	HR	RBI	BA	OBA	SA
1	82	7	56	.243	.312	.319
2	99	6	58	.284	.340	.359
3	108	23	81	.256	.368	.427
4	96	18	92	.253	.373	.411
5	102	24	125	.288	.366	.496
6	83	21	101	.299	.387	.474
7	69	22	83	.263	.361	.434
8	56	9	65	.262	.352	.379
9	45	6	42	.177	.249	.254

BATTING BY DEFENSIVE POSITION

	R	HR	RBI	BA	OBA	SA
C	59	21	84	.263	.365	.454
1B	81	20	90	.251	.351	.417
2B	67	5	47	.253	.317	.335
3B	85	17	103	.298	.374	.455
SS	96	6	60	.277	.332	.350
LF	94	25	99	.282	.353	.458
CF	93	10	87	.252	.347	.376
RF	103	24	87	.265	.414	.441
DH	9	1	4	.206	.341	.353
PH	23	4	25	.253	.337	.369
P	18	3	17	.142	.186	.200

TEAM PITCHING

	W-L	CG	QS	QS%	<6	>6	IPS	IP	ERA	OPR
ROTATION	64-49	12	95	59	28	61	6.1	988.1	3.76	.709

	W-L	GR	SV	BSV	HD	BHD	IRS%	IP	ERA	OPR
BULLPEN	28-21	404	39	20	150	69	33	458.1	3.97	.738

THE SPY: BASEBALL '98

1998 PROJECTIONS

BATTING

PLAYER	BA	G	AB	R	H	2B	3B	HR	RBI	BB	SO	SB	CS	SA	OBA
Bonilla, Bobby	.290	150	557	83	161	33	4	20	97	67	84	3	4	.474	.366
Booty, Josh	.216	9	32	3	7	1	0	1	5	2	14	0	0	.389	.259
Cangelosi, John	.269	69	144	26	39	6	1	1	10	22	25	8	3	.345	.365
Castillo, Luis	.263	71	255	31	67	7	0	0	9	27	60	20	9	.290	.334
Counsell, Craig	.267	93	341	50	91	20	5	3	41	33	42	6	0	.382	.332
Dunwoody, Todd	.234	90	322	52	75	12	6	15	45	29	129	14	0	.454	.298
Eisenreich, Jim	.306	80	212	27	65	14	1	3	26	21	21	3	0	.415	.368
Floyd, Cliff	.232	115	244	35	57	15	2	8	31	38	59	9	2	.415	.335
Johnson, Charles	.242	146	484	49	117	26	1	20	64	64	121	0	2	.422	.331
Knorr, Randy	.251	16	51	5	13	2	0	1	6	5	10	0	0	.351	.313
Kotsay, Mark	.250	76	292	55	73	15	2	9	40	40	52	9	0	.406	.341
Lee, Derek	.278	66	236	37	65	13	1	6	27	27	75	6	0	.417	.352
Milliard, Ralph	.264	23	87	13	23	2	1	1	9	7	14	3	0	.371	.320
Natal, Bob	.225	12	37	4	8	2	0	1	6	2	6	0	0	.413	.273
Renteria, Edgar	.292	152	609	93	178	22	3	5	51	46	106	31	12	.365	.342
Sheffield, Gary	.263	147	480	94	126	24	1	27	86	124	74	14	8	.488	.414
Zaun, Greg	.275	52	126	18	35	8	1	2	16	19	16	1	0	.408	.372

141

PITCHING

PITCHER	W	L	SV	ERA	G	GS	IP	H	HR	BB	SO
Alfonseca, Antonio	4	3	2	3.88	49	0	65	67	8	22	41
Barrios, Manuel	6	3	0	3.30	58	0	85	72	5	35	66
Fernandez, Alex	5	4	0	3.76	11	11	77	72	9	24	62
Heredia, Felix	7	4	0	4.38	88	0	86	83	4	46	78
Henriquez, Oscar	5	3	7	3.08	65	0	79	71	4	32	70
Hernandez, Livan	8	8	0	4.10	27	27	149	142	9	73	90
Larkin, Andy	4	4	0	4.62	15	15	74	75	11	35	44
Leiter, Al	11	9	0	3.93	27	27	160	135	12	95	142
Ludwick, Eric	5	4	0	3.79	26	12	83	79	10	31	67
Powell, Jay	6	2	7	3.83	75	0	80	75	4	35	63
Stanifer, Rob	1	2	1	4.51	34	0	42	40	8	14	26
Medina, Rafael	4	4	0	4.36	15	15	78	80	11	35	48

MANAGEMENT

Manager	General Manager	Owner
Felipe Alou Career Record 470-399 .541	Jim Beattie	Claude Brochu

1997 RECORD

Won-Lost	Pct.	Division Finish/GB	Wild Card Finish/GB
78-84	.481	4 E -23	6 -14

Preseason Consensus Projection	4 (3.43)

1st Half	2nd Half	Home	Road	Intradivision	Interleague
45-35	33-49	45-36	33-48	18-30	12-3

Comebacks	Blowouts	Nailbiters
11-9	16-25	37-44

142

AN EXCRUCIATING SEASON

The 1997 season was the darkest of several dark recent seasons for the overachieving but under-funded Expos. Reaching a new low since the club was rebuilt in the early 1990s, a weak club stumbled to a poor 78-84 record and a fourth-place finish, showing little of the spirit, drive, or competence that has marked manager Felipe Alou's clubs. Things got so bad that, at times, it seemed as if a parody of the Expos, rather than the club itself, was on the field.

It wasn't that the team's record was so bad, it was the way the year ended that had Expos fans tearing their hair out. Montreal has had worse records several times in the '90s (most recently in '95), but there was something for fans to hang their hopes on after those losing campaigns.

Continuing the club's longtime policy of scraping the barrel for fringe players to fill in, veteran righthander Anthony Telford (out of the majors since 1993!) led the Expos' staff by making 65 appearances. He was at least of acceptable quality. Other last-chancers tried but found wanting in the bullpen included Salomon Torres and Lee Smith. Fellow trash-can pickup Marc Valdes pitched reasonably well in a minor role.

The Shop-N-Save approach also netted opening day starting pitcher Jim Bullinger, who was predictably horrible, and Dustin Hermanson, who was quite promising after being acquired from San Diego in spring training.

Besides being bad, Montreal was unlucky. Lefthander Rheal Cormier pitched but one game for the Expos before being diagnosed with an elbow injury that ended his season. He left the club after the season via free agency. Promising righthander Matt Wagner, acquired from Seattle in the Jeff Fassero deal, missed all of 1997 with back and shoulder injuries. Meanwhile, sore-shouldered third baseman Shane Andrews crashed and burned (sent down after fanning 20 times in 64 at bats), which forced yet another veteran fill-in, Doug Strange, to man the hot corner almost every day.

The only regulars who played above-average ball were first baseman David Segui (.307, 21 homers), second baseman Mike Lansing (.281, 20 homers), and catcher Darrin Fletcher (.277, 17 homers). All have now departed.

Other everyday players put up some flashy numbers but were, ultimately, disappointments. Rondell White, finally healthy, played in 150 games for the first time in his career. However, he did not have a particularly good year despite hitting .270 with 28 homers. He wasn't much on the basepaths and walked just 31 times while whiffing 111, posting a subpar .316 on-base. He did show above-average range in center field, though.

Shortstop Mark Grudzielanek smacked 54 doubles to lead the major leagues but was a mediocre offensive player anyway. Asked to lead off, he made nearly 700 plate appearances and walked just 23 times and, oddly, batted but .224 against lefthanders. Certainly it isn't Grudzielanek's fault that Felipe Alou asked him to bat first—something he can't do—but "G" didn't do anything as well in '97 as he had in '96. Like White, however, he plays excellent defense. He and Lansing formed perhaps the best double-play combination in baseball.

Left fielder Henry Rodriguez, a 1996 All Star, reverted back to form, hitting .244 with 26 homers. While he will hit home runs this season for the Cubs (to whom he was traded in the off-season), Rodriguez is not a particularly good player, playing bad defense and having little speed.

Rookie Vladimir Guerrero, given the everyday right field job in spring training, was disabled three times but still managed to hit .302 with 11 homers when able. He had 10 assists, but he also made 12 errors. Guerrero symbolizes hope for the future, which this club badly needs.

If not for the outstanding performances of Lansing and pitcher Pedro Martinez, this team might have ended up worse than the Phillies. Lansing, having his best season yet, hit .281 with 45 doubles and 20 homers. He made just nine errors in 144 games at second while displaying good range.

In previous years when the team's lineup lacked a true superstar, a quality bench helped keep the Expos in the

TEAM MVP

Pedro Martinez was the best pitcher in baseball during 1997, and (despite some competition) the Expos' best player. How he could finish "only" 17-8 while posting a major league best 1.90 ERA and striking out 305 in 241.1 innings is hard to understand, but then again, without Pedro the Expos' record was just 61-76.

BIGGEST SURPRISE

Acquired from Florida in spring training, righthanded pitcher **Dustin Hermanson** made 28 starts and four relief appearances, finishing with a 3.69 ERA and an 8-8 record. He fanned 136 batters in 158.1 frames after having spent his entire professional career in the bullpen. Hermanson is raw but has the stuff to be a rotation anchor. He will get a chance to take that job in 1998.

BIGGEST DISAPPOINTMENT

Shane Andrews was supposed to take the third base job and run with it in 1997, but instead he batted .203 in 18 games before missing the rest of the year with a sore left shoulder. In his absence the Expos used Doug Strange, Jose Vidro, and others in what was a weak spot on the diamond all season.

143

hunt. But stretched beyond its capabilities, the 1997 Montreal reserve corps was poor.

Fan favorite F.P. Santangelo was pressed into action at six positions and could not duplicate the magic of his rookie season. He hit .249, though he did manage a .379 on-base percentage due to his good eye. Andy Stankiewicz hit .224 in 107 at bats, while 25-year-old first base hopeful Ryan McGuire showed some offense (.299 average, .410 on-base) without a lot of power (3 homers in 184 at bats). Not-ready-for-prime-time third baseman Jose Vidro, 22 years old, was yanked up from the minors in desperation, but played poorly in 67 games. The performances of out-fielders Hensley "Bam Bam" Meulens, Sherman Obando, and Joe Orsulak are best left undiscussed.

WAIT TILL NEXT YEAR—AGAIN

Rookie catcher Chris Widger, brought over in trade for Jeff Fassero last year, was perhaps the Expos' biggest disappointment. He was expected to throw far better than platoon partner Darrin Fletcher, but didn't, allowing 84 percent of baserunners to steal. NL runners took full advantage of his weakness, stealing 116 times against Widger, averaging more than 1.5 stolen bases per game. This was by far the worst rate in the league, and he made 11 errors in 85 games to boot!

Widger also didn't hit, batting just .234 overall and .209 against righthanded pitching. The Expos, however, want him to succeed, so even though prospect Raul Chavez is in waiting, expect to see Widger play regularly in '98.

The people throwing the ball to Widger, Fletcher, and Chavez were a motley mix of good talent and fortunate flotsam getting another chance. Montreal is the best rehabilitation clinic in Major League Baseball—maybe the team should change its name to the St. Elsewheres—but it couldn't do anything for Jim Bullinger, who finished with the NL's third-worst ERA among qualifying pitchers. Multi-organization bad boy Jeff Juden won 11 games before being traded to Cleveland for Steve Kline in midseason. (Even the patient Felipe Alou could no longer stand having Juden around; the beefy righthander allowed 41 runners to steal in just 130 innings, and he walked nearly four hitters per game.)

However, veteran southpaw Carlos Perez came back after

144

missing a full season due to serious elbow problems to pitch 206.2 innings with a 3.88 ERA, and 24-year-old Dustin Hermanson showed why he was considered a top prospect a few years earlier. Both should perform well for Les Expos in 1998, although there is a legitimate question about whether Perez can stand such a heavy workload with his recent injury history.

Sadly, the spectacular performance turned in by Pedro Martinez was often the only reason to watch the Expos play last year. Fanning an incredible 305 hitters in just 241 innings (11.37 per game, an NL best), he managed to lose eight games while winning 17, despite holding opponents to a league-leading 1.90 ERA and a league-low .184 batting average. He could have sued his mates for nonsupport, as Montreal scored just 3.45 runs per game for him, the lowest figure among any of the team's starters. Pedro hurled 13 complete games to lead the NL by a wide margin.

It was the best season by a Montreal pitcher in the club's history, far better than those of Bill Stoneman and Carl Morton in the early '70s, Steve Rogers in the late '70s and early '80s, or Dennis Martinez, Ken Hill and Jeff Fassero in the 1990s. Pedro was so good that even pitching for a bad team in a media backwater couldn't keep people from thinking that he might have been the best pitcher in the game. He has gotten better every year he's been in the majors, and he's just 26.

Unfortunately for Montreal fans, the Expos decided to manage their annual fiscal crisis by dumping their two best players. Both Martinez and Lansing were traded for comparatively little, to Boston and Colorado, respectively, marking the latest episode in Montreal's wait-till-next-year philosophy.

No major league team has so consistently hemorrhaged talent like this for such a long, long time. While the Expos aren't the 1998 version of the 1899 Cleveland Spiders (20-134), the continued plundering of their talent-rich roster by wealthier teams has reached the point of absurdity. Right now, the Expos are little more than a perpetual tryout camp for good young players who, if they prove they can play, will be picked off by teams with a chance of winning the pennant.

The only exception of note in recent years has been center fielder Rondell White, signed to a five-year deal in spring 1996. Admittedly, Montreal must engage in a baseball kind of triage, in which management has to make difficult decisions about who to keep and who to let walk—or trade before they walk.

Why the team hasn't distinguished between overrated players who clearly should be traded (e.g., Henry Rodriguez and Wil Cordero), excellent players who were legitimately too expensive to keep (e.g., Larry Walker, John Wetteland, and Pedro Martinez), and excellent players who they might have tied up in cost-effective, long-term deals, a la Rondell White (e.g., Marquis Grissom, Jeff Fassero and Mike Lansing), is the $72 million question.

FAN SUPPORT IS A TWO-WAY PROPOSITION

One of the common refrains of baseball pundits and professionals alike is that Montreal fans just won't support their team. Let's get real: Why should they? If the Expos won't take the financial risk to lock up some of their homegrown talent so that they can win a championship, why should the fans take the emotional risk and care about the team?

Watching quality players leave the team year after year has to be incredibly frustrating for Montreal fans. Why should people buy tickets to see the Expos if every time a veteran player gets to the peak of his game, he's traded for prospects or allowed to leave as a free agent? Baseball fans want to be emotionally attached to their players, and this constant turnover cruelly denies them that emotional bond.

One of the saddest legacies of the 1994 strike is the fact that the Expos were poised to make it to the World Series for the first time ever when the season ended prematurely. The Expos were leading the NL East by six games over the defending division-winning Braves on August 12, and they had the best record in either league at the time.

Who knows how many lifelong Expos fans would have been created in Quebec by a chance to root for Montreal in the World Series? Since Expos ownership had thrown its lot in with the hard-liners who wanted to break the union, it may have been just punishment for them, but surely not for their fans.

THE MOMENT OF TRUTH

Montreal was actually 11 games over .500 (40-29) on **June 18** after Carlos Perez shut out the Orioles 1-0. From that point on, however, the club was dreadful, dropping from 3.5 games back in the NL East to 10.5 back in just 17 days. The Expos never again resembled a contending club.

BEST DEAL

Marc Valdes was a Florida first-round pick in 1993, but never was able to break through with the Marlins. Claimed off waivers in December 1996, he found a place in Montreal and pitched well enough to enter the running for a rotation berth for 1998. Valdes made 48 appearances for the Expos, including seven starts, and finished with a 4-4 mark and a fine 3.13 ERA.

145

WORST DEAL

The Expos' decisions to trade **Pedro Martinez** and **Mike Lansing** once again gutted a rebuilding club. At least Montreal got something for Martinez in ready-to-go hurler Carl Pavano; the booty for Mike Lansing—two highly regarded low minor league pitchers and a minor league outfielder—may be good on paper for the player development department, but why couldn't the Expos pick up at least one quality major league regular in exchange for their best regular?

TOP PROSPECTS
SPRING 1998

1. **Brad Fullmer, 1B.** Slated to start for the Expos, Fullmer had an outstanding 1997 at three levels. In 94 games at Double A he batted .311 with 19 homers and 62 RBIs. Sent to Triple A, Fullmer hit .297 with three homers in 24 games. Finally, a 19-game promotion to Montreal produced a .300 average and three homers. While Fullmer doesn't walk that often, he makes contact and his power has greatly improved. Defense won't be a strong point.

2. **Carl Pavano, P.** Pavano is a six-foot, five-inch righthander with an excellent fastball, and good command. At Triple A Pawtucket in 1997, he was 11-6 with a 3.12 ERA in 28 starts after beginning the season disabled with a sore elbow. The 22-year-old Pavano has proven that he is ready to advance to the next level, and after the trade from Boston he could be a rotation anchor for Montreal as early as this season.

3. **Orlando Cabrera, IF.** The trade of Mike Lansing opens up a spot at second base for the Expos, and Cabrera could fill it. The 23-year-old infielder is a fine defensive player with good instincts and an improving bat. He played for four teams in 1997: Class A West Palm Beach (.276, 32 steals in 69 games), Double A Harrisburg (.308, five homers in 35 games), Triple A Ottawa (.262 in 31 games), and, Montreal. He is fast, and has some pop.

4. **Hiram Bocachica, SS.** The Expos are very excited about his ability. A first-round 1994 draft pick, Bocachica has a very strong arm, good range, and very fine speed. Unfortunately, he made 32 errors at Harrisburg last year and may be switched to second base. The 23-year-old Bocachica's bat is improving; he hit 11 homers with a .278 average at Harrisburg.

5. **Ben Fleetham, P.** Fleetham led the Eastern League in 1997 with 30 saves, picking up 11 in a row at one point. Striking out 69 men in 50 innings is a good way to get noticed, and Fleetham's stuff has improved since he signed in 1994. He had pitched in just 70 pro games before 1997 and is a step away from the majors.

6. **Trey Moore, P.** Seattle's second-round draft pick in 1994 came over in the 1996 deal that sent Jeff Fassero west. The 25-year-old righthander had a solid 11-6 season at Double A, and at this point, if he can improve his control just a little, he could be in the majors.

7. **Mike Thurman, P.** A first-round pick in 1994, Thurman is a pitcher rather than a thrower—his fastball isn't dominating but he knows what he needs to do to be successful. He did well at Harrisburg (9-6, 3.81, 30 walks in 116 innings) but struggled both at Ottawa and with the Expos. Thurman could win a job in the Montreal rotation this spring.

8. **Javier Vazquez, P.** Aside from Pavano, Vazquez is the top mound prospect in the Montreal system. He's only rated this low because he's 22 this summer and relatively inexperienced. Last season he was 6-3 with a 2.16 ERA in 19 starts for West Palm Beach, fanning 100 and walking 28 in 112.2 innings. Sent to Harrisburg, Vazquez piled up a 4-0 record.

9. **Shayne Bennett, P.** The Australian righthander has been effective in a short relief role although his control has occasionally deserted him. Bennett began his career with the Red Sox; moving to Montreal gives him a clearer route to the majors. Bennett needs to have command of his breaking ball.

10. **Israel Alcantara, 3B.** There is no question about Alcantara's power. He hit .283 at Harrisburg last season with 27 homers in just 300 at bats, though he did fan 84 times and hit just nine doubles. The real problem may be that he has no defensive position, failing to impress at either third or first. The 25-year-old Alcantara has some real holes.

11. **Jon Saffer, OF.** A lefthanded hitter with moderate physical gifts, Saffer, 25 this season, does a bit of everything: get on base, hit for line drive power, and steal a few bases. He hit only .267 at Triple A, but the Expos' outfield reserves last year were bad, meaning there is opportunity for him to move up.

146

WHO ARE THESE GUYS?

Shayne Bennett
Jose Paniagua
Mike Thurman
Mike Johnson
Everett Stull
Steve Falteisek
Steve Kline
Rick DeHart

All eight were rookie pitchers used by Montreal last season. None was especially effective. If even one of these pitchers turns out to be a real major leaguer, the Expos will be very happy. The best bet was Paniagua, but he won't be pitching for Montreal, having been selected by Tampa in the expansion draft. The impressive farm-system talent that the Expos have depended upon to help prop up a weak big league club is currently very thin—thinner than it's been in years.

MEN OF LETTERS

While Montreal may not have led the league in anything else, they did in letters used. Alou could run this lineup out on any given night:

P   Dustin Hermanson
C   Darrin Fletcher
1B   Ryan McGuire
2B   Andy Stankiewicz
SS   Mark Grudzielanek
3B   Shane Andrews
LF   Henry Rodriguez
CF   F.P. Santangelo
RF   Vladimir Guerrero

That doesn't even include closer Ugueth Urtain Urbina, the first player in big-league history with the initials U.U.U. The farm system has Israel Alcantara, Orlando Cabrera, Fernando Seguignol, Hiram Bocachica, and Benjamin Fleetham on the way, so keep your pencils sharpened and your guidebook handy.

OH, I SEE

Cubs announcer Ron Santo doesn't like F.P. Santangelo. It's not because he's a Cub-killer (though he has shown signs of being one) or that he doesn't hustle enough for Santo's taste (he does). In Santo's words, "Those initials, that F.P., really bother me. I don't like that F.P."

The rumor that the Expos can't afford to buy him an entire first name is not true; the 29-year-old utility player simply prefers F.P. to his given name of Frank-Paul.

BRAD FULLMER: THE REAL DEAL?

Many people thought first baseman David Segui was the best position player the Expos had in 1997, before he, predictably, left to sign with Seattle this past winter. Now that Segui's gone, Montreal is bound by league rules to put somebody at first base. That somebody could be Brad Fullmer, who was the organization's 1997 minor league player of the year.

Fullmer did indeed blow through the minors in 1997, batting .311 with 19 homers in 94 games at Double A Harrisburg before a 24-game trial at Triple A Ottawa, where he batted .297 in 91 at bats with three homers. Brought up to Montreal, Brad homered in his first big league plate appearance on September 2, against Boston's Bret Saberhagen. He finished with a .300 average and three homers in 40 at bats for the Expos.

A sandwich pick in the 1993 draft, Fullmer enters 1998 at age 23. He has hit for a good average his entire pro career. However, his ultimate value will depend on whether his power increase of 1997 is real and whether he will be disciplined enough to work the count in his favor. Of course, doing so will make his power numbers better as well.

Fullmer's seasonal home run totals as a pro are eight, nine, and 22. He took only 33 walks in nearly 500 plate appearances last year, though he fanned only 25 times. Obviously, Fullmer is an interesting young player who is still developing. If his power is legit, the Expos have a winner.

SEE YA' LATER

In November the Expos sent out their 1997 *Postseason Media Guide*, containing photos of 16 Expos players, manager Felipe Alou, and Youppi!, the team's mascot. Only seven of the players remained with the team by this January—the mascot is apparently not yet eligible for arbitration.

147

1997 TEAM STATISTICS

BATTING/BASERUNNING

	Raw	Rank	+/- %		Raw	Rank	+/- %		Raw	Rank	+/- %
R	691	10	-7	BA	.258	11	-2	SB	75	14	-42
R/G	4.27	10	-7	HR	172	4	+11	CS	46	14	-23
OBA	.316	14	-5	LH	373	1	+19	SB%	62.0	13	-8
SA	.425	3	+4	BB	420	14	-24				
PRO	.741	8	0	SO	1,084	7	-1				

PITCHING/FIELDING

	Raw	Rank	+/- %		Raw	Rank	+/- %		Raw	Rank	+/- %
OR	740	7	-1	BA	.251	4	-4	OSB	192	14	+52
RA/G	4.57	7	-1	HR	149	6	-4	OCS	42	1	-29
OOB	.325	4	-2	LH	291	7	-7	OSB%	82.1	14	+21
OSA	.393	6	-4	BB	557	6	0	FA	.979	14	0
PRO	.718	5	-3	SO	1,138	6	+3	GDP	130	10	+9

BATTING BY LINEUP SLOTS

	R	HR	RBI	BA	OBA	SA
1	84	5	53	.274	.331	.375
2	101	20	73	.279	.336	.462
3	84	26	93	.270	.317	.468
4	93	25	88	.276	.345	.465
5	80	31	105	.274	.326	.489
6	74	17	72	.262	.320	.427
7	74	22	76	.235	.307	.402
8	70	18	64	.259	.329	.444
9	31	8	35	.174	.217	.267

BATTING BY DEFENSIVE POSITION

	R	HR	RBI	BA	OBA	SA
C	68	23	93	.262	.310	.458
1B	91	26	91	.300	.373	.496
2B	95	20	72	.271	.324	.445
3B	74	19	69	.243	.312	.395
SS	76	4	52	.275	.307	.385
LF	74	27	89	.245	.319	.455
CF	94	31	90	.277	.324	.492
RF	83	14	67	.267	.350	.426
DH	2	1	1	.188	.297	.281
PH	13	4	22	.211	.275	.351
P	14	3	13	.140	.166	.198

TEAM PITCHING

	W-L	CG	QS	QS%	<6	>6	IPS	IP	ERA	OPR
ROTATION	57-57	27	82	51	40	62	6.0	965.2	3.93	.697

	W-L	GR	SV	BSV	HD	BHD	IRS%	IP	ERA	OPR
BULLPEN	21-27	390	37	18	121	93	34	481.1	4.54	.758

148

1998 PROJECTIONS

BATTING

PLAYER	BA	G	AB	R	H	2B	3B	HR	RBI	BB	SO	SB	CS	SA	OBA
Andrews, Shane	.226	58	176	23	40	8	0	10	28	15	58	2	0	.443	.287
Cabrera, Orlando	.257	79	263	49	68	15	3	7	32	20	44	11	0	.417	.310
Chavez, Raul	.276	43	136	14	38	8	0	2	22	8	22	1	0	.389	.318
Fullmer, Brad	.273	104	374	53	102	23	2	18	58	23	39	3	0	.485	.315
Grudzielanek, Mark	.289	149	614	80	178	45	3	4	48	24	79	26	8	.395	.316
Guerrero, Vladimir	.293	131	470	62	138	30	2	16	56	26	56	4	6	.469	.329
McGuire, Ryan	.280	75	214	33	60	14	2	4	18	31	42	3	0	.414	.372
Santangelo, F.P.	.259	123	328	49	85	18	5	5	35	44	61	6	4	.387	.346
Stankiewicz, Andy	.253	58	78	10	20	6	0	1	6	5	17	2	1	.368	.301
Vidro, Jose	.270	104	333	40	90	19	1	10	44	23	54	1	0	.428	.317
White, Rondell	.277	151	583	82	161	31	5	22	77	35	105	19	8	.463	.318
Widger, Chris	.242	123	358	39	87	26	4	9	47	28	81	2	0	.412	.297
Stovall, Darond	.263	39	142	20	38	8	1	4	25	15	48	2	0	.412	.335

149

PITCHING

PITCHER	W	L	SV	ERA	G	GS	IP	H	HR	BB	SO
Batista, Miguel	4	4	0	4.64	20	9	72	70	10	28	46
Bennett, Shayne	4	3	2	4.02	37	1	60	59	5	32	37
Dehart, Rick	1	1	0	3.73	15	0	22	20	3	8	17
Falteisek, Steve	2	2	0	5.39	7	5	32	40	3	16	12
Hermanson, Dustin	10	9	0	4.14	44	29	181	160	19	78	152
Johnson, Mike	2	6	1	6.01	26	16	93	102	21	36	59
Kline, Steve	4	4	0	4.47	46	3	72	81	9	23	45
Perez, Carlos	12	12	0	3.97	32	29	186	189	20	43	109
Telford, Anthony	3	4	1	3.81	51	0	73	68	10	27	52
Thurman, Mike	6	4	0	4.28	19	16	95	84	14	27	58
Urbina, Ugueth	5	7	25	4.06	47	5	73	64	11	32	82
Valdes, Marc	4	5	0	3.84	56	12	124	126	5	56	63
Pavano, Carl	9	7	0	4.03	19	19	136	141	12	32	103

MANAGEMENT

Manager	General Manager	Owner
Bobby Valentine Career Record 681-698 .494	Steve Phillips	Fred Wilpon/ Nelson Doubleday

1997 RECORD

Won-Lost 88-74	Pct. .543	Division Finish/GB 3 E -13	Wild Card Finish/GB 2 -4

Preseason Consensus Projection	3 (3.30)

1st Half 2nd Half 45-35 43-39	Home Road 50-31 38-43	Intradivision Interleague 29-19 7-8

Comebacks 17-10	Blowouts 26-19	Nailbiters 40-40

150

FLUSHED WITH SUCCESS

Luckily for the Mets their 1997 season wasn't a Broadway show. If it had been, it'd have closed the first night—if not before. The team had already lost much fan interest after an awful 71-91 season in 1996, its sixth straight sub-.500 campaign. With the world champion Yankees on the other side of town, the team could hardly afford another bad year.

But medical problems crippled the Mets from the start. All three of the club's three top pitching prospects—righthanders Paul Wilson and Jason Isringhausen and left-hander Bill Pulsipher—had gone under the laser the winter before. Wilson had undergone shoulder surgery after the 1996 season, while Pulsipher had elbow surgery. Isringhausen bested them both, having procedures on both his shoulder and his elbow.

Neither Wilson nor Pulsipher would pitch in the major leagues during 1997, and Isringhausen was largely unsuc-

cessful in his attempts to do so. He will sit out all of 1998 as he undergoes reconstructive surgery on his right elbow.

Righthanded reliever Derek Wallace was diagnosed with an aneurysm in his pitching shoulder in March and was lost for nearly the entire season as well.

Without the big three or Wallace, the Mets began the season in San Diego on April 1 in grand fashion, losing 12-5 as the Padres scored 11 runs in the fifth inning.

The club's opening day starting pitcher, Pete Harnisch, had already been experiencing serious problems sleeping, due to his attempts to quit smokeless tobacco. His difficulties got worse and he was ultimately disabled after being diagnosed not only with the shakes but also with depression. Harnisch did not pitch again until August 5, and when he did take the mound he was so bad that he was soon waived; he was claimed by the Brewers.

After a three-game sweep by visiting San Francisco, the

Mets were 3-9 on April 14. A week later they lost to the 0-14 Cubs.

However, the Mets began to win in May. A three-game sweep at St. Louis brought them over .500, and the club never again was under the magic mark. The Mets jousted with the Expos for third place the rest of the first half, then took it over for good in July. A hot streak later that month even brought them into a second-place tie with the Marlins for four days, but a streak in which they lost eight of 10 finished off the club's playoff plans.

Despite that, 1997 was an encouraging year in Flushing. Despite poor seasons from outfielders Bernard Gilkey and Carl Everett, and a traumatic deal sending Lance Johnson, Mark Clark, and Manny Alexander to the Cubs for Brian McRae, Mel Rojas, and Turk Wendell, the Mets finished the season 88-74. New York tied for fifth in the league in runs and finished sixth in ERA. Shea Stadium was a slightly above average park for hitters.

Third sacker Edgardo Alfonzo emerged as a star-quality offensive and defensive player, while first baseman John Olerud had an encouraging comeback season. Pitchers Rick Reed, Brian Bohanon, Bobby Jones, John Franco, and Dave Mlicki all performed well. Todd Hundley played All Star ball with the bat and glove, and Butch Huskey hit 24 homers. Manager Bobby Valentine finally had a good year, using his bench well and getting the most that he could out of his healthy starters.

How much of the Mets' fine 1997 play is sustainable? That depends on several factors:

•Can left fielder Gilkey, center fielder McRae, right fielder Huskey and new arrival Rich Becker provide sufficient offense?

•Can the starting pitchers hang tough? With former hotshots Paul Wilson, Jason Isringhausen, and Bill Pulsipher now yesterday's news, New York was on the prowl over the winter for a top starting pitcher. The Mets traded some prospects for Florida southpaw Al Leiter, the hard throwing, sometimes brilliant lefthander who has led both leagues in walks and was getting hit hard at the end of last year. And the team signed Japanese righthander Yoshii Masato, a 10-year veteran, in January to an inexpensive deal loaded with incentive bonuses. Masato is not a hard thrower, but he is a polished pitcher who has improved in

TEAM MVP

The Mets' best player is **Todd Hundley**, a catcher with good defensive skills who has become a fearsome hitter. Last season he clouted 30 home runs and batted .273, taking 83 walks as well. Unfortunately for New York, he underwent right elbow surgery two days before the end of the season and may not be back in 1998.

BIGGEST SURPRISE

Following two mediocre seasons spent in utility roles, 23-year-old **Edgardo Alfonzo** was given the everyday third base assignment in 1997 and exploded. He lifted his batting average 54 points to .315, hit 27 doubles and 10 homers, took 63 walks, and played Gold Glove–caliber defense.

151

BIGGEST DISAPPOINTMENT

After signing a big four-year contract, left fielder **Bernard Gilkey** went into the tank. He hit .249 with 18 home runs and 78 RBIs, numbers far below those expected of him after a fine 1996 season—a year which was actually far above his norm, and therefore isn't likely to ever be repeated.

recent seasons and had impressed Mets manager Bobby Valentine when he was working in Japan.

A rotation composed of the likes of Bobby Jones, Rick Reed, Brian Bohanon, Al Leiter, Dave Mlicki, and Juan Acevedo, Masato or Armando Reynoso might be short on impressive names, but it should be good-to-excellent. As Reed shows (see below), all it takes sometimes is the right amount of trust from management.

•Can the refurbished bullpen, which lost Cory Lidle this off-season but gained John Hudek and Dennis Cook, provide more reliable performance in the late innings?

•How about power? The Mets hit 153 home runs last year, sixth in the NL. That is expected to decrease in 1998 due to the elbow injury Todd Hundley suffered late in '97 (after hitting 30 homers). Hundley may not play at all in '98, depending on how his rehabilitation from surgery progresses.

The club spent much of the winter trying to trade for a power hitter, with no success. Last year's other 20-homer Mets—Butch Huskey (24) and John Olerud (22)—still left something lacking in the power department and, at least in Huskey's case, will be expected to provide more sock in '98. Huskey's professional home-run peak was 28 in 109 games at Triple A in '95, while Olerud's was 24 in '93 with Toronto.

•And how about getting on base? One thing the Mets must do to keep their offense productive is put more runners on. Poor seasons from Rey Ordonez (.255 on-base percentage), Carl Everett (.308), Alex Ochoa (.300), Brian McRae (.317), and Bernard Gilkey (.338) all did substantial damage to the offense. With Everett and Ochoa now gone in trades and Rich Becker on board, things should improve. McRae and Gilkey are likely to rebound somewhat in '98, and it's hard to see how Ordonez could be much worse.

•And then there's the catching. Minus Hundley, New York's catching situation is still a mess. Alberto Castillo, a good defender who can't hit, is available, as is the current favorite to start in Hundley's absence, veteran Todd Pratt. Castoff Tim Spehr has also been added to the mix. Pratt has always been capable of hitting for power, but his defense and low batting average kept him from playing. He surprised everyone by hitting .301 at Triple A Norfolk and

.283 for the Mets in '97 while throwing better than expected. Nevertheless, counting on Pratt at 31, to repeat that performance over a full season is questionable, and a spring trade for a more productive receiver may be in the cards.

FINALLY BREAKING THROUGH

The Mets entered 1997 with starting pitching as a weakness. They ended the season with starting pitching as a strength.

The men who made the starting pitching a strength included: Bobby Jones, who had a fine 15-9 campaign; Dave Mlicki, who was the staff workhorse, making 32 starts; and two veterans whom no one could logically have expected to have a big impact: Brian Bohanon and Rick Reed.

Bohanon was the Rangers' first-round draft pick in 1987 out of high school in Houston. A stocky lefthander with a decent fastball, a good curve, and a deceptive sidearm delivery, Bohanon began to have injury problems almost immediately after signing. He had an elbow ligament transplant in 1988, an operation to repair torn shoulder cartilage in 1991, and biceps and finger injuries in 1991.

Also working against him was the developmental philosophy of his own team, one frequently driven by desperation due to an unproductive farm system. Bohanon was 5-0 in 11 starts for the Rangers' Double A club at Tulsa in 1989 after recovering from his elbow surgery, and he appeared to be on track. The next year, however, Texas vaulted him immediately to the majors and into the rotation, and Bohanon got shelled. Sent back to the minors, he returned to the disabled list with a sore rotator cuff.

In both 1990 and 1991 he spent his time shuttling between the hospital, the trainer's table, rehabilitation starts in the minors, and Arlington Stadium. As could have been predicted for a young lefthander, Bohanon was excellent in his minor league starts but had a rocky time getting adjusted to the majors.

Between the injuries and the Rangers' chronic unwillingness to simply let him pitch enough to gain needed experience in the big leagues, Bohanon's career stagnated. He spent much of 1993 with the club as a long reliever, getting nowhere, and after 1994 he was allowed to leave as a free agent.

152

Detroit signed him for 1995 and used him as a long reliever/spot starter. Somehow Bohanon managed to pitch 52 games (10 starts) and 105.2 innings but still compile only a 1-1 record. He was dreadful as a starter, racking up a 7.40 ERA, but pitched well in relief.

At this point Bohanon was in desperate straits. Even the Tigers no longer wanted him, and he signed with the Jays. After working effectively in 31 games at Triple A Syracuse as a spot reliever, Bohanon was called up for 20 games with Toronto and was—you guessed it—terrible.

Coming into '97 Bohanon hadn't been used exclusively as a starter since 1991-92 when still with the Rangers' organization. The Mets had very few lefthanded options in spring 1997. With Bill Pulsipher out for the year, southpaws of all descriptions were hauled into camp, including Joe Crawford, Yorkis Perez, Rico Jordan, and Kashiwada.

Bohanon sneaked in with them and made the opening day roster as a reliever. He gave up two earned runs in each of his first five appearances, all out of the bullpen. After his fifth game on April 20, Bohanon was sent down.

At this point somebody in the Mets organization decided to use Bohanon as a starter. He was excellent at Triple A Norfolk, going 9-3 with a 2.63 ERA and 84 strikeouts in 96 innings. The Mets brought him up in late July and from that point on reaped the benefits of their patience.

Bohanon made 14 starts for the Mets from July 29 through the end of the season and allowed just 30 runs in those starts. He ended the season with a 6-4 record and a 3.82 ERA, becoming perhaps the most surprising lefthanded starter in the major leagues. Bohanon fanned 66 in his 94.1 innings and continued his pattern of pitching as well (even slightly better) to righthanders as lefthanders.

It seems that he's been around forever, but Bohanon is just 29. If he stays healthy (a big if), he's going to be a steady starter for several years. He is in some ways comparable to Jamie Moyer, another lefty who had decent stuff but kicked around with mediocre clubs for a long time before settling in with one that knew what it was doing.

Exhibit B in this paean to perseverance is Rick Reed. A former replacement player, the righthander is now 32 years old and has finally won himself a job in the majors.

Reed spent three years at Marshall University (Huntington, West Virginia) before being drafted by the

THE MOMENT OF
TRUTH

Two weeks into the season the Mets were already seven games out of first, nestled not-so-comfortably in fourth place. One of the more frustrating days of the season came on **April 13**, in a home-opener doubleheader loss to the visiting Giants. Just four days after that, the Cubs, losers of their first 14 games, beat the Mets to gain their first win of the year.

BEST DEAL

For some reason the Braves no longer thought righthanded reliever **Greg McMichael** could help them, and dumped him on the Mets last winter for righthanded reliever Paul Byrd, who has never been effective in the majors for any extended stretch. Byrd was mediocre-to-poor for the Braves and was sent down to Triple A in July, while McMichael had a fine season in his first go-round in Mets pinstripes (2.98 ERA, 73 hits and 81 strikeouts in 87.2 innings).

WORST DEAL

The decision to sign **Bernard Gilkey**, a 30-year-old outfielder, to a four-year deal with an option for a fifth year was one of the worst decisions the Mets have made in recent memory. While Gilkey has always been an average-to-good player, he had his first big season (1996) at an advanced age (he turned 30 that year), and his signing ties up the club both financially and on the field for a long time.

153

Pirates in the 26th round in 1986. He never had much of a fastball, but quickly climbed up the ladder because he could get hitters out. On August 4, 1988, he got the call to Pittsburgh and shut down the Mets for eight scoreless innings to get his first big league win. After another start in which he allowed four runs in four innings, he was returned to Triple A.

Reed spent the next three years bouncing back and forth between Pittsburgh and Buffalo. Having long established that he could get minor league hitters out, Reed dominated Triple A even after leaving the Pirates, organization for Kansas City after the 1991 season.

However, his lack of premier stuff meant that he was viewed essentially as a career Triple A player and was thus rarely given much of a chance. The 1992 Royals (70-92) allowed him 18 starts, but despite a fine 3.68 ERA, Reed's 3-7 record just didn't look good on his resume. There were many on that staff who pitched worse than Reed, yet the veteran righthander got the boot anyway.

He received look-sees from the Royals and Rangers in 1993 and 1994, then took the bait when offered a chance to be a replacement player in 1995. Stories later reported that Reed's parents were destitute and that the veteran pitcher felt he had nothing to lose by seizing the opportunity.

So Reed signed with the Reds and was sent to Triple A when the replacement baseball sham ended. Called up to the big club later that summer, Reed was shunned by most of his teammates (as all the replacement

154

TOP PROSPECTS
SPRING 1998

1. **Derek Wallace, P.** The righthander came up with an aneurysm in his pitching shoulder during 1997 spring training and pitched just 14 times, all in the minors. His slider, splitter, and four-seam fastball are big league pitches, and Wallace ought to be in the New York bullpen this year. However, he hasn't yet shown, even when healthy, that he deserves more than a setup role.

2. **Jay Payton, OF.** The club's top prospect spent all of 1997 out of action due to a bad elbow. He has only played the schedule once in four pro years due to frequent physical problems. If he is healthy Payton is a high-average hitter with speed and line-drive power. The Mets believe he is best suited for left field. If he is healthy, that is. At age 25, he's going to go from prospect to suspect awfully soon.

3. **Ed Yarnall, P.** A star lefthander out of LSU, Yarnall began playing pro ball last season. He reached Triple A. After going 5-8, 2.48 in 18 starts at St. Lucie, he made five strong starts at Binghamton and one bad one at Triple A. All told, Yarnall fanned 148 men in 143 innings last season, using four pitches, a funky delivery, and solid control. The Mets might call on him as soon as this summer.

4. **Benny Agbayani, OF.** An organizational favorite, the 26-year-old Agbayani batted .310 at Triple A Norfolk with 67 walks, and could be in line for a bench job. He has good speed and some power, having swiped 29 bases and clouted 11 homers in 1997. The righthanded-hitting Agbayani was born and still resides in Hawaii.

5. **Preston Wilson, OF.** At age 17 in 1992 he was the Mets' first-round pick. He has suffered plenty of injuries and, when healthy, has showed power at bat but never conquered his problem of chasing bad pitches. He socked 11 homers in 63 games at Class A St. Lucie, a good total, but fanned 66 times and walked only eight. After a promotion to Double A Binghamton, Wilson then smacked 19 homers in 259 at bats, but also whiffed on 71 occasions. He is a good rightfielder blessed with speed, but unless he cuts down on his swing, Wilson won't make it.

players were when they first made the majors after the strike) and was not retained after the season.

After inking with the Mets for '96 he enjoyed another fine Triple A season, running his career minor league record to 97-58. By that time he had fanned 917 hitters and walked just 249 in 1,379 minor league innings, because he was 31 years old and without much big league experience or stuff, Reed was again stuck.

However, new manager Bobby Valentine saw something in Reed that he liked and employed him as a starter in spring training. Reed came north with the team and quickly became the surprise performer on the staff. By season's end he was 13-9 with a terrific 2.89 ERA (sixth in the NL), finishing first or second on the club in almost all pitching categories. Walking just 31 hitters in 208 innings, Reed finally showed that if put in the right ballpark with the right infield behind him, he could be an extremely effective pitcher. By the end of the year he had even apparently won over most of his teammates.

While neither Reed nor Bohanon were as exciting or flashy as top pitching prospects like Pulsipher, Paul Wilson, or Jason Isringhausen, they've both done something these kids haven't done much of and may never do in the future: pitch effectively in the major leagues.

TRUE GRIT

In honor of those guys who aren't "scouts' players"—those without that 95-mph fastball or that smooth stroke, those who have stayed sharp as they got older and worked hard because they had to—here's a team composed of the real grinders in baseball.

SP	Rick Reed, Mets
SP	Armando Reynoso, Mets
SP	Greg Maddux, Braves
SP	Orel Hershiser, Indians
SP	Steve Karsay, Athletics
SP	Brian Bohanon, Mets
RP	Jeff Brantley, Reds
RP	Bob Patterson, Cubs
RP	Ed Vosberg, Marlins
C	Jason Kendall, Pirates
1B	David Segui, Expos
2B	Mark Lemke, Braves
SS	Omar Vizquel, Indians
3B	Jeff Cirillo, Brewers
3B	Dave Hollins, Angels
OF	Darren Bragg, Red Sox
OF	Brian Jordan, Cardinals
OF	Rusty Greer, Rangers
UT	Tony Phillips, Angels
UT	Darren Daulton, Phillies

155

NEW YORK METS
1997 TEAM STATISTICS

BATTING/BASERUNNING

	Raw	Rank	+/- %		Raw	Rank	+/- %		Raw	Rank	+/- %
R	777	5	+4	BA	.262	6	0	SB	97	12	-25
R/G	4.80	5	+4	HR	153	6	-1	CS	74	1	+23
OBA	.332	7	0	LH	302	10	-4	SB%	56.7	14	-16
SA	.405	7	-1	BB	550	7	0				
PRO	.737	9	-1	SO	1,029	2	-6				

PITCHING/FIELDING

	Raw	Rank	+/- %		Raw	Rank	+/- %		Raw	Rank	+/- %
OR	709	6	-5	BA	.262	8	0	OSB	106	3	-16
RA/G	4.38	6	-5	HR	160	7	+3	OCS	44	2	-25
OOB	.326	5	-2	LH	317	8	+2	OSB%	70.7	11	+4
OSA	.411	7	+1	BB	504	2	-10	FA	.981	6	0
PRO	.737	7	-1	SO	982	13	-11	GDP	135	12	+13

156

BATTING BY LINEUP SLOTS

	R	HR	RBI	BA	OBA	SA
1	103	10	56	.265	.340	.383
2	102	11	74	.293	.355	.398
3	115	28	125	.295	.396	.497
4	112	37	113	.273	.371	.519
5	82	15	85	.277	.358	.412
6	77	22	95	.270	.313	.441
7	67	15	80	.255	.308	.390
8	64	5	63	.247	.292	.324
9	55	10	50	.174	.228	.266

BATTING BY DEFENSIVE POSITION

	R	HR	RBI	BA	OBA	SA
C	89	32	112	.265	.380	.493
1B	108	26	118	.307	.402	.502
2B	76	12	72	.271	.308	.387
3B	93	12	78	.292	.363	.401
SS	56	3	54	.236	.281	.310
LF	95	19	74	.250	.336	.403
CF	99	9	60	.274	.349	.395
RF	82	24	99	.264	.306	.453
DH	6	2	7	.303	.410	.515
PH	40	11	45	.247	.311	.393
P	19	3	22	.139	.174	.199

TEAM PITCHING

	W-L	CG	QS	QS%	<6	>6	IPS	IP	ERA	OPR
ROTATION	61-48	7	96	59	23	62	6.1	993.2	3.90	.733

	W-L	GR	SV	BSV	HD	BHD	IRS%	IP	ERA	OPR
BULLPEN	27-26	376	49	25	108	72	39	465.2	4.06	.748

1998 PROJECTIONS

BATTING

PLAYER	BA	G	AB	R	H	2B	3B	HR	RBI	BB	SO	SB	CS	SA	OBA
Alfonzo, Edgardo	.297	153	505	69	150	25	3	8	65	50	59	8	4	.407	.360
Baerga, Carlos	.285	130	487	61	139	27	1	11	62	23	43	3	4	.412	.317
Becker, Rich	.260	133	459	65	119	23	3	9	49	57	122	16	6	.381	.342
Franco, Matt	.276	56	84	11	23	3	0	3	10	6	12	0	0	.398	.327
Gilkey, Bernard	.272	143	524	88	143	34	2	20	85	65	106	10	9	.460	.352
Hundley, Todd	.258	83	271	45	70	13	1	19	53	46	70	1	2	.517	.365
Huskey, Butch	.281	107	360	43	101	17	1	16	58	21	65	4	3	.474	.320
Lopez, Luis	.278	67	203	25	56	12	1	3	19	10	45	2	0	.385	.312
McRae, Brian	.260	141	543	88	141	31	6	12	48	61	80	23	9	.406	.335
Olerud, John	.280	154	520	81	146	32	1	20	86	81	59	0	0	.460	.377
Ordonez, Rey	.268	135	421	49	113	8	4	1	38	23	50	9	5	.313	.305
Paquette, Craig	.241	46	152	19	37	7	1	7	23	7	38	2	1	.424	.275
Pratt, Todd	.241	78	251	36	61	9	2	7	34	26	77	1	0	.383	.313

PITCHING

PITCHER	W	L	SV	ERA	G	GS	IP	H	HR	BB	SO
Acevedo, Juan	5	5	0	3.72	25	12	97	94	8	32	65
Bohanon, Brian	7	7	0	3.65	21	17	121	124	13	45	80
Cook, Dennis	2	2	0	4.18	56	0	62	60	4	30	60
Crawford, Joe	3	3	0	3.94	12	6	50	53	4	16	28
Franco, John	6	3	31	2.45	68	0	70	64	3	25	61
Hudek, John	2	3	4	5.22	52	0	53	48	10	36	50
Jones, Bobby	13	9	0	4.10	30	30	193	196	24	58	122
Kashiwada, Takashi	4	2	0	4.46	45	0	40	45	5	23	25
McMichael, Greg	6	7	4	3.17	69	0	82	74	7	27	75
Mlicki, Dave	7	10	0	4.06	37	23	162	165	18	62	133
Reed, Rick	12	9	0	3.30	34	31	207	193	21	33	113
Reynoso, Armando	6	5	0	4.83	19	18	102	114	12	33	53
Rojas, Mel	2	5	21	4.27	71	0	78	69	10	32	85
Mercado, Hector	4	3	0	3.49	17	10	72	67	6	29	56

157

PHILADELPHIA PHILLIES

MANAGEMENT

Manager	General Manager	Owner
Terry Francona Career Record 68-94 .420	Lee Thomas	Bill Giles

1997 RECORD

Won-Lost	Pct.	Division Finish/GB		Wild Card Finish/GB	
68-94	.420	5 E	-33	10	-24

Preseason Consensus Projection	5 (4.70)				

1st Half	2nd Half	Home	Road	Intradivision	Interleague
23-56	45-38	38-43	30-51	19-29	5-10

Comebacks	Blowouts	Nailbiters
8-9	16-34	39-31

THE ISLAND OF DR. MARONE

There is a little-known island in the Schuylkill River, not far from Veterans Stadium in south Philadelphia, called the Island of Dr. Marone. The island, named after Phillies team physician Phillip Marone, cannot be found on any map. In the top-secret laboratories there, crackerjack teams of orthopedic surgeons and research scientists work around the clock in an attempt to create new forms of life.

The first hybrid to come from the island's labs was a minor league baseball player who looked and acted like a major leaguer. Many early models have been extensively field-tested with the Phillies in the past few years, with decidedly mixed results.

The second hybrid, field-tested in 1997, was a baseball manager with a hide so thick that he was impervious to criticism. That prototype performed well under grueling test conditions in 1997 with the last-place Phillies.

The third hybrid, yet to be tested, is a pitcher who is able to shed an injured arm and regrow a healthy limb when he suffers a serious arm injury. Success in this effort is viewed as a key to the future by the Phils, who, rumor has it, have considered changing their name to the Philadelphia Fugitives because they have so many one-armed men.

TAKING THE FALL

On December 9, 1997, the Phillies fired general manager Lee Thomas. Considering the wretched seasons the team has had since 1995, the fact that it took so long for the understandable frustration to boil over into internecine squabbling was remarkable. Far too many baseball teams panic after a long losing streak or a bad season, well before their careful plans have a chance to blossom. However, at some point such stability becomes detrimental to progress. Something drastic needs to be done when your team is at the bottom of the league, when your veteran players spend much of their time on the DL, when your farm system is unproductive, and when the fans have stopped showing up. The ax fell first on manager Jim Fregosi's neck after the 1996 season, then on Thomas's neck after 1997.

With their most recent last-place finish in the NL East, the Phillies have finished at the bottom of their division four times in the past nine years. They have also finished next-to-last two other years. The Phils have also placed third once and second once, though neither of these teams was a contender and both had sub-.500 records. To balance the unsuccessful years the team had only the magical 1993 season to point to. And point to it they did, for too long, as if it were the standard and all the miserable years the aberrations, instead of the opposite.

Where did this team go off the tracks? What crucial decisions led to this train wreck of a franchise? There are three primary reasons that the Phillies are in their current plight.

First, it is no secret that the Phillies' player development system has utterly failed in the '90s. The lack of quality players in the minors has led the parent team to focus on making trades and signing veteran free agents to fill the gaps in its lineup and rotation.

Second, the Phillies have spent their salary money unwisely, signing three veterans to huge multiyear contracts. It is no accident that the collapse of the team came as Lenny Dykstra's and Darren Daulton's talents were silenced by serious injuries and as free agent Gregg Jefferies flatly failed to produce.

Third, the Phillies have consistently relied on underachieving pitchers whose pasts were full of injury or failure. When the organization was able to resurrect these projects and get them to produce, it patted itself on the back for getting something for nothing.

The downside of this policy was watching these same questionable hurlers suffer through injury-ridden or unproductive seasons. From 1990 to '97 the Phillies suffered 135 disabling injuries, 64 of them to pitchers. Half of the pitcher disablements were for 60 days or more.

Who made the crucial decisions to commit the organization's resources to a living-on-the-edge outfielder at the peak of his career, to a thirtysomething catcher with a long history of knee problems, and to an unpopular line-drive

TEAM MVP

Rookie of the Year Scott Rolen was a wonderful addition to the team, fielding well and hitting .292 with 35 doubles, 21 homers, 76 walks, and 16 steals. However, the team's heart and soul was hard-throwing, super-competitive right-hander **Curt Schilling**, who tied for the league lead with 35 starts and fanned a major-league-best 319 batters en route to a 17-11, 2.97 finish. At the All Star break Schilling was 9-8. The rest of the team's pitchers had a combined 15-53 record at that point.

BIGGEST SURPRISE

The development of two young players happily surprised the Phillies. Catcher **Mike Lieberthal**, a real question mark at the start of the year and a real disaster for the first half of the season, rallied to post a 27-double, 20-homer season at age 25. Former Orioles farmhand **Garrett Stephenson**, an unsung righthander, pitched extremely well for the Phillies (8-6, 3.15 in 20 games, 18 of them starts). Stephenson, now 26, has been up and down in the minors but certainly looked good in 1997, walking only 27 in 117 innings.

BIGGEST DISAPPOINTMENT

The performance of the team's veteran free agents was extremely distressing. Even worse, however, was the performance of **Gregg Jefferies**. The 30-year-old left fielder continued his steady decline last season, as his batting average (.256) dropped precipitously for the fourth straight year and he hit just 11 home runs for the Phillies in 130 games. It's truly a wonder that rookie skipper Terry Francona could stand to watch Jefferies play.

hitter who was given power-hitter money? Who made the repeated decisions to stick with, trade for, or sign broken-down or second-rate moundsmen?

At some point, you must look for and pay for the security which comes with consistent, productive players. There's a reason that Greg Maddux and Barry Bonds and other top-flight players cost a lot: they're durable and dependable, a quality sorely lacking in almost all of the Phillies' front-line players.

Here the buck stops at the desk of owner and former CEO Bill Giles. As agreeable a person as could inhabit an executive suite, Giles became Philly's favorite punching bag, partly because his team was at its nadir, partly because he was willing to admit he'd made mistakes, partly because he refused to blame his subordinates, and partly because he owned a baseball team. Baseball is now routinely bashed by the sports media for sins real and imagined, while the other sports skate over similar problems.

Giles, the leader of the ownership group, certainly deserves his share of blame. He's the one who hired (and failed to fire) the GM, he was the one who set the overall budgets, and he was the one at the helm while the S.S. *Philadelphia* slid not-so-slowly under the waves. Fortunately for the few remaining baseball fans in the area, Giles did in '97 what few owners have the good sense to do: fire themselves. (Technically, he resigned as CEO and managing partner while sticking around to secure funding for the club's proposed baseball-only ballpark.)

However, the collapse has been so total that there is more than enough blame to go around for everyone. Thomas, the general manager, largely managed to escape blame till the day he was canned last winter. There were two standard defenses for his role in the debacle: first, he wasn't given the budget he needed to compete with teams like Atlanta; and second, he was a victim of the failure of his previous director of scouting, the oft-criticized Jay Hankins. Both defenses have merit; neither is sufficient to absolve Thomas of his large portion of responsibility.

JUST SAY NO

Let's examine the circumstances under which the Phils signed their three big player contracts. The decisions made in 1993 and 1994 should have affected the last, devastat-ing deal the team inked with Gregg Jefferies. Three strikes and the Phils were out—for years to come.

The easiest signing to justify on paper was the Lenny Dykstra deal. Coming off a season in which he was arguably the best player in the league (though some other guy named Barry Bonds managed to win the MVP award), Dykstra was the poster boy for the brash, crass, blue-collar underdogs who fought their way to the World Series.

The argument for signing Lenny was that he was at the peak of his game at 29 and was the best leadoff hitter in baseball. The arguments for not signing Lenny were also very sound. Dykstra was prone to injuries, and his kamikaze style of play, which so endeared him to the fans, also made for bone-shattering collisions with outfield walls and other fixed objects, rendering him a good bet to collect a large amount of his new-found wealth while on the DL.

Dykstra was still under contract through the end of 1994. A gutsy but sound strategy would have been to let him play '94 without agreeing to a huge extension. If he had played as well as in '93, he could have shopped himself to the highest bidder, and the Phils would have risked a major PR blow if they lost him. And if he played that well, they would probably end up paying him more than they agreed to at the end of 1993. Not much more, however, since his $5 million per annum deal was certainly not below-market value for a non-power-hitter in those days.

If Dykstra slumped from his 1993 peak, or if he were injured, he could probably have been signed by the Phils for substantially less money than they paid. And if he chose to go elsewhere, the PR hit would be a lot less if he weren't at the top of his game. As it turned out, Dykstra was disabled by a congenital condition called spinal stenosis, though he is now attempting a comeback. Since no baseball player has ever attempted to play after surgery for such a condition, it's impossible to know Dykstra's chances.

The earlier Darren Daulton deal was an emotional decision with a clear risk. The team captain, scarred by many surgeries but widely admired for his determination and resistance to pain, was given a four-year contract extension before the '93 season. The same factors were present as with Dykstra: the popular 31-year-old Daulton had one more year on his current contract and was coming off his career year. By locking him up for four more years,

Philadelphia seemingly ensured he would finish his career there, but the risk of Darren blowing out one of his knees was huge. And it happened.

The coup de grâce was signing Jefferies in December of 1994. The Phils were looking for a No. 3 hitter to replace the departed John Kruk. They fooled themselves into thinking that the 27-year-old Jefferies was likely to reprise his peak .342 and .325 averages (of 1993-94). Then they fooled themselves into thinking that Gregg could play the outfield—not because they had any evidence that he could, but because they needed him to. Last, they fooled themselves into thinking that his malcontent attitude wouldn't negatively affect the tightly knit clubhouse.

Such is the way in which major league teams are hobbled for years by the legacy of bad decisions. The Phillies were obligated to pay $16 million to these three in '97, and it was killing them (even allowing for some relief via insurance payments) to the point where they couldn't rebuild.

To say that re-signing Dykstra or Daulton was a mistake is a tough call. Waiting a year on either might have gotten the team a better deal, but the 1994-95 strike makes it hard to evaluate. Nevertheless, there was no excuse for the Jefferies signing, which, on top of the two previous long-term obligations, pushed the sinking team under the waves.

These three deals are perfect examples of the crucial decisions baseball executives routinely face, when refusing the demands of a veteran player will certainly be unpopular even if it's a smart move. Multiply the effects of the Dykstra-Daulton-Jefferies deals by 28 and you have one of the biggest reasons why baseball as an industry is in such a pickle. Unless team presidents and general managers (who, let's not forget, are paid good salaries to make these tough decisions) stop looking for someone else (the players) or something else (a salary cap) to bail them out, nothing will change. It's long past time to just say no.

REASONS FOR HOPE

The outlook in south Philadelphia over the off-season was the rosiest it has been in years, which isn't saying a lot. Though the team never quit on rookie manager Terry Francona, its first-half record was a pathetic 24-61, 32 games off the pace, saved only by the brilliant play of vet-

THE MOMENT OF TRUTH

Something happened to the Phillies at the All-Star break. Destitute, desperate, and a disgraceful laughing stock at 24-61 (.282 winning percentage), the Phils came out charging after their mid-summer night's dream. Their 44-33 record after the break was fourth-best in the major leagues. While the Phillies couldn't succeed in making a silk purse out of a sow's tail, the surge was almost enough to make the club's few remaining fans forget about the miserable first half.

BEST DEAL

Picking up two outfielders helped the Phillies. Receiving **Billy McMillon** in trade from Florida for **Darren Daulton** gave the club a promising top-of-the-order candidate, while waiver pickup **Midre Cummings** played surprisingly well across the Keystone State from his former home in Pittsburgh.

WORST DEAL

Free agents **Danny (Tartabull)** and the three Marks (**Leiter**, **Portugal**, and **Parent**) might have made a good name for a doo-wop group, but the quartet brought only misery to the Phillies. Tartabull missed almost the entire season with a fractured foot, while Portugal was disabled twice with elbow problems and didn't pitch after May 3. Parent hit .150 in 113 at bats, while Leiter was 10-17, leading the NL in losses, with a 5.17 ERA.

161

eran ace Curt Schilling and rookie Scott Rolen.

To everyone's amazement, the team charged out of the blocks in the second half, fashioning a 44-33 record that was just one game behind Atlanta's second-half pace. Philadelphia's second-half rise from the ashes was keyed by good performances from several pitchers and hitters.

Shortstop Kevin Stocker, batting just .250 with one homer before the All-Star break, batted .286 with three homers afterward. Catcher Mike Lieberthal, who had 12 homers but just a .227 average before the midsummer classic, hit .265 with eight homers and 28 walks in 68 games after it. Midre Cummings, cut loose by Pittsburgh, assumed the Phils' center field job and hit .303 with 23 walks after the break, replacing the offensive ciphers Wendell Magee, and Ricky Otero.

Several pitchers improved dramatically in the second half. Garrett Stephenson, who had a 4.02 ERA and a 2-4 record in nine pre–All Star break games, was 6-2 with a 2.57 mark in 11 appearances after the hiatus. Matt Beech, 0-4, 5.72 with 38 strikeouts and 23 walks in 45.2 innings in his first nine games, improved even more dramatically after the break. In 15 starts after July 6 Beech fanned 82 in 91 innings, walked just 34, and posted a 4-5 record with a 4.75 ERA.

Even Curt Schilling, the team's best pitcher (9-8, 3.59, 159 Ks in 133 innings) during the first half, improved. He was 8-3 in the second half with a 2.30 mark in 16 starts, striking out 160 and walking only 21.

TOP PROSPECTS
SPRING 1998

1. **Desi Relaford, SS.** The Phillies are likely to give Relaford the everyday shortstop job this spring. Relaford's 1997 season at Triple A Scranton wasn't bad; he hit .267 with 34 doubles, nine homers, and 29 stolen bases. Defense, something of a problem in the past, is now stronger for him. Although he has always been viewed as something of a disappointment, Relaford is still only 24.

2. **Bobby Estalella, C.** A young power hitter with solid average defensive skills, Estalella won't win a starting job for the Phillies this season. He may stay at Triple A after a 1997 season (.233, 32 doubles, 16 homers) that featured a thumb problem. However, Estalella belongs in the big leagues somewhere and will be there soon.

3. **Marlon Anderson, 2B.** A decent hitter with some power, Anderson doesn't walk enough (42 times last season in 137 games at Double A Reading) or steal bases well enough (27 for 42) to be a quality leadoff man. However, his speed and ability to play second base should get him a job in the majors, perhaps as a utilityman. He is 24 this season and is expected to be a regular within a year.

4. **Carlton Loewer, P.** The Phillies made him their 1994 first-round pick. Loewer has three pitches, including a fastball he isn't afraid to throw inside, but has been hit hard at every level. However, the Phillies have moved him through the system quickly, and in 1997 he was 5-13 with a 4.60 ERA at Scranton. At this point Loewer does not seem to be ready to pitch in the majors, but if he gets it together this year, he'll get a call-up.

5. **Steve Carver, OF.** The 25-year-old is right on the cusp. He was a bit too old for Double A last season, where a hit .262 with 15 homers in 79 games (he was injured part of the season) and struggled to play adequate outfield defense. The Phillies like his power, however, and have a barrel of vacancies in the outfield. With a good spring training, Carver could make a serious impression.

6. **Tony Fiore, P.** A totally unheralded 26-year-old righthander, Fiore is a workhorse without any outstanding pitch. He was 8-3 at Reading in 1997 before a promotion to Scranton, where he made nine starts with a 3-5, 3.86 result. Fiore has gotten no attention, but could slip into the picture if he has a good spring.

7. **Wayne Gomes, P.** The former first-round pick has just an average fastball but is blessed with a fine hard curve. Unfortunately, he has command of neither pitch. In 1997 he was being used as the second-line closer at Scranton, not a great accomplishment for the fourth overall pick in 1993.

Another big post–All Star contributor was pitcher Tyler Green. He spent the first half of the season rehabilitating his right shoulder at Triple A Scranton/Wilkes-Barre, racking up an unimpressive 4-8, 6.10 mark. However, when called up to Philadelphia in July, he pitched well. Green's final record was 4-4 with a 4.93 ERA in 14 starts—not great, but better than those who preceded him.

Whether the Phillies can sustain their second-half progress this coming season depends on several factors, but it is clear that having four healthy and effective starting pitchers (Schilling, Beech, Stephenson, and Green) would go a long way toward getting the club to .500. It is very unlikely, however, that all four members of that checkered quartet (plus the oft-injured Mike Grace) will be both healthy and effective.

Moreover, if the team gets off to a bad start, the pressure to trade staff ace Schilling and closer Ricky Bottalico will mount once more. The off-season Mickey Morandini and Kevin Stocker deals showed that the new execs aren't afraid to deal fan favorites if it means saving salary. It was no secret that Big Schill was anxious to leave town by midsummer 1997; he may well get his wish by midsummer 1998. It was also no secret that the 27-year-old Bottalico was offered to Seattle for Jose Cruz, Jr., in July; Ricky will be on the trading block again this year.

The Phils are still looking to develop a big-threat power hitter, but they're hoping that Rolen, Lieberthal and Rico Brogna will provide the necessary juice (all hit at least 20 homers in '97). They also have to figure out what to do with the unpopular and unproductive Gregg Jefferies and find enough fans who have been out of the country in recent years to sell season tickets to.

The winter acquisitions of center fielder Doug Glanville (for Morandini), outfielder Bob Abreu (for Stocker), and second baseman Mark Lewis (a free agent bridge to prospect Marlon Anderson), combined with the promotion of shortstop prospect Desi Relaford, show that the brain trust is looking for long-term improvement. Glanville and Relaford have the gloves to help, but their bats will be disappointing; Lewis has a decent bat and an iron glove; Abreu is a risky but worthwhile gamble with a lot of upside. Veteran utility infielder Alex Arias, signed as a free agent, will provide insurance at short and second.

If Rolen develops into a bona fide superstar, if some of these new players pan out, if the young starters stay healthy, and if the team makes smart trades and draft picks, the 1999 or 2000 Phillies might be contenders again. That's a big bundle of ifs, however.

DUTCH TREAT

The skeptics were in full cry when Darren Daulton tried to come back last spring from a long series of knee injuries. At age 35 he was trying to return to action after missing all but six games the previous season due to a knee injury suffered in August 1995. Luckily for Daulton, his popularity in Philadelphia was such that he was allowed to try to play a completely new position (right field) when opening day starter Danny Tartabull was immediately injured.

Despite the odds, Daulton showed he could still hit. He was disciplined and hit for power; most importantly, he gritted his teeth and kept on going out there. The Phillies didn't have much else to offer their fans, and Daulton played hard in his last hurrah.

It was appropriate, however, for the club to deal Daulton in July in exchange for outfield prospect Billy McMillon. The Marlins needed a first baseman to platoon with the sagging Jeff Conine, and Daulton was willing to move to a contender near his Florida home. On the day the trade was announced, there wasn't a dry eye in the front office or in the broadcast booth, nor many in the stands.

Daulton's iron will and no-nonsense personality had ruled the Phillies' clubhouse for most of the 1990s. The positive side of his leadership was the wildly popular Macho Row crew which won the '93 pennant against long odds; the negative side was a querulous crew of limping veterans who froze rookies out of their clique while the team plunged into the abyss.

On the last day of the season, GM Lee Thomas also obliquely referred to another benefit of the Daulton deal. Without implying any disparagement of Daulton, he said it seemed that when Darren was traded and took his "clubhouse presence" with him, the younger guys, Mike Lieberthal and Scott Rolen specifically, were able to assert themselves and take on leadership roles.

163

1997 TEAM STATISTICS

BATTING/BASERUNNING

	Raw	Rank	+/ %		Raw	Rank	+/ %		Raw	Rank	+/ %
R	668	13	10	BA	.255	12	3	SB	92	13	29
R/G	4.12	13	10	HR	116	14	25	CS	56	11	7
OBA	.322	11	3	LH	325	4	+4	SB%	62.2	12	8
SA	.385	14	6	BB	519	9	6				
PRO	.707	14	5	SO	1,032	3	6				

PITCHING/FIELDING

	Raw	Rank	+/- %		Raw	Rank	+/- %		Raw	Rank	+/- %
OR	840	12	+13	BA	.265	9	+1	OSB	107	4	15
RA/G	5.19	12	+13	HR	171	10	+10	OCS	57	6	3
OOB	.342	11	+3	LH	384	14	+23	OSB%	65.2	5	4
OSA	.437	13	+7	BB	616	13	+10	FA	.982	3	0
PRO	.780	12	+5	SO	1,209	2	+9	GDP	103	5	13

BATTING BY LINEUP SLOTS

	R	HR	RBI	BA	OBA	SA
1	81	8	54	.263	.331	.377
2	92	3	50	.292	.357	.383
3	103	16	80	.259	.342	.412
4	97	25	101	.280	.370	.482
5	67	19	85	.227	.286	.370
6	78	19	84	.267	.329	.416
7	61	16	82	.257	.307	.400
8	58	6	48	.270	.340	.379
9	31	4	38	.171	.214	.233

BATTING BY DEFENSIVE POSITION

	R	HR	RBI	BA	OBA	SA
C	71	24	94	.236	.306	.417
1B	76	23	95	.256	.292	.434
2B	92	4	44	.282	.349	.369
3B	96	22	97	.281	.371	.460
SS	55	4	47	.270	.337	.358
LF	87	15	75	.261	.332	.397
CF	67	5	51	.262	.321	.361
RF	79	15	80	.278	.360	.437
DH	4	1	2	.184	.205	.289
PH	21	3	26	.183	.266	.285
P	13	0	11	.151	.171	.175

TEAM PITCHING

	W-L	CG	QS	QS%	<6	>6	IPS	IP	ERA	OPR
ROTATION	51-71	13	80	49	34	65	6.0	971.2	4.63	.768

	W-L	GR	SV	BSV	HD	BHD	IRS%	IP	ERA	OPR
BULLPEN	17-23	409	35	16	112	81	38	448.2	5.38	.803

PHILADELPHIA PHILLIES
1998 PROJECTIONS

BATTING

PLAYER	BA	G	AB	R	H	2B	3B	HR	RBI	BB	SO	SB	CS	SA	OBA
Abreu, Bob	.269	100	364	47	98	20	6	4	47	41	113	10	0	.390	.343
Amaro, Ruben	.258	39	63	7	16	3	0	1	8	7	9	0	0	.355	.331
Arias, Alex	.269	62	111	14	30	4	1	1	13	11	13	1	0	.353	.337
Barron, Tony	.272	48	167	20	45	9	1	6	29	11	39	1	0	.456	.317
Brogna, Rico	.263	125	456	57	120	29	1	17	70	32	102	8	2	.443	.310
Cummings, Midre	.265	91	254	29	67	16	4	4	25	22	47	1	2	.409	.324
Estalella, Bobby	.218	31	105	15	23	7	0	4	16	13	32	1	0	.402	.305
Glanville, Doug	.292	143	435	70	127	20	5	4	33	21	45	17	9	.384	.324
Hudler, Rex	.269	44	122	20	33	6	0	5	14	5	25	5	2	.436	.296
Jefferies, Gregg	.276	124	470	68	129	24	3	10	52	47	26	14	7	.404	.342
Jordan, Kevin	.276	35	80	9	22	4	0	3	12	2	12	0	0	.431	.292
Lewis, Mark	.275	118	368	51	101	18	4	9	44	28	70	3	2	.423	.327
Lieberthal, Mike	.250	141	476	61	119	27	1	20	78	44	80	3	3	.440	.313
Magee, Wendell	.248	30	100	12	25	6	0	3	12	10	22	1	0	.393	.317
McMillon, Billy	.247	70	227	33	56	16	1	7	33	26	69	5	0	.422	.325
Parent, Mark	.208	19	54	5	11	2	0	2	7	4	18	0	0	.358	.263
Relaford, Desi	.253	76	285	42	72	17	3	5	29	24	51	12	0	.389	.310
Rolen, Scott	.275	160	575	88	158	35	3	21	91	74	136	14	6	.456	.357
Sefcik, Kevin	.287	71	149	14	43	5	1	2	9	7	15	2	2	.366	.320

PITCHING

PITCHER	W	L	SV	ERA	G	GS	IP	H	HR	BB	SO
Beech, Matt	4	9	0	5.02	23	23	129	137	24	50	112
Bottalico, Ricky	3	5	34	3.53	68	0	76	63	7	39	88
Brewer, Billy	1	3	0	4.93	37	0	33	31	4	19	25
Gomes, Wayne	4	1	0	4.95	31	0	36	38	3	20	20
Grace, Mike	4	5	0	4.28	14	14	80	84	4	26	45
Green, Tyler	4	5	0	4.44	14	14	83	76	11	38	46
Harris, Reggie	1	2	0	5.40	33	0	37	37	1	29	31
Leiter, Mark	7	12	0	4.99	26	25	150	164	21	49	118
Maduro, Calvin	3	5	0	4.86	15	13	78	72	10	45	37
Portugal, Mark	4	4	0	4.30	12	12	69	71	8	20	37
Schilling, Curt	14	11	0	3.32	33	33	236	200	23	58	276
Spradlin, Jerry	3	6	1	4.86	60	0	65	68	8	21	52
Stephenson, Garrett	10	8	0	3.59	26	22	145	138	14	50	100
Winston, Darrin	2	2	0	3.93	14	3	30	25	4	12	19
Welch, Mike	4	3	3	3.75	46	0	53	55	6	16	30

CHICAGO CUBS

MANAGEMENT

Manager	General Manager	Owner
Jim Riggleman Career Record 329-430 .433	Ed Lynch	Tribune Co.

1997 RECORD

Won-Lost	Pct.	Division Finish/GB	Wild Card Finish/GB
68-94	.420	5 C -16	10 -24

Preseason Consensus Projection	3 (2.87)		

1st Half	2nd Half	Home	Road	Intradivision	Interleague
32-49	36-45	42-39	26-55	21-27	9-6

Comebacks	Blowouts	Nailbiters
6-15	16-22	41-44

HORROR SHOW

Another season, another disaster for the Chicago Cubs. This team lost its first 14 games of the year and was out of the race immediately. The free-agent pitchers either bombed or spent most of the year on the disabled list; the $10 million right fielder batted .251 and lead the league with 174 strikeouts (which also set a club record), and the pitcher who led the team in wins (11) spent the first two months of the season in the minor leagues.

Perhaps worse than the debacle of the season itself was the sobering fact that there was a frighteningly small amount of talent on the roster by the end of the season. The Cubs had below-average players at catcher, second base, shortstop, third base, and two outfield positions in 1997. Only first baseman Mark Grace and erratic right fielder Sammy Sosa were above par, and, although they are

both good, neither is ultimately an MVP-caliber player.

By the end of the year the Cubs had no closer but a few good and healthy starting pitchers. That abundance of good arms is their sole hope for 1998. Otherwise, it's going to be another rotten season at Wrigley.

LEFT OUT

Coming into spring training in 1997, the Cubs had no left fielder. They did, however, have several rookie candidates for the position:

•Brooks Kieschnick, a 24-year-old former first-round draft pick with power.

•Robin Jennings, a 24-year-old overachiever with a line-drive bat who was fairly impressive in a 1996 trial.

•Doug Glanville, 26, another former No. 1 pick, a speedster with a good arm but a suspect stick.

•Pedro Valdes, 23, who was coming off three straight

years of hitting .280 or better in the high minor leagues.

Veteran Dave Clark and still-prospect Ozzie Timmons were also in camp, but were never really under consideration for a regular position.

Considering the above choices, it came as somewhat of a surprise that the opening day left fielder was converted first baseman Brant Brown, a line-drive hitter who had a surprisingly good stint with the Cubs late in '96, following a very undistinguished minor league career.

While Brown accepted the position switch and worked hard, he predictably didn't hit enough to stick around. He also played left field about as well as most of the fans who watched him from the bleachers. Exit, Brown.

Before summer arrived, Glanville was given the job. He showed outstanding speed, played good defense, and, as a bonus batted .300. However, he hit for negligible power, did not steal bases effectively, and posted a very poor on-base percentage. A mixed bag, to say the least.

Kieschnick and Jennings had short, unimpressive late-season trials with Chicago; Brown returned as well and fared no better than he had the first time around. Valdes was nowhere to be seen.

At season's end, neither Kieschnick, Valdes, nor Jennings appeared to be in the team's plans any longer. Kieschnick was picked by Tampa Bay in the expansion draft. Brown's future is also in doubt.

There's a lesson here about how not to squander young talent. If you're afraid to give young players a chance to prove themselves—knowing full well that many will fail—they can easily end up as nobodies with little or no value. If you don't have faith in a young player, or don't have the time or the room to let him struggle, it's better to trade him for something you lack rather than watch his value slowly dissipate.

SOME POP OFF THE PINE

Despite having a terribly unproductive everyday lineup, Chicago actually sported a decent bench. Utility infielder Jose Hernandez had his third straight strong year off the pine, hitting with power (his .486 slugging average was six points higher than that of Sammy Sosa), while Rey Sanchez provided a very good glove both at second and short before being traded to the Yankees.

TEAM MVP

You could easily argue that **Mark Grace** was not only the Cubs' MVP, but also that he was the only truly valuable player they had. Grace batted .319 to finish sixth among NL hitters, and his .409 on-base percentage ranked 10th. While Grace hit just 13 homers, he's far from the only NL first sacker without big power. He does almost everything well and plays fine defense.

BIGGEST SURPRISE

Righthanded pitcher **Jeremi Gonzalez**, never an organization favorite due to his average fastball, began the year in the minors and didn't come up until late May. From that point on, he piled up a team-leading 11 wins. Still only 23, he is the most immediately impressive young pitcher the Cubs have brought up in several years, although his ceiling may not be very high.

BIGGEST DISAPPOINTMENT

Perhaps the worst season of all came from center fielder **Brian McRae**, who started badly and never got hot. By the time he was traded to the Mets late in the season, he had lost the considerable good will he had accumulated over the previous two years with both the fans and the media.

Dave Hansen hit .311 and chipped in with line-drive power and a good on-base percentage (.429) in a platoon role at third, while Dave Clark was again one of the game's best outfield reserves and pinch hitters, batting .301 and driving in 32 runs in just 143 at bats. Tyler Houston hit as well as most backup catchers and was also able to play third base although he threw out just 18 percent of opposing base thieves.

Of course, these veterans found their opportunities because so many of the regulars simply stunk.

TURNABOUT

Playing half of their games in Wrigley Field, the Cubs' pitching staff usually seems worse than it really is. In 1997 the usual pattern was reversed, as the pitchers were hit harder on the road than at home. The Chicago staff ERA was 4.44 overall (4.77 on the road), which ranked ahead of only San Diego, Philadelphia, and, of course, Colorado.

But by the end of the season the Cubs were getting excellent pitching from starters Mark Clark (acquired from the Mets) and Kevin Tapani (recovered from a finger injury which cost him two-thirds of the season). The two were superb, combining for a 15-4 record and 3.16 ERA in Cubs garb. Both are durable and, if healthy (which is usually the case with both), capable of pitching 200 innings.

The younger pitchers were more of a problem. Amaury Telemaco, still rehabilitating his shoulder, never got untracked; Frank Castillo was so bad he was traded to Colorado for minor league flotsam in midseason; and Miguel Batista didn't show enough command to impress, despite several opportunities to do so.

Steve Trachsel allowed 32 homers, the most in the majors, and struggled all year with his mechanics—and, therefore, his control. At times he worked quickly, dominating the opposition, but too often he fidgeted, hemmed, hawed—and got hit hard. Kevin Foster, meanwhile, won 10 games by July 2 and showed some signs of recapturing his fine 1994-95 form. However he also was bedeviled by the gopher ball and appeared lost at times. (Foster took the 1996 firing of pitching coach Fergie Jenkins hard.) After his excellent start, he didn't win a game in his last eight starts and was disabled from mid-August until late September due to a sore right shoulder.

Finally, rookie Jeremi Gonzalez led the staff with 11 wins, despite not being called up until May 27. His positive traits include a willingness to pitch inside, a moving fastball, and a strong arm. His weak points include inexperience, poor control, and a long delivery that allows runners to get a good jump. Gonzalez is not going to be the savior of the pitching staff, as his stuff just isn't that good, but he could be a solid No. 3 starter—just like everyone else in the Cubs' rotation. That's one of their problems.

TRADER ED DOES HIS THING

Following their disastrous start the Cubs decided by mid-season to cut salaries. They therefore became active in the late-season and postseason market, dumping several free agents and some previous club fixtures. The most significant comings and going as orchestrated by GM Ed Lynch:

•Terry Mulholland, who was claimed on waivers by San Francisco on August 8. At the time of the move Mulholland had pitched as well as anyone on the staff, compiling a 6-12 record despite a decent 4.07 ERA, largely because the Cubs scored fewer than three runs per game for him. It is almost impossible to believe that Lynch didn't have offers for him, and Cubs players and fans were rightfully outraged.

•Frank Castillo, traded to Colorado for Double A pitcher Matt Pool. Castillo compiled the same ERA for the Rockies (5.42) that he had for Chicago. The team gave up on Castillo way too late and couldn't expect anything in return for him.

•Mel Rojas, Turk Wendell, and Brian McRae, traded to the Mets for Mark Clark, Lance Johnson, and Manny Alexander. This was a classic Cubs trade, in which the team unloaded two expensive, underachieving players and one valuable reliever when the value for all three was quite low. Although Clark pitched extremely well for the Cubs, the trade is still questionable at best.

Clark is an on-again, off-again starter who has now toiled for four big league teams and has had hot streaks for all of them. He's not chopped liver, but he's not prime steak, either.

Johnson, formerly a crowd favorite across town with the White Sox, is a good player when healthy. Last year he was bothered by shin splints and couldn't run often or effectively. His on-base average was a career-high .370 (40 points above his previous career average); if he can't repeat that performance, he won't be an ideal leadoff hitter.

Alexander had made four errors in 54 games with New York, playing mostly second base and some shortstop. After coming over to Chicago, he committed seven errors—almost all of them costly—in 33 games, mostly at short. By season's end few were convinced that he could play regularly, though he did hit .293 for the Cubs, 45 points better than he had for the Mets.

McRae was the one player the Cubs needed to trade. Angry and often bitter even when playing well in '96, he seemed to lose focus in '97. Not only did he play poorly (.242 overall, his lowest average in five years), he also brought little intensity to his game. That kind of negative example can be poisonous, and McRae had his disciples in the Cubs' clubhouse. His was the most disappointing performance of anyone in a Chicago uniform in 1997.

The Cubs finished 1996 with an acceptable bullpen (Wendell, Adams, Patterson) that had no outright closer. Rojas was signed to be that closer, as if he alone could make the team a contender. Of course, it didn't happen: Rojas didn't get a save opportunity until the club's 19th game. All season, he had problems with walks and home runs; he allowed three times as many round-trippers in '97 (15) as he did in '96!

Although Turk Wendell wasn't a closer, he showed that he had substantial value as a middle reliever and an emergency closer. The bullpen, which was strong at the start of last year, had degenerated to the point of using Mark Pisciotta, a 27-year-old rookie with serious control problems, as the setup pitcher for an ineffective Adams by season's end.

•Miguel Batista, traded to Montreal for Henry Rodriguez. The Cubs have long coveted an outfielder to "protect" Sammy Sosa in the order, and they acquired Rodriguez virtually for a song. While the former Dodgers' and Expos' fly chaser can hit the ball a long way, he may strike out as often as Sosa; Rodriguez paced the NL with 160 whiffs in 1996. Batista's career might be salvaged by the Expos, but even Montreal can't turn some guys around.

•Jeff Blauser, signed as a free agent. Blauser's addition puts an end to the Alexander experiment, though he could

THE MOMENT OF
TRUTH

While it is tempting to say that the Cubs' season was defined by their first game of the year, losing 4-2 on April Fools' Day in Florida, the most representative contest of 1997 came on **April 24** at Wrigley Field. The Cubs held a 3-2 lead in the ninth over Pittsburgh, but the Pirates had the tying run on third with two out. Mel Rojas had two strikes on Jason Kendall and appeared to strike him out on a check swing. The pitch, however, was ruled a ball. Kendall followed immediately with a game-tying double, and then he scored when Rey Sanchez threw wildly on Jose Guillen's roller. Pirates win, 4-3.

BEST DEAL

Free-agent signees **Dave Hansen** and **Dave Clark** played well off the bench in reserve roles.

WORST DEAL

Sammy Sosa's four-year contract extension, worth $42.5 million. The reward for Sosa, a popular and talented, if erratic, player, is thoroughly out of proportion to his production. His sky-high salary also drives up the market for anyone with comparable power—a significant number of players. Sosa is simply not a superstar, regardless of his 35-40 homers per season. A batting average of .251 with an on-base percentage of .300 and a slugging average of .480 don't add up to more than $10 million a year.

169

1. **<u>Kerry Wood, P.</u>** The righthanded flamethrower has raw stuff as good as anyone in the minor leagues and made it to Triple A in 1997, just his third pro season. He has a high-90s fastball, a power curve, and a change. Wood, who turns 21 in June, still needs a lot of work on control; in 57.2 innings at Iowa last season, he walked 52 (but fanned 80). He could make the Cubs later this season.

2. **<u>Justin Speier, P.</u>** He is not highly rated by scouts, but the 24-year-old son of former big league shortstop Chris Speier is well-regarded by the organization. Last season the righthanded reliever, who throws mostly sinkers and sliders, was 6-5, 4.48 at Double A Orlando before a promotion to Iowa, where he threw 12.1 scoreless innings, fanning nine and walking one. Speier is a possibility for long relief this spring.

3. **<u>Robin Jennings, OF.</u>** A solid all-around player without any exceptional tools, Jennings appears to have slipped off the Cubs' depth chart. The lefty hitter has enjoyed two productive seasons at Iowa without earning a real shot in Chicago. Jennings, who hit .276 with 20 homers last season, will be 26 this April.

4. **<u>Mark Pisciotta, RP.</u>** The hard-throwing 27-year-old righthander was a six-year veteran of the Pittsburgh organization before being waived to the Cubs in November 1996. Pisciotta has a mid-90s fastball and keeps the ball down—often, unfortunately, in the dirt. He saved 22 last summer at Iowa and was impressive (3-1, 3.18) in 24 games for the Cubs despite walking 16 in 28 innings. With closer Rod Beck on board, Pisciotta will probably end up in a setup role.

5. **<u>Pat Cline, C.</u>** Chicago's catcher of the future has a powerful righthanded bat and a strong arm. However, he is still raw both at the plate and behind it. There is little chance he will see regular duty in the majors until at least 1999; last season Cline spent time at Double and Triple A, batting a combined .246 with 10 homers and 102 strikeouts in 366 at bats.

6. **<u>Terrell Lowery, OF.</u>** The former college basketball star is now 27 but could win a bench job with the Cubs this spring. An impressive season at Iowa (.301, 17 homers) was followed by a 4-for-14 trial with Chicago in September. The righthanded hitter runs well, has improved his hitting, and plays decent defense.

7. **<u>Rod McCall, 1B.</u>** McCall is a six-foot, seven-inch, 235-pound, lefthanded-hitting 26-year-old who played more than seven years in the Cleveland organization hooking on with the Cubs last summer. He hit .300 with six homers in 70 at bats at Orlando before a promotion to Iowa, where he batted .284 with 14 homers in just 148 at bats. McCall strikes out too often, which is why he hasn't yet been able to reach the majors. He's not going to crowd Mark Grace.

8. **<u>Earl Byrne, P.</u>** Another pitching hopeful who has performed well despite a low ranking from scouts, Byrne finished fifth in the Double A Southern League last year with a 3.95 ERA. He also led the loop in strikeouts (128). Byrne, a southpaw from Australia, was more effective in relief but is likely to remain in the rotation this year at Iowa. He turns 26 this summer.

9. **<u>Marty Gazarek, OF.</u>** At age 24 the righthanded hitter was enjoying a big year at Double A before breaking the hamate bone in his left hand last July. A 12th-round pick in 1994, Gazarek has moved steadily through the Cubs system, but it is unlikely that he will be a starter in the majors.

10. **<u>Terry Joseph, OF.</u>** A speedy righthanded hitter with on-base ability, Joseph hit .277 with 22 doubles, 11 triples, and 11 homers at Double A Orlando (a good hitters' park) in 1997. He also swiped 17 bases and took 59 walks. Joseph was a 13th-round pick in 1995 and has never been highly regarded despite his tools. He will start at Triple A this spring.

170

be helpful in a utility role if he sticks around. Blauser is a very good hitter (at least he has been in his two option years) and was a big favorite of manager Bobby Cox in Atlanta due to his toughness and underrated defensive play.

At 32, Blauser is coming off a terrific season (.308, 17 homers, 70 RBIs). He has always hit well in Chicago and has more homers in Wrigley Field than in any other park but Fulton County Stadium. Given the pickings the Cubs have in the minors at shortstop—slim and none—this was a fine move.

•Doug Glanville, traded to Philadelphia in December for Mickey Morandini. This was an excellent trade in which the Cubs parted with a player they did not need and who had a limited upside while acquiring a solid veteran who will stabilize the infield defense and contribute at bat. It's a deal the Cubs needed to make and one that along with the signing of Blauser, will pay big dividends for several years.

To bolster the short relief, the Cubs signed veteran closer Rod Beck on January 15. He received a one-year $3.5 million contract with an option for 1999 (which is guaranteed if he appears in 53 games this season). Beck, who won't be 30 until August, had trouble getting a long-term deal despite his 37 saves last season.

Although Beck still gets his strikeouts and has been effective for the most part, he does not throw as hard as most other closers. Roberto Hernandez and Randy Myers, both significantly older, received multiyear deals this winter, but Beck struggled to get even this modest (by 1998 standards) contract. He has survived in recent seasons by relying on pinpoint control and a devastating forkball as his velocity has declined to below-average. Some veteran closers can pitch effectively for years like this (e.g., Dennis Eckersley), but big league teams prefer dominating, hard-throwing closers if they can get them.

KEVIN ORIE: THE KID IS ALL RIGHT

Despite the club's terrible season, there were a couple of bright spots among the rookies. Jeremi Gonzalez showed he can pitch in the big leagues, and Kevin Orie made a good showing at third base.

Entering the season with no big league experience, Orie endured a trial by fire. He was victimized on opening day in Florida when he charged a bunt by Edgar Renteria, let it roll down the line, and watched the ball pick up speed and bounce past third base and into left field for a double. The play was on all the highlight shows, and Orie became the focus of much unwanted attention during the team's 14-game, season-opening losing streak.

The rook hung in there, though. Manager Jim Riggleman stuck with him all the way and, as the season progressed, Orie steadily improved. He hit .275 on the year with a little bit of power (8 homers) and a batting eye that drew praise from everyone involved. It's been a while since the Cubs had any young, disciplined hitters, and Orie knows how to work the count in his favor and take the walk. Disciplined young hitters will frequently improve their power if they can force pitchers to come in to them when behind in the count, so Orie could blossom into a pretty good player.

Add to this package a good arm and glove: Orie has first-step quickness and a very strong arm at third. A former shortstop, he showed good movement to both sides and overall, actually charged the bunt extremely well. As a result he showed the best range of any regular NL third baseman in '97.

Orie is neither Brooks Robinson at third base nor Matt Williams at bat. He is probably not going to hit more than 15-20 homers per season. However, he should be a solid hitter and play strong defense. If the Cubs had more players as good as he is, they might even be contenders.

171

CHICAGO CUBS
1997 TEAM STATISTICS

BATTING/BASERUNNING

	Raw	Rank	+/- %		Raw	Rank	+/- %		Raw	Rank	+/- %
R	687	12	-8	BA	.263	5	0	SB	116	9	-11
R/G	4.24	12	-8	HR	127	13	-18	CS	60	6	0
OBA	.321	12	-4	LH	308	6	-2	SB%	65.9	10	-3
SA	.396	11	-3	BB	451	13	-18				
PRO	.717	12	-4	SO	1,003	1	-8				

PITCHING/FIELDING

	Raw	Rank	+/- %		Raw	Rank	+/- %		Raw	Rank	+/- %
OR	759	8	+2	BA	.266	10	+2	OSB	146	12	+15
RA/G	4.69	8	+2	HR	185	13	+19	OCS	59	9	0
OOB	.339	9	+2	LH	335	11	+8	OSB%	71.2	12	+5
OSA	.435	11	+6	BB	590	11	+6	FA	.981	5	0
PRO	.774	11	+4	SO	1,072	10	-3	GDP	94	2	-21

172

BATTING BY LINEUP SLOTS

	R	HR	RBI	BA	OBA	SA
1	93	11	45	.275	.321	.399
2	101	10	51	.274	.334	.388
3	96	17	84	.284	.370	.425
4	90	33	122	.278	.331	.511
5	78	15	93	.276	.331	.412
6	71	14	77	.258	.313	.393
7	63	11	66	.262	.314	.389
8	52	10	62	.270	.324	.373
9	43	6	42	.175	.228	.238

BATTING BY DEFENSIVE POSITION

	R	HR	RBI	BA	OBA	SA
C	50	8	64	.255	.299	.339
1B	95	13	85	.311	.398	.452
2B	71	14	80	.266	.309	.400
3B	63	13	68	.282	.363	.434
SS	74	11	56	.282	.313	.391
LF	93	13	59	.273	.329	.403
CF	96	12	44	.262	.330	.395
RF	91	36	119	.252	.301	.480
DH	2	1	7	.375	.423	.500
PH	29	6	47	.249	.308	.382
P	15	0	15	.113	.157	.133

TEAM PITCHING

	W-L	CG	QS	QS%	<6	>6	IPS	IP	ERA	OPR
ROTATION	56-61	6	83	51	32	56	5.9	958.2	4.43	.770

	W-L	GR	SV	BSV	HD	BHD	IRS%	IP	ERA	OPR
BULLPEN	12-33	441	37	18	151	100	33	470.1	4.46	.782

1998 PROJECTIONS

BATTING

PLAYER	BA	G	AB	R	H	2B	3B	HR	RBI	BB	SO	SB	CS	SA	OBA
Alexander, Manny	.257	63	156	23	40	7	2	2	14	11	36	8	2	.357	.308
Blauser, Jeff	.278	147	506	84	140	28	3	17	62	68	101	7	2	.444	.364
Brown, Brant	.248	52	175	27	43	11	2	9	27	15	39	2	0	.478	.309
Grace, Mark	.312	149	556	86	173	36	3	12	78	75	43	2	3	.452	.394
Hansen, Dave	.284	90	144	15	41	6	1	2	15	25	29	1	1	.386	.389
Hardtke, Jason	.252	20	71	8	18	4	0	2	8	6	11	0	0	.398	.314
Hernandez, Jose	.260	77	151	26	39	7	2	6	21	11	40	1	2	.450	.309
Houston, Tyler	.286	60	145	14	41	8	0	2	23	7	27	1	1	.382	.320
Jennings, Robin	.252	35	125	16	31	6	1	5	17	13	23	1	0	.435	.325
Johnson, Lance	.312	119	475	75	148	18	11	6	46	35	30	29	10	.434	.359
Lowery, Terrell	.255	61	205	31	52	12	1	7	31	30	61	4	0	.423	.349
Martinez, Sandy	.252	15	48	5	12	2	0	1	5	5	14	1	0	.333	.322
Mieske, Matt	.266	80	227	33	60	14	2	7	30	17	45	1	2	.440	.319
Morandini, Mickey	.294	146	550	80	161	37	5	2	41	59	91	19	10	.390	.362
Orie, Kevin	.274	137	435	48	119	28	6	10	52	47	68	2	2	.432	.344
Rodriguez, Henry	.252	134	483	61	122	31	2	27	86	40	146	2	2	.491	.309
Servais, Scott	.269	130	424	43	114	23	0	9	57	30	69	0	1	.390	.318
Sosa, Sammy	.257	149	593	88	152	26	3	38	114	44	157	23	10	.501	.308

PITCHING

PITCHER	W	L	SV	ERA	G	GS	IP	H	HR	BB	SO
Adams, Terry	2	7	18	4.13	63	0	72	78	3	38	60
Clark, Mark	13	9	0	3.98	31	30	194	208	22	55	120
Foster, Kevin	11	9	0	4.80	27	26	148	144	28	63	116
Gonzalez, Jeremi	9	9	0	4.25	26	26	163	142	20	74	100
Morel, Ramon	2	2	0	4.23	12	7	40	45	5	15	24
Myers, Rodney	2	2	0	4.64	7	7	39	42	5	12	18
Patterson, Bob	2	6	4	3.54	91	0	69	58	9	17	65
Pisciotta, Marc	6	2	0	3.45	50	0	60	43	2	35	44
Swartzbaugh, Dave	3	3	0	4.29	8	7	44	50	4	20	26
Tapani, Kevin	11	7	0	4.37	23	23	148	155	19	44	98
Telemaco, Amaury	3	3	0	4.51	10	8	56	60	8	17	32
Trachsel, Steve	8	10	0	4.29	30	30	182	193	28	65	135
Speier, Justin	2	2	0	3.72	23	0	36	32	3	9	24
Wood, Kerry	5	3	0	3.47	14	14	70	37	2	52	71

173

CINCINNATI REDS

174

KNIGHTFALL

The Reds entered last season on fire, and the flames spread as the year went on. Having signed or traded for a basketful of low-cost veterans, including Kent Mercker, Stan Belinda, Terry Pendleton, Ricky Bones, and Ruben Sierra (the Tigers were eating almost all of the latter's salary), the Reds stumbled out of the gate and never recovered. Manager Ray Knight, already criticized for his performance in 1996 (when the Reds, who had finished atop the NL Central for two straight years, fell to third), was almost immediately rumored to be on his way out.

Knight said he would use a set lineup as the season began, but didn't, much to the consternation of his projected regulars. Instead, when the offense sputtered, the skipper decided to use the whole roster every day, rotating players around the field in an attempt to score runs.

The result: no one was producing and most of the line-up was hitting well below .200 by May. Sierra, whose signing was a shot in the dark with a rusty cap gun anyway, was summarily dumped, and a procession of outfielders began to wind its way through the Queen City. Ozzie Timmons, Mike Kelly, Lenny Harris, and Curtis Goodwin dutifully trooped into the outfield, and when Reggie Sanders suffered his annual injury, the parade continued.

Fourteen men played the outfield for the Reds in '97, including Willie Greene (39 games), Eduardo Perez (12 games), and catcher Eddie Taubensee (11 games). It appeared as if Knight didn't know anything about his talent, so he had to rotate everyone in and out of every position on the field and back and forth from Triple A so that he could say he'd tried everything he could to win.

The pressure kept mounting on Knight, and it showed. The NL suspended the Reds' manager early in the season after he went bonkers during a losing streak and verbally (and almost physically) assaulted an umpire. GM Jim Bowden sent Knight home to rest, which led the media to speculate that the skipper would soon be canned. For his part, Bowden claimed that Knight's job was safe.

Knight really did try his best, and he took the losses harder than anyone. (Too hard, probably.) He bunted, stole, ordered intentional walks, argued and cajoled, benched players, used spot starters and rotated relievers in and out of the pen, but he couldn't get his team to perform. These types of panicky tactics almost never work, and inspired only eye-rolling from the regulars, resentment from the bench players (who could and would be sent out at any moment), and mockery from the press.

A storm of bad karma rained on the team. Closer Jeff Brantley missed most of the season with a shoulder injury. Captain and shortstop Barry Larkin ended the year playing just 73 games. Second baseman Bret Boone never got his bat going and ended the season at an almost unbelievable .223. Starter Pete Schourek's elbow never got any better, and he went 5-8 with a 5.42 ERA. Former ace Jose Rijo never came back.

By July, Knight seemed to have lost all control. He announced a six-man starting rotation, a move that lasted about 48 hours until he ditched the idea on advice from Don Gullett, his pitching coach. Meanwhile, the clubhouse was in open revolt. Pitcher Mike Morgan said, as others before him had, that he didn't respect Knight and wouldn't pitch for him; Knight sniped back that Morgan shouldn't talk, given his sub-.500 career record.

Finally, Knight was relieved of his duties in late July. With that explosion came an end to Knighttime in Cincinnati, and ballplayers were soon scattered all over the landscape. Trades, releases, promotions, and Deion Sander's departure to play football quickly followed in the wake of Knight's firing and the hiring of "Trader Jack" McKeon as manager.

By the time the cool autumn breezes began to blow through the Queen City, what remaining fans there were looked at their club and said, "They aren't that bad." By the end of the year the Reds had made several major improvements:

•Underachieving reliever Hector Carrasco, long unhappy with Knight, was traded to Kansas City in exchange for

TEAM MVP

Closer **Jeff Shaw** (and who would ever have put those three words together before 1997?) was excellent, saving 42 games in 49 tries to lead the NL. Taking over the job after Jeff Brantley went down with shoulder trouble, Shaw struck out 74 and walked 12 in 94.2 innings and held opponents to a .227 average. The emergence of Shaw, who made less than one-fourth of the $2.8 million the Reds paid Brantley last year, allowed Cincinnati to deal Brantley this winter for Dmitri Young.

BIGGEST SURPRISE

Shaw's big year was a big surprise. Other than that, the emergence of rookie starting pitcher **Brett Tomko** (11-7, 3.43 ERA), the return to excellence of setup man **Stan Belinda** (114 K's in just 99 innings), and the blossoming of third sacker **Willie Greene** (.253, 26 homers, 78 walks) were the high points of the Reds' season.

BIGGEST DISAPPOINTMENT

Injuries to shortstop **Barry Larkin** and right fielder **Reggie Sanders** put a crimp in the Reds' offense, as did the decline of veteran first baseman **Hal Morris** (who fell from 16 homers to 1) and second baseman **Bret Boone** (.223). Starting pitchers **Mike Morgan**, **Dave Burba**, **John Smiley**, and **Pete Schourek** (hampered by injury) were awful, and the club struggled all year to find someone who could lead off effectively.

Chris Stynes and Jon Nunnally.

•Hal Morris departed via free agency after hitting just one homer in 333 at bats, making it easier for the Reds to let him go. Eduardo Perez hit 16 homers, third on the team, and won the first base job.

•Willie Greene blossomed into a big-league power hitter, slamming 26 homers and drawing 78 walks. He also lived through two managers who didn't seem to believe in his talent.

•Jeff Shaw and Stan Belinda had borderline spectacular years in relief. Shaw saved 42 games, while Belinda fanned 114 in just 99.1 innings.

•Brett Tomko, a promising rookie righthander, went 11-7 in 22 games with a staff-best 3.43 ERA. He showed the potential to become a staff ace.

•A trade with Cleveland brought over infielder Damian Jackson and pitchers Danny Graves, Scott Winchester and Jim Crowell. The days of "Just who was that masked reliever—Felix Rodriguez, Pedro A. Martinez, Richie Lewis, Jeff Tabaka, or Joey Eischen?" may finally be over.

With their late-season overhaul and the jettisoning of unproductive veteran free agents, the Reds look a whole lot better now than they did at the start of the 1997 season. In fact four-fifths of the Reds' 1997 opening-day starting rotation (Dave Burba, John Smiley, Mike Morgan, Pete Schourek, and Kent Mercker) are now gone. Only Burba remains, joined for 1998 by converted reliever Mike Remlinger, last year's rookie star Brett Tomko, and new acquisitions Mark Hutton, Pete Harnisch, and Jim Crowell. Lefthander Gabe White might also inch his way into the picture.

Tomko and Burba are quality pitchers. Hutton has a very good arm, and Remlinger proved himself worthy last season. Harnisch's ability to come back is a serious question, while White and Crowell could be helpful if not asked to do too much too soon.

Amazing what a little surgery can do to relieve the pressure on all parties. Meanwhile, Knight, currently convalescing inside the studios of ESPN's "Baseball Tonight," is said to be resting comfortably.

Even though he was considered an interim manager when he replaced Knight, McKeon received and deserved much of the credit for the Reds' turnaround—which shows what being decisive can do. For that, he was rewarded with a contract for 1998.

Ominously, though, Cincinnati hired former Kansas City manager Bob Boone over the winter as a player-personnel adviser to the general manager. If the Reds stumble, the death watch for McKeon will start immediately, even if Boone's stormy tenure in K.C. looked a lot like Knight's stormy tenure in Cincy.

This will mark the third time in the 1990s that the Reds have apparently hired the current manager's replacement long before firing the manager. Davey Johnson was hired by the Reds as a consultant while fall-guy Tony Perez was managing; when Perez got the ax, Johnson stepped in without missing a beat.

Johnson then saw the same thing happen to him, as the Reds hired Ray Knight to be their third base coach and "assistant manager" while Johnson was at the helm. At least in Davey's case, he knew it was coming, as owner Marge Schott announced a year in advance that Knight would be taking over from Johnson when his contract expired.

Maybe Cincinnati should take the lead and create a formal new position for major league teams to fill: manager-in-waiting. Good luck, Jack. With Bob Boone upstairs and two Boones on the field, you'll be surrounded.

DEION SANDERS: THE WANDERER

After Deion Sanders sat out the 1996 baseball season (he was quoted as saying he didn't miss the game at all; the feeling is mutual among many baseball fans), he was enticed back for the 1997 season by his love for the city of Cincinnati, his love for his teammates, and, oh, maybe a couple of million dollars. It's not as if Deion really likes baseball that much, as he's said so many times. What he really loves is the camaraderie.

Well, most of his teammates seem to like him, and GM Jim Bowden seems almost to have a teenage crush on him (Bowden's family's dog is named Prime Time). The media loves Neon Deion too, because he's the proverbial good story, both for his on-field speed and his telegenic personality.

Anyway, Deion came back and stole 56 bases to go with his usual .329 on-base average. He also left the team to go play football in the fall (as usual), and found God while

176

browsing in a jewelry store. Are the Reds really any better for having had Deion Sanders? Is he really a championship-caliber baseball player? Or did they just waste time and money that they could have used evaluating other players?

At least his September departure meant that the Reds could look at Pat Watkins, Jon Nunnally, and Chris Stynes. Stay away, Deion, and all will be forgiven.

SHORT STORY

Injuries to Barry Larkin gave Calvin "Pokey" Reese the opportunity to play shortstop for the Reds in '97. He was by observation and statistical evidence an excellent defensive player and, as a bonus, showed good baserunning speed. But he is a very poor hitter. Reese has never hit .270 at any pro level and was nearly useless at the plate for the Reds.

Reese turns 25 in June and may improve a bit, but he should never be expected to be an offensive threat. It is more likely that he will be a No. 8 hitter for most of his career, as he is now.

What kind of team can afford to play such a below-average offensive player? One that has above-average production at most other positions. The Reds are not likely to be that team in 1998. Over the winter, it was not clear whether Barry Larkin would be at shortstop, at another position, or in another city come April, and the fates of others, including, but not limited to, Reese, Damian Jackson, and Chris Stynes, hang in the balance.

The Reds have plenty of options: Eduardo Perez is penciled in at first base, while Taubensee is slated to be behind the plate. Other than that, three infield and all three outfield spots are up for grabs between Reese, Jackson, Larkin, Stynes, Willie Greene, Mel Nieves, Aaron Boone, Reggie Sanders, Eric Owens, Ozzie Timmons, Jon Nunnally, and Pat Watkins.

There are no big boppers in that group. Sanders and Greene, while good power hitters, are not going to be superstars capable of carrying a team. Nieves will play, but will strike out at least once a game. If Larkin is physically capable of playing shortstop, then he has to play shortstop. He's most valuable there, because he allows other capable hitters to fill less demanding defensive positions.

THE MOMENT OF
TRUTH

The firing of **Ray Knight** and the hiring of **Jack McKeon** as manager. During 1997 manager Ray Knight fought with umpires and several of his players, while his boss, GM **Jim Bowden**, said he wouldn't fire Knight, then sent him home for a "rest" before eventually firing him. Once McKeon took over and cut through the chaos, the Reds stabilized and played good ball down the stretch. This should be an improved club in 1998.

BEST DEAL

GM **Jim Bowden** made several good moves. His best was a July trade that sent **Hector Carrasco** and **Scott Service** to Kansas City for **Chris Stynes** and **Jon Nunnally**. Carrasco and Service are no longer with the Royals, while Stynes (.348, 6 homers for the Reds) and Nunnally (.318, 13 homers with Cincinnati) are penciled in for outfield duty in '98.

WORST DEAL

Signing and trading for veteran "names" like **Deion Sanders**, **Terry Pendleton**, **Ricky Bones**, and **Ruben Sierra** just mucked everything up. Only Sanders was even passable on the field. The Reds were better after all of them set sail.

177

THE BOONIES

Bret and Aaron Boone got to play together for a while last year, but if Bret is with the Reds this spring, it will be quite a surprise. Aaron, on the other hand, doesn't seem to have much left to learn in the minors. He will be 25 when the season starts and is coming off a .290, 22-homer, 75-RBI season at Triple A Indianapolis. At his age Boone should be dominating minor league pitching, but he still appears to be a legitimate big league hitter. He won't walk much, but he should hit for a good average with line-drive power.

Defensively Boone is excellent at third base with a strong arm and a good first step. He has more speed than his older brother. Assuming Aaron works his way through the confusion and lands himself an everyday job somewhere in the Reds infield, he should be considered a strong candidate for Rookie of the Year.

If Aaron plays second, he won't be as good as his brother, but he should provide more offense. If Aaron supplants Willie Greene at third, it means the Reds will be on their way to repeating the confusion of the past two years, because they would likely end up giving Greene a full-time job elsewhere.

PLAYING HARDBALL

Pete Rose, Jr., tried to fly the Cincy coop in the off-season after he was taken off the Reds' major league roster. However, no one expressed any interest in him, so he ended up signing a minor league deal for 1998 with Indianapolis, the Reds' Triple A affili-

TOP PROSPECTS
SPRING 1998

1. **Aaron Boone, 3B**. Last season was the first in which the 24-year-old third baseman hit for power. He slugged 30 doubles and 22 homers for the Triple A Indianapolis Indians and won himself a shot at the Reds' job for 1998. The knock on Boone is that he is an impatient hitter who rarely walks, a weakness that could be exploited in the majors as it has been for his brother Bret. Defensively, Boone is a smooth, solid third baseman but doesn't have the fielding gifts of his older sibling. Assuming Aaron is healthy and shows well this spring, he could 1) move Willie Greene off third base, 2) move Greene out of town, or 3) position himself to be traded.

2. **Damian Jackson, IF.** A very good defensive infielder, Jackson has not shown much power in the minors. He is fast, gets on base some, and has the skill to play either shortstop or second base for the Reds. While Jackson could be a regular, he might also get lost in the team's glut of infielders. At the very least he should be a valuable utility player. He got into 12 games for Cincy late last summer after batting .288 with 24 steals at Triple A.

3. **Jim Crowell, P.** A lefthander signed as a nondrafted free agent out of the University of Indianapolis, Crowell has been a pro for only three years. Like Scott Winchester, he jumped all the way from Kinston of the Carolina League (where he was 9-4, 2.37 with 94 strikeouts in 114 innings) to the majors after being sent to the Reds in the John Smiley deal. An overachiever with a high-80s fastball, a curve, a change, and a screwball, Crowell could start in the majors this year.

4. **Danny Graves, P.** The 24-year-old righthanded reliever also came to the Reds from Cleveland in the John Smiley trade. He has one of the best sinking fastballs in the game and has had nothing but success climbing the minor league ladder. Graves, who is not a strikeout artist but has dominated hitters anyway, picked up seven saves last season at Triple A but was also used as a starter in three games. Setup duty looks to be his major league destination.

5. **Scott Winchester, P.** His streak of 18 straight games in which he collected either a win or a save, not his big fastball, brought him attention. A 14th-round draftee in 1995, Winchester vaulted all the way from the Carolina League to the majors last season, coming to the Reds via trade and pitching for them in five late-season games. He mixes a good sinking fastball with a tough breaking ball and has averaged a strikeout an inning in his professional career. He might need a full season at Triple A, but Winchester is already quite polished.

ate. Since his 1997 promotion was publicity-driven, the very marginal 28-year-old prospect is unlikely to see much, if any, big league action.

THE YEAR'S WEIRDEST PLAYS

Only two of which involved the Reds...

April 27, Dodgers at Marlins. On a Sunday night ESPN game, Dodgers third baseman Todd Zeile reacted oddly to Moises Alou's two-out, first-inning grounder. With men on second and third, he thought there was a force out and simply tagged third. But there was no such force out, and a run scored.

May 9, Royals at Yankees. In the sixth with the bases loaded, Jeff King of the Royals grounded to Charlie Hayes, who stepped on third to force out Jose Offerman as Tom Goodwin scored from third. Hayes then made a wild throw to first, and Jay Bell advanced from first to third. Umpire Dale Ford incorrectly called Bell out for passing Offerman—who was already out. Crew chief Rich Garcia overruled Ford, sending Bell back to third despite a protest by the Yankees.

May 12, Mariners at Brewers. With runners at first and second in the ninth, Ken Griffey, Jr., topped a single between home and third base. Brewers pitcher Doug Jones threw the ball away, allowing the runner on second to score, and then was called for obstruction when he ran into the other runner, who was waved home by the umpires. One 40-foot single, two errors, two runs.

May 13, Yankees at Twins. With Yankee Mariano Duncan at bat, Kevin Jarvis's wild pitch caromed into a tunnel near the Twins dugout, preventing further advance of the two Yankee runners.

July 6, Braves at Expos. With men on first and second in the last of the seventh, Vladimir Guerrero singled to right field. The runner on second scored. Braves right fielder Michael Tucker nailed the other runner with a fine throw to third, but third baseman Keith Lockhart dropped the ball. That runner scored. Lockhart, seeing Guerrero trying for second, then heaved the ball back into right field. Tucker backed up the play and threw back to Lockhart at third to finally retire Guerrero.

July 15, Mets at Pirates. Pittsburgh shortstop Kevin Polcovich drove a pitch into the right-center-field gap in the bottom of the seventh. Jose Guillen, on first, did not touch second base. Mets shortstop Rey Ordonez saw this happen and instructed second baseman Carlos Baerga to take the relay throw and step on second base. Guillen was called out, and Polcovich lost a triple.

August 6, Yankees at Rangers. Domingo Cedeno came up in the eighth for Texas with men on second and third. He singled to right, scoring a run. On the play, plate umpire Ted Hendry was hit in head when Joe Girardi threw off his catcher's mask. Hendry left the game while Larry Barnett took his place for the ninth inning.

August 8, Orioles at Angels. Anaheim second baseman Luis Alicea dropped Mike Bordick's line drive. Harold Baines, on second base, thought the ball had been caught and that he had been doubled off second after Alicea ran to second to force out Chris Hoiles, the runner on first. Baines was actually ruled out for leaving the basepath, completing a 4 unassisted double play.

August 28, Astros at Braves. Tim Bogar hit a fly ball to left-center in the seventh inning. Expecting to be retired, Bogar kept his head down after rounding first and headed towards the visitors' dugout on the third base line. Left fielder Ryan Klesko, who had dropped the ball, still had plenty of time to throw out Bogar, who was tagged by the third baseman as he headed for the dugout.

September 2, Royals at Reds. Cincinnati's Dave Burba batted in the second with Willie Greene and Bret Boone on the bases. Burba bunted to the mound. When Dean Palmer at third dropped pitcher Jose Rosado's throw, Greene was safe. However, Boone kept steaming toward third, where he was tagged out by Palmer. Burba, who tried to advance to second base, was thrown out Palmer to Shane Halter. One error, one double play.

September 14, Reds at Phillies. Cincinnati pitcher Bret Tomko dropped Tony Barron's fourth-inning popup, then scrambled down the line to pick up the ball. Tomko was then flattened by Barron running toward first. The luckless Tomko was given an error and Barron was allowed to take first.

September 19 (Game 2), Indians at Royals. With Jeff King at bat in the first inning and rookie Jed Hansen on third, Matt Williams pulled the hidden-ball trick to pick off Hansen.

179

1997 TEAM STATISTICS

BATTING/BASERUNNING

	Raw	Rank	+/- %		Raw	Rank	+/- %		Raw	Rank	+/- %
R	651	14	-13	BA	.253	14	-4	SB	190	1	+46
R/G	4.02	14	-13	HR	142	9	-8	CS	67	3	+12
OBA	.321	13	-4	LH	296	12	-6	SB%	73.9	2	+9
SA	.389	13	-5	BB	518	10	-6				
PRO	.710	13	-4	SO	1,113	9	+2				

PITCHING/FIELDING

	Raw	Rank	+/- %		Raw	Rank	+/- %		Raw	Rank	+/- %
OR	764	10	+3	BA	.256	6	-2	OSB	139	11	+10
RA/G	4.72	10	+3	HR	173	12	+12	OCS	48	3	-18
OOB	.330	7	-1	LH	340	12	+9	OSB%	74.3	13	+10
OSA	.417	10	+2	BB	558	7	0	FA	.982	2	0
PRO	.747	8	+1	SO	1,159	5	+5	GDP	101	3	-15

BATTING BY LINEUP SLOTS

	R	HR	RBI	BA	OBA	SA
1	81	8	37	.250	.308	.341
2	92	14	62	.270	.332	.396
3	94	16	71	.271	.351	.416
4	96	33	103	.270	.343	.506
5	79	17	90	.257	.337	.399
6	74	22	95	.274	.339	.441
7	53	20	69	.256	.327	.409
8	49	10	48	.246	.317	.357
9	33	2	37	.169	.214	.221

BATTING BY DEFENSIVE POSITION

	R	HR	RBI	BA	OBA	SA
C	51	23	68	.256	.317	.424
1B	81	17	85	.271	.334	.414
2B	59	7	53	.222	.292	.318
3B	75	21	93	.250	.337	.414
SS	81	10	48	.254	.343	.370
LF	78	13	67	.291	.346	.408
CF	83	14	47	.284	.341	.414
RF	99	34	107	.270	.350	.507
DH	2	0	0	.227	.261	.318
PH	23	2	25	.201	.262	.277
P	10	1	19	.131	.159	.172

TEAM PITCHING

	W-L	CG	QS	QS%	<6	>6	IPS	IP	ERA	OPR
ROTATION	60-66	5	74	46	38	45	5.6	914.1	4.67	.761

	W-L	GR	SV	BSV	HD	BHD	IRS%	IP	ERA	OPR
BULLPEN	16-20	423	49	14	139	86	40	534.2	3.99	.723

CINCINNATI REDS
1998 PROJECTIONS

BATTING

PLAYER	BA	G	AB	R	H	2B	3B	HR	RBI	BB	SO	SB	CS	SA	OBA
Boone, Aaron	.250	64	230	32	57	12	2	8	30	16	45	4	0	.425	.299
Boone, Bret	.246	125	425	45	104	24	2	9	52	38	92	4	3	.376	.308
Greene, Willie	.246	153	467	62	115	18	3	25	88	70	112	5	0	.461	.344
Harris, Lenny	.275	61	130	18	36	7	1	2	15	10	12	4	2	.378	.326
Jackson, Damian	.243	47	158	26	38	8	1	2	8	19	36	8	0	.340	.323
Larkin, Barry	.295	110	369	68	109	23	4	15	46	64	36	26	6	.500	.399
Nieves, Melvin	.237	111	349	50	83	17	2	20	58	37	143	1	5	.468	.310
Nunnally, Jon	.245	106	336	49	82	14	3	17	44	43	110	7	0	.458	.330
Owens, Eric	.267	51	175	24	47	6	2	4	17	17	31	8	0	.387	.333
Perez, Eduardo	.248	110	300	45	74	18	0	16	51	31	74	5	1	.463	.319
Reese, Pokey	.231	71	221	28	51	9	0	2	15	18	48	15	4	.302	.289
Sanders, Reggie	.256	119	429	72	110	27	3	24	71	59	121	24	11	.500	.346
Stynes, Chris	.297	73	298	47	89	16	1	7	42	16	25	7	0	.424	.332
Taubensee, Ed	.277	121	313	37	87	20	0	12	46	27	73	1	2	.460	.334
Timmons, Ozzie	.257	28	89	10	23	3	0	3	12	13	26	0	0	.389	.351
Watkins, Pat	.274	49	179	26	49	10	3	5	20	12	31	6	0	.444	.319
Young, Dmitri	.270	113	334	40	90	14	3	5	35	40	65	6	6	.372	.348

PITCHING

PITCHER	W	L	SV	ERA	G	GS	IP	H	HR	BB	SO
Belinda, Stan	3	4	6	4.02	70	0	80	69	8	31	83
Borland, Toby	2	1	1	4.57	26	0	33	32	3	21	25
Burba, Dave	11	10	0	4.40	35	26	162	154	19	77	130
Cooke, Steve	8	14	0	4.58	31	29	159	178	17	70	101
Crowell, Jim	4	6	0	5.29	17	14	92	106	11	49	36
Graves, Danny	3	3	2	4.61	36	3	64	76	5	29	24
Hutton, Mark	4	3	0	3.69	39	5	78	76	10	30	49
Jordan, Ricardo	1	2	0	4.56	30	0	34	35	1	20	23
Remlinger, Mike	6	6	1	4.43	61	11	106	87	10	54	120
Shaw, Jeff	4	4	26	2.88	65	0	81	75	6	17	60
Sullivan, Scott	3	2	1	3.39	41	0	66	56	8	22	64
Tomko, Brett	10	7	0	3.81	26	24	151	140	18	49	105
Weathers, David	2	2	0	3.93	11	5	41	44	4	12	27
White, Gabe	4	5	0	4.67	18	14	89	107	11	18	40
Glauber, Keith	3	2	1	3.70	38	0	44	40	3	18	33

181

HOUSTON ASTROS

MANAGEMENT

Manager	General Manager	Owner
Larry Dierker Career Record 84-78 .519	Gerry Hunsicker	Drayton McLane Jr.

1997 RECORD

Won-Lost 84-78	Pct. .519		Division Finish/GB 1 C		Wild Card Finish/GB	
Preseason Consensus Projection		2 (2.22)				
1st Half 40-42	2nd Half 44-36		Home 46-35	Road 38-43	Intradivision 31-17	Interleague 4-11
Comebacks 6-11	Blowouts 27-11		Nailbiters 39-46			

182

A JOB WELL DONE

Many barrels of ink were spilled over Houston's risky decision to move Larry Dierker out of the broadcast booth and into the dugout last season. While many broadcasters have previously moved into managerial roles, what made Dierker's case so interesting is that he had had no experience as a manager or coach at any level before his hiring last winter.

Many others, ranging from Lou Boudreau to Joe Torre to Bobby Valentine, have moved from the booth back to the field with varying levels of success. Of course, all of them had been managers before going to the booth.

Dierker and the Astros came through the year with flying colors, though, winning the weak NL Central title. The 24-year-fixture of the Astros' organization showed a refreshing no-B.S. attitude with the press, gained the respect of his players, and—most importantly—accom-

plished what his predecessor, Terry Collins, couldn't by riding a fairly weak team into the postseason. Not bad for his first year.

What did Dierker do? He gave his starting pitchers the reins and expected them to work hard and produce. They did. He gave Billy Wagner the closer job and expected him to save games. He did. He platooned where he had to, gave up offense for defense where he had to, and got a title out of a club that, on paper, was hardly a winner.

POWER OUTAGE

The Astros' team weakness was shown in the Division Series, when neither Craig Biggio nor Jeff Bagwell hit, and as a result all was lost. Derek Bell, the other third of the so-called "Killer B's," had a poor series as well.

Given that only first base and second base were above-average offensive positions for the Astros in 1997, how did the team win? There were two things that carried the Astros to victory: the great seasons from Biggio and Bagwell, and a strongly improved starting rotation.

The two B-boys were spectacular offensive players despite spending half their season in a poor hitters' park. Both batted .311 in road games; Biggio hit 15 of his 22 round-trippers away from home, while Bagwell batted only .258 in the Astrodome despite hitting 22 homers.

The club's offensive instability is shown by the fact that Dierker used 10 No. 2 hitters last year, six of them for 15 or more games. Luis Gonzalez batted cleanup for most of the season despite being better suited to a platoon role. Billy Spiers would have been an ideal No. 2 hitter, except for the fact that nobody had counted on him to hit as well as he did—he only played because regular third baseman Sean Berry was hurt for much of the season.

The Astros were able to score enough runs to win the NL Central because both Bagwell and Biggio stayed healthy and had spectacularly good seasons. While both could reprise their stellar performances in '98, Houston's chances of repeating will be measurably improved if the team can upgrade offensively at several positions. It has the potential to do so.

In the outfield, after trying several ultimately unsatisfactory options in center field (Pat Listach, Thomas Howard, James Mouton), Houston wound up the season with young Richard Hidalgo and reclamation project Chuck Carr splitting the position. Hidalgo is ready for a full shot in the bigs in '98, and he should get it.

Bob Abreu, another young hopeful, deserves a chance to play every day, but didn't get it in Houston. A lefthanded batter with seven years of pro experience, he turns just 24 in March and could be the top-of-the-order help the Phillies need. He could have been the top-of-the-order help the Astros needed, since he's been a very patient hitter in the minors and took 21 walks in only 210 plate appearances in 1997. The Astros left him unprotected in the expansion draft and Tampa Bay gladly grabbed him, then traded him to Philly for shortstop Kevin Stocker.

Left fielder Gonzalez is a good defensive player, but didn't offer enough offense to play every day. His .261 average, seven homers, and .348 on-base percentage against righthanders make him marginal as an everyday player.

TEAM MVP

While Jeff Bagwell had another superb season, this Astros team depended more than anything else on the multidimensional skills of leadoff man/second baseman **Craig Biggio**. The Houston sparkplug scored 146 runs, the highest total in the majors since 1985 and the most in the NL since 1932. Biggio hit .309 with 84 walks, 47 steals, 37 doubles, and 22 homers— and knocked in 81 runs despite batting first in all 156 of his starts. He also won the Gold Glove award.

BIGGEST SURPRISE

Righthander **Darryl Kile**'s ascent toward Cy Young territory propelled the Astros to their division title. He had never before pitched as well as he did for as long as he did. He didn't completely iron out his control problems, but Kile did improve enough to finally have earned the title of "staff ace."

BIGGEST DISAPPOINTMENT

Several players had disappointing seasons due to injury, such as Shane Reynolds, Sean Berry, Bob Abreu, and Tim Bogar. However, the biggest bummer may have been the continuing decline of former top prospect **James Mouton**. Despite several chances to establish himself in Houston's lineup, Mouton has failed to hit and played himself out of the organization's plans permanently.

183

However, he could be very helpful this season as a fourth outfielder for Detroit, with whom he signed as a free agent this winter, due to his decent speed, strong defense, and ability to get on base.

Derek Bell, the everyday right fielder, posted some adequate numbers—a .276 average, 15 homers, 71 RBIs, and 15 steals. Unfortunately, he was caught stealing seven times, did not put together good power numbers for a right fielder, had more errors (8) than assists (5), and walked only 40 times.

In his defense, Bell did suffer a hematoma in his left calf, which kept him out of action for nearly a month. However, in 1996 he was healthy, and did the same thing—compile an impressive RBI count (largely because of his lineup slot), hit some doubles, and steal some bases while hitting for a mediocre average (.263).

The Astros are tied to him through 1999, even though at 29 his best years appear to be behind him. He's not a good outfielder, and is prone to terrible slumps, and his contract is hobbling the team's ability to improve.

Houston's dissatisfaction with Bell is not atypical; just look at how weak the current NL crop of outfielders is. No team had three good offensive players in its outfield. Even Atlanta struggled along with Michael Tucker and Ryan Klesko having only slightly above-par seasons, and the Rockies' outfield looks good only if you throw out Dante Bichette's and Ellis Burks' mediocre-to-poor statistics on the road. Most good teams had at least one key player in their outfield suffer from a subpar season—Gary Sheffield in Florida, Todd Hollandsworth in L.A., Glenallen Hill in San Francisco, Ron Gant in St. Louis, Greg Vaughn in San Diego, an injury-plagued Al Martin in Pittsburgh, and whoever was playing center field for Houston—while the really bad teams like the Cubs, Cincinnati, and Philadelphia were almost laughably weak in the power-hitting corner positions. How hard can it be to find someone who can hit 20 homers and stick him in left field? Very hard, apparently.

On the left side of the infield the Astros were totally in flux. There was no regular at shortstop in '97, with Pat Listach, Ricky Gutierrez, Bill Spiers, and Tim Bogar all jousting for playing time during the year.

Finally, Bogar—waived by the Mets on March 31—was given the job in June. Even if he wasn't going to hit, he provided a good glove until his forearm was broken by a pitch on September 4. Although he surprised everyone, Bogar still hit only .249 and is not a championship-quality shortstop. Gutierrez is a good utility player, but was certainly out of place as a regular. Spiers is best as a third baseman due to his shoulder troubles. Listach, mercifully, was released July 1. The club's best hope for the future improvement at shortstop is Carlos Guillen.

Spiers did very well subbing for Berry at the hot corner last season, but neither one really supplied enough offense to help the team. Berry was re-signed at a much lower salary for '98 and will play regularly if healthy.

Overall, when looking at the Astros' record, their good fortune in winning a weak division, and the telling three-and-out playoff loss to the Braves, the answer to the question "How far can a team go with only two good offensive players?" turns out to be "However much it takes to win a weak division, and no further."

PITCHING PROBLEMS

During the '97 season Houston reliever John Hudek (trying to recover from two years of shoulder injuries) complained that manager Larry Dierker's policy of letting starting pitchers work out of their jams and, therefore, pitch more innings was playing havoc with the bullpen.

While Hudek, the former Astros closer, may be right about some members of the bullpen atrophying—himself, for instance—Dierker really had no other choice. Given a starting staff of young, strong arms that was underachieving, what option did he have other than to try to make them better? It is far more important for the future of the franchise that Darryl Kile, Shane Reynolds, and Mike Hampton become quality starters than it was for John Hudek, Jose Lima, and Russ Springer to get in their innings.

Kile had shown flashes of brilliance before but never could step up to become a staff ace. In '97, however, he threw a career-high six complete games (including four shutouts), while only a September slump kept him from winning 20. Last season Dierker gave Kile the responsibility of working out of his own jams—and he did. Kile also was able to put the ball where he wanted far more often; in

184

seven of his wins he walked only one batter. While Kile had his ups and downs, he remained healthy and mechanically sound.

One thing that Dierker did not receive enough credit for was his use of Ramon Garcia as a starter. During the first half Garcia worked largely as a middle reliever, making just two emergency starts as Kile, Reynolds, Hampton, Chris Holt, and Donne Wall filled out the rotation. When Reynolds went out in mid-June for knee surgery (he returned a month later) and Wall was bombed back to the minors, Dierker stuck Garcia in the rotation, where he made an immediate impact.

With a 1-3 record out of the bullpen, Garcia ended up 8-5 as a starter and was especially effective in the second half. After the All Star break Garcia went 6-1 with a 3.07 ERA in 14 starts. During September, Garcia won four of his five starts and lost none, compiling a 1.95 ERA. None of this was accomplished by his taking unusual advantage of the Astrodome.

As for the relievers, closer Billy Wagner's August slump can hardly be blamed on Dierker. Wagner had a regular work pattern, but just couldn't get strike one. Even the best relief pitchers sag sometimes, and one or two bad outings can easily fluff up a closer's ERA. By September, Wagner had turned the corner: he saved 23 games in 29 chances, along the way setting a single-season record for strikeouts per nine innings (14.40) for hurlers throwing 50 or more innings.

Middle relief was often a weak point for Houston. Springer fanned an outstanding 74 in 55 innings, consistently throwing a mid-90s fastball. However, he did have his problems in June and July, when he was cuffed around with some regularity. Springer did so well that he was one of Arizona's prize picks in the expansion draft.

The club's two lefthanded middle relievers, veteran Mike Magnante and rookie Tom Martin, acquitted themselves reasonably well. Martin, a soft-tossing southpaw, was more effective against righties and allowed nearly half of his inherited runners to score, but he did post a good 2.09 ERA. He was also taken in the expansion draft. Magnante was much more effective than Martin against lefthanders (.154).

Detroit refugee Jose Lima also had his moments but got

THE MOMENT OF
TRUTH

On **April 4** the 2-1 Astros scored the first of three straight come-from-behind wins at the Astrodome against chief divisional rival St. Louis in a series that set the tone for both clubs for the year. The April 4 victory, finally won on Jeff Bagwell's 11th-inning single, lifted the 'Stros into sole possession of first place, where they would spend nearly the entire season.

BEST DEAL

The Astros made a deal last winter that went largely unnoticed but that had a huge impact on the club, claiming pitcher **Ramon Garcia** in the Rule V draft from Milwaukee. Garcia began the season as a junk reliever, but moved into the rotation at midseason due to injured and ineffective teammates. He established himself as a presence during the late part of the season, going 4-0 in September.

WORST DEAL

Free agent **Pat Listach** came on board and was given the shortstop job in spring training. He proved to be an utter waste of time, showing neither hitting skill, acceptable range, nor the kind of baserunning that once made him valuable. The Astros released him on July 1.

185

1. **Richard Hidalgo, OF.** Houston has been loath to give him the everyday job in center field because of doubts that he can actually play the position adequately. The 22-year-old Hidalgo has been a very consistent minor league hitter, batting between .270 and .292 and hitting between 10 and 14 homers each year from 1993 to 1997. If he reaches those levels in the majors, Hidalgo will be only adequate, because he does not walk often and has only average speed. The Astros' recent acquisition of Moises Alou is not particularly good news for him.

2. **Russ Johnson, SS/3B.** Johnson, the Astros' top pick in 1994, hit .276 at Triple A New Orleans but disappointed with just four homers. However, he makes good contact and is regarded as smart. It's not likely that he will explode into a power machine as Jeff Bagwell did, but Johnson is expected to increase his production. He is prized for his fiery attitude, but even that may not make him a productive third baseman unless he either hits above .300 and takes walks or ratchets up his power considerably. The club does not believe he has the arm or range to play shortstop every day.

3. **John Halama, P.** John Thadeuz Halama is a six-foot, five-inch lefthander from Brooklyn who led the American Association in wins (13) and ERA (2.58) during 1997, making 24 starts and two relief appearances. He had finished second in the Texas League ERA race in 1996 with a 3.26 mark. Obviously Halama does not throw hard, because no noise has been made about him despite his obvious ability to get hitters out. He walked just 32 men in his 171 innings last season, struck out 126, and showed a fine pickoff move to boot. Halama is in the mix for a starting spot this spring.

4. **Daryle Ward, 1B.** Brought over from the Tigers in last off-season's mammoth trade, Ward increased his standing in 1997 with a 19-homer, 90-RBI year at Double A. He turns 23 this season with nowhere to go in the organization as a first baseman, but with a lot more home runs to come out of his bat. Ward also hit .329 at Jackson and continued to improve his strikeout and walk numbers. The son of former slugger Gary Ward is a tremendous talent.

5. **Scott Elarton, P.** A first-round pick in 1994, the six-foot, eight-inch Elarton throws three pitches, the best of which is a sharp curve. His velocity and command have both been up and down, but last season at Jackson, Elarton fanned 141 in 133 frames while going 7-4 with a 3.24 ERA. If Larry Dierker sees something he likes this spring, Elarton could get a call if other pitchers are injured or slumping.

6. **Carlos Guillen, SS.** A 22-year-old from Venezuela, he hit .254 with 10 homers at Jackson in 1997. He stayed healthy for the first time in three years and turned a lot of heads. Guillen may get a look this spring due to his speed, defensive skills, and developing power. Unfortunately, he's not going to hit big league pitching well for another couple of years; his pre-1997 pro experience consisted of 18 games in the Dominican Summer League, 30 games in the Gulf Coast League, and 29 games in the Midwest League. Suffice it to say that he's raw.

7. **Mitch Meluskey, C.** The switch-hitting catcher added power to his developing offensive game in 1997 and established himself as a prospect. He hit .340 with 14 homers at Jackson in just 73 games before heading to New Orleans, where he batted .250 with three more homers in 172 at bats. Meluskey will also take a walk. However, defense is a question: the 24-year-old Meluskey has a strong arm but is still raw around the plate.

murdered in road games (6.60 ERA), and righthanders batted .302 against him. He's no cinch to make the team in '98, even in a reprise of his middle role. Hudek walked 33 in 40 innings and posted a 5.98 ERA. He was dealt to the Mets in December for outfielder Carl Everett.

PAGING DR. DIERKER

The Astros' staff will be put to the test in 1998 with last year's big gun, Darryl Kile, gone. Therefore, righthander Shane Reynolds and lefthander Mike Hampton, both of whom should be fully recovered from various surgeries, will head up the rotation. Chris Holt and Ramon Garcia will probably start as well. That's a decent four-man base.

Management is hoping that two reclamation projects and one rookie can bolster the rotation. Southpaw Pete Schourek, hampered for two years by elbow problems, has come over as a free agent. Righthander Sean Bergman, who never has performed at a level his raw talent would indicate, was acquired in the off-season from San Diego. Finally, rookie lefthander John Halama, a two-time minor league ERA champ, hopes to break into the picture.

In the outfield the Astros have added Moises Alou and Carl Everett and subtracted Luis Gonzalez, James Mouton, and Chuck Carr. Alou in left will provide a lot more production than 1997's regular, Gonzalez. Everett, who can play all three pasture spots, will probably battle with Richard Hidalgo for the everyday job in center field, with Derek Bell remaining in right. However, if Bell slumps or the team gets a chance to unload his contract, Everett could end up seeing time in right field.

Alou should provide the Astros what Bell hasn't been able to supply: consistent extra-base punch in the fourth spot. Pro Player Stadium wasn't a good home run park last year, but Alou hit 12 of his 23 dingers there nonetheless.

Everett, 27 in June, has hit for power, gotten on base, played good defense, and run the bases well in his pro career—but rarely in the same season. He also comes with personal baggage and a damaged reputation, and has something to prove.

Both the rotation and the outfield will be challenging cases for sophomore manager Dierker. If he enjoys the success he experienced in 1997 with such projects, the Astros should end up in the catbird seat in the NL Central.

THE "ISN'T HE SELLING ALUMINUM SIDING BY NOW?" TEAM

The Astros were bedeviled by shortstop problems in 1997. Pat Listach didn't work out. Tim Bogar played well until injured. Chris Spiers fielded a stellar .932. Ricky Gutierrez did the job with the glove, but didn't hit. Finally, Luis Rivera got the call on September 1, at age 33 making his first appearance in the majors since 1994.

Therefore, Rivera became eligible to join the following motley cast of characters forgotten by most fans, but not by the teams who called them out of mothballs and back into the majors last season. (Yes, Berryhill did play one game at first base for the Giants.)

P	Scott Bailes	Rangers
C	Carlos Hernandez	Padres
1B	Damon Berryhill	Giants
2B	Tripp Cromer	Dodgers
SS	Luis Rivera	Astros
3B	Darnell Coles	Rockies
OF	Russ Morman	Marlins
OF	Hensley Meulens	Expos
OF	Rob Ducey	Mariners

187

1997 TEAM STATISTICS

BATTING/BASERUNNING

	Raw	Rank	+/- %		Raw	Rank	+/- %		Raw	Rank	+/- %
R	777	5	+4	BA	.259	8	-1	SB	171	2	+32
R/G	4.80	5	+4	HR	133	11	14	CS	74	1	+23
OBA	.344	3	+3	LH	354	2	+13	SB%	69.8	6	+3
SA	.403	9	-2	BB	633	3	+15				
PRO	.747	6	+1	SO	1,085	8	-1				

PITCHING/FIELDING

	Raw	Rank	+/- %		Raw	Rank	+/- %		Raw	Rank	+/- %
OR	660	3	-11	BA	.251	5	-4	OSB	92	1	-27
RA/G	4.07	3	-11	HR	134	4	-14	OCS	57	6	-3
OOB	.319	3	-4	LH	278	3	-11	OSB%	61.7	3	-9
OSA	.380	2	-7	BB	511	3	-8	FA	.979	11	0
PRO	.699	2	-6	SO	1,138	6	+3	GDP	131	11	+10

188

BATTING BY LINEUP SLOTS

	R	HR	RBI	BA	OBA	SA
1	149	22	82	.307	.412	.497
2	103	17	90	.294	.361	.450
3	116	44	138	.289	.426	.597
4	80	11	85	.254	.333	.361
5	89	15	75	.246	.317	.395
6	63	6	67	.255	.330	.342
7	60	8	78	.269	.342	.380
8	74	9	59	.255	.329	.382
9	43	1	46	.148	.203	.201

BATTING BY DEFENSIVE POSITION

	R	HR	RBI	BA	OBA	SA
C	57	5	59	.268	.332	.347
1B	115	44	136	.288	.429	.595
2B	149	22	81	.310	.417	.501
3B	79	14	86	.261	.339	.411
SS	69	5	64	.257	.327	.361
LF	89	12	81	.263	.349	.388
CF	81	12	63	.248	.316	.384
RF	80	15	85	.266	.331	.403
DH	5	2	3	.440	.462	.800
PH	19	2	38	.223	.315	.317
P	22	0	24	.113	.152	.148

TEAM PITCHING

	W-L	CG	QS	QS%	<6	>6	IPS	IP	ERA	OPR
ROTATION	62-50	16	97	60	26	85	6.4	1,043.0	3.61	.706

	W-L	GR	SV	BSV	HD	BHD	IRS%	IP	ERA	OPR
BULLPEN	22-28	354	37	22	105	81	42	416.0	3.83	.680

1998 PROJECTIONS

BATTING

PLAYER	BA	G	AB	R	H	2B	3B	HR	RBI	BB	SO	SB	CS	SA	OBA
Alou, Moises	.277	151	550	86	152	29	3	22	105	61	85	8	4	.461	.349
Ausmus, Brad	.266	125	397	47	106	22	1	5	41	38	76	12	7	.363	.331
Bagwell, Jeff	.278	159	566	103	157	39	2	35	120	118	113	25	8	.541	.403
Bell, Derek	.279	135	524	71	146	30	3	15	86	39	99	20	7	.433	.329
Biggio, Craig	.291	157	596	126	173	31	6	19	75	76	90	37	8	.460	.371
Bogar, Tim	.257	117	234	31	60	13	3	3	29	23	44	4	2	.376	.323
Butler, Rob	.260	51	102	15	26	7	1	0	12	8	12	1	1	.344	.312
Clark, Dave	.271	57	101	13	27	5	0	3	17	13	22	1	1	.417	.353
Eusebio, Tony	.283	67	192	18	55	6	1	2	25	21	30	0	1	.361	.355
Everett, Carl	.250	102	296	41	74	17	2	8	38	26	72	10	5	.409	.311
Gutierrez, Ricky	.276	85	240	29	66	11	2	2	25	19	44	5	2	.367	.328
Hidalgo, Richard	.272	88	338	45	92	24	3	7	47	21	52	3	0	.417	.315
Howell, Jack	.245	79	176	25	43	6	0	12	30	13	37	1	0	.491	.299
Johnson, Russ	.259	46	162	23	42	5	2	2	17	21	36	2	0	.338	.345
Phillips, J.R.	.244	22	79	10	19	5	0	4	12	6	27	0	0	.435	.300
Rivera, Luis	.238	14	43	5	10	3	1	1	5	4	7	1	0	.363	.299
Spiers, Bill	.287	137	274	41	79	20	3	4	41	47	40	8	3	.432	.392
Guillen, Carlos	.237	32	108	13	26	4	0	3	9	9	26	1	0	.348	.298

PITCHING

PITCHER	W	L	SV	ERA	G	GS	IP	H	HR	BB	SO
Cabrera, Jose	3	2	0	2.97	27	0	42	31	3	18	36
Garcia, Ramon	9	8	1	4.37	49	19	165	166	24	54	114
Hampton, Mike	13	10	0	3.88	32	32	204	207	15	69	131
Henry, Doug	3	6	5	4.33	61	0	64	63	5	33	60
Holt, Chris	7	11	0	3.68	31	28	191	196	15	58	85
Lima, Jose	2	5	1	5.28	34	3	58	63	8	14	46
Magnante, Mike	3	1	1	3.58	47	0	60	57	4	19	47
Reynolds, Shane	10	9	0	3.96	29	29	179	184	17	41	154
Wagner, Billy	6	7	27	2.92	62	0	71	50	6	35	106
Halama, John	5	5	0	3.74	15	14	101	107	7	22	61
Miller, Trever	5	5	0	4.31	14	14	79	97	9	29	40
Nitkowski, C.J.	5	4	0	3.65	12	12	76	78	5	24	52

MILWAUKEE BREWERS

MANAGEMENT

Manager	General Manager	Owner
Phil Garner Career Record 437-469 .482	Sal Bando	Bud Selig

1997 RECORD

Won-Lost	Pct.	Division Finish/GB	Wild Card Finish/GB
78-83	.484	3 C -8	5 -17.5

Preseason Consensus Projection	4 (3.83)		

1st Half	2nd Half	Home	Road	Intradivision	Interleague
37-40	41-43	47-33	31-50	22-25	8-7

Comebacks	Blowouts	Nailbiters
10-4	16-19	40-48

190

MIXED BAG

While most of the baseball news coming out of Milwaukee in recent seasons has been about the interim commissioner or the struggle to fund and build new Miller Park, the Milwaukee Brewers have—unknown to many—continued to play baseball games on the field. Brewers manager Phil Garner has continued to run an underfunded club that he manages to keep in contention, but for the third consecutive season, the Brew Crew slumped in the late going to fall out of the postseason hunt.

By the end of the '97 season the Brewers had slipped sharply and dropped out of contention. The offense just plain up and died, and Garner complained that some of his players weren't hustling and weren't executing.

It was an unfortunate end to what had been a most interesting and competitive season for the Brewers, one that came despite crippling injuries to first baseman John Jaha, left fielder Marc Newfield, starter Ben McDonald, second sacker Fernando Vina, and shortstop Jose Valentin.

Jaha's injury, which cost him more than 100 games, took a huge bite out of the team's offense. Dave Nilsson and Jeromy Burnitz had good years, but couldn't carry the load alone. Valentin, missing close to a month, declined from his big 1996 performance, and Vina was a serious offensive liability when healthy. Newfield's absence led to such unknowns as Jack Voigt and Todd Dunn seeing duty in left field; the Brewers used 11 players at the position in 1997.

Meanwhile, staff ace McDonald, going through another on-again, off-again season, was shut down in mid-July due to a torn rotator cuff. However, the Brewers got good pitching even in his absence, finishing fourth in the AL with a 4.22 ERA, a big improvement from eighth place and a 5.14 mark the season before.

It was clearly the anemic offense that sank the Brewers' pennant hopes. Only Toronto scored fewer runs than the Brewers did, even though a .260 team average made things seem not so bad. What killed the offense?

Besides Jaha's injury, the real culprit was a lack of plate discipline from most positions, including second base, center field, left field, catcher, and shortstop. Milwaukee had the second-fewest walks and the second-lowest on-base percentage in the league and, as most Milwaukeeans could tell you, it's hard to make weinerschnitzel without the veal.

The acquisition of Marquis Grissom, which popped the ejector seat on Gerald Williams in center field, will certainly help the Brewers. With Grip in center, Nilsson in left field, and Burnitz in right, the Brewers will have an outfield that scares people for a change—although the most frightened might actually be the fans in the left field seats watching Nilsson, attempt to ply his trade.

Another offensive-oriented change for 1998, which raised some eyebrows, was the Brewers' signing of veteran DH-first baseman Bob Hamelin. After all, Milwaukee isn't in the AL anymore; why did it want Hamelin, who isn't going to displace regular John Jaha at first?

Jaha has had only two healthy seasons out of five, which is one reason to want Hamelin around. The fact that Hamelin, a lefty, can platoon at first if necessary is another reason. The fact that Brewers pinch hitters hit only two home runs in 140 at bats last season is yet another reason. In fact, being in the NL, where pinch hitting and double switches are much more common, is the best reason of all to add Hamelin to the roster.

FERNANDO VINA: SECOND BEST?

The injuries to Fernando Vina and Jose Valentin gave Mark Loretta a chance to play, and he responded, batting .287 with five homers in 132 games. He played all four infield positions at least 15 times apiece, spending the most time (63 contests) at second base.

Loretta is a tough, gritty, versatile player who could be a regular for some teams. He isn't a championship-quality everyday player, however, and probably shouldn't be in there for Milwaukee. He is not the defensive player that either Valentin or Vina is, and he lacks Valentin's potentially explosive offensive production. Given a chance to hit

TEAM MVP

After false starts with the Mets and Indians, outfielder **Jeromy Burnitz** blossomed in 1997. He batted .281 in 153 games, pacing the Brewers in most critical offensive categories, including triples (8), homers (27), RBIs (85), and walks (75). He also threw out 13 runners from right field. Burnitz isn't superstar material, but he is the best everyday outfielder the Brewers have had for several years.

BIGGEST SURPRISE

The Brewers made 40-year-old **Doug Jones** their closer in 1997 out of desperation. He responded with perhaps his best season ever, saving 36 games with a 2.02 ERA and an amazing 82 K's and nine walks in 80.1 innings. Whether Jones can keep this up is almost irrelevant; the guy has had more comebacks than Maurice Chevalier.

BIGGEST DISAPPOINTMENT

Injuries to **John Jaha**, **Ben McDonald**, **Fernando Vina**, and **Marc Newfield** were extremely disappointing to Milwaukee, who were contending for a playoff spot in a relatively weak AL Central. Of the players that stayed healthy but didn't perform, No. 1 in manager Phil Garner's doghouse was center fielder **Gerald Williams**, whose inability to work the strike zone led to a mediocre .253 average in 155 games. He hit 32 doubles and swiped 23 bases, but took just 19 walks and had more than his share of mental lapses. The Brewers dealt him to Atlanta in December.

191

leadoff when Vina suffered a broken leg, Loretta posted just a .317 on-base percentage. He did much better hitting in the second slot, and batted a surprising .302 overall against righthanded pitchers.

Vina is truly outstanding at second base. But if Milwaukee is going to stick with Fernando (which they are, since they signed him to a multiyear deal last year), they must get him out of the leadoff slot. All but two of Vina's plate appearances in 1997 were in the top spot, and his .312 on-base percentage in that role is plainly inexcusable. Never a patient hitter, Vina drew only 12 walks and was caught stealing in seven of his 15 tries. Unfortunately for the Brewers, they simply don't have anybody else who can fill the leadoff role, either. Grissom may get the call, even though his skills are best suited for other slots in the order, as was shown in Cleveland.

THE MOUND CREW

The Brewers began the season with Cal Eldred, Ben McDonald, Scott Karl, and rookie Jeff D'Amico in the starting rotation. Jose Mercedes also made some spot starts.

Eldred was expected to supply both a lot of innings and good performance. But by the end of the season the pitcher his teammates call "Cornfed" because of his "workhorse" approach had the highest ERA (4.99) of any of the starters, although his 202 innings were an important contribution. Early-season slumps from Karl and Mercedes were evened out by their strong late-season performances, and D'Amico had an excellent first season.

Along the way such perennial enigmas as Angel Miranda and Al Reyes were disposed of, while low-cost gambles like Paul Wagner and Pete Harnisch were snapped up. Lefthander Joel Adamson, only 26 years old, was picked up on waivers from Florida, and showed excellent potential.

The deep bullpen, featuring big performances from ancient Doug Jones, Bob Wickman, Ron Villone, and Adamson, was a pleasant surprise and one of the more effective relief corps in the league. It could have been even better had Bryce Florie not had injury trouble. However, Wickman has had his ups and downs in the past, and counting on another big year from the 41-year-old Jones is hardly a sound idea. The Brewers need to get a hard-throwing righthander into the picture

somehow; Wagner could fit into this equation, assuming he's healthy.

By the end of the season the Milwaukee pitching picture looked much better than it had earlier. However, the series of off-season trades that brought Jeff Juden, Chad Fox, and Mike Myers to the team and sent away Florie, McDonald, Villone, and Mike Fetters hurt the staff. The loss of Adamson in the expansion draft was another blow.

The Brewers' 1998 rotation will be built from a group including Eldred, Karl, Mercedes, Wagner, Juden, Steve Woodard, Kyle Peterson, Brad Woodall, and Tim Van Egmond. In January the team announced that D'Amico would be sidelined at least until July due to surgery on a torn labrum in his right shoulder. D'Amico's career has been full of injury, but he is a key part of the team's future.

MILWAUKEE RETURNS TO THE SENIOR CIRCUIT

It is more than a little curious that the Milwaukee Brewers (Bud Selig, proprietor) could not forge a successful heritage as an American League team. After all, the franchise spent 28 years in the AL, which is more than twice the amount of time that the Milwaukee Braves played in the National League. In essence, the franchise decided that the three-decade-old Braves tradition was more appealing to fans than the current team.

The only conclusion that can be drawn is that the Brew Crew's lack of success in the past decade, plus the controversial struggle to get a new ballpark, has turned off most Wisconsin fans. After all, when you continually tell the locals that you're leaving town if they don't open their wallets, you incur no small amount of ill will.

It is true that the old Braves, led by Henry Aaron, Eddie Mathews, Warren Spahn, Lew Burdette, Johnny Logan, Del Crandall, and Joe Adcock, won two NL pennants, and beat the heavily-favored New York Yankees in the 1957 World Series in one of the bigger upsets in history. However, the Brewers won an AL pennant of their own in 1982 and had their fair share of local and national heroes, including Robin Yount, Paul Molitor, Ben Oglivie, Mike Caldwell, Cecil Cooper, Pete Vuckovich, and Gorman Thomas, as well as former NL stars like Don Sutton, Ted Simmons, and, briefly, Henry Aaron.

192

The Brewers' new home, the NL Central, is often referred to as the weakest division in baseball. This, in itself, gives Milwaukee more hope of winning a title in the next few years.

DOUG JONES: ANOTHER SHOT

Closer Doug Jones had a spectacular '97 season in Milwaukee, saving 36 games in 38 chances and putting together an amazing 82-9 strikeout-to-walk ratio. He also allowed just four homers in 80.1 innings.

Can Jones do it again? Since coming to the major leagues in 1987, he has stumbled several times, alternating fine seasons with terrible ones. Considering his complete lack of stuff, what's surprising is not that he has periods where hitters tattoo him to the outfield wall, but that he has periods where he baffles even the best hitters with his varied changeups. When was the last time you heard of a major league closer whose only effective pitch was a changeup?

In 1991 Jones pitched his way out of Cleveland after four terrific campaigns with a 4-8, 5.54 performance. After coming back for a great 1992 in Houston he was 4-10, 4.54 in 1993. After taking his tonic, he found his effectiveness again for the '94 Phillies, then he moved on to Baltimore, where he was pounded in '95.

The desperate Cubs signed him for 1996 but disposed of him after 28 games, just two saves, and a 5.01 ERA. That's when the Brewers disinterred him, got him back on his feet at Triple A, and brought him north.

With this kind of record, Jones is certainly not a pitcher that any monied club is going to gamble on. Even his supporters would admit that when he's not on his game, Jones is as hittable as a batting practice pitcher. However, if it's a question of him or the now-departed Mike Fetters, the Brewers would have been crazy to take the ball out of Jones' hand. The ancient junkballer will now get the ball until he proves he can't handle the job anymore. Which, based on his history, could be May 1998 or August 2000.

UPS AND DOWNS

Two Brewers outfielders, both of whom have long been considered talented enough to start in the majors, finally got their chances at everyday play in 1997. One proved he was a big league regular, and one didn't.

THE MOMENT OF TRUTH

The high point of Milwaukee's season came in late July and early August. The Brewers won nine in a row, closing the gap between themselves and first-place Cleveland from eight games to just 2.5 before fading for good. In their string the Brew Crew swept two doubleheaders from the visiting Blue Jays on consecutive days. In the first game of the first twin bill, on **July 28**, pitcher **Steve Woodard** made his big league debut by shutting out Roger Clemens and the Jays 1-0. Woodard fanned 12 in eight innings and allowed only one hit.

BEST DEAL

The Brewers made fine deals in 1996, acquiring young players like Jeromy Burnitz, Ron Villone, Bryce Florie, and Marc Newfield for veterans. However, last year the club did almost no dealing. The best move was probably the decision to finally let go of pitcher **Angel Miranda**, which cleared space for youngster **Steve Woodard**.

WORST DEAL

Acquiring veterans **Julio Franco** and **Darrin Jackson** down the stretch made little impact for the Brewers in 1997, but Jackson showed enough (.272 in 26 games) to earn a new contract for 1998. This can only spell trouble—if Jackson plays often, that means that either Marc Newfield, Jeromy Burnitz, or Dave Nilsson doesn't.

193

TOP PROSPECTS
SPRING 1998

1. **<u>Ron Belliard, 2B.</u>** Defense is Belliard's strong suit. The 23-year-old slumped early in 1997 at bat in Triple A, but came on late to hit .282 with 35 doubles and 61 walks at New Orleans. He is not an especially good basestealer, but Belliard still has potential to be a major league leadoff man. He's currently stuck behind Fernando Vina.

2. **<u>Geoff Jenkins, OF.</u>** The Brewers made Jenkins their No. 1 draft pick in 1995 in the hope that he would turn his power potential into results. He has not yet done that. Playing just 93 games last season at Triple A after undergoing knee surgery, he hit .236 with 10 homers. Jenkins, also bothered by a bad shoulder since 1996, is not going to get to the majors unless he hits. He turns 24 this summer.

3. **<u>Steve Woodard, P.</u>** Posting a 3.17 ERA and going 14-3 at Double A El Paso will get a pitcher noticed, even if, like Woodard, he doesn't have much of a fastball. Woodard, who will be 23 in July, wins with his ability to change speeds and throw strikes on the corners. He will begin the 1998 campaign in the Brewers' rotation. Originally a fifth-round pick in 1994, Woodard has a 45-19 professional record.

4. **<u>Sean Maloney, P.</u>** Not a hard thrower, the 26-year-old righthander saved 38 games and struck out 57 men in 59 innings in the Texas League in 1996, then fanned 21 and walked just three in 18.2 innings at Triple A Tucson in 1997. He uses a very good split-finger pitch, of which he has excellent control, to get his K's. Last season he pitched just 18 times (three in the majors) because he was forced to undergo an appendectomy. He's got a good chance to be in Milwaukee's bullpen this spring.

5. **<u>Valerio de los Santos, P.</u>** Disabled for much of the season with a staph infection, the hard-throwing lefthander went 6-10 at El Paso. He was moved from starting duty to the bullpen late in the season and is now considered a future closer candidate. The Brewers aren't worried by his 5.74 ERA in a hitter's park, but were dismayed by his low strikeout total (61 in 114 innings). He won't be 23 until December, so he has time to get back to the level he was in 1996 (10-8, 3.55 at Class A Beloit).

6. **<u>Antone Williamson, 1B.</u>** So far the former No. 1 pick, who turns 25 in July, has been a disappointment. He did not play third base effectively in the minors and had to be shifted to first, and isn't producing enough to play there regularly. Batting .283 with five homers at Triple A, as he did in 1997, isn't going to cut it. Williamson also didn't impress when called up to Milwaukee (.203 in 24 games). A first baseman who has never reached double figures in homers in a season and has hit .300 only once doesn't have a lot of value.

7. **<u>Mike Kinkade, 3B.</u>** He made 60 errors—yes, 60 errors—at El Paso, but the Brewers are more impressed with his .385 average and 109 RBIs. Kinkade, who will be 25 in May, had a good year at Class A in 1996, but his '97 El Paso explosion may be due to the great hitting environment in his home park. This year at Triple A, Kinkade will try and sustain the bat and improve the glove. He may shift to the outfield.

8. **<u>Travis Smith, P.</u>** The smallish righthander has an above-par fastball as well as a usable curve, changeup, and slider. Coming from nowhere, he was 16-3 at El Paso with a 4.15 ERA. He may not be a major league starter, but Smith could get the call sometime this year if he performs effectively at Triple A.

194

Jeromy Burnitz, who never got a real shot with either the Mets or the Indians, had an outstanding year for Milwaukee as its right field fielder (and occasional center fielder). Burnitz led the Brewers in almost every offensive category and threw out 13 baserunners to boot.

Gerald Williams, formerly a platoon player, got his chance and didn't make anything out of it. He played 155 games, 129 of them in center field, and showed good defense but very poor overall offense. His 32 doubles and 23 steals were all he could boast about; Williams had an awful .282 on-base percentage and slugged a weak .369. Phil Garner was very unhappy at his lack of plate discipline, but this shouldn't have been a surprise to anyone familiar with his career record.

THE LITTLE PARK THAT COULD

The Brewers' top hitting prospect is Double A third baseman Mike Kinkade, who despite making 60 errors at third base in the Texas League, is rated as a hopeful because of a big offensive year at El Paso. Kinkade, a 24-year-old former catcher, batted .385 with 180 hits, 23 doubles, 12 triples, 12 homers, and 109 RBIs.

Big deal. El Paso has long been the locus of inflated batting statistics among minor league ballparks. Let's take a quick look at the record.

These are the top hitters at El Paso, 1987-96. (An asterisk indicates a player led the league in that category.)

Year	Player	BA	HRs	RBIs
1996	Todd Dunn	.340	19	78
	Brad Seitzer	.319	17	87
1995	Brian Banks	.308	12	78
	Antone Williamson	.309	7	90
1994	Rodney Lofton	.331*	2	54
	Scott Talanoa	.259	28*	88
	Tim Unroe	.310	15	103*
1993	Bo Dodson	.312	9	59
	Ed Smith	.294	8	69
1992	Troy O'Leary	.334*	5	79
	Edgar Caceres	.312	2	52
	John Byington	.306	4	64
1991	John Jaha	.344	30*	134*
	Jim Tatum	.320	18	128
	Shon Ashley	.308	24	100
1990	Jesus Alfaro	.301	16	88
	Craig Cooper	.282	11	63
1989	Tim McIntosh	.300	17	93
	Ramon Sambo	.322	2	34
1988	Mario Monico	.342	8	52
	Greg Vaughn	.301	28*	105*
1987	Lavell Freeman	.395*	24	96
	Todd Brown	.330	13	82

With a couple of exceptions, the big question is, "Who are these guys?" Only O'Leary, Jaha, and Vaughn have enjoyed any major league success.

In 1992 O'Leary led the Texas League in average, hits, total bases, and runs. The year before, Jaha paced the TL in homers, RBIs, runs, total bases, and finished second in hitting. In '88 Vaughn led the league in doubles, runs, total bases, homers, and RBIs. The conclusion is unavoidable: if you play in El Paso and don't blow the league away, you're not much of a hitter.

El Paso almost annually leads the Texas League in team batting average, so a high average there means little. Remember Billy Jo Robidoux? He hit .342 in 1985 at El Paso with 46 doubles and 132 RBIs. His career major league average in 173 games: .209.

More evidence? In 1983 somebody named Carlos Ponce batted .348 at El Paso with 50 doubles and 111 RBIs. Somebody named Billy Max hit .336 with 28 homers and 112 RBIs. Earnest Riles won the batting title that year, hitting .349 for El Paso. In 1981 two guys named Stan Davis (.313) and Johnny Evans (.312) finished seventh and eighth in the TL batting race, combining for 46 homers and 216 RBIs. Ever hear of them?

Before the 1997 season Milwaukee shifted its Triple A franchise from New Orleans (a pitcher's park, but good for home runs) to Tucson (a hitter's park). Should Kinkade have big numbers in Triple A for 1998, that won't necessarily mean he's very good. The Brewers have the unfortunate circumstance of annually having to drain the air out of the batting statistics posted by their upper-level minor league hitters. That should be easy, right? If it were such a snap, how would Vinny Castilla and Dante Bichette ever gotten to be considered good hitters?

195

MILWAUKEE BREWERS
1997 TEAM STATISTICS

BATTING/BASERUNNING

	Raw	Rank	+/- %			Raw	Rank	+/- %			Raw	Rank	+/- %
R	681	13	-15		BA	.260	11	-4		SB	103	8	-3
R/G	4.23	13	-14		HR	135	13	-24		CS	55	6	+7
OBA	.325	13	-4		LH	321	7	0		SB%	65.2	11	-3
SA	.398	13	-7		BB	494	13	-13					
PRO	.723	13	-6		SO	967	6	-7					

PITCHING/FIELDING

	Raw	Rank	+/- %			Raw	Rank	+/- %			Raw	Rank	+/- %
OR	742	4	-7		BA	.261	3	-4		OSB	106	7	-3
RA/G	4.61	4	-7		HR	177	7	0		OCS	52	7	-2
OOB	.333	4	-2		LH	299	4	-8		OSB%	67.1	7	+1
OSA	.418	4	-3		BB	542	6	-3		FA	.980	10	0
PRO	.751	4	-2		SO	1,016	7	-1		GDP	146	13	+12

196

BATTING BY LINEUP SLOTS

	R	HR	RBI	BA	OBA	SA
1	92	11	61	.269	.315	.371
2	96	20	83	.274	.363	.456
3	72	14	80	.285	.355	.422
4	89	29	95	.257	.342	.450
5	80	21	82	.247	.319	.425
6	69	16	82	.260	.329	.406
7	73	13	67	.260	.304	.389
8	57	6	45	.235	.283	.323
9	53	5	48	.247	.308	.332

BATTING BY DEFENSIVE POSITION

	R	HR	RBI	BA	OBA	SA
C	46	5	50	.257	.321	.342
1B	78	25	83	.241	.324	.408
2B	76	8	66	.287	.332	.386
3B	83	12	93	.292	.369	.438
SS	72	17	65	.251	.315	.384
LF	77	16	66	.241	.292	.384
CF	69	10	46	.248	.292	.380
RF	95	26	84	.271	.352	.503
DH	68	14	71	.263	.336	.379
PH	9	2	19	.231	.317	.325
P	0	0	0	.000	.053	.000

TEAM PITCHING

	W-L	CG	QS	QS%	<6	>6	IPS	IP	ERA	OPR
ROTATION	57-62	6	70	43	27	51	5.9	950.0	4.47	.756

	W-L	GR	SV	BSV	HD	BHD	IRS%	IP	ERA	OPR
BULLPEN	21-21	367	44	15	132	66	35	477.1	3.75	.741

BATTING

PLAYER	BA	G	AB	R	H	2B	3B	HR	RBI	BB	SO	SB	CS	SA	OBA
Banks, Brian	.268	24	84	11	23	5	1	2	13	7	23	1	0	.414	.325
Burnitz, Jeromy	.268	157	463	78	124	33	6	23	78	68	101	16	10	.515	.361
Cirillo, Jeff	.291	155	555	80	162	42	3	11	76	59	69	4	4	.440	.359
Diaz, Eddy	.271	14	52	7	14	3	1	1	9	3	5	0	0	.398	.309
Dunn, Todd	.250	23	78	12	19	6	1	3	11	6	25	1	0	.459	.305
Grissom, Marquis	.278	139	558	80	155	26	6	15	62	41	77	24	11	.426	.328
Jackson, Darrin	.282	47	151	18	43	7	1	4	22	7	26	3	1	.411	.316
Jaha, John	.272	87	314	54	85	16	0	19	59	45	68	2	0	.506	.364
Levis, Jesse	.274	100	209	22	57	7	0	1	20	29	16	1	0	.320	.361
Loretta, Mark	.287	103	302	42	87	11	3	3	32	33	42	3	3	.377	.357
Matheny, Mike	.250	124	328	32	82	17	2	5	41	18	78	1	2	.360	.289
Newfield, Marc	.263	65	193	22	51	12	0	4	28	15	36	0	0	.394	.317
Nilsson, Dave	.287	139	494	70	142	30	1	18	78	57	75	2	3	.464	.361
Valentin, Jose	.253	138	489	69	124	26	3	19	68	47	117	19	7	.434	.318
Vina, Fernando	.283	117	440	64	125	15	5	5	40	25	32	12	7	.380	.322
Williamson, Antone	.265	46	155	23	41	10	2	2	20	22	26	1	0	.390	.358

PITCHING

PITCHER	W	L	SV	ERA	G	GS	IP	H	HR	BB	SO
D'Amico, Jeff	11	9	0	4.82	29	29	164	167	33	54	111
Eldred, Cal	10	12	0	4.77	29	29	172	173	25	75	104
Fox, Chad	0	2	0	3.53	53	0	48	44	7	29	49
Jones, Doug	6	5	29	3.08	73	0	79	75	6	15	78
Juden, Jeff	9	5	0	4.37	40	19	140	133	18	64	116
Karl, Scott	10	11	0	4.56	31	30	185	203	23	66	110
Mercedes, Jose	6	10	0	4.21	30	20	143	137	23	49	72
Misuraca, Mike	1	1	0	4.24	5	1	17	17	2	6	8
Myers, Mike	0	4	2	5.11	90	0	60	62	11	29	58
Reyes, Al	2	2	0	3.25	20	0	30	23	4	12	28
Ruffcorn, Scott	0	2	0	5.41	13	3	28	26	3	22	23
Wickman, Bob	6	4	3	3.55	66	0	86	87	7	38	67
Woodard, Steve	7	6	0	4.16	18	18	117	127	10	23	73

PITTSBURGH PIRATES

MANAGEMENT

Manager	General Manager	Owner
Gene Lamont Career Record 337-293 .535	Cam Bonifay	Kevin McClatchy

1997 RECORD

Won-Lost	Pct.	Division Finish/GB		Wild Card Finish/GB	
79-83	.488	2 C	-5	5	-13

Preseason Consensus Projection	5 (4.65)				

1st Half	2nd Half		Home	Road		Intradivision	Interleague
37-43	42-40		43-38	36-45		24-24	7-8

Comebacks	Blowouts		Nailbiters				
9-8	23-24		40-40				

198

DOING A LOT WITH A LITTLE

A great deal of credit for Pittsburgh's 1997 success must go to manager Gene Lamont, who took hamburger and nearly made lemonade out of it. Given a club picked to lose more than 100 games by most analysts, he kept it in the running for the (admittedly weak) NL Central Division title until late September.

Lamont made some gutsy choices, giving rookie right fielder Jose Guillen a job straight out of Class A, dipping into Triple A repeatedly for has-beens and never-weres like Kevin Polcovich, Turner Ward, Mark Smith, and Marc Wilkins, and making rookie Rich Loiselle his closer when veteran John Ericks came up lame. He did a good job handling a raw corps of starting pitchers and induced good performances out of a modestly talented bullpen.

While Lamont's performance as ringmaster of the Chicago White Sox circus drew mixed reviews, he did win

a division title and finished his term 48 games over .500. With low-budget Pittsburgh in 1997, he had few alternatives, so he made a plan—let the kids play and try to win with pitching, speed, and defense—and stuck with it.

If the Pirates hope to contend again this year, Lamont needs to do some big work on the offense. There are very specific places in which Pittsburgh must improve: power hitting and getting on base.

The Pirates hung in contention until the last week of the season despite an offense that scored only 725 runs, eighth in the NL. Pittsburgh batted .262, a point under the league average, but walked just 481 times, fewer than any team in baseball besides Montreal and the Cubs; its on-base percentage of .329 was four points below the NL average.

The Bucs rapped only 129 homers, fewer than any club besides Philadelphia (119) and, again, the Cubs (127). Led by Tony Womack (60 steals), the Pirates did finish fourth in the majors in stolen bases with 160.

A Pirates rally, then, usually consisted of a few singles and a stolen base. Few Pittsburgh hitters had power or patience, and those who had one rarely possessed the other. Kevin Young led the club by hitting a surprising 18 homers, but took only 16 walks. Guillen tried his best to match Young's more-homers-than-walks feat, but could only manage 14 round-trippers to go with his 17 walks. Veteran Shawon Dunston, acquired in a late-season deal with the Cubs, finished the season with 14 homers and an almost incredible eight walks. Leadoff hitter Womack's 43 free passes ranked fourth on the club, only a handful behind club leader Jason Kendall, who walked just 49 times.

Fortunately for the Pirates, there is help on the way. If Pittsburgh gives Jermaine Allensworth an everyday outfield job in 1998, he will most likely walk 60 or 70 times. Hot prospects Ron Wright (at first base) and Chad Hermansen (now in the outfield) have proved to be disciplined hitters in the minors. Veteran left fielder Al Martin, third-year catcher Kendall, and Allensworth are probably around for the long term. Young probably isn't going to be around for the long haul, although his 1997 performance will give him first crack at the starting job at first or third base in 1998.

As for Womack and Guillen, they have a lot of work to do if they want to be productive big league hitters.

CAN THEY DO IT AGAIN?

Young teams that make big leaps forward one year often fall back the next. How the Pirates handle the growing pains they are likely to encounter this year will determine their long-term success or failure. How could the Pirates fall back? Let us count the ways:

Starting pitching. Pittsburgh had five healthy pitchers last season who combined to start all but five of the club's games. That isn't likely to continue, simply because the list of teams with five reliable and healthy starting pitchers for more than a year is very, very short.

Hitting. As weak as the Pirates' attack was in 1997, it could be even worse this season. Tony Womack may have had a career season at second base, and the same easily can be said for Kevin Polcovich at shortstop. Kevin Young and Jose Guillen have serious problems with the strike zone,

TEAM MVP

It isn't easy to select one player as Pittsburgh's MVP. In truth, they lacked a star-caliber player but were adequate at most positions. However, one player best exemplified the Bucs' grittiness and never-give-up quality: catcher **Jason Kendall**. He led the Pirates with a .389 on-base percentage, beefed up in large part because he was hit by pitches 31 times (second in the league). Kendall scored more runs than anyone else on the team but leadoff man Tony Womack, and he is one of the league's better defensive catchers.

BIGGEST SURPRISE

That **Gene Lamont** was able to fashion a good five-man rotation out of **Jon Lieber**, **Esteban Loaiza**, **Jason Schmidt**, **Steve Cooke**, and **Francisco Cordova** was perhaps the biggest surprise of the Pirates' season. While none of those pitchers was of Cy Young caliber, none of them were bombed out of the rotation either, and each made 29 or more starts. Only five of the Bucs' 162 games were started by anyone other than those five.

BIGGEST DISAPPOINTMENT

After batting .274 with 13 homers in 1996, first baseman **Mark Johnson** came into the '97 season with a job for the first time. Unfortunately for the Pirates, he never got untracked in 1997, hitting just four homers in 78 games and striking out in more than a third of his at bats. Johnson backslid so far that he fell back to Triple A and, eventually, out of the organization's plans.

199

THE MOMENT OF
TRUTH

The high point for the 1997 Pirates came on July 12. The first-place Astros were in town with the Bucs just one game behind. A sellout crowd of 44,119 jammed the rafters of Three Rivers Stadium to watch **Francisco Cordova** pitch nine innings of no-hit ball against Houston. The Pirates couldn't score either, so extra innings were needed. After reliever **Ricardo Rincon** sent down the Astros in the tenth, **Mark Smith** smashed a dramatic, game-winning three-run homer to left-center that sent the crowd into hysterics, elevating the Pirates into a first-place tie with the Astros and ending the first extra-inning combined no-hitter in major league history.

BEST DEAL

Two big deals last winter with Toronto and Kansas City brought the Pirates several young arms and third baseman **Joe Randa**, but the trade that perhaps benefited Pittsburgh the most in 1997 was an August 1996 deal that brought **Rich Loiselle** over from Houston for veteran hurler **Danny Darwin**. The hard-throwing Loiselle stepped into the breach when projected closer **John Ericks** got hurt in May, and all Loiselle did was save 29 games.

WORST DEAL

The Pirates haven't made too many bad trades of late. One player they perhaps should have held on to was infielder **Nelson Liriano**, whom the Pirates waived last winter. He is a good pinch hitter with some speed and the ability to play three infield spots. Pittsburgh could have used him last summer.

which pitchers are likely to exploit this season. Bench players Turner Ward and Mark Smith will probably sag as well. Players that are likely to improve their performance this year include Al Martin, who was injured for much of 1997, and Jermaine Allensworth. Newly acquired third baseman–second baseman Doug Strange was very productive with Montreal in 1997, but he will be 34 in April.

At times in 1997 the Pirates seemed to run on adrenaline, and they certainly liked being underdogs. This year, Pittsburgh isn't going to sneak up on anybody. The league knows they can play ball, and the young Bucs will be forced to make adjustments. Some will, some won't.

Of course, the Bucs will also be working more outstanding prospects into the equation, which is why this club will ultimately win a few division championships. Shortstop candidates Lou Collier and Abraham Nunez, third base hopeful Aramis Ramirez, outfielder Chad Hermansen, and pitchers Jose Silva, Jose Pett, Kris Benson, Jimmy Anderson, and Jeff Wallace are all on track for big league jobs, some of which could open up this spring.

Pittsburgh general manager Cam Bonifay is now seeing the fruits of his trades. He successfully traded a truckload of veteran players for a boatload of prospects. As a result the Pirates' farm system is now widely regarded as having the most talent of any organization.

TONY WOMACK: HOW GOOD IS HE?

Infielder Tony Womack's hot September in 1996 gave him an inside track on a starting job in 1997.

The real reason the Pirates wanted to give Womack a regular job was his speed. The Pirates, who knew they'd be short on offense, decided to do what many power-short teams do: add speed as a substitute. Womack played every day and led the NL with 60 steals in 67 attempts, hit .278, and established himself as a major league regular.

That's the good news. The bad news is that, despite hitting leadoff and playing 155 games, Womack scored just 85 runs. This is due mostly to a subpar .326 on-base percentage a direct result of Womack's walking just 43 times in nearly 700 plate appearances.

Now 28, Womack is not likely to improve that much as a hitter, so is he really valuable? In a word, no. There is no substitute for getting on base. Speed can win a game here and a game there, but it's almost a certainty that a hitter with a .375 on-base percentage and 20 steals will score more runs than Womack did in 1997 if the two were surrounded by the same hitters.

However, while Womack may not be a good leadoff hitter, he could still help win ballgames as a lower-order hitter—if he plays good defense. So how was Womack's glovework? He showed below-average range and committed 20 errors, the highest total of any NL second baseman. The Pirates might need to find another option if they want to contend.

THE DOLLAR STORE

The 1997 Pirates benefited from the performances of two bargain-basement free-agent pickups, Turner Ward and Mark Smith. Both were released by other clubs and signed Triple-A deals with the Pirates (who, by the way, had 70 roster or nonroster players in their spring camp). That's to say nothing of Dale Sveum, who played great ball in '97 after joining the organization as a minor league free agent back in 1994 after his big league career had flamed out.

Ward, who came up to the majors in midseason, hit .353 in 167 at bats with 16 doubles and seven homers. He slugged .587, and he showed he could play all three outfield positions.

Smith was dumped by San Diego in the spring but joined Pittsburgh during the year when injuries struck. All Smith did was hit .285 with nine homers in 193 at bats. He also posted a .374 on-base percentage, second highest on the team.

TOP PROSPECTS
SPRING 1998

1. **Kris Benson, P.** A first-round pick, Benson began his pro career last season at Class A Lynchburg and was 5-2, with 72 K's and 13 walks in 59 innings. At Double A Carolina, Benson posted a 4.98 ERA and a 3-5 record in 14 games. He has a blazing fastball, a sharp curve, a developing changeup and could be in the majors this season.

2. **Lou Collier, SS.** A good defensive shortstop, the 24-year-old Collier hit .330 last season at Triple A Calgary but with no power and few walks. Collier, Kevin Polcovich, and Abraham Nunez will be in the mix this spring, and Collier has a chance to win the job.

3. **Abraham Nunez, SS.** He came from Toronto in last winter's Orlando Merced trade and became one of the organization's prized prospects. Nunez, just 22 this year, hit .260 with 29 steals at Lynchburg, then batted .328 in a 47-game promotion to Carolina. He also played 19 games for Pittsburgh. Nunez has no power, but has tremendous defensive skills, a good eye, and could be a leadoff man.

4. **Jimmy Anderson, P.** The 22-year-old southpaw has an average fastball with outstanding movement and a terrific slider. He should be a successful big league pitcher even if his control doesn't improve. Anderson has been successful everywhere he has pitched.

5. **Chad Hermansen, IF/OF.** Hermansen was the Bucs' first-round draft pick in 1995, out of high school. He runs well and has hit everywhere. Originally a shortstop, Hermansen has been tried in center field but ended 1997 playing second base.

6. **Jose Silva, P.** After five years with Toronto, Silva was traded to the Pirates in November 1996. The hard-throwing righthander is being considered for a starting job. The keys to his success are throwing his slider and changeup more often and more effectively.

7. **Ron Wright, 1B.** Limited to just 91 games due to injury, Wright whomped 16 homers at Calgary and knocked in 63 runs, but fanned 91 times. Wright is still an outstanding prospect because of his pure power, and will be just 22 this season.

8. **Jeff Wallace, P.** The lefthander made the majors last year at age 21. Converted to relief last spring, the Pirates recalled him for 11 games, in which he allowed one earned run in 12 innings and fanned 14 men. Wallace throws in the upper 90s, but does have control troubles.

9. **Aramis Ramirez, 3B.** At the tender age of 19 Ramirez was the Class A Carolina League's MVP. The Pirates have given some thought to promoting him all the way up to the majors in 1998. Ramirez hit 29 homers and drove in 114 runs last season at Lynchburg.

201

1997 TEAM STATISTICS

BATTING/BASERUNNING

	Raw	Rank	+/- %			Raw	Rank	+/- %			Raw	Rank	+/- %
R	725	9	-3		BA	.262	7	0		SB	160	4	+23
R/G	4.48	9	-3		HR	129	12	-17		CS	50	12	-17
OBA	.329	9	-1		LH	343	3	+9		SB%	76.2	1	+13
SA	.404	8	-2		BB	481	12	-13					
PRO	.733	10	-1		SO	1,161	13	+6					

PITCHING/FIELDING

	Raw	Rank	+/- %			Raw	Rank	+/- %			Raw	Rank	+/- %
OR	760	9	+2		BA	.271	12	+4		OSB	109	6	-14
RA/G	4.69	9	+2		HR	143	5	-8		OCS	66	10	+12
OOB	.343	12	+3		LH	331	10	+6		OSB%	62.3	4	-8
OSA	.415	9	+2		BB	560	8	0		FA	.979	12	0
PRO	.757	10	+2		SO	1,080	9	-2		GDP	113	6	-5

202

BATTING BY LINEUP SLOTS

	R	HR	RBI	BA	OBA	SA
1	95	8	60	.275	.332	.380
2	92	9	69	.261	.333	.369
3	101	18	84	.272	.356	.440
4	94	22	97	.262	.334	.429
5	83	23	106	.289	.354	.484
6	85	17	82	.303	.374	.474
7	66	16	83	.263	.310	.413
8	73	10	58	.260	.340	.392
9	36	6	47	.156	.205	.236

BATTING BY DEFENSIVE POSITION

	R	HR	RBI	BA	OBA	SA
C	81	8	56	.288	.381	.426
1B	94	24	102	.265	.342	.440
2B	88	7	58	.279	.330	.381
3B	77	16	85	.279	.338	.441
SS	73	19	80	.271	.336	.449
LF	97	20	91	.270	.345	.447
CF	91	7	72	.260	.333	.357
RF	70	21	89	.266	.320	.435
DH	4	2	5	.304	.333	.609
PH	27	5	29	.230	.309	.390
P	12	0	19	.109	.142	.128

TEAM PITCHING

	W-L	CG	QS	QS%	<6	>6	IPS	IP	ERA	OPR
ROTATION	53-57	6	90	56	38	60	5.8	943.0	4.25	.752

	W-L	GR	SV	BSV	HD	BHD	IRS%	IP	ERA	OPR
BULLPEN	26-26	451	41	18	146	91	36	493.0	4.34	.767

1998 PROJECTIONS

BATTING

PLAYER	BA	G	AB	R	H	2B	3B	HR	RBI	BB	SO	SB	CS	SA	OBA
Allensworth, Jermaine	.263	110	383	58	101	18	3	4	48	45	85	15	8	.359	.340
Brown, Adrian	.289	52	192	36	56	8	2	1	16	22	29	10	0	.368	.361
Brown, Emil	.184	20	29	5	5	1	0	1	2	3	10	2	0	.293	.264
Collier, Lou	.275	58	192	26	53	12	2	0	20	14	30	5	0	.356	.324
Garcia, Freddy	.224	67	234	32	52	10	1	12	35	13	59	0	0	.429	.265
Guillen, Jose	.270	150	524	62	142	21	5	15	75	18	94	1	2	.417	.295
Kendall, Jason	.290	157	520	72	151	35	5	7	52	49	50	15	5	.418	.351
Martin, Al	.290	126	483	74	140	28	5	14	59	47	92	26	9	.453	.353
Nunez, Abraham	.259	47	170	21	44	5	2	1	12	14	33	5	0	.325	.315
Osik, Keith	.277	42	100	11	28	9	1	0	8	9	18	0	1	.385	.338
Polcovich, Kevin	.274	87	254	39	70	17	1	5	22	22	47	2	2	.401	.332
Smith, Mark	.270	79	217	30	58	13	1	9	36	27	42	3	2	.468	.350
Strange, Doug	.253	118	299	36	76	14	2	9	42	30	64	0	2	.406	.321
Ward, Turner	.248	80	232	34	57	15	2	7	34	19	32	4	0	.419	.304
Womack, Tony	.285	148	591	84	169	25	9	5	50	43	102	56	6	.384	.334
Young, Kevin	.280	118	379	61	106	20	2	20	76	20	100	11	3	.497	.315
Wright, Ron	.248	38	139	17	35	10	0	5	21	8	40	0	0	.430	.291

203

PITCHING

Burrows, Terry	2	2	0	4.09	21	0	26	26	2	12	18
Christiansen, Jason	3	2	0	4.46	56	0	54	60	5	28	53
Cordova, Francisco	11	10	5	3.85	48	26	189	191	16	50	140
Granger, Jeff	2	2	0	3.82	12	4	28	31	2	10	19
Lieber, Jon	10	11	0	4.50	40	27	174	187	22	43	138
Loaiza, Esteban	9	10	0	4.31	30	29	177	197	18	53	105
Loiselle, Rich	1	5	28	3.31	67	1	73	80	8	25	63
McCurry, Jeff	1	3	0	4.25	30	0	36	38	6	16	16
Peters, Chris	4	3	0	3.22	31	7	62	52	6	29	41
Rincon, Ricardo	4	9	6	3.54	66	0	63	55	5	26	75
Schmidt, Jason	10	10	0	4.75	34	30	184	190	16	81	135
Silva, Jose	7	5	0	3.32	29	16	106	115	6	35	73
Tabaka, Jeff	2	1	0	3.01	30	0	30	23	3	11	29
Wallace, Jeff	0	0	0	0.86	38	0	42	30	0	30	48
Wilkins, Marc	7	4	2	3.92	58	1	69	64	7	32	47
Williams, Mike	2	2	0	3.90	11	4	35	30	3	15	24
Anderson, Jimmy	5	4	0	4.05	17	17	84	85	6	44	52
Benson, Kris	3	3	0	4.07	11	11	53	56	8	22	42

MANAGEMENT

Manager	General Manager	Owner
Tony LaRussa Career Record 1481-1346 .524	Walt Jocketty	Limited Partnership

1997 RECORD

Won-Lost 73-89	Pct. .451	Division Finish/GB 4 C -11	Wild Card Finish/GB 9 -19

Preseason Consensus Projection	1 (1.52)		

1st Half	2nd Half	Home	Road	Intradivision	Interleague
39-41	34-48 •	41-40	32-49	20-28	8-7

Comebacks	Blowouts	Nailbiters
8-17	23-19	34-52

204

RUNNING OUT OF GAS

The 1997 Cardinals were never close to repeating their 1996 success. Even though new leadoff hitter Delino DeShields had an excellent comeback season and veteran Ray Lankford put up some great numbers, the offense was dysfunctional from opening day, and even vaunted manager Tony LaRussa couldn't squeeze runs out of his undermanned, overaged, injury-ravaged squad.

While left fielder Ron Gant's performance (.229, 17 HRs, 62 RBIs) was a terrible disappointment to the team, other factors—Dmitri Young's failure to produce at first base, the retention of elderly Gary Gaetti at third, and injuries to right fielder Brian Jordan and catcher Tom Pagnozzi—were equally damaging to the Redbirds' offense.

The 38-year-old Gaetti played hard, continued to field his position well, and hit 17 homers. However, all in all he had one of those seasons that look worse the closer they are

examined. For a cornerman playing 148 games, 17 homers and 69 RBIs aren't much; a .251 average, just 36 walks, and 20 double-play groundouts put a terrible drain on the team's offense.

Meanwhile, Jordan's injury problems were destructive, disabling him three times during the year. Thoroughly unable to play the field or provide any power at bat (just five doubles, no homers, and no triples in 145 at bats) due to serious back troubles, he left an offensive hole that John Mabry couldn't fill.

What went right? The midseason trade for Mark McGwire injected some excitement into an otherwise dull season, and the club's decision to sign McGwire to a long-term deal showed loyal Redbirds fans that the Cards are serious about regaining their place at the top of the NL Central.

Except . . . there are several excepts. McGwire is the best

home run hitter in the game, but he is now 34 years old and, improbably, has been healthy for most of the last two seasons. Signing an older player with a serious injury history to a long-term deal is a huge gamble, one the Cardinals lost in 1997 with Gant.

The inability of the St. Louis system to produce young position players in recent years means that the club will again have to build through trades and free agency to be successful. The skill of an experienced and veteran-oriented manager like LaRussa, then, is appropriate for this team.

However, even LaRussa, regarded as a managerial genius by many others besides himself, can't work miracles with a club this thin. The injuries and inefficiency of several regulars forced the bench into action, and LaRussa's crop of reserves for 1997—many of whom he brought in himself—was well below average. A bench that contained, at different times, Steve Scarsone, Mike Gallego, Phil Plantier, Danny Sheaffer, Scott Livingstone, Willie McGee, and Tom Lampkin seems more like a parody of a bench Tony LaRussa would select rather than one he really did. Only McGee and Lampkin were even average performers.

UPWARD ROTATION

St. Louis suffered a setback when the team and ace pitcher Andy Benes couldn't reach agreement on a new contract before the December deadline for re-signing free agents. Exit the elder Benes. However, in midwinter, there were plenty of rumors that he would sign with another club and be traded back to St. Louis.

Even without Andy Benes, however, the Cardinals starting staff looks impressive. Todd Stottlemyre, Alan Benes, and 1997 rookie Matt Morris make a strong front three, while Kent Mercker (who signed with the Redbirds after a healthy if not impressive year with Cincinnati) and rookie Manny Aybar will fill out the rotation. Other youngsters such as Brady Raggio and Sean Lowe could work if needed. Most teams would be happy to have a rotation like that.

THE FARM REPORT

St. Louis's farm system has not come up with many quality position players in the last decade, which is one reason why the Cards have held on to veterans like Gary Gaetti and Ron Gant.

TEAM MVP

The Cardinals got poor production from most of their everyday players in 1997, but center fielder **Ray Lankford** was very effective. He hit .295 with 31 homers and 95 walks while fielding a difficult position with skill. Lankford has never been very consistent, and it's almost impossible to predict what he'll do in 1998.

BIGGEST SURPRISE

Rookie righthander **Matt Morris**, the Cardinals' first-round pick in 1995, made the rotation out of spring training and wound up leading the club with 33 starts, 217 innings, and 12 wins. His fine performance bolstered a surprisingly brittle staff for which nobody else took the ball more than 28 times.

205

BIGGEST DISAPPOINTMENT

There were several candidates for this "honor" in 1997. Southpaw Donovan Osborne's inability to contribute (3-7, 4.93) hurt the team's rotation, and the failure of Dmitri Young to develop at first base made him expendable. However, the award must go to left fielder **Ron Gant**, whose limp bat (.229, 17 homers) blunted the team's offense all season. He was just awful.

Several Cardinals youngsters have played in the last two years without making much impact. Catcher Mike "Pigboy" Difelice showed in his rookie year that he isn't afraid to get dirty, but he's already gone to Tampa Bay. Mike Gulan, Terry Bradshaw, Luis Ordaz, Jeff Berblinger, and Aaron Holbert have been hailed as comers but haven't come yet, and Scarborough Green's defense probably won't be enough to support his weak bat.

The Cardinals have always been a "draft the best available athlete" organization. They were able to develop some quality outfielders, such as Ray Lankford, Brian Jordan, and Bernard Gilkey (and trade the excess, like Lance Johnson, Alex Cole, and Allen Battle) in the past, but have struck out in recent seasons. The relative failures of John Mabry and Dmitri Young, the only new regulars the system has developed in five years, simply underscore the point.

However, the St. Louis organization has done a good job of developing pitchers. Matt Morris and Alan Benes are both potentially top performers, and Donovan Osborne is a solid third starter when healthy. Second-liners like John Frascatore, Rigo Beltran, and Curtis King are more than capable of filling out a bullpen. The departed T.J. Mathews and Eric Ludwick were both developed in-house as well. Other current big league hurlers developed by the St. Louis system include Allen Watson, Rheal Cormier, and Jeff Fassero.

ROYCE CLAYTON: THE BEST IS YET TO COME?

The Cardinals have been using Royce Clayton as their regular shortstop for two seasons now since acquiring him from San Francisco for three players: Rich DeLucia, Allen Watson, and Doug Creek. None of the three is still with the Giants, but the booty was still significant to acquire a shortstop who had batted but .236 and .244 in the two seasons preceding the trade.

How well has Clayton worked out for St. Louis? As a regular at a key position, he is a borderline player, and much of the perception of Clayton's talent depends on what standards are used to determine value.

Clayton is durable and will play every day if given the opportunity. He is fast enough to beat out infield choppers

and is a frequent and good basestealer, swiping 30 sacks last year at a 75 percent success rate. He showed more power than ever before; his 39 doubles and nine homers in '97 were career highs. Clayton is also proficient at bunting for hits and can sacrifice when asked. As a defensive player he is slick, usually with a league-average or better fielding percentage, and turns the double play well.

However, there are significant problems with his game. His range has never been at the top of the list of shortstops, and as a hitter he has real weaknesses. Clayton has never walked more than 38 times in a season, and his career on-base average is a puny .306. He strikes out often enough that both the Cardinals and Giants decided he can't help out at the top of the order, so Clayton is likely to spend much of the rest of his career in the seventh or eighth slot.

As a shortstop Clayton is in the middle of the pack both offensively and defensively. He's been a regular since he was 23 and has played on one division championship club in his career to date. Suffice it to say that if Royce Clayton hits .266 with 39 doubles and nine homers, as he did in 1997, he's a helpful player. He hasn't done that well every year, but heads into this season at age 28. Clayton could well elevate his game in 1998 and break out of the pack.

OUT WITH THE OLD

Fifteen of the players on the Cardinals' 40-man roster heading into 1997 spring training were gone by the end of the year. Nine of the dearly departed were members of the pitching staff. Several of them were up there in years (Tony Fossas, Dennis Eckersley, Rick Honeycutt, Danny Jackson), while some were pitchers in their prime or approaching it (T.J. Mathews, Andy Benes, Eric Ludwick). St. Louis has the talent in its system to bring more pitching to the big leagues, but a complete rebuilding of the bullpen overnight will be difficult. Newly acquired Jeff Brantley, tabbed to be the closer this season, is a good pitcher if healthy—he saved 44 games for the Reds in '96—but not a long-term solution. He'll be 35 by season's end.

Did anyone notice that the 1997 Cardinals used two players who were already in the majors when Tony LaRussa, a big league manager since 1979, was still learning his craft in the minors? Eckersley and Honeycutt each preceded LaRussa to the major leagues by a fairly healthy margin.

JOHN MABRY: OUT AT THIRD?

St. Louis has never figured out what to do with John Mabry. He has the throwing arm to play right field, but he has been crowded out of that picture by the multitalented Brian Jordan. Playing Mabry at first base isn't much of an option, since it wastes his arm—his best tool—and he doesn't hit enough to fill that position anyway.

Faced with a third baseman in his dotage (Gary Gaetti) and no prospects on the way, the Cardinals have now decided to convert the 27-year-old Mabry to third base. This transition almost never works, which doesn't stop desperate teams from trotting out the instructors and fungo bats anyway. Supposedly one reason that Gaetti was re-signed for 1998 was to help Mabry with the learning process, but the unspoken reason is that Gaetti can always step back in and play every day if the transplant fails.

The throw from third should be no problem for the strong-armed Mabry. The real question is, can he field the position? Luckily for Mabry, third basemen don't need to be fast, but they must be quick. Does he have the first-step quickness essential for the job? As an outfielder he has shown adequate range in the past, although he does not accelerate particularly well. The jury is out.

Hitting is another matter. Even in his best season, 1996, Mabry was only average offensively. He runs poorly, lacks power, and won't be on base enough to help the team unless he bats .300. There are a lot of maybes here for such a critical position. If Mabry isn't doing well by May, look for him to move back to the outfield, especially if Jordan is still having problems staying healthy.

REBIRTH

The St. Louis Cardinals, arguably the most successful franchise in NL history, hit bottom in 1994 and 1995, finishing third and fourth with records well below .500. The '95 club, at 62-81, was especially embarrassing, so Manager Joe Torre was canned that June and replaced on an interim basis by director of player development Mike Jorgensen.

The Cardinals had been run since the death of the legendary owner "Gussie" Busch in 1989 by his son August

THE MOMENT OF TRUTH

On **July 3** the Cardinals were clinging to first place with a 41-41 mark. Third-place Pittsburgh came to town that weekend for four games, hoping to make progress. Did they ever. The Pirates swept the series, leaving Busch Stadium in first place and pushing the Cardinals all the way down to third. The Redbirds never recovered, going 32-44 the rest of the way.

BEST DEAL

St. Louis made two special infield acquisitions in 1997. Second baseman **Delino DeShields** signed as a free agent before the season after three poor years in Los Angeles had left him on the scrap heap. DeShields batted .295 and collected 51 extra base hits, 55 stolen bases, and 55 walks in a big comeback season. First baseman **Mark McGwire** came over from Oakland in July and hit a spectacular 24 homers in just 51 games, establishing himself as the big man in town both with fans and teammates.

WORST DEAL

The Cardinals' 73-89 finish cannot be blamed on any deals or signings made after the 1996 season. Mistakes like **Ron Gant**'s long-term deal, the failure to acquire or develop a third baseman, and the decline of closer **Dennis Eckersley** were problems already extant for more than a year.

207

1. **<u>Eli Marrero, C.</u>** The 24-year-old receiver has an excellent throwing arm and hits with pop. Nineteen homers and a .270 average at Double A Arkansas in 1996 were followed in 1997 by 20 more homers and a .273 mark at Triple A Louisville. Marrero, a righthanded hitter with a good defensive package, is likely to get the first shot at the Redbirds' catching job in 1998 after a 17-game trial with St. Loius last year (2 HRs, 7 RBIs). While he doesn't walk often, he also doesn't strike out very much.

2. **<u>Manny Aybar, P.</u>** Aybar, an ex-shortstop, throws hard and has outstanding control of three pitches. The 23-year-old righty's best offering is a hard slider, which he used to strike out 114 men in 137 innings at Louisville last year. That total ranked fifth in the American Association. The Cardinals think Aybar can be a helpful big league starter in 1998 and are likely to give him some of the departed Andy Benes's innings.

3. **<u>Curtis King, P.</u>** The six-foot five-inch King attended Pennsylvania Textile College before being drafted by the Cardinals in the fifth round in 1994. He began his career as a starter but was converted to short relief in 1996 at Class A St.

Petersburg, where he saved 30 games despite mediocre control. King, a righty, saved 16 more at Double A in 1997 before promotions to Triple A and, finally, St. Louis. He pitched well in 30 games for the Cardinals in a setup role. King rarely strikes out hitters, instead using a heavy sinker to induce groundouts. He'll begin 1998 in the Cards' bullpen.

4. **<u>Luis Ordaz, SS.</u>** A 22-year-old from Venezuela, Ordaz has excellent defensive tools. That alone may have to get him to the majors, because outside of a good batting average Ordaz isn't a good offensive player. He batted .272 at St. Petersburg in 1996 and .287 at Arkansas in 1997, but without power, walks, or stolen bases. He isn't fast, but does have above-average range.

5. **<u>Brady Raggio, P.</u>** His best pitch is a sinker, but Raggio's top marker is his bulldog attitude and the fact that while he's not overpowering, he isn't afraid to pitch to his strengths. The righthander slumped late last season to an 8-11 record and a 4.24 ERA at Louisville, but he made 15 appearances for the Cardinals and could get another shot this season if other options fail.

Busch III. The team's status clearly slipped during those years as GM Walt Jocketty was forced to work with fewer resources. The proud St. Louis franchise, run by a rich brewery and blessed with loyal fans and an excellent farm system, suddenly started behaving as if it were the Montreal Expos—bereft of an audience in a small market.

From 1986 through 1992, St. Louis ranked in the top three in NL attendance every year. Starting in 1993, however, Cardinals attendance dipped sharply relative to that of other clubs in the league. The franchise responded in a most uncommon way—by cutting budgets rather than by aggressive moves to repair the stadium or the team.

By 1995, the Cardinals were trying to contend with a starting rotation of Mark Petkovsek, Allen Watson, Donovan Osborne, and Danny Jackson. Ken Hill and Todd Zeile, two of the club's more productive (and high-salaried) players, were unloaded at midseason for virtually nothing. The team's winningest pitcher was middle reliever Rich DeLucia, at 8-7. Legendary shortstop Ozzie Smith was 40 years old and plagued with shoulder problems, but he refused to bow out gracefully, batting .199.

Happily for Redbird fans, change was in the wind. After almost running the team into the ground, the Busch family decided to get out of the baseball business.

208

Bill DeWitt, Jr., son of the former St. Louis Browns owner and longtime big league executive, made an offer for the team. Presumably with assurances that DeWitt's offer would be approved, Tony LaRussa came on board to manage the club.

With DeWitt in the owner's suite and LaRussa on the field, things changed quickly and dramatically. The team confronted the Ozzie problem head-on, acquiring short-stop Royce Clayton. Pitchers Dennis Eckersley, Todd Stottlemyre, and Rick Honeycutt followed LaRussa from Oakland, and third baseman Gary Gaetti and outfielder Ron Gant were signed as free agents.

The club also made improvements to Busch Stadium itself, ripping out the turf and replacing it with grass, opening amusement and picnic areas, lowering ticket prices for children, putting in hundreds of new seats closer to the action, and reconfiguring other seats so that they faced the the infield.

The Cardinals won the NL Central in 1996 and advanced to the NLCS. Attendance improved by nearly a million that year, rising to fourth in the league, where it stayed in 1997, despite slippage in the standings.

In 1997, the Cardinals made another commitment to its fans by acquiring slugging first baseman Mark McGwire—about to turn free agent—from the Oakland Athletics. Big Mac promptly made a rush at Roger Maris's record of 61 homers.

Many analysts said that McGwire would never sign with a Midwestern team, supposedly because he wanted to live in southern California to be close to his son. But when the smoke had cleared, McGwire, impressed with the organization and bowled over by the enthusiasm of Cardinals fans, signed a long-term deal with St. Louis and set up a local foundation to combat child abuse.

Not all of these moves have worked out, but St. Louis has certainly come a long way in just two seasons. Nothing changed but the management team, which is something to remember the next time an owner starts crying about how his team can't compete with the big boys in New York or L.A. because it is stuck in a relatively small market without a new stadium. The Cardinals are an object lesson in the value of good management.

PRESENTING THE HARD-ASS CLUB

Who better to manage our fictional team full of tough, rough, sometimes mean guys than Tony LaRussa? A manager who has always gotten a lot out of his players, LaRussa is known almost as much among the media for his dancing, suspicious eyes and carefully considered answers as for his on-field success. His first lieutenant with this team? Phil Garner. Here are our picks for the players, with their 1997 team(s):

SP	Todd Stottlemyre	Cardinals
SP	Cal Eldred	Brewers
SP	Randy Johnson	Mariners
SP	Danny Darwin	White Sox/Giants
RP	Troy Percival	Angels
C	Mike Difelice	Cardinals
C	Tony Pena	White Sox/Astros
1B	David Segui	Expos
2B	Jeff Kent	Giants
SS	Shawon Dunston	Cubs/Pirates
3B	Dave Hollins	Angels
OF	Tony Phillips	White Sox/Angels
OF	Barry Bonds	Giants
OF	Curtis Goodwin	Reds
OF	Chad Curtis	Indians/Yankees

1997 TEAM STATISTICS

BATTING/BASERUNNING

	Raw	Rank	+/- %		Raw	Rank	+/- %		Raw	Rank	+/- %
R	689	11	-8	BA	.255	13	-3	SB	164	3	+26
R/G	4.25	11	-8	HR	144	8	-7	CS	60	6	0
OBA	.324	10	-3	LH	308	6	-2	SB%	73.2	3	+8
SA	.396	10	-3	BB	543	8	-1				
PRO	.720	11	-3	SO	1,191	14	+9				

PITCHING/FIELDING

	Raw	Rank	+/- %		Raw	Rank	+/- %		Raw	Rank	+/- %
OR	708	5	-5	BA	.259	7	-1	OSB	134	10	+6
RA/G	4.37	5	-5	HR	124	2	-20	OCS	66	10	+12
OOB	.328	6	-1	LH	264	2	-15	OSB%	67.0	6	-1
OSA	.380	3	-7	BB	536	4	-4	FA	.980	9	0
PRO	.709	4	-4	SO	1,130	8	+2	GDP	117	8	-2

BATTING BY LINEUP SLOTS

	R	HR	RBI	BA	OBA	SA
1	104	10	69	.275	.332	.401
2	89	13	56	.255	.298	.380
3	105	39	109	.280	.387	.541
4	87	22	91	.245	.356	.421
5	74	18	85	.250	.310	.380
6	77	16	71	.284	.352	.415
7	54	10	60	.254	.315	.350
8	58	12	69	.243	.298	.395
9	41	4	44	.201	.254	.272

BATTING BY DEFENSIVE POSITION

	R	HR	RBI	BA	OBA	SA
C	46	14	61	.245	.314	.367
1B	85	31	80	.262	.357	.462
2B	95	9	61	.289	.350	.427
3B	74	16	79	.238	.287	.366
SS	81	10	66	.268	.307	.396
LF	83	22	83	.249	.327	.412
CF	104	31	109	.281	.391	.522
RF	67	8	60	.270	.334	.355
DH	0	0	3	.160	.160	.240
PH	22	3	29	.186	.259	.285
P	20	0	23	.197	.235	.240

TEAM PITCHING

	W-L	CG	QS	QS%	<6	>6	IPS	IP	ERA	OPR
ROTATION	50-58	5	95	59	25	73	6.2	1,001.0	3.92	.697

	W-L	GR	SV	BSV	HD	BHD	IRS%	IP	ERA	OPR
BULLPEN	23-31	399	39	19	145	78	26	454.2	3.80	.736

1998 PROJECTIONS

BATTING

PLAYER	BA	G	AB	R	H	2B	3B	HR	RBI	BB	SO	SB	CS	SA	OBA
Bell, David	.242	41	97	8	23	5	1	1	9	7	19	1	1	.339	.294
Clayton, Royce	.273	143	538	70	147	33	4	8	54	34	106	30	11	.395	.317
DeShields, Delino	.273	153	572	87	156	22	12	9	52	59	92	53	14	.401	.341
Gaetti, Gary	.261	103	363	48	95	18	1	15	55	27	65	4	2	.441	.312
Gant, Ron	.241	131	463	71	112	19	3	23	71	65	136	15	5	.444	.334
Green, Scarborough	.263	34	113	17	30	6	2	1	10	14	29	3	0	.363	.343
Howard, David	.245	51	126	17	31	5	2	1	12	11	24	2	2	.331	.305
Jordan, Brian	.285	73	256	39	73	14	0	8	39	14	41	12	2	.431	.321
Lampkin, Tom	.245	76	162	21	40	6	1	5	19	20	21	1	1	.386	.328
Lankford, Ray	.272	150	536	98	146	37	4	29	96	89	130	27	10	.519	.376
Mabry, John	.292	113	382	40	112	20	1	7	42	33	66	1	1	.403	.348
Marrero, Eli	.229	68	232	29	53	10	3	10	33	12	42	3	0	.429	.267
McGee, Willie	.300	69	175	22	53	10	2	2	21	12	35	4	1	.419	.344
McGwire, Mark	.263	155	524	92	138	24	0	56	118	106	138	2	0	.627	.387
Ordaz, Luis	.267	23	76	8	20	4	1	1	10	4	9	2	0	.361	.304
Sheaffer, Danny	.258	42	89	7	23	4	1	1	10	7	13	1	1	.355	.310

PITCHING

PITCHER	W	L	SV	ERA	G	GS	IP	H	HR	BB	SO
Aybar, Manuel	6	6	0	3.80	18	18	109	106	10	40	69
Beltran, Rigo	5	3	0	3.02	30	8	74	65	7	27	55
Benes, Alan	11	9	0	3.97	30	30	193	178	16	75	171
Brantley, Jeff	2	2	25	2.86	41	0	44	34	5	18	47
Busby, Mike	3	3	0	4.41	8	7	45	46	6	13	25
Frascatore, John	4	2	0	3.16	52	2	77	80	6	35	55
King, Curtis	3	3	3	4.18	55	0	62	75	6	21	30
Lowe, Sean	2	2	0	3.44	8	7	37	35	3	13	26
Mercker, Kent	8	12	0	4.24	33	26	153	146	18	67	82
Morris, Matt	12	9	0	3.42	33	33	216	214	12	71	149
Osborne, Donovan	6	9	0	4.26	21	21	129	130	16	37	87
Painter, Lance	3	1	0	4.91	31	0	42	42	7	17	34
Petkovsek, Mark	4	3	1	4.50	30	4	62	66	8	20	33
Raggio, Brady	3	3	0	3.86	13	9	58	59	6	15	32
Stottlemyre, Todd	12	9	0	4.15	28	28	184	168	20	72	165

211

ARIZONA DIAMONDBACKS

MANAGEMENT

Manager	General Manager	Owner
Buck Showalter Career Record 313-268 .539	Joe Garagiola, Jr.	Jerry Colangelo

A FORCE TO BE RECKONED WITH

Jerry Colangelo didn't get into baseball to lose money. He didn't get into it to lose games, either although that's almost incidental, and the Arizona Diamondbacks are going to *make* money, a lot of money, because Colangelo knows how to sell an experience. Having built the NBA's Phoenix Suns from a sub-.500 club into a winner and a perennial arena-filler, he knows what fans want out of a ballpark experience, so he built a park to give them just that.

Colangelo is also smart enough to hire good baseball people who can ensure that the team will have a philosophy and a brand of its own. Colangelo and his efficient, shiny, purple, gold, and green operation may be fabulously successful on and off the diamond.

However, Colangelo may not be so successful in revolutionizing baseball. First of all, what he did to the salary structure this fall with the Jay Bell and Matt Williams contracts showed that all his talk about bringing "common-sense" ideas to the game was a lot of hot air. The idea to move the World Series to a different warm-weather site every year—as the Super Bowl is—is his, too. That one didn't go over too well, thankfully.

Since joining the owners' club three years ago, Colangelo has been heard every so often commenting about how this game isn't run well, how things aren't done right in baseball, and why don't these guys listen to new ideas anyway?

Colangelo was one of the biggest advocates of the so-called "radical realignment" plans, which would have changed a century of baseball tradition and remade the game in the image of the NBA.

Welcome to the major leagues, Jerry. It's going to be interesting to watch as you attempt to make stodgy old baseball a different game.

BUCK SHOWALTER: FINALLY IN COMMAND

Buck Showalter is respected by most people in baseball; he is a very smart manager. Players love to play for him, as long as they "respect the game," as he is fond of saying. The Diamondbacks went to great lengths to let everyone know that they not only wanted good players, but also good guys in the clubhouse. (So why did they get Devon White?)

Looking back on Showalter's tenure managing the Yankees, it's clear that he did an excellent job. He turned the club from an also-ran to a contender within two years and a playoff team within three. And Showalter was winning in spite of some big weaknesses: Don Mattingly was deteriorating physically; the starting pitchers were old, infirm, or just plain bad; Wade Boggs was posting some mediocre seasons at third; and there always seemed to be a starting outfielder—Luis Polonia, Dion James, or even Randy Velarde—hitting .302 with five home runs.

Showalter chafed at the control that George Steinbrenner wanted, and got, over the on-field operation of the Yankees. Showalter seems to be getting more of a free hand in Phoenix, having spent much of the past two years on the road scouting players while also having a great deal of input in the overall decision-making process. Leaving a successful skipper like Showalter alone while he does his job is a smart move.

CATCHING UP AFTER THE DRAFT

So what kind of club will Buck Showalter be managing?

The Diamondbacks don't look like a bad team at first glance. The starting pitchers are young and inexperienced (32-year-old ex-Tiger Willie Blair, with a 41–49 career record, is expected to be the ace), but most of them have something to contribute and, most importantly, have ceilings that haven't yet been reached. (Many of these guys will never reach those ceilings, but that's to be expected.) The relievers are solid role players, and 28-year-old Hector Carrasco, who came from Kansas City in the expansion draft, has the inside track on the closer's job.

In contrast to the pitching staff, many of the position players are seasoned veterans. This lineup will definitely score some runs: super prospect Travis Lee and veterans Jay Bell and Matt Williams will anchor one of the best expansion infields ever. Whoever ends up in the outfield—maybe Brent Brede and Karim Garcia flanking Devon White—will catch the ball and provide some offense as well. Garcia, in particular, is a fascinating gamble because of his age (just 22) and his obvious physical gifts. If he succeeds, it will be a real triumph for Showalter. The catching is decent; Jorge Fabregas was one of the better players chosen in the draft.

On paper, this is a much stronger team than the Devil Rays, not only because of the money spent on veterans, but also because the Diamondbacks had a better draft than Tampa—a much better draft.

While the Devil Rays were burning picks on Triple A roster fillers like Aaron Ledesma, Andy Sheets, Vaughn Eshelman, Dan Carlson, and Luke Wilcox, the Diamondbacks were actually drafting young talent. (Of course, Arizona's selection of 28-year-old second-line receiver Damian Miller was an anomaly; maybe somebody

in the rear of the D-backs' war room was smoking a little wacky tobacky.)

To its credit, Arizona did not use its draft picks on the kind of players who are routinely available as six-year minor league free agents. Tampa Bay did. The Diamondbacks smartly used the draft to get players they could use and players they could trade. While Arizona did burn a draft pick on one pitcher, Scott Winchester, just to acquire another, Felix Rodriguez from the Reds, at least it doesn't have delusions that Mike Kelly (whom Tampa acquired from the Reds for a player to be named, first baseman Dmitri Young) can be a 25-homer outfielder, as the Devil Rays seem to.

A ONE-OF-A-KIND BALLPARK

BancOne Ballpark (already nicknamed "The Bob") will have interesting dimensions. The left field line is 328 feet, while the right field line is 335. The power alleys range to 376 feet, while center field is 402 feet. This is not a large ballpark. With the 1,090-foot elevation in Phoenix (third in the majors, behind Denver and Atlanta), the Diamondbacks could potentially become the Rockies South.

The stadium will be the only one in the world with all three of the following components: a retractable dome, grass, and air conditioning. The air conditioning and roof are both designed for the fans' comfort. The roof will be opened at particular angles to keep too much sun from heating the stadium, therefore preventing it from overheating. Decisions about when to open and close the roof will have a big impact on the games themselves.

Arizona management seems to have tailored their talent somewhat to a ballpark with short dimensions and a grass surface. Their infielders are solid but unspectacular defensively (except for Matt Williams), as the D-backs have followed the prevailing wisdom that grass fields allow for slow infielders, while artificial turf necessitates fast ones.

Arizona's outfielders range from fast to, uh, not fast, and the pitchers are a mixed bag. The majority of potential starters (Willie Blair, Jeff Suppan, Bob Wolcott, and Brian Anderson) induce ground balls most of the time. However, the more experienced relievers, like Hector Carrasco, Russ Springer, and Clint Sodowsky, are "blow-it-by-'em" types.

213

1. **Travis Lee, 1B.** Almost certain to start the Diamondbacks' inaugural season at first base, Lee has blown away every league in which he has played. A power hitter with great strike-zone judgement, Lee hit .363 with 18 homers at Class A High Desert before being loaned to the Triple A New Orleans club. All Lee did at that level, at age 22, was club 14 more homers and bat .300.

2. **Vladimir Nunez, P.** A Cuban refugee, Nunez says he is 23. He was 10-0 in the Rookie-level Pioneer League in 1996 and followed that up with an 8-5 campaign last season at Class A. His 5.17 ERA isn't terrible for that ballpark, and he fanned 142 men in 158 innings. Nunez has the fastball and curve to pitch in the majors, and could be in the rotation this summer.

3. **Karim Garcia, OF.** Disciplinary problems have taken some of the luster off Garcia, the 22-year-old who had been the Dodgers' best prospect until Paul Konerko and Adrian Beltre passed him in 1997. Garcia hit .305 with 20 homers in his second year at Triple A Albuquerque—not particularly good numbers in that park—and was suspended for behavioral reasons as well. Whether Garcia, who has a tremendous arm, gets a shot at center field in 1998 depends on his attitude; Buck Showalter is a stickler for "respecting the game."

4. **Edwin Diaz, 2B.** At age 22 Diaz repeated at Double A and hit .275 with 15 homers. However, he continued to struggle with the strike zone, fanning 102 times and walking just 33. His 76 at bats at Triple A were disastrous (.105), and the Rangers decided they could live without him. Diaz and the Diamondbacks might make Texas regret that decision. Diaz has genuine power, is still fairly young, and has improved his defense.

5. **Chris Clemons, P.** A first-round pick in 1994 from Texas A&M, Clemons was pushed through the White Sox system despite having problems with control. He has a fastball and a slider, but hasn't thrown as hard as advertised. After just 19 games at Double A in 1996, he moved to Triple A Nashville last year and had some growing pains. He was 5-5 with a 4.55 ERA, fanning just 70 and walking 65 in 125 innings.

6. **Dave Dellucci, OF.** Dellucci, a tenth-round draft pick, blew it out at Double A Bowie at age 24, hitting .327 with 20 homers in 385 at bats. He even got into 17 games with Baltimore, where he smacked a home run. As a lefthanded hitter who can play both left and right field, Dellucci could make a lot of sense as a reserve in the major leagues. He's in the running for a job in Arizona, and he has a good attitude and a dependable bat working in his favor.

7. **Mike Bell, 3B.** At age 22 he hit .285 at Double A Tulsa with eight homers in 123 at bats, but just .235 with five homers at Triple A Oklahoma City. After the season he was traded from Texas to Anaheim, which, despite having an awful farm system, let him go in the expansion draft. Bell is a good defensive third baseman and could be a fine major league hitter.

8. **Danny Klassen, SS.** Klassen, just 22, appears to have recovered from his 1995 knee problems. He is a slash hitter who batted .331 with 14 homers last season at Double A El Paso—inflated numbers in this hitter's park, to be sure, but with his range and hands, Klassen's offense should be good enough to carry him to the majors.

9. **Todd Erdos, P.** The hard-throwing righthander has improved his command in the last couple of seasons and is thought of as a closer candidate due to a very good fastball. He saved 27 games at Double A Mobile in 1997 before a short stint with the Padres.

ARIZONA DIAMONDBACKS
1998 PROJECTIONS

BATTING

PLAYER	BA	G	AB	R	H	2B	3B	HR	RBI	BB	SO	SB	CS	SA	OBA
Batista, Tony	.247	89	259	36	64	13	1	6	27	21	49	5	4	.378	.303
Bell, Jay	.272	155	572	82	156	29	3	17	82	65	107	8	5	.425	.346
Benitez, Yamil	.252	84	298	42	75	10	1	15	47	17	91	6	0	.443	.293
Brede, Brent	.278	97	349	61	97	21	3	7	56	38	80	5	0	.411	.349
Dellucci, Dave	.253	50	167	24	42	9	1	6	19	20	37	3	0	.434	.334
Fabregas, Jorge	.287	133	392	38	112	13	1	7	55	21	51	1	1	.378	.323
Frias, Hanley	.268	26	91	13	24	3	1	1	9	10	16	5	0	.346	.342
Garcia, Karim	.232	79	276	44	64	12	5	16	55	22	93	8	0	.480	.288
Jones, Chris	.260	76	133	22	35	7	0	5	22	13	38	4	1	.429	.326
Miller, Damian	.262	36	127	14	33	6	1	3	25	9	29	2	0	.393	.310
Stinnett, Kelly	.241	70	183	30	44	11	2	6	27	26	49	1	0	.416	.337
White, Devon	.269	101	383	55	103	23	3	10	53	35	82	16	5	.421	.331
Williams, Matt	.273	146	573	87	156	28	2	32	105	39	109	9	3	.495	.320
Diaz, Edwin	.238	55	227	30	54	14	0	7	21	16	68	2	0	.391	.287
Lee, Travis	.241	95	367	54	88	20	3	19	59	41	90	2	0	.468	.317

PITCHING

PITCHER	W	L	SV	ERA	G	GS	IP	H	HR	BB	SO
Adamson, Joel	4	3	0	3.86	27	5	65	70	11	18	47
Anderson, Brian	6	7	0	4.50	19	19	116	129	19	25	59
Blair, Willie	13	8	0	4.32	47	21	171	176	19	50	99
Carrasco, Hector	2	6	5	4.18	57	0	75	68	6	39	63
Clemons, Chris	2	3	0	4.31	9	7	46	42	6	23	21
Daal, Omar	4	4	1	5.45	55	4	73	83	8	29	59
Erdos, Todd	3	2	1	3.50	42	0	46	39	3	16	32
Hansell, Greg	2	1	0	3.90	16	3	35	35	6	9	26
Janzen, Marty	4	4	0	4.28	27	7	71	66	10	33	48
Lidle, Cory	7	2	2	3.89	50	2	76	84	7	19	50
Manuel, Barry	2	2	0	4.09	16	3	35	34	6	12	25
Ojala, Kirt	4	3	0	4.19	11	10	64	71	7	29	42
Rodriguez, Felix	1	1	0	4.17	32	1	52	54	3	31	37
Sodowsky, Clint	3	3	0	4.83	46	4	65	68	9	44	55
Springer, Russ	2	4	5	4.87	46	2	65	67	8	30	72
Suppan, Jeff	7	8	0	4.77	26	26	143	154	16	42	73
Wolcott, Bob	6	7	0	5.42	23	22	121	146	24	38	67

COLORADO ROCKIES

MANAGEMENT

Manager	General Manager	Owner
Don Baylor Career Record 362-384 .485	Bob Gebhard	Jerry McMorris

1997 RECORD

Won-Lost 83-79	Pct. .512	DivisionFinish/GB 3 W -7	Wild Card Finish/GB 4 -9
Preseason Consensus Projection 3 (2.70)			

1st Half 43-39	2nd Half 40-40	Home 47-34	Road 36-45	Intradivision 13-23	Interleague 9-7

Comebacks 8-13	Blowouts 22-22	Nailbiters 35-35

PITCHING-POOR OR SHELL-SHOCKED?

Five years into Colorado's successful foray into big league baseball, what do we know about the types of pitchers who can succeed in the rarified air? The Rockies have spent their five years trying to find healthy sinkerball pitchers. This type of pitching has always been assumed to be the secret to winning games at the mile-high altitude of Mile High Stadium and Coors Field. But is it?

The short answer is that good pitching wins anywhere, even in Colorado. However, when dealing with the best hitters' park baseball has ever seen, one that boosts offensive production to a much higher level than any other big league park, definitions of good must be radically adjusted.

Even the best pitchers are not going to win ERA titles in Colorado, but the perception that they are pitching badly when allowing five runs per game keeps them from completing games or racking up a lot of innings. Therefore, it essentially kills their chances of posting good individual strikeout or win totals.

To no one's surprise, Colorado has had the most active bullpen in the game. This paid off in 1994 and '95, when the team had arguably the best relief corps in the majors. However, possibly from overuse, Colorado's relievers have slumped in the past two seasons, and the rest of the team has stumbled along with them.

Many feel that manager Don Baylor wants his pitchers to do the impossible in Denver: pitch normal stints while not giving up runs. Anyone who thinks that pitchers can do this in Coors Field needs to take a close look at the evidence. Rockies pitchers can go a long way and post ugly ERAs, or the team can keep going through five pitchers every game.

The truth is that a starting pitcher who gives up five runs a game in Colorado is a good pitcher. Baylor apparently can't accept that, often jerking his pitchers—especially the young ones—in and out of the rotation and complaining about their lacking the "guts" to stay in games. He seems trapped into thinking that allowing five runs at 5,280 feet is the same as allowing them at sea level.

The NL earned run averages in Coors Field are truly shocking: 6.40 in its inaugural year of 1995, a whopping 7.06 in the peak offensive year of 1996, and a relatively modest 6.05 last season. (AL pitchers were not included in '97 numbers for comparison purposes.)

A quick look at NL batting stats in Coors show why. The altitude in Denver makes ordinary hitters everywhere else into .300 hitters; the league has hit .315, .323, and .318 there in the past three seasons! It also can make any decent power hitter into an MVP candidate, as the Blake Street Bombers have demonstrated. The NL on-base plus slugging (OPS) figures make your eyes pop: .916 in 1995, .931 in 1996, and .899 last season.

To be fair to Baylor, he's not much different than most others in baseball. Players, coaches, managers, executives, and writers pay lip service to the obvious fact that ballparks dramatically influence individual statistics, but they still don't make realistic allowances when evaluating players. If people don't understand that pitchers with ERAs in the threes in the Astrodome and hitters with 20 homers in Wrigley aren't anything special, then how long will it take for realistic adjustments to be made for the best hitters' park the game has ever seen?

A WELCOME PAIR

Pedro Astacio and Frank Castillo combined for an 11-4 record with the Rockies after coming over in separate trades. Astacio (4.25 ERA) allowed nine homers in 48.2 innings with Colorado, while Castillo (5.42 ERA) served up 16 in just 86.1 frames. However, both were stingy with walks, and Castillo (who signed with Detroit as a free agent after the season) cut down on the running game, helping to keep the damage under control.

The deal to get Astacio, a quality pitcher, from Los Angeles for Eric Young was one of the most underrated trades of last season. Young has been a mediocre player at best anywhere except Denver, while Astacio, who still throws hard, could become the ace the Rockies have

TEAM MVP

There's really no choice here. **Larry Walker** won the National League MVP with a spectacular year. He hit .346 with 29 home runs and 62 RBIs—in road games. Walker played hard and productively through nagging injuries. It's hard to imagine his ever having another season like 1997, but Walker showed again last year that he is by far the best player ever to wear a Rockies uniform.

BIGGEST SURPRISE

The emergence of relievers **Jerry DiPoto** and **Mike DeJean** in 1997 was part of the reason the Rockies felt they could afford to let go of veterans Steve Reed and Darren Holmes in the off-season. DiPoto led the club with 16 saves by pitching some of his best baseball ever, while DeJean, part of the booty in the deal that sent Joe Girardi to the Yankees in 1995, provided solid work in the middle.

BIGGEST DISAPPOINTMENT

Pitcher **Bill Swift** earned his release on August 20 with a 4-6 record and 6.34 ERA, ending a Rockies career long on injuries and short on quality performance. In three well-paid seasons with Colorado, Swift won a grand total of 14 games and made only 40 appearances. Meanwhile, rotation anchor **Kevin Ritz** pitched only 18 times because of a torn right labrum (a shoulder muscle) that required surgery.

217

needed since their debut.

These are the 34 pitchers who have started games for the Rockies in their five-year history (those asterisked are still with the team): Juan Acevedo, Andy Ashby, Pedro Astacio*, Roger Bailey*, Willie Blair, Kent Bottenfield, John Burke*, Frank Castillo, Mike Farmer*, Marvin Freeman, Joe Grahe, Mike Harkey, Greg Harris, Butch Henry, Darren Holmes*, Bruce Hurst, Mark Hutton*, Bobby M. Jones*, Curt Leskanic*, David Nied, Omar Olivares, Lance Painter, Jeff Parrett, Armando Reynoso, Kevin Ritz*, Bruce Ruffin*, Bret Saberhagen, Mo Sanford, Keith Shepherd, Bryn Smith, Bill Swift, Mark Thompson*, John Thomson*, Jamey Wright*.

As the Rockies have bemoaned their poor mound performances throughout their history, several effective pitchers have slipped through their fingers. Exhibit A is Andy Ashby, a first-round pick of the Rockies in the 1993 expansion draft. After 20 games (0-4, 8.50), the 26-year-old righthander was dealt to San Diego with Brad Ausmus and Doug Bochtler (another fine arm) in a disastrous deal that netted broken-down veterans Greg W. Harris and Bruce Hurst. Given time to sort out his troubles in San Diego, Ashby has become one of the league's best starting pitchers.

Armando Reynoso, another charter member of the Colorado staff, was arguably the team's best pitcher in its first four seasons. Allowed to declare free agency in 1997, he pitched well for the Mets before hurting his right shoulder. He'll be back this year and should continue to be effective (he suffered a serious elbow injury back in 1994 and came back strong).

After a good season (6-10, 4.75 in Colorado is a good season) as a swingman in 1993, Willie Blair (another first-round expansion pick) found himself shunted to middle relief. He pitched poorly in that role in 1994 and was allowed to leave for San Diego as a free agent.

Juan Acevedo was 17-6 for the Rockies' Double A club in 1994. Halfway through 1995 he was traded to the Mets with fellow prospect Arnold Gooch in exchange for Bret Saberhagen, who pitched nine games for Colorado before blowing out his shoulder. Acevedo remains a good prospect who might finally get his chance in the Mets rotation in 1998.

Kent Bottenfield spent the past two years with the Cubs

as a middle reliever and was very good in that role. The Rockies had tried him as a starter in 1993 and '94 without overwhelming success and released him. He signed with the Cardinals this winter.

KILE HIGH STADIUM

The Rockies weren't going to be overbid in their efforts to land former Houston righthander Darryl Kile. The 29-year-old power pitcher had his best season in 1997, going 19-7 with a 2.57 ERA and 205 strikeouts for the Astros.

Can he continue to be effective pitching in Coors Field? Over the past three years he has pitched just 13.1 innings in Colorado, allowing only one run in that span, so there isn't much of a track record to examine.

Kile's best pitch is a hard-breaking curve. Baseball people believe that the curve simply does not break as well in thin air, so that's strike one. If he's not getting the calls from the umpires, Kile could be hit hard. Darren Holmes, another curveball pitcher, had plenty of problems in Coors Field.

Very few pitchers escape Coors without their ERAs ballooning. In the last three years, only three pitchers (Steve Reed, Bruce Ruffin, and Tom Glavine) have pitched more than 40 innings in Denver with ERAs under 4.00. Among starting pitchers in that period, only Glavine, Frank Castillo, and Armando Reynoso have managed ERAs lower than 5.50.

Kile, unlike many of the other Rockies' better starters of the last few years (Bret Saberhagen, Bill Swift, Kevin Ritz, Reynoso), comes to Colorado with a clean bill of health and the ability to simply overpower hitters. While Kile has the stuff to be successful, he has a career ERA of 4.08 outside the Astrodome, so he is highly unlikely to win any Cy Young Awards.

The remainder of Colorado's rotation includes youngsters Jamey Wright and John Thomson and veterans Astacio and Roger Bailey. Wright and Thomson have plenty of skill, but two years ago, the same could be said for Bryan Rekar. The Rockies haven't yet proven they can develop a young pitcher. Astacio's ERA in Denver from 1995-97 was 8.58 in 31 innings, but he is better than that (see above). Bailey, a sinkerballer whose big strength is durability and grit, is a solid fourth or fifth starter.

218

ROAD WORRIERS

The Rockies scored far more runs (923) than anyone else in the NL last year. They also had by far the worst ERA (5.25) of any team in the league. However, a simple breakdown will show where the problem truly was.

At Coors Field, the Rockies scored 6.73 runs per game. Their pitchers had a 5.67 ERA. The club had a 47-34 record at home. In road games, the Rockies scored an average of only 4.67 runs. The pitchers compiled a road ERA of 4.81. The club's road record? 36-45.

Colorado pitchers were nearly a run better in road games than at home, while their hitters were more than two runs worse. While the pitching staff wasn't great in either location, the hitters' production looked deceptively good at home.

One big reason is that despite playing half the time in Coors Field, where pitchers work very carefully, the aggressive Rockies hitters ranked just sixth in the league in walks. On the road they didn't do much except hit homers, and the team suffered for it. In road contests, the Rockies' .253 average was 10 points below the NL average, while their .327 on-base percentage on the road was six points below par. It's hard to score runs with nobody on base.

THE PRESSURE'S ON THE PEN

Don Baylor, Colorado's manager for its entire history, uses his bullpen more than any other manager. Each season, he runs through dozens of pitchers looking for that elusive combination. An astonishing 25 men pitched for the Rockies in their inaugural campaign of 1993, while in 1995, Colorado had four men pitch more than 60 games in relief and another three make at least 30 relief appearances.

In 1996 Baylor used three relievers 70 or more times, as well as two others 50 or more times. Five Rockies relievers made 55 or more appearances last season, with Darren Holmes kicking in another 36 and Jeff McCurry making 33. The man counted on to be the club's top reliever, Bruce Ruffin, suddenly couldn't find the plate and spent some of the season in the minors and some on the disabled list. He pitched just 23 times for the Rockies and may not be able to come back.

Colorado used 13 starting pitchers in 1997, as did the Cardinals and Giants; the Phillies used 15 to lead the NL.

Colorado hung around close to the NL West lead through the halfway point of the season. They won a big game, 11-7, against Anaheim on **June 30** to remain just 4.5 games back of the Giants. But the next day **Chuck Finley** shut down the Rockies, 4-1, starting Colorado on a string of seven straight losses and 15 defeats in 16 games. By the time they won on July 20, the Rox were 10.5 games out, buried for good.

BEST DEAL

Trading **Eric Young** to Los Angeles for **Pedro Astacio** last summer worked out just fine. Young, never a favorite of Don Baylor's, just wasn't that good of a player for Colorado, while Astacio was a spectacular 5-1 with a 4.25 ERA in seven starts for the Rockies. While Astacio may not duplicate his great numbers in 1998, he is a solid pitcher who may eventually be the best starter that Colorado has ever had.

WORST DEAL

While the Rockies may not have had much use for second baseman **Craig Counsell**, whom they traded to Florida on July 27, the world champion Marlins did. **Mark Hutton**, who came over in exchange, didn't pitch often or particularly well for the Rockies and was dumped after the season, while Counsell won an everyday job with gritty play and a surprisingly good bat. He's not going to be a star, but Counsell is at least a quality fifth infielder—something the Rockies lack.

219

A good indication of the Rockies' season-long pitching instability was the fact that only three pitchers (Roger Bailey, John Thomson, and Jamey Wright) made as many as 20 starts for Colorado.

The Rockies' bullpen, however, will be going into 1998 without two of its most valuable members. On-again, off-again closer Darren Holmes, who saved 46 games for the Rockies in five years, now takes his big curveball to the Yankees. Steve Reed, who took the ball 265 times in the last four years with Colorado, is also history, having signed with San Francisco.

Colorado management, which showed little interest in keeping Reed, apparently didn't realize how good he was. Coming into 1997 with a 2.36 career ERA in road games, Reed slumped to 4.65 in away contests while posting an excellent (and unusual) 3.45 mark at Coors Field. The sidewinding Reed, who is durable and reliable, has been extremely consistent during his five years with the Rockies. The Giants (who originally signed him in 1988 and lost him to Colorado in the expansion draft) were very happy to snare Reed this winter.

Holmes, who also pitched very well for the Rox, never seemed to get his due, either. He struggled last season, but most of the damage came immediately before he went on the disabled list with a bad elbow and in one horrible start at Los Angeles. Still blessed with an outstanding curve, Holmes can serve as a closer or setup reliever and also made a half-dozen starts in 1997.

TOP PROSPECTS
SPRING 1998

1. **Todd Helton, 1B.** Helton, the Rockies' first-round draft pick in 1995, takes over for the departed Andres Galarraga this season. A 24-year-old lefthanded batter, Helton will hit for average, draw walks, and play a premium first base. Last season at Triple A Colorado Springs, he batted .352 with 16 homers and 61 walks in only 99 games, then added five more homers in 93 at bats with the Rockies.

2. **Derrick Gibson, OF.** A fine athlete who is learning how to play baseball, Gibson had his best pro year in 1997, batting .317 with 23 homers and 20 steals at Double A New Haven and then hitting .423 in 78 at bats for Colorado Springs. Defense is a problem, and strike-zone judgement is another, but Gibson is only 23 this season and could force his way into the Rockies' outfield picture.

3. **Steve Shoemaker, P.** A fourth-round pick of the Yankees in 1993, Shoemaker came over in the Joe Girardi trade. He has an outstanding fastball and has fanned over a man per inning for the last two years. However, the lack of other quality pitches has kept him from advancing as quickly as the Rockies would like. He did notch a 6-4 record and a 3.02 ERA last year at New Haven (in the pitching-friendly Eastern League) before a shaky five-game trial at Colorado Springs.

4. **Mike Vavrek, P.** The lefty, who turns 24 in April, has the usual southpaw arsenal and "crafty" approach, but he burst out with a 12-3 season at New Haven in 1997 to become a prospect. He walked just 34 in 123 innings and fanned 101. Vavrek, in just his third year of pro ball, will make the jump to Colorado Springs, where many pitching prospects have gone to die.

5. **Mark Brownson, P.** Spending a second full season at New Haven, Brownson was 10-9 with a 4.19 ERA. Despite middling velocity, Brownson gets nearly a strikeout per inning with a decent moving fastball and fine changeup, and he has shown very good control throughout his career. However, he did allow 24 homers in 1997, and might suffer for the combination of good location but mediocre velocity this year, either at Coors Field or Colorado Springs.

6. **Mike Saipe, P.** Fanning 129 and walking just 23 at New Haven, Saipe continued in 1997 to work his way into the Rockies' plans. A 4-3 record, despite a 5.52 ERA, in 10 starts at Colorado Springs didn't hurt. Saipe has never been highly thought of and doesn't have great stuff, but he has pitched impressively with good control since being signed. Only in mid-1996 did he work his way out of middle relief. The Rockies now think he could be at least a fourth starter.

220

With Curtis Leskanic, who is coming off elbow and shoulder problems, still trying to recover his 1995 form, and with Bruce Ruffin having made only 23 appearances in 1997 due to elbow problems that required surgery, the success of the Rockpen this season will depend on some slightly less-experienced arms.

Jerry DiPoto, who led the Rockies with 16 saves in 1997, is an ex-Mets and ex-Indians hurler who throws hard. While DiPoto's performance was encouraging, it is questionable whether he has the ability to be a dominating closer. Behind DiPoto, things look pretty thin. Lefthander Mike Munoz, another five-year Colorado bullpen vet, has been up and down. Ruffin and Leskanic have to prove they are capable of staying healthy and helping out. Mike DeJean, a rookie last season, wasn't bad but doesn't look like anything more than a middle reliever. Former Pittsburgh righty Jeff McCurry was average at best.

The rotation got a boost when Colorado signed free agent Darryl Kile in the off-season; he will be expected to carry a very heavy load. The Rox will also count on relatively new acquisitions like Pedro Astacio and Mark Hutton to pitch more innings. However, it's hard for a tiger to change his stripes, and one would expect that Baylor will continue to use his pen heavily. If he does, he'll need more quality pitching.

The Rockies added one reliable righthander, taking Dave Veres off the Expos' hands in a postseason deal. Although Veres appears to have lost something off his fastball due to heavy use in his first two seasons with Houston, he should be helpful in Colorado. Newly acquired southpaw Chuck McElroy should bolster the Rockies' relief corps from the left side.

MOST VALUABLE (AND OVERRATED) PLAYERS

Larry Walker did it all last season: he was healthy and happy and on top of his game. Walker hit .366 with 74 walks, 99 extra-base hits, and 33 stolen bases in 41 attempts. He paced the NL in both on-base percentage (.452) and slugging average (.720). His 49 homers also led the league. For all this, he was chosen the NL's Most Valuable Player.

Of course, Walker was helped by playing half his games in Coors Field. What hitter wouldn't be? The real test is what a Colorado player does in road games. While Dante Bichette, often viewed as a talented hitter, batted .246 with six homers in 70 away games during 1997 (and .362 with 20 homers in Denver), and Ellis Burks hit .247 with 15 homers on the road (while hitting .337, with 17 homers at home), Walker was the real deal. He batted .346 with 29 homers away from Coors Field.

A quick look at the Rockies' main offensive threats and their 1997 home/road stats is quite illuminating. Galarraga, who hit .342 at home and .295 on the road, is a good hitter who takes full advantage of his home field, while the images of Vinny Castilla (.320/.287) and Bichette as sluggers have largely been illusions created by Coors Field.

Bichette's second-place finish in the 1995 MVP voting was a joke, and he's gotten worse in the past two years. Burks finished third in the MVP sweepstakes in his big year, 1996, with a lot more to recommend him than his teammate had the previous season.

Walker has only played three seasons in Colorado, one an injury-riddled 1996 campaign. At 31, whether he can repeat his spectacular 1997 is an open question. However, one thing is very clear: his MVP season was the best a Rockies' player has had so far, and it was a legitimately great season even considering his homefield advantage, as the numbers show.

221

| | 1997 | | 1996 | |
	BA	HRs	BA	HR
Bichette/H*	.362	20	.366	2
Bichette/R**	.246	6	.253	9
Burks/H	.337	17	.390	23
Burks/R	.247	15	.291	17
Castilla/H	.320	21	.345	27
Castilla/R	.287	19	.259	13
Galarraga/H	.342	21	.359	32
Galarraga/R	.295	20	.245	15
Walker/H	.384	20	.393	12
Walker/R	.346	29	.142	6

*Home

**Road

COLORADO ROCKIES
1997 TEAM STATISTICS

BATTING/BASERUNNING

	Raw	Rank	+/- %			Raw	Rank	+/- %			Raw	Rank	+/- %
R	923	1	+24		BA	.288	1	+9		SB	137	6	+6
R/G	5.70	1	+24		HR	239	1	+55		CS	65	4	+8
OBA	.357	1	+7		LH	309	5	-2		SB%	67.8	7	0
SA	.478	1	+17		BB	562	6	+2					
PRO	.835	1	+12		SO	1,060	4	-3					

PITCHING/FIELDING

	Raw	Rank	+/- %			Raw	Rank	+/- %			Raw	Rank	+/- %
OR	908	14	+22		BA	.300	14	+15		OSB	130	9	+3
RA/G	5.60	14	+22		HR	196	14	+26		OCS	54	4	-8
OOB	.367	14	+10		LH	383	13	+23		OSB%	70.7	10	+4
OSA	.479	14	+17		BB	566	9	+1		FA	.983	1	0
PRO	.846	14	+14		SO	870	14	-21		GDP	179	14	+50

222

BATTING BY LINEUP SLOTS

	R	HR	RBI	BA	OBA	SA
1	112	8	63	.275	.368	.394
2	146	34	93	.300	.377	.498
3	149	49	136	.347	.430	.662
4	121	39	138	.309	.376	.552
5	107	39	149	.309	.351	.550
6	97	41	116	.303	.366	.551
7	74	19	75	.267	.323	.412
8	64	5	57	.259	.338	.362
9	53	5	42	.200	.259	.274

BATTING BY DEFENSIVE POSITION

	R	HR	RBI	BA	OBA	SA
C	63	18	72	.256	.328	.390
1B	126	42	145	.313	.382	.566
2B	98	8	61	.283	.354	.409
3B	99	42	115	.300	.353	.543
SS	84	9	61	.269	.361	.397
LF	99	36	136	.298	.332	.521
CF	132	28	96	.295	.374	.474
RF	151	49	140	.358	.447	.685
DH	6	1	1	.258	.343	.355
PH	25	4	25	.268	.349	.405
P	26	2	17	.154	.199	.188

TEAM PITCHING

	W-L	CG	QS	QS%	<6	>6	IPS	IP	ERA	OPR
ROTATION	54-59	9	62	38	30	51	5.9	954.1	5.48	.876

	W-L	GR	SV	BSV	HD	BHD	IRS%	IP	ERA	OPR
BULLPEN	29-20	426	38	22	125	89	38	478.1	4.80	.785

BATTING

PLAYER	BA	G	AB	R	H	2B	3B	HR	RBI	BB	SO	SB	CS	SA	OBA
Bates, Jason	.244	66	138	19	34	9	1	3	13	18	31	1	2	.392	.332
Bichette, Dante	.305	134	518	80	158	29	2	25	108	28	82	12	6	.516	.341
Burks, Ellis	.294	127	453	92	133	24	4	30	85	47	82	13	3	.564	.361
Castilla, Vinny	.294	157	609	90	179	28	1	38	107	39	97	3	4	.529	.336
Colbrunn, Greg	.313	77	251	32	78	15	0	9	39	12	40	2	2	.484	.345
Echevarria, Angel	.281	44	150	27	42	11	0	5	34	13	30	2	0	.461	.338
Helton, Todd	.286	93	340	59	97	19	2	13	59	41	67	1	0	.465	.364
Goodwin, Curtis	.292	74	228	31	67	10	1	1	13	24	50	21	10	.354	.359
Lansing, Mike	.302	148	587	92	177	46	2	18	71	47	88	17	5	.477	.354
Manwaring, Kirt	.251	105	327	22	82	10	3	2	30	30	76	1	3	.319	.313
Perez, Neifi	.305	103	420	73	128	24	8	8	49	24	57	6	0	.463	.343
Reed, Jeff	.283	102	280	38	79	12	0	12	41	38	55	2	1	.457	.368
Vander Wal, John	.233	41	50	6	12	2	0	1	9	6	16	1	1	.356	.317
Walker, Larry	.318	161	587	129	187	42	5	45	121	67	90	30	6	.635	.388

223

PITCHING

PITCHER	W	L	SV	ERA	G	GS	IP	H	HR	BB	SO
Astacio, Pedro	10	9	0	4.03	35	27	181	182	20	56	136
Bailey, Roger	8	9	0	4.64	34	24	167	183	22	69	76
Burke, John	4	8	0	5.76	34	13	100	131	22	41	74
DeJean, Mike	5	0	2	4.09	53	0	66	73	4	23	37
DiPoto, Jerry	4	3	12	4.42	55	0	73	81	4	30	52
Jones, Bobby	4	4	0	5.11	11	10	58	61	7	30	35
Kile, Darryl	16	10	0	4.46	37	35	250	263	21	120	216
Leskanic, Curt	4	1	7	5.07	55	0	60	59	7	25	59
McElroy, Chuck	3	3	1	5.49	57	0	64	72	6	25	53
Minchey, Nate	1	1	0	5.35	4	3	20	23	2	7	11
Munoz, Mike	3	3	1	5.24	74	0	55	63	6	18	41
Ritz, Kevin	7	6	0	5.05	16	16	96	110	12	42	52
Ruffin, Bruce	2	3	13	4.44	42	0	40	33	4	24	46
Thomson, John	7	8	0	4.70	25	25	157	182	14	48	100
Thompson, Mark	5	5	0	5.37	18	14	84	94	14	35	43
Veres, Dave	3	2	3	4.24	49	0	59	69	6	27	52
Wright, Jamey	7	9	0	5.34	22	22	128	155	15	57	53
Brownson, Mark	4	3	0	4.38	9	9	53	51	7	16	41

LOS ANGELES DODGERS

MANAGEMENT

Manager	General Manager	Owner
Bill Russell Career Record 137-111 .552	Fred Claire	Peter O'Malley

1997 RECORD

Won-Lost	Pct.	Division Finish/GB		Wild Card Finish/GB	
88-74	.543	2 W	-2	2	-4

Preseason Consensus Projection	1 (1.09)				

1st Half	2nd Half	Home	Road	Intradivision	Interleague
39-42	49-32	47-34	41-40	18-18	9-7

Comebacks	Blowouts	Nailbiters
11-7	27-12	37-41

224

DAWNING OF A NEW ERA

There will be big changes in Los Angeles for 1998. Veteran clubhouse and on-field leaders Todd Worrell and Brett Butler have retired. Knuckleball specialist Tom Candiotti signed with Oakland. Shortstop Greg Gagne declared free agency and has been replaced by slick-fielding veteran Jose Vizcaino.

What kind of team will this be? It depends on what direction the club decides to take in the spring. If youngsters Roger Cedeno, Paul Konerko, and Mike Judd get their chances to play, and players like Antonio Osuna, Darren Dreifort, and Dennis Reyes can expand their roles, the Dodgers could field a team that will both develop for the future and win in the present.

However, Los Angeles has shown at times in the past that it is too eager to deal for veteran solutions. (There are plenty of established players available on the market this win-

ter, and a lot of over-the-hill types who can be had cheaply. This approach hasn't worked in the past, but some teams never seem to learn. Have the Dodgers learned?)

UP AND DOWN IN L.A.

The Dodgers had a hot-and-cold offense last year. They scored 742 runs, which ranked seventh in the league, while playing their home games in the league's best pitcher's park in 1997. Four L.A. players—catcher Mike Piazza, first baseman Eric Karros, third sacker Todd Zeile, and right-fielder Raul Mondesi—hit 30 or more homers last year. All four of them scored at least 85 runs, with Piazza tallying more than 100.

But the rest of the offense was pretty much a bust, so there will be changes in 1998. The power core is still one of the best if Piazza and Mondesi stay healthy, although Karros and Zeile are overrated. If the team can figure out who should set the table (Roger Cedeno and Eric Young?), the offense could be even better. They won't win the NL West, though, if they have as many offensive black holes as they did last season.

One question yet to be answered is what the team plans to do with Zeile and Karros now that Paul Konerko is ready to step in and play either first or third. It would be unfortunate for the Dodgers if the questionable contracts to which the club signed Zeile and Karros keep Konerko, the organization's top prospect, from advancing.

LOOKS CAN BE DECEIVING

The Dodgers pitching staff once again had superficially good statistics on the year, posting a 3.63 ERA, second-best in the NL. However, their home ERA of 3.00 contrasted sharply with a road ERA of 4.26.

Dodgers pitchers tossed only six complete games all season, the same number they threw in 1996. Bill Russell likes going to his bullpen and likes to keep that bullpen well-stocked. But both lefty Mark Guthrie and closer Todd Worrell were far below average last season, each serving up a horrible 12 homers, in 69.1 and 59.2 innings of work, respectively.

Russell hasn't shown much trust yet in hard-throwing young pitchers Antonio Osuna and Darren Dreifort, but this season should be the time that both of them get a chance to prove their merit. Both are better pitchers than the recently retired Worrell or Darren Hall, the other top righthander in the Dodgers pen.

Of course, the Dodgers have enjoyed good pitching at home ever since their home stadium opened, as "Chavez Ravine," in 1962. What is now called Dodger Stadium was the best park for pitchers in the National League every year from 1962-71, and again in 1974, 1986, 1994, 1995, 1996, and 1997.

Part of this park effect is the tail wagging the dog—such standouts as Sandy Koufax, Don Drysdale, Johnny Podres, Ron Perranoski, Don Sutton, Bill Singer, Fernando Valenzuela, Ramon Martinez, Ismael Valdes, and Orel Hershiser are part of the reason that the Dodgers had the best home pitching records in the league those years, and often the best pitching staffs in toto. However, of course, it is necessary to point out that the spacious dimensions of

TEAM MVP

Catchers who bat .362 with 40 home runs aren't a plentiful commodity. **Mike Piazza** isn't and may never be a top-notch defensive catcher, but his hustle, as well as his spectacular offensive ability, make him an annual MVP candidate. Piazza finished in the top three among NL hitters in batting average, slugging average, and on-base percentage and ended fourth in home runs and RBIs.

BIGGEST SURPRISE

Chan Ho Park emerged as a first-rate starting pitcher in 1997, winning 14 and losing eight with a fine 3.38 ERA. He improved his control and showed the ability to dominate with four above-average pitches. Park might vault into the upper echelon of National League starters as early as this season.

BIGGEST DISAPPOINTMENT

Outfielder **Todd Hollandsworth** had a terrible sophomore season, batting just .247 with four home runs and five steals. He started out well but suffered a knee injury and went into a terrible slump. After returning from a spell at Triple A, Hollandsworth fractured his right elbow and did not play much the rest of the season. The Dodgers expect Hollandsworth to come back 100 percent in 1998, and don't have too many options in the outfield if he can't.

225

are also a major reason that the pitching staff's performance was so good.

The best pitchers the Dodgers have—Martinez, Valdes, Darren Dreifort, Al Osuna, and Chan Ho Park—all had ERAs lower than 4.00 on the road last season and pitched well at home. Others, like Worrell, Candiotti, and Astacio, struggled in games away from Los Angeles and are now gone. Hideo Nomo, who had a 4.99 ERA on the road last season, and Guthrie, who allowed 28 earned runs in 39.2 innings in away games, need to get themselves together.

WILTON GUERRERO: THE YEAR THAT WASN'T

The Dodgers expected to capture their sixth straight Rookie of the Year Award in 1997. Their hopes were pinned on second baseman Wilton Guerrero, a slick fielder with a slashing, high-average bat. He had shown good defense and high batting averages in the minors, and he continued showing them in the majors. The 24-year-old batted .291 and made but four errors all season.

Still, Guerrero was deemed a disappointment. The Dodgers were so unhappy with him, in fact, that they traded with the Rockies in August for Eric Young and consigned Guerrero to the bench. Young, a product of the Dodgers' system, had been taken in the expansion draft by Colorado after the 1992 season. He returned to L.A. and held down the second base job for the final six weeks of the season.

It wasn't Guerrero's fault that he wasn't considered a success. It was the fault of the Dodgers, who asked the youngster to do something he was not capable of: batting at the top of the order. Guerrero had never walked often enough in the minors to be a top-of-the-order hitter, and he was a fair-to-awful percentage basestealer to boot.

While leading off for the Dodgers, Guerrero walked once in nearly 100 plate appearances. Batting first and second, he hit .279 (58 for 208), but walked only three times. Overall, Guerrero walked only eight times all season in nearly 400 plate appearances. That could have been predicted.

It was a tough year for Guerrero. Surely one of the most painful things to watch all season was an incident on June 1, when the rookie's bat exploded, spraying cork all over the St. Louis infield. Guerrero, who became flushed and embarrassed when umpires and fans figured out what had happened, was suspended for eight games. The ugly incident made what was expected to be a banner year even more difficult.

The Dodgers made a decision in the off-season to stick with Eric Young, signing him to a long-term contract. Since they also signed free agent Jose Vizcaino to play shortstop, Guerrero will now be the odd man out. However, Young won't be nearly the player in Los Angeles that he was in Colorado; history has already proven that.

Young's road numbers while with the Rockies from 1993-97 show just how overrated he was: 1,049 at bats, 56 doubles, eight triples, seven homers, 69 RBI, and 103 walks. That's a poor .245 batting average and weak .334 slugging average without the compensation of a good on-base percentage or good defense. After being dealt to Los Angeles, Young hit .273 in 37 games with but eight extra-base hits and a .347 on-base. Unless he can radically adjust his game now that he's not cosseted by Coors Field, he's going to seriously disappoint the Dodgers.

The Dodgers are now faced with a decision. Do they stay with Young (whom they signed to a four-year contract this winter) and either trade or demote Guerrero? Guerrero has the advantages of youth, defensive prowess, and a low salary. He is seven years younger (23 to 30), a better defensive second baseman, and several million dollars cheaper. Of course, Guerrero won't blossom until the Dodgers use him properly.

TODD HOLLANDSWORTH: FROM LEFT FIELD TO LEFT OUT

Entering the '97 season the Dodgers' outfield picture looked quite bright. Left fielder Todd Hollandsworth was the 1996 NL Rookie of the Year, Brett Butler was primed and ready to go in center after his remarkable comeback from cancer, and young star Raul Mondesi was set in right.

But by season's end only Mondesi was left standing. He played 159 games in right and had a very good season, batting .310 with excellent power and stolen base production (the first 30–30 season in Dodgers history) and 10 assists. (His assist totals have declined dramatically from a league-leading 16 each in 1994 and 1995, both strike-shortened

226

years, because fewer runners dare challenge his arm.)

No one else played even as many as 90 games at any other outfield position for L.A. Hollandsworth slumped, lost his job, was sent to the minors, and finished the year trying to wedge himself in between retreads Darren Lewis and Billy Ashley. Butler played as often as he could, but was forced to share time with veterans Otis Nixon and Wayne Kirby and prospect Roger Cedeno. None of the center fielders contributed much offensively.

Hollandsworth is an obviously talented hitter who became overanxious when he encountered a sophomore slump. His career is at a crossroads, because the Dodgers can't afford to let him work out his problems in the majors. With veteran Todd Zeile a candidate to move to left field (a move not likely to work well), Hollandsworth may not have a regular job on opening day 1998.

NEW OWNERSHIP, NEW RULES

Proposed organizational changes for 1998, when Rupert Murdoch, owner of the Fox Television Network, takes over running the Los Angeles Dodgers:

1. The Dodgers will have new uniforms, designed to resemble clothes worn by the cast of "Beverly Hills 90210."

2. Fox sponsor Little Caesar's will buy the rights to Mike Piazza's name and market a new "Mike Pizza."

3. Fans will only be allowed into the ballpark in Parties of Five.

4. Dodger Stadium is to be renamed Chan Ho Park to appeal to the city's Korean community.

5. The mysterious abduction of Pedro Astacio by aliens from Colorado is to be dramatized on "The X-Files."

6. Two Dodgers utility infielders will star in the new "buddy" TV series "In the Dugout With Tripp & Chip."

7. Recently retired Brett Butler will be signed to star in a new Fox comedy with comedienne Brett Butler.

8. A different celebrity visit to every Dodgers batting practice will be televised as part of Fox's weeknight lineup. Week one: Gillian Anderson.

9. All Dodgers players already not named "Todd" will be required to change their first names to conform.

10. All Los Angeles home games will start at 8:00 Eastern, 5:00 Pacific time. Check your local listings.

THE MOMENT OF TRUTH

The Dodgers led the NL West by two games over San Francisco on **September 17** but lost two one-run games to the Giants at 3 Com Park, falling into a first-place tie. Los Angeles then dropped three straight games at home to third-place Colorado—two of them after jumping out to early leads—which sealed their fate as a second-place club.

BEST DEAL

Los Angeles did not make many significant deals in 1997. A good one, however, was acquiring veteran **Otis Nixon** to play center field. He hit .274 with the Dodgers and scored 30 runs in 42 games—a terrific ratio—before signing with the Twins in the off-season.

227

WORST DEAL

Trading hurler **Pedro Astacio** for second baseman **Eric Young** will probably improve Los Angeles' offense, but with Tom Candiotti gone and Pedro Martinez on the trading block, Astacio's ability to start or relieve would have been valuable to the Dodgers this year. He will be missed.

1. **Paul Konerko, 3B/1B.** Whether Konerko succeeds (most likely at the hot corner) depends only on whether the Dodgers will take a gamble on the 22-year-old. The 1994 first-round pick is ready to be an excellent offensive player right now. He has power, a good slashing bat, excellent strike-zone judgement, and a good head on his shoulders. Even at Albuquerque, his 37 homers, 127 RBIs, and .323 average of 1997 are head-turning numbers. Konerko is going to be a big contributor, either now or later.

2. **Dennis Reyes, P.** Called a "Fernando Valenzuela look-alike" despite being four inches taller, and 40 pounds heavier, Reyes blazed through the system in 1997, combining for a 14-4 record at Double A and Triple A. He then went 2-3 in 14 games with the Dodgers, fanning 36 in 47 innings and posting a 3.83 ERA. Lefthanded starters with good stuff don't grow on trees, even in this organization, and Reyes will be up again soon if he's not on the opening day roster.

3. **Adrian Beltre, 3B.** Those who feel that Beltre is the best prospect in the minors have a good argument. Beltre is a Gold Glove–caliber third baseman who hit .317 in 1997 at the obscene age of 19 and clubbed 26 homers, collected 25 steals, and took 67 walks in the pitching-dominant Florida State League. While it isn't likely he'll be in Los Angeles this year, similar promotions have come for players with far less talent. Beltre is one of the few minor leaguers to show signs of true superstardom.

4. **Mike Judd, P.** Judd reached the majors in just his third pro season. Originally in the Yankees organization, he came over in trade in mid-1996 and has been outstanding ever since. Owner of an excellent fastball, Judd blew away the Florida State League and was 4-2 at San Antonio before the Dodgers purchased his contract in late September. Judd might spend the season at either Double A or Triple A to smooth out some occasional command problems, but could also sneak into the Los Angeles rotation with a strong spring.

5. **Adam Riggs, 2B.** The 25-year-old infielder is fast and can hit. He batted .304 with 13 homers and 12 steals in 57 games last year for Albuquerque after returning from a fractured hamate bone suffered in April. He made it to L.A. for nine games, but won't be a starter now that Eric Young is in the picture. The hard-working Riggs's defense at second base is now average.

6. **Kevin Gibbs, OF.** This outfielder, who turns 24 in April, is quickly maturing into an outstanding leadoff man. Advancing from the Class A Florida State League in 1996 to the Double A Texas League last year, Gibbs hit .335 with 72 walks and 49 stolen bases—numbers that will lead to years with more than 100 runs scored. In '97 he tallied 89 times in just 101 games. Though he has no power, Gibbs is incredibly fast, bunts well, and is progressing in a hurry.

7. **Brian Richardson, 3B.** He was well over his head in a 1996 Triple A trial, but found himself last year at Double A San Antonio. Richardson collected 23 doubles, 13 triples, and 13 homers, batting .298. He still has problems with the strike zone, but is improving in that area. Possessing a strong arm, he is only 22 and remains on the way to the majors—if not with the Dodgers, who have plenty of third base options, then with someone else.

8. **Jeff Kubenka, P.** The lefty's numbers at Class A San Bernadino (5-1, 0.92 in 34 games, 19 saves, 62 strikeouts and 11 walks in 39 innings) and Double A San Antonio (3-0, 0.70, four saves in 19 games, 38 K's and six walks in 25.2 innings) indicate a dominating power pitcher. This he isn't. The 23-year-old has just a high-80s fastball. Kubenka's big pitch is an outstanding screwball that he throws with excellent confidence and command. The test comes this year with a full season in the high minors.

228

IMPORTED GOODS

The whole Hideki Irabu mess was only the ugliest part of a breakthrough 1997 season for Asian pitchers. Four Japanese and one Korean pitcher worked in the major leagues last year, the most ever. Three of these hurlers were appearing in the majors for the first time.

It's no secret that major league teams are desperate for pitching. Believing the domestic supply to be inadequate, teams have been scouring foreign countries during the 1990s, looking for promising kids with good fastballs and, to a lesser extent, for Japanese professionals with stuff and moxie. The fact that foreign prospects can generally be signed for a small percentage of what an American prospect wants doesn't slow down the global pitching search one bit.

How did the great experiment turn out? What will happen in the future? Let's look at each of the hurlers in some detail, in order of their arrival in the majors.

•Hideo Nomo, Dodgers. "The Tornado" threw harder than almost all other Japanese pitchers and was a dominating strikeout artist in Japan. He's been good here as well at whiffing enemy hitters. Reports of his impending decline have been exaggerated, as in his three years Nomo has remained a solid big-league starter with an above-average fastball and an excellent split-finger pitch.

Pitching in Dodger Stadium is a big advantage for him; he might not be as successful in another park. Nomo had a 4.99 ERA on the road last season, and was thoroughly miserable down the stretch.

•Chan Ho Park, Dodgers. It now appears that the 24-year-old Korean-born righty is going to be better than Nomo. Park began to put it together in 1997, harnessing his fastball and using his breaking pitches better than previously. Park is death on righthanders and is often overpowering. Now that his command (of his pitches and himself) has improved, he could move quickly into 20-win territory. He struggled a bit down the stretch however.

•Makoto Suzuki, Mariners. The only one on this list who didn't pitch in the majors last year, Suzuki was signed by the Mariners in 1992 when he was just 17. The baby-faced lefthander throws extremely hard but lacks any command of the strike zone and continues to founder in the minor leagues. He pitched one game with the Mariners in 1996. Obviously, the jury is still out on Suzuki.

•Shigetoshi Hasegawa, Angels. Brought over from the Orix Blue Wave with the caveat that he was not a hard thrower and not expected to be a starter, Hasegawa had a decent season for Anaheim. He showed more media savvy and friendliness than other imports. The Angels were happy to have Hasegawa due to his versatility, presence, and good arm, but expectations are not high.

•Takashi Kashiwada, Mets. A six-year Japanese minor league lefthander with only limited experience with the Yomiuri Giants, Kashiwada was purchased by the Mets to help solve their bullpen problems. He only added to them. He was 3-1 in 35 games, but walked 18 hitters in 31.1 innings and fashioned a 4.35 ERA. Kashiwada does not yet appear to be ready for the major leagues in this country.

•Hideki Irabu, Yankees. This one smelled bad from the start, as Irabu burned bridges in his country with his mercenary, egotistical stance while angering a lot of people in America due to the brusqueness of agent Don Nomura.

Once Irabu got a basketful of George Steinbrenner's money and America's attention, it was time for him to show what he could do. He didn't do much. Irabu blew quickly through the minor leagues but had trouble adjusting to the majors. In his most embarrassing start, Irabu got the stuffing knocked out of him on national television in Milwaukee on July 20, then raged at the celebrating fans.

Irabu has outstanding stuff. However, he clearly has a lot to learn, especially about overusing his fastball. He struck out more than a hitter per inning with the Yankees, but also allowed 15 home runs in 13 games. Final ERA: 7.09.

Obviously, most of these pitchers will be back in 1998. Nomo, Park, and Irabu are expected to be in their clubs' starting rotations. Several teams signed young Japanese pitchers during the off-season, but much depends on how these three fare. It is intriguing that only coastal teams (Mets, Yankees, Dodgers, Angels, Mariners, and—let's not forget—Irabu's original owners, the Padres) have taken on Asian pitchers, which suggests that marketing to Asian communities is at least part of the consideration.

Of course, being Asian, will only get a player so far if he doesn't do the job. If international scouts are doing their jobs, we'll be seeing many of the world's best players from all countries in the next few years.

229

1997 TEAM STATISTICS

BATTING/BASERUNNING

	Raw	Rank	+/- %		Raw	Rank	+/- %		Raw	Rank	+/- %
R	742	7	0	BA	.268	4	+2	SB	131	7	+1
R/G	4.58	7	0	HR	174	2	+13	CS	64	5	+7
OBA	.330	8	-1	LH	275	14	-12	SB%	67.2	8	-1
SA	.418	4	+2	BB	498	11	-10				
PRO	.748	5	+1	SO	1,079	6	-1				

PITCHING/FIELDING

	Raw	Rank	+/- %		Raw	Rank	+/- %		Raw	Rank	+/- %
OR	645	2	-13	BA	.241	1	-8	OSB	118	7	-7
RA/G	3.98	2	-13	HR	163	9	+5	OCS	58	8	-1
OOB	.313	2	-6	LH	289	6	-7	OSB%	67.0	7	-1
OSA	.389	5	-5	BB	546	5	-2	FA	.981	8	0
PRO	.702	3	-5	SO	1,232	1	+11	GDP	85	1	-29

BATTING BY LINEUP SLOTS

	R	HR	RBI	BA	OBA	SA
1	106	3	52	.276	.336	.356
2	102	18	71	.276	.318	.407
3	115	46	136	.330	.391	.604
4	95	26	97	.286	.353	.460
5	86	31	95	.298	.354	.515
6	87	27	85	.259	.353	.437
7	67	15	78	.253	.315	.390
8	48	4	57	.250	.313	.327
9	36	4	35	.165	.214	.226

BATTING BY DEFENSIVE POSITION

	R	HR	RBI	BA	OBA	SA
C	116	43	130	.335	.407	.597
1B	87	32	105	.266	.328	.462
2B	78	9	67	.277	.315	.387
3B	89	31	90	.267	.366	.456
SS	56	11	69	.248	.296	.352
LF	71	11	56	.252	.315	.364
CF	97	4	55	.283	.347	.364
RF	100	31	90	.302	.353	.527
DH	4	0	7	.441	.444	.588
PH	19	2	28	.186	.282	.273
P	17	0	9	.141	.167	.179

TEAM PITCHING

	W-L	CG	QS	QS%	<6	>6	IPS	IP	ERA	OPR
ROTATION	63-52	6	96	59	17	67	6.3	1,014.1	3.73	.706

	W-L	GR	SV	BSV	HD	BHD	IRS%	IP	ERA	OPR
BULLPEN	25-22	412	45	20	167	78	24	445.0	3.40	.692

LOS ANGELES DODGERS
1998 PROJECTIONS

BATTING

PLAYER	BA	G	AB	R	H	2B	3B	HR	RBI	BB	SO	SB	CS	SA	OBA
Blanco, Henry	.238	17	54	5	13	3	0	1	6	5	14	1	0	.340	.303
Castro, Juan	.212	27	50	5	11	2	1	0	3	5	15	0	0	.292	.288
Cedeno, Roger	.267	119	277	41	74	14	2	3	24	34	63	11	1	.371	.348
Cromer, Tripp	.263	27	87	10	23	4	0	2	10	4	18	0	0	.390	.298
Guerrero, Wilton	.298	87	274	31	82	8	7	3	25	6	42	5	4	.414	.314
Hollandsworth, Todd	.270	139	405	56	109	24	3	9	47	29	85	11	6	.408	.319
Hubbard, Trenidad	.256	57	203	32	52	10	0	7	26	25	35	10	0	.406	.338
Karros, Eric	.267	148	573	79	153	26	1	29	99	54	110	11	4	.470	.330
Konerko, Paul	.229	77	280	39	64	13	0	15	52	26	44	1	0	.440	.294
Mondesi, Raul	.294	158	621	95	183	38	6	27	87	38	108	26	11	.507	.335
Otero, Ricky	.262	43	142	19	37	4	2	1	7	15	13	4	3	.339	.330
Piazza, Mike	.331	161	595	100	197	26	1	40	119	71	85	3	1	.578	.401
Prince, Tom	.250	37	73	11	18	4	0	2	11	5	13	0	0	.381	.300
Riggs, Adam	.226	18	68	13	16	2	0	3	6	7	14	3	0	.377	.297
Vizcaino, Jose	.278	148	558	74	155	19	7	2	51	43	88	11	8	.355	.330
Young, Eric	.293	138	539	96	158	27	7	7	57	57	41	43	15	.406	.361
Zeile, Todd	.261	120	443	62	115	17	0	21	67	59	81	4	3	.441	.348

PITCHING

PITCHER	W	L	SV	ERA	G	GS	IP	H	HR	BB	SO
Dreifort, Darren	4	5	10	3.71	52	0	65	58	3	36	65
Guthrie, Mark	2	4	1	4.36	58	0	64	64	8	25	46
Hall, Darren	3	3	3	2.88	69	0	62	70	4	31	45
Judd, Mike	4	3	0	2.98	11	10	67	64	0	29	46
Martinez, Ramon	13	6	0	3.76	25	25	158	146	15	79	130
Nomo, Hideo	13	10	0	3.80	29	29	187	160	19	79	207
Osuna, Antonio	4	5	5	2.95	61	0	73	59	7	27	79
Park, Chan Ho	13	8	0	3.61	42	26	187	148	21	82	171
Radinsky, Scott	5	1	2	3.35	76	0	64	63	5	23	47
Reyes, Dennis	6	6	0	3.68	22	17	112	116	8	47	75
Scott, Tim	2	2	1	3.83	37	0	40	36	3	13	31
Valdes, Ismael	12	11	0	3.17	32	31	210	197	18	53	155
Lankford, Frank	2	3	0	4.49	8	8	50	56	2	15	20

231

SAN DIEGO PADRES

MANAGEMENT

Manager	General Manager	Owner
Bruce Bochy Career Record 237-231 .506	Kevin Towers	John Morris

1997 RECORD

Won-Lost	Pct.		Division Finish/GB		Wild Card Finish/GB	
76-86	.469		4 W	-14	7	-16

Preseason Consensus Projection		2 (2.22)				

1st Half	2nd Half		Home	Road	Intradivision	Interleague
36-45	40-41		39-42	37-44	19-17	8-8

Comebacks	Blowouts	Nailbiters				
14-7	16-27	41-33				

232

FROM FIRST TO WORST

San Diego tumbled from first to last in 1997, with terrible pitching and an injury bug combining to subvert a good overall offensive performance. Pitching helped carry the Padres to their 1996 NL West title, and it helped destroy them last year. After finishing with the third-best ERA in the NL in '96, San Diego's pitching sagged last season, ranking 13th (above only Colorado) with an awful 4.99 ERA. That was the Padres' worst team mark ever, including their first six seasons when the club lost 95 or more games and finished last each year. San Diego pitchers didn't notch a single complete-game shutout in 1997, and went the distance just five times, tied for fewest in the NL.

There was little quality among the starting pitchers. Joey Hamilton won 12 games and was the team's best pitcher, but even he sagged to a 4.25 ERA. Andy Ashby, who led the team with 30 starts, was 9-11. Lefthander Sterling Hitchcock, well on his way to proving that his detractors are right, made 28 starts and racked up a 5.20 ERA.

Injuries to several pitchers and ineffectiveness by others forced the team to use four spot starters: Tim Worrell, Sean Bergman, rookie Will Cunnane, and sore-armed veteran Pete Smith. Only Smith was effective, and he didn't move into the rotation until midseason.

Worst of all was the performance of purportedly 36-year-old southpaw Fernando Valenzuela, whose 1996 comeback helped the Padres win the division. It was a different story for the likable lefty last year; he got hammered early and often and had to be unloaded, and the Cardinals also dumped him after an 0-4 mark in five more starts.

The pitcher whom the Padres got for Valenzuela, Danny Jackson, delivered an even more amazing performance. Fernando was 2-8 with a 4.75 ERA for the Padres, while

Danny was 1-7 with a nifty 7.53 mark. That's a combined 3-15 mark in 22 starts from San Diego's No. 2 lefthanded starter, Danando Jacksonuela.

And if you think the starting pitching was bad, how about that bullpen? It is not an exaggeration to say that closer Trevor Hoffman was the only effective reliever the Padres had in 1997. Had San Diego not been able to count on Hoffman, they would have been a far worse team. Reassuming his place at the top of the NL closers' list, Hoffman saved 37 games in 44 tries and fanned 111 in 81.1 innings. So much for losing his fastball.

One of the club's strengths in 1996 was a slew of hard-throwing relievers who performed unexpectedly well. Rookie Dario Veras assumed a setup role after coming up in July; Doug Bochtler and Tim Worrell pitched quite effectively in the middle. Of course, unexpectedly good performances from unheralded players are quite commonly followed by expectably bad performances the next season.

In 1997 Veras hurt his shoulder and was never effective, Worrell was lousy, and Bochtler lost whatever command he had in '96 and got cuffed around regularly. The result: 20 blown saves.

In addition to the slumps by the remaining arms, several pitchers who had provided bullpen depth in 1996 were traded late that season or shortly afterward. Ron Villone and Bryce Florie, both usable pitchers with talent, were packed off to Milwaukee in the ill-fated Greg Vaughn deal. Willie Blair, who had not pitched well in 1996, was sent to Detroit, where he won 16 games.

In place of the departed came well-traveled and largely useless arms like those of Tim Scott, Rich Batchelor, Jim Bruske, and Terry Burrows, along with equally unimpressive youngsters Marc Kroon, Todd Erdos, and Joey Long. Kroon has been touted as a potential closer for three years but still shows no sign of gaining the requisite command to be effective in the bigs.

So when the pitching falls apart and the young arms don't develop—and in fact regress—and the team finishes last, what happens? The pitching coach gets fired.

While many of San Diego's pitchers defended Dan Warthen and said that he wasn't to blame, it would have been very difficult to ashcan ten pitchers and keep Warthen

TEAM MVP

Who else but **Tony Gwynn** deserves this award? Last year's NL MVP, Ken Caminiti, slumped sharply, and none of the pitchers did the job. At age 37 Gwynn had perhaps his greatest season ever, capturing his eighth NL batting crown with an unreal .372 mark. He also kicked in career highs of 49 doubles, 17 homers, and 119 RBIs as well. The amazing season he enjoyed in 1997 only further confirms that Tony Gwynn is one of the greatest hitters of recent times.

BIGGEST SURPRISE

First baseman **Wally Joyner**, his professional life threatened after a poor 1996 season (.277, eight homers), bounced back last season for a .327 average that was his best ever. Joyner also clouted 13 homers and drove in 83 runs. He's still just an average offensive performer at his position, but good defense makes Joyner a plus player if he can remain close to his 1997 level.

BIGGEST DISAPPOINTMENT

Two veteran pitchers led the Padres' tumble in 1997. **Tim Worrell** and **Sean Bergman**, both of whom at one time had been considered possible starters, instead punted their chances with ERAs of 5.16 and 6.09, respectively. Both ended the year as middle relievers.

233

instead. Somebody had to take responsibility for the disappointing performances of Bochtler, Worrell, Bergman, and Veras. All this despite the fact that Qualcomm Stadium was one of the better pitcher's parks in the NL in 1997.

Former Oakland pitching stalwart Dave Stewart, who had been an assistant to GM Kevin Towers, was hired to take Warthen's place for 1998. Stewart is expected to bring a tough, in-your-face attitude to the Padres. He did have a tremendously intimidating presence on the mound in his day, but he also had a hell of a lot of talent.

In the off-season the Padres completely razed the bullpen, releasing Bruske, Burrows, and Batchelor and trading Bergman, Bochtler, and Worrell. In their place came Ed Vosberg, Donne Wall, Dan Miceli, Don Wengert, and Brian Boehringer. All five of those pitchers have talent, but the Padres may be hoping for too much by pushing Miceli as a future setup man.

After redoing the relief corps, a huge off-season trade brought starter Kevin Brown to San Diego in exchange for prospects Derrek Lee and Rafael Medina. Brown, one of the few truly dominating pitchers in baseball, has been helped by pitching in Florida (1.69 ERA at home in 1996, 2.51 in 1997), but he was pretty damn good in road games as well (2.19 ERA on the road in 1996, 2.89 in 1997). Qualcomm Stadium is a friendly park for home run hitters, but overall a good park for pitchers. Since sinkerballer Brown keeps the ball low (allowing only 10 homers in 1997), he shouldn't be hurt by the park's home run habit.

Brown's contract is up after the 1998 season, and it's quite possible he won't be re-signed to a long-term deal by San Diego. If, however, the addition of an ace like Brown leads to the NLCS or beyond, the trade will be a success regardless of what happens long-term. Padres management is acutely aware that a successful 1998 season will greatly increase their chances of getting voters to approve funding for a new ballpark—which the team maintains is essential to their remaining in San Diego.

Other off-season acquisitions were outfielder James Mouton, who should get playing time as a fourth outfielder, and veteran lefthander Mark Langston, bothered for most of the last two years by knee and elbow problems. Mouton came over for disappointing pitcher Sean Bergman; he adds speed and the ability to hit lefthanders.

Langston is a fierce competitor and will work hard to come back, but he has not had a truly fine season since 1993.

TONY GWYNN: IT WAS A VERY GOOD YEAR

The Padres did score some runs in 1997. They ranked third in the NL in tallies, largely because of Steve Finley's 28 homers, great leadoff work from Rickey Henderson (.422 on-base), solid year from '96 NL MVP Ken Caminiti and, most importantly, a world-class season from Tony Gwynn.

At age 37, the Padres' legend won his fourth consecutive batting crown with a .372 mark, the second-best average of his career. Gwynn also added a career-high 17 homers and 119 RBIs and swiped 12 bases. He played 149 games despite having a bad left knee and a blood clot in his right leg. What more could one ask from any player than a season like the one Gwynn enjoyed in 1997?

THE FALL GUY

When your MVP third baseman misses 25 games because of injury, and pitchers can't stay healthy, and the disabled list looks as big as the active roster, what happens?

Larry Duensing had been in the Padres organization since 1977 and had been the team's head trainer since 1993. Unfortunately for Duensing, San Diego had to disable 18 players last year for a total of 549 days. Following the season, Duensing was fired.

Of course, this wasn't all the trainer's fault. How could it have been? The Padres had several injury-prone veterans on the club, including pitchers like Andy Ashby, Fernando Valenzuela, and Pete Smith, infielder Craig Shipley, and outfielders Tony Gwynn and Greg Vaughn.

Right or wrong, Duensing is gone. All three Padres starting outfielders underwent surgery after the season, and Ken Caminiti, who played most of the season on a torn-up right knee, also went under the laser. If this club is healthy in 1998, it should contend, as the NL West doesn't figure to be a really strong division. Even so, the addition of another team, the Arizona Diamondbacks, will ultimately make it harder for the Padres or anyone else to sneak into the postseason merely by squeaking by three other weak teams.

In addition to the pitching coach, the head trainer, and the middle relievers, one other head of note rolled in San

234

Diego in 1997. The Padres tried to be patient, but they finally had to dump Don Slaught on May 20, since he had not yet collected a base hit. He played in 20 games, 16 of them as a pinch hitter, and was 0-for-20 with five walks. No one picked up the 38-year-old receiver after San Diego let him go. That's a pretty sad way to end a good career.

GREG VAUGHN: A LONG-TERM MISTAKE

Perhaps the worst big-dollar contract of 1997 was the three-year deal the Padres gave Greg Vaughn in February. After two injury-marred off-years, Vaughn had a very good year in 1996, though it ended with him playing unexpectedly poorly after being traded to San Diego. He collected his booty in the form of a rich new contract, and then went out and had a miserable season.

San Diego was under substantial pressure to sign Vaughn to a long-term deal in the 1996-97 off-season, but it was pressure that could have and should have been resisted. While the team had a legitimate worry about having enough power, it also needed a bona fide leadoff hitter and was unwilling to eat Rickey Henderson's contract by cutting him loose or trading him for little in return. It was also looking at Vaughn's .206 batting average in 43 games in the NL in '96.

By signing Vaughn the Padres were left with both Henderson and Vaughn competing for playing time in left. As it turned out, Vaughn hit only one more homer in 1997 than feared power threat Tony Gwynn, and as a bonus Vaughn batted 156 points lower. Henderson played much better than Vaughn, but he was unloaded to save some money after the team was out of the race.

By July the Padres were offering their white elephant left fielder to anyone who would take on his hefty contract. San Diego worked out a six-player deal with the Yankees, but the Bronx crew voided the deal after claiming that Vaughn's surgically repaired right shoulder didn't pass their physical exam. While New York's excuse was suspect, the deal was dead and no one else was willing to take on the financial burden Vaughn represented.

If San Diego management had wanted to know about the wisdom of giving Vaughn a long-term deal, they should have asked Milwaukee GM Sal Bando. The Brewers signed

THE MOMENT OF TRUTH

San Diego was 9-7, four games out, on April 20. They didn't win again until May 1, after they had dropped eight straight. Opponents outscored San Diego 53-28 in the eight-game loss string as the pitching began its season-long slide toward a 4.99 staff ERA. The Padres spent almost the entire season in last place in the NL West.

BEST DEAL

Dumping unhappy hurler **Hideki Irabu** on the Yankees was a good move; the trade netted San Diego outfielder **Ruben Rivera**, still considered a very good prospect, and pitcher **Rafael Medina**, later used to pry Kevin Brown away from the Marlins.

235

WORST DEAL

Who in their right mind would have given veteran left fielder **Greg Vaughn** a multiyear contract? The Padres did after an encouraging 1996, and were rewarded for their misplaced faith with a .216 average and 18 homers in 120 games.

Vaughn to a lucrative three-year deal after his career year in 1993, then watched as he slumped for two years, partly due to injury.

If Padres GM Kevin Towers had resisted the pressure, he could have gone to arbitration with Vaughn and thereby signed him to a one-year deal. Whether he won or lost the arbitration hearing, the team would have won in the long run by being free of its $10-million-plus commitment to Vaughn for 1998 and '99. And if Vaughn had gone out and hit 40 homers as he did in '96, San Diego could have re-signed him during or after the '97 season. Sure, it would have cost more then than it would have in February, but that's a risk the team had to take in order to avoid the possibility of signing an expensive, unloadable contract.

When one looks at the distortions in the salary structure in baseball (after separating out the whining of the owners about how much they're being victimized by the guys they see in the mirror every morning), contracts like Vaughn's stand out. Players in Vaughn's position—and, of course, their agents—depend on a team's fear of being taken to arbitration, in order to extract much more lucrative deals than they might otherwise obtain.

Arbitration is almost always unpleasant, and it can leave a player with long-term feelings of resentment about how management criticized his performance. That is one reason why many teams sensibly try to avoid it. However, avoiding it at all costs doesn't solve any problems, as the threat of going to arbitration also gives the club

TOP PROSPECTS
SPRING 1998

1. **Matt Clement, P.** Last season, the 23-year-old righthander blossomed into a top-flight mound prospect. A 6-3 record and 1.60 ERA over 14 starts in the hard-hitting California League impressed the Padres, as did his 109 strikeouts in just 101 innings. Sent to Double A Mobile, Clement was 6-5. 2.56 in 13 more starts, whiffing 92 men in 88 frames. He has command of three solid pitches, including a fine slider, and could be in San Diego by midseason if his progress continues. Management feels Clement can eventually be a No. 1 starter.

2. **Ruben Rivera, OF.** Many say he has the best physical tools—bat, power, arm, and legs—of any player in baseball. Unfortunately, a combination of injuries and disciplinary problems have taken some years out of Rivera's career. 1997 was spent on the disabled list; Rivera got only 45 at bats at Triple A and 20 for the Padres. He is now 24 with everything to prove. Luckily for him, he will also have the opportunity.

3. **Heath Murray, P.** Formerly the Padres' top pitching prospect, the lefthander slumped in 1997 at Triple A Las Vegas, falling to 6-8 with a 5.45 ERA after a 13-9 1996 season at Double A Memphis. When called to San Diego he was cuffed around in 17 games (14 in relief). Murray sports four pitches, the best of which his curve, and has good command of his stuff. Unfortunately, Las Vegas is a bad place to pitch, and Murray struggled with men on base. He'll be in somebody's rotation sooner or later.

4. **Marc Kroon, P.** The Padres have been talking about the hard-throwing reliever for years now, but Kroon is still trying to get his game together at Triple A. In 1997 Kroon—a classic fastball/slider reliever—saved 15 games and fanned 53 men in 42 innings. He also walked 22. He could see setup duty for San Diego this season.

5. **Juan Melo, SS.** While his range is only average, and he does not add speed, Melo's hands are good and his arm is very strong. He will go to Triple A this season after hitting .287 with seven homers at Double A Mobile. Melo, a switch hitter, is not yet selective at the dish, but at age 21 is still developing. Assuming he plays well this season, Melo will be asking for Chris Gomez' job in 1999.

real leverage when setting salary disputes, especially when negotiating a multiyear deal.

This was a classic case where going to the mat with a player was the smart thing to do. Vaughn was 31, he wasn't a franchise player, his value rested almost solely on his power hitting, he played only a minor role in the team's '96 division title he played poorly after changing leagues, he had one good season in the last three, he had a serious injury history, and he wanted a lot of guaranteed money. Forcing Vaughn to prove that he could repeat his '96 Milwaukee performance would have been a tough decision, but it would have also left the Padres unencumbered with his big salary in 1998 and 1999 when they needed to retool the team.

Mistakes aside, Vaughn still has power in his bat and could conceivably stage another comeback; he hit better after getting contact lenses late in the season. With Henderson gone, Vaughn will have left field to himself unless Ruben Rivera recovers from his injury problems and is ready for "The Show." Vaughn did throw out seven baserunners in 94 games last season—not a bad number for someone whose shoulder hangs by a thread—and made just one error.

Almost inevitably when a big, muscular slugger has an unexpected sharp drop in performance, there is talk that he has gotten too bulked-up and that his muscle mass makes him less flexible at the plate. Questions about the wisdom of extra weight and excessive muscle development in baseball will likely become more prevalent in the next few years, as the debate has been simmering quietly for some time now. The Padres' clubhouse has been one of the most conscious in the big league about weight-training, and, if Vaughn, Ken Caminiti, et al. have future problems with injuries or reduced performance, the issue could soon come to the forefront in San Diego.

RICKEY HENDERSON: HE KNOWS THE SCORE

The Padres may not fare as well offensively in '98 as they did in '97 because they'll be lacking the best leadoff hitter in baseball history. Whatever else anyone says about Rickey Henderson (and people had gossiped about him a lot over his career, much of it unjustified), he has been a supreme run-scoring machine.

Before he was traded to Anaheim on July 31, Rickey was having another outstanding season. He hit .274, took 71 walks, and stole 29 bases in 33 tries. As a result he scored 63 runs in 88 games. That's a great ratio, but not unusual for him.

Even being absent from the Pads for the last two months, Rickey still scored more runs in his 88 games with San Diego than Chris Gomez, Wally Joyner, or Greg Vaughn did over the full season.

A HANDY-DANDY CHART FOR JERRY COLEMAN

Player, Pos., Team	Pronunciation
Quilvio Veras, 2B, Padres	KILL-vee-oh VARE-us
Dario Veras, P, Padres	DARR-e-oh VARE-us
Randy Veres, P, TBA	RAN-dee VARE-ess
Dave Veres, P, Rockies	DAVE VEERZ

237

1997 TEAM STATISTICS

BATTING/BASERUNNING

	Raw	Rank	+/- %		Raw	Rank	+/- %		Raw	Rank	+/- %
R	795	2	+7	BA	.271	2	+3	SB	140	5	+8
R/G	4.91	2	+7	HR	152	7	-2	CS	60	6	0
OBA	.342	5	+3	LH	291	13	-7	SB%	70.0	5	+3
SA	.407	6	-1	BB	604	4	+10				
PRO	.749	4	+1	SO	1,129	11	+3				

PITCHING/FIELDING

	Raw	Rank	+/- %		Raw	Rank	+/- %		Raw	Rank	+/- %
OR	891	13	+20	BA	.280	13	+7	OSB	171	13	+35
RA/G	5.50	13	+20	HR	172	11	+11	OCS	75	14	+28
OOB	.352	13	+6	LH	327	9	+5	OSB%	69.5	8	+3
OSA	.435	12	+6	BB	596	12	+7	FA	.979	13	0
PRO	.787	13	+6	SO	1,059	11	-4	GDP	102	4	-14

BATTING BY LINEUP SLOTS

	R	HR	RBI	BA	OBA	SA
1	119	13	58	.250	.363	.352
2	117	20	72	.311	.372	.457
3	100	18	138	.324	.373	.496
4	118	31	109	.294	.391	.504
5	94	27	119	.271	.336	.456
6	60	12	77	.261	.331	.364
7	60	8	70	.245	.308	.334
8	64	13	67	.278	.331	.396
9	63	10	51	.186	.250	.276

BATTING BY DEFENSIVE POSITION

	R	HR	RBI	BA	OBA	SA
C	57	13	63	.273	.314	.390
1B	78	17	91	.308	.382	.457
2B	90	7	57	.266	.349	.350
3B	103	28	111	.279	.371	.471
SS	73	5	62	.257	.327	.332
LF	98	19	79	.246	.348	.377
CF	114	31	102	.252	.317	.454
RF	115	20	126	.363	.409	.534
DH	6	3	8	.216	.310	.486
PH	34	7	44	.247	.332	.371
P	18	2	18	.127	.160	.175

TEAM PITCHING

	W-L	CG	QS	QS%	<6	>6	IPS	IP	ERA	OPR
ROTATION	47-62	5	67	41	37	50	5.8	933.2	4.98	.793

	W-L	GR	SV	BSV	HD	BHD	IRS%	IP	ERA	OPR
BULLPEN	29-24	426	43	20	117	80	41	516.1	5.00	.775

1998 PROJECTIONS

BATTING

PLAYER	BA	G	AB	R	H	2B	3B	HR	RBI	BB	SO	SB	CS	SA	OBA
Arias, George	.241	39	137	20	33	8	1	3	18	11	21	1	0	.375	.296
Caminiti, Ken	.289	130	470	83	136	28	0	27	90	68	96	10	3	.518	.379
Cianfrocco, Archi	.262	63	154	19	40	9	1	3	23	14	52	3	1	.391	.326
Finley, Steve	.274	141	560	102	153	30	6	24	81	47	81	19	6	.475	.330
Giovanola, Ed	.260	35	111	16	29	5	2	1	11	16	19	1	0	.358	.355
Gomez, Chris	.260	134	462	56	120	19	2	6	50	51	101	4	6	.346	.334
Gwynn, Tony	.349	143	566	86	197	40	2	12	95	40	23	12	5	.491	.392
Hernandez, Carlos	.293	94	227	23	67	10	1	5	23	8	49	0	3	.419	.318
Joyner, Wally	.302	139	478	62	144	30	1	12	81	61	61	3	5	.442	.381
Myers, Greg	.266	87	252	31	67	15	1	6	37	19	44	0	0	.409	.316
Romero, Mandy	.217	24	76	12	16	4	0	3	11	8	17	1	0	.384	.290
Sheets, Andy	.230	57	194	27	45	9	0	7	22	19	62	2	0	.382	.299
Sweeney, Mark	.276	73	112	14	31	5	0	2	16	16	21	2	1	.368	.368
Vaughn, Greg	.231	107	351	62	81	11	0	21	64	54	96	7	3	.442	.334
Veras, Quilvio	.267	146	531	80	141	22	2	4	42	82	84	36	15	.341	.365

239

PITCHING

PITCHER	W	L	SV	ERA	G	GS	IP	H	HR	BB	SO
Ashby, Andy	8	8	0	3.92	26	26	170	173	15	43	118
Bergman, Sean	3	4	0	5.18	29	10	76	90	9	28	56
Boehringer, Brian	3	4	0	4.11	32	2	57	51	6	37	56
Brown, Kevin	15	10	0	2.79	32	32	232	211	10	58	183
Cunnane, Will	3	1	0	5.44	26	4	43	52	5	22	37
Hamilton, Joey	10	7	0	4.15	28	27	178	179	18	64	124
Hitchcock, Sterling	10	8	0	5.00	29	26	151	164	21	54	102
Hoffman, Trevor	7	5	38	2.89	70	0	81	59	9	26	105
Kroon, Mark	0	4	0	4.74	39	0	38	38	6	15	39
Long, Joey	0	0	0	6.72	23	0	25	36	2	17	19
Menhart, Paul	3	3	0	4.78	9	8	45	47	5	16	26
Miceli, Dan	3	3	3	4.69	50	2	65	63	10	30	58
Murray, Heath	5	4	0	3.47	20	13	80	85	5	27	55
Smith, Pete	7	8	0	4.95	39	18	136	142	22	53	75
Veras, Dario	4	2	0	4.20	38	0	43	44	7	19	35
Vosberg, Ed	3	3	2	4.05	64	0	55	61	4	23	41
Wall, Donne	3	3	0	4.42	8	8	49	51	7	13	29
Wengert, Don	3	5	1	4.97	23	8	71	84	11	22	35
Clement, Matt	5	4	0	3.14	11	11	77	81	4	31	67

SAN FRANCISCO GIANTS

MANAGEMENT

Manager	General Manager	Owner
Dusty Baker Career Record 383-362 .514	Brian Sabean	Peter Magowan

1997 RECORD

Won-Lost	Pct.	Division Finish/GB	Wild Card Finish/GB
90-72	.556	1 W	

Preseason Consensus Projection	4 (3.57)

1st Half	2nd Half	Home	Road	Intradivision	Interleague
47-34	43-38	48-33	42-39	22-14	10-6

Comebacks	Blowouts	Nailbiters
11-8	17-20	42-32

SMOKE AND MIRRORS?

At first glance, the 1997 Giants looked like anything but a championship club. Most of their players did not sport impressive statistics. Their opening day starting pitcher was Mark Gardner. Their top RBI man batted .250. Only three pitchers won in double figures. Their top pinch hitter was Marvin Benard.

But it didn't matter. The Giants topped the NL West, winning 90 games and losing just 72, despite being outscored by their opponents! San Francisco finished fourth in the NL in runs and just ninth in team ERA, but wound up an astonishing 18 games over .500 anyway, racking up the third-best record in the National League.

How the hell did they do that?

Sometimes, a few really good seasons from a few really good players can carry a team to the top (especially in a weak four-team division), and that's what the Giants had.

Most of the team's players were of just average or slightly above-average quality. There were really four irreplaceable Giants in 1997, and they were:

Barry Bonds. Ho-hum. Another great year: 40 homers, 123 runs, 101 RBIs, .291 average, and 145 walks. A .446 on-base percentage. Of his 40 homers, six tied games and 13 gave the Giants the lead, and almost all of them were real-live, honest-to-goodness late-inning shots. He also threw out ten baserunners from left field.

Shawn Estes. He came from (nearly) nowhere to serve as the Giants' ace, posting 19 victories in 32 starts. He's still raw, even though he's a seven-year pro, but last summer at age 24 he came into his own. Estes should be an outstanding pitcher for years.

J.T. Snow. Finally giving the Giants good production from first base—something they hadn't had in five years—Snow had the finest season of his career, albeit in almost total obscurity. He may be the game's best defensive first baseman, and he both drove in runs and got on base.

Kirk Rueter. His 13-6 record was good, and his 3.45 ERA was fine as well, but what was most important about Rueter's performance was the way he picked it up down the stretch. With Mark Gardner unable to pitch due to a tired arm and a family illness, Rueter was 4-0 in September with a 1.97 ERA in five starts. There were times when he was absolutely untouchable, something that few who had seen him in his early years with Montreal would ever have thought the finesse southpaw could be.

Those were the four most important players on the team. Some may argue that Jeff Kent's 121 RBIs were irreplaceable, but that's not so. The point isn't that the RBIs were replaceable, but that Kent himself was. He happened to have his best year, a good year but well short of a great year, batting behind the best player in the NL. A really good player would have driven in 140. It is silly to suggest, as some did in September, that Kent was having an MVP-type season. He had nothing of the kind.

Darryl Hamilton, Bill Mueller, Jose Vizcaino, and Stan Javier were all solid or better defenders who made consistent if unspectacular offensive contributions. Brian Johnson came over in July and hit 11 homers in 179 at bats.

The supporting cast of pitchers was important as well. Closer Rod Beck (signed by the Cubs in the off-season) had some rough times, blowing eight save chances but still converting 37. Roberto Hernandez came over in a trade from the White Sox and went 5-2 with four saves and a 2.48 ERA. Wilson Alvarez, acquired in the same deal, had some good and some poor games, while Gardner started hot and faded. Julian Tavarez pitched 89 times for the Giants, while Rich Rodriguez took the hill 71 times. Both were unheralded but important contributors, and righthander Doug Henry had his moments as well.

When you look carefully at the season, not to take anything away from the team's achievement, the Giants were really an average team that was carried to glory by a handful of outstanding performers. That's certainly not something they should be ashamed of, however; most major league teams have average players plus a few stars. But not all those teams pull together and win, and few of them have their own Barry Bonds.

TEAM MVP

The big performances from Shawn Estes, J.T. Snow, and Jeff Kent were happy surprises for the Giants. The monster year from **Barry Bonds** (.291, 40 homers, 143 walks, 37 steals) was not, but San Francisco wouldn't have been close without him. Bonds, media disdain and all, is still one of the three best all-around players in baseball.

BIGGEST SURPRISE

In previous years **J.T. Snow** had shown sparks of talent, but had never sustained a full-season pace. In 1997 he was spectacular (as usual) in the field and hit very well. Although Snow batted just .188 with one homer against lefthanders, he really cleaned up against righties (.312, 27 homers in 398 at-bats) and was on base all year. He was worth two Allen Watsons last year, although the Giants had to give up just one.

BIGGEST DISAPPOINTMENT

San Francisco benefited from a strong team effort in 1996, but two players didn't make the cut. Right fielder **Glenallen Hill**'s mediocre, uninspired play led to a late-summer benching, and he will not be back in 1998. Meanwhile, young righthander **William VanLandingham**, considered a potential No. 1 starter two years ago, was 4-7 with a 4.96 ERA in 18 games before being outrighted to Triple A in August.

241

THE MOMENT OF TRUTH

On September 17 the Giants stood two games behind the Dodgers with 11 to play. Los Angeles invaded Candlestick Park for two critical games. After pulling out a 2-1 squeaker, the Giants stood one out on September 18. That night the Giants jumped out to a 5-1 lead but allowed two in the sixth and two in the seventh. The game stayed tied 5-5 until the bottom of the twelfth, when catcher **Brian Johnson** led off with a homer that sent 52,000 crazed San Francisco fans screaming into the night and killed the Dodgers. While the Giants won seven of their next nine, Los Angeles lost its next three and fell permanently out of the race.

That's the legacy of the 1997 Giants: they won. Of course, doing it again in '98 will be a bigger challenge.

ARE YOU SURE THESE ARE THE GIANTS?

Well, they're not the 1996 Giants, that's for sure. That club was a truly awful, ugly aggregation, and its memory has already been almost fully eradicated. Rookie general manager Brian Sabean did a remarkable job remaking the team.

Back in '96, the Giants finished in last place in the NL West with a pathetic 68-94 record, their second straight season bringing up the rear. Not too good. The team was unathletic, often hurt, and just plain bland. The infield consisted of first basemen Mark Carreon and David McCarty, second baseman Robby Thompson, shortstop Shawon Dunston, and third baseman Matt Williams. The outfield? Barry Bonds, Stan Javier, and Glenallen Hill. The catchers were Tom Lampkin, Kirt Manwaring, and Rick Wilkins.

Sabean redid almost the entire starting lineup through a series of trades, signings, and promotions. He picked up Mark Lewis and Jose Vizcaino for the left side of the infield

and Jeff Kent and J.T. Snow on the right side. He ended up with an excellent unit, although it cost the team Bay Area fan favorite Williams (for which Sabean took a lot of heat until it was clear the team was a contender).

In the pasture, Bonds remained a fixture in left field. Darryl Hamilton took over in center while Hill (one of the '97 Giants' few outright disappointments) ultimately lost his job in right to Javier. Taking over behind the plate were Wilkins and, at midseason, Brian Johnson, brought over in a trade from Detroit.

Of the 49 players the Giants used in 1996, just 19 of them wore the uniform in 1997, with several of those not finishing the season with the club. The makeover was completed by the beginning of August. On July 31 the Giants skimmed Wilson Alvarez, Roberto Hernandez, and Danny Darwin from the White Sox in exchange for some half-good prospects and a couple of really hot ones. The next day, Wilkins, another letdown, was waived to Seattle.

Left to mold this new cast into a cohesive club was manager Dusty Baker. Many of Baker's present and former players profess deep respect and admiration for his ability to balance egos and get the most out of his players. After two years of finishing last with a cruddy club, he took an average club to the top.

NO MIGHT FROM THE RIGHT

The Giants used righthanded starting pitchers only 82 times last year, and the tally board isn't encouraging:

Pitcher	Starts	By End of Season Was ...
Mark Gardner	30	On leave to be with his ailing wife
W. VanLandingham	17	Waived, then re-signed to a Triple A deal
O. Fernandez	11	Injured
Keith Foulke	8	Traded
Danny Darwin	7	In the rotation
Pat Rapp	6	In the rotation
Joe Roa	3	Back in the minors

Gardner is signed for 1998. The Giants hope Fernandez can recover from his elbow problems and make a comeback, though the team's original expectations for the now 29-year-old finesse pitcher were unrealistically high. Rapp might be

242

back in 1998, but he was cut loose after the season.

To shore up the staff, San Francisco signed the consummate veteran pitcher, Orel Hershiser, in the off-season. No one around the game questions Hershiser's determination, intelligence, work ethic, experience, or record. None the less, by the end of the World Series, a lot of people around the game were questioning his ability to get good hitters out: his 4.47 ERA in '97 was the worst of his long career. If it is true, as was reported in October, that Orel is doctoring the ball to survive, the Giants may be very disappointed.

POLE-AXED

The Giants canned pitching coach Dick Pole at the end of the season. The talk around Baghdad by the Bay was that former Dodgers pitching coach Ron Perranoski (brought in for '97 to be Dusty Baker's bench coach) had a better rapport with the players and the media. (Baker, however, wanted both men to stay.) San Francisco's pitching has generally been very good in the last few years, even though many of the pitchers themselves have been young and unheralded.

The thinking behind this move and the Orel Hershiser signing may be that, because Estes and Rueter have developed, the Giants can afford to go after some veteran pitchers. As the staff matures, someone older and more relaxed like Perranoski may be needed, rather than an aggressive younger teacher, as Pole is. Salary could have also had something to do with the decision.

THINK LONG-TERM

GM Brian Sabean's trade register since July 1996, when he effectively took over from departing GM Bob Quinn:

Gained	Given Up
Kirk Rueter, Tim Scott	Mark Leiter
Jeff Kent, Julian Tavarez, Jose Vizcaino, Joe Roa	Matt Williams, Trent Hubbard

BEST DEAL

Getting **J.T. Snow** from Anaheim for **Allen Watson** was a tremendous trade, although one couldn't have predicted so at the time; Snow had never had a good full season in the major leagues. Another terrific deal was snagging **Jose Vizcaino**, **Julian Tavarez**, **Jeff Kent**, and **Joe Roa** from the Indians last winter for **Matt Williams** and **Trent Hubbard**. In addition to acquiring three players who played major roles in the club's NL West win, dealing Williams eased the payroll and opened up third base for **Bill Mueller**.

WORST DEAL

At the time, it looked like a fine trade. The July 31 blockbuster that brought **Wilson Alvarez**, **Roberto Hernandez**, and **Danny Darwin** to San Francisco for six prospects looked like a great way to bolster the Giants' pitching not only for the short haul but the long haul. But San Fran showed little apparent interest in inking either Alvarez or Hernandez, and what they got was a two-month rental of three pitchers in exchange for a couple of terrific prospects (righthanded pitcher **Lorenzo Barcelo** and shortstop **Michael Caruso**). As a result of this and other deals, the Giants' farm system is now almost totally decimated.

243

Gained	**Given Up**
J.T. Snow	Allen Watson
Mark Lewis	Jesse Ibarra
Travis Thurmond	Rich DeLucia
Brian Johnson	Marcus Jensen
Pat Rapp	Brandon Leese, Bobby Rector
Wilson Alvarez, Danny Darwin, Roberto Hernandez	Keith Foulke and six minor-leaguers
Robb Nen	Joe Fontenot, Mike Villano, Mick Pageler
Charlie Hayes	Chris Singleton, Alberto Castillo

No one who looks at that list should fail to be suitably impressed. However, trading well is not the only job of a GM, and it's not even the most important job if you're team isn't close to the top. Building and maintaining a solid organization from top to bottom is critical to long-term success, as the Dodgers have shown for a half-century. Several general managers have made big reputations by hornswoggling other teams for a few years, only to find that it doesn't matter when your team is at the bottom of the league. Bill Lajoie and Lee Thomas are good recent examples.

Lajoie was king of the hill in Detroit in 1984, with a reputation as a fearsome trader and an astute judge of talent. Yet his talented world champion Tigers lapsed into mediocrity after their only World Series victory, and all of Lajoie's desperation moves couldn't compensate for a wretched farm system. Lajoie never got another management job after leaving Detroit.

Thomas was king of the hill in Philadelphia in 1993, with a trade résumé that looked so good people, wondered why other GMs even answered the phone when he called. Yet his one World Series team, the overachieving and over-the-hill Phillies, collapsed so swiftly that it seemed like '93 was a mirage. Thomas built his reputation on trades while neglecting player development; in return, he produced

only one winning season in nine years and lost his job last winter. Whether he gets another chance at the helm remains to be seen.

THE PROGNOSIS

This Giants team may not be ready to win again in 1998. Bonds, if healthy, will have another big season, and the young pitchers should continue to perform well. However, some of the other players on the team are getting up there in years, and a lot of potential free agents are really old already. Sabean won't have much time to rest on his laurels. There are a lot of questions about the '98 Giants yet to be answered:

Can the relief pitching hold up? It's not clear who will set up for new closer Robb Nen. Who will be the Giants' top righthanded starter? Can young Dante Powell break into the outfield this season? They won't need to sign or trade for Terry Mulholland again, will they? Can Charlie Hayes stay happy and contribute if he's platooning with Bill Mueller at third? The club is short on the bench as well, despite having added a steady veteran backup/platoon catcher in Brent Mayne.

The Giants were apparently never in the running to re-sign either Wilson Alvarez or Roberto Hernandez, both of whom were loaded down with sacks of gold by Tampa Bay. Orel Hershiser, signed in early December, is a gamble due to his age (39) and recent decline.

Jose Vizcaino's departure to the Dodgers as a free agent in December indicates that the Giants intend to give Rich Aurilia a chance at the everyday shortstop job in spring training (if they don't sign Shawon Dunston instead). Aurilia clearly has the defensive skills to start in the major leagues. His bat has always been the question: Aurilia hit just .234 in a full season at Double A in 1994 and only .239 in 318 at bats for the Giants in 1996.

Last year Aurilia batted .275 for the Giants in 102 at bats, evenly split against lefties (.280) and righties (.269). If Aurilia, who is 28 in September, hits .270 with eight homers, he'll be an improvement over Vizcaino because he'll be millions of dollars cheaper and just as good.

Despite the plethora of questions, this franchise is immeasurably stronger, more secure, and more fun to watch than it was one short year earlier.

244

LUMBER PARTY

Three Giants drove in more than 100 runs in 1997: Jeff Kent, J.T. Snow, and Barry Bonds. The last time the Giants had three 100-RBI guys was in 1947. Who were they? (Answer below.) Clue: one's a Hall of Famer, one was a six-time All Star catcher, and the other was a three-time All Star outfielder.

Answer: Johnny Mize, Walker Cooper, and Willard Marshall.

TOP PROSPECTS
SPRING 1998

1. **Russ Ortiz, P.** Ortiz has one of the best fastballs in the minor leagues and is on course to become either a starter or a power closer in the majors. The Giants used him as a starter this year at both Double A and Triple A in order to help him further develop his breaking and off-speed stuff. He didn't dominate in 1997 as he had in his two previous seasons (6-6, 4.96 combined at Double A and Triple A), but he made significant progress toward becoming a more complete pitcher. He could start this season in San Francisco's rotation.

2. **Jacob Cruz, OF.** The lefthanded-hitting Cruz, 25, was way ahead of the Pacific Coast League competition last year and belongs in the majors in some capacity. However, since he has only line-drive power and average speed and range, his claim as an everyday player is tenuous. If he could play center field, Cruz would certainly have a job. He does have the arm strength to play right.

3. **Wilson Delgado, SS.** Delgado, just 22, is a slick defensive shortstop who came from Seattle in the Shawn Estes deal. He hit .288 at Triple A Phoenix last season with nine homers and can play a big league shortstop. While Delgado does not yet draw walks or steal bases, his tools are excellent and he is expected be a major-league starter within two years. Watch for him in a bench role with the Giants sometime this season.

4. **Dante Powell, OF.** A first-round draft pick in 1994, Powell stalled last year at Triple A Phoenix after ripping apart the Texas League the season before. Powell has the speed, arm, and range to play center field and is expected to hit 20-plus homers in the big leagues. He needs to make progress if he wants the job by 1999.

5. **Darrin Blood, P.** The Giants like Blood because he has four quality pitches, but are alarmed by his control troubles. Last season he was 8-10 at Double A Shreveport, walking 83 men in 156 innings. He wins with his breaking pitches, but must establish his fastball in order to advance. Just 23, the righthander still has time to move up.

6. **Calvin Murray, OF.** He has disappointed since being the Giants' first-round pick in 1992. Last season, his third at Double A Shreveport, Murray stole 52 bases in 58 tries and batted .272 with 10 homers. A patient hitter who can play center in the bigs, Murray is an outstanding athlete who turns 27 this year and must turn it on quickly if he wants to have any kind of a major league career.

245

1997 TEAM STATISTICS

BATTING/BASERUNNING

	Raw	Rank	+/- %		Raw	Rank	+/- %		Raw	Rank	+/- %
R	784	4	+5	BA	.258	10	-2	SB	121	8	-7
R/G	4.84	4	+5	HR	172	4	+11	CS	49	13	-18
OBA	.337	6	+1	LH	303	9	-3	SB%	71.2	4	+5
SA	.414	5	+1	BB	642	2	+17				
PRO	.751	3	+1	SO	1,120	10	+2				

PITCHING/FIELDING

	Raw	Rank	+/- %		Raw	Rank	+/- %		Raw	Rank	+/- %
OR	793	11	+6	BA	.270	11	+3	OSB	108	5	-15
RA/G	4.90	11	+6	HR	160	7	+3	OCS	73	13	+24
OOB	.340	10	+2	LH	279	4	10	OSB%	59.7	2	-12
OSA	.412	8	+1	BB	578	10	+4	FA	.980	10	0
PRO	.752	9	+1	SO	1,044	12	-6	GDP	135	12	+13

BATTING BY LINEUP SLOTS

	R	HR	RBI	BA	OBA	SA
1	105	7	54	.255	.342	.340
2	93	7	57	.271	.337	.360
3	111	30	106	.287	.399	.527
4	111	35	119	.262	.359	.501
5	100	30	115	.258	.347	.471
6	90	23	107	.285	.357	.468
7	65	12	72	.258	.320	.399
8	60	23	75	.250	.309	.411
9	49	5	41	.188	.246	.246

BATTING BY DEFENSIVE POSITION

	R	HR	RBI	BA	OBA	SA
C	58	21	67	.229	.290	.376
1B	83	29	108	.271	.373	.488
2B	106	34	133	.264	.324	.501
3B	76	11	67	.278	.349	.412
SS	91	10	66	.266	.321	.373
LF	128	41	107	.289	.441	.579
CF	108	6	57	.278	.363	.362
RF	78	18	96	.260	.317	.409
DH	5	0	5	.242	.257	.333
PH	25	1	27	.267	.365	.367
P	16	1	13	.126	.161	.144

TEAM PITCHING

	W-L	CG	QS	QS%	<6	>6	IPS	IP	ERA	OPR
ROTATION	60-48	5	81	50	32	46	5.7	920.2	4.25	.743

	W-L	GR	SV	BSV	HD	BHD	IRS%	IP	ERA	OPR
BULLPEN	30-24	481	45	24	156	94	38	525.1	4.75	.769

1998 PROJECTIONS

BATTING

PLAYER	BA	G	AB	R	H	2B	3B	HR	RBI	BB	SO	SB	CS	SA	OBA
Aurilia, Rich	.266	96	253	30	67	12	0	7	33	21	41	3	1	.397	.322
Benard, Marvin	.255	38	89	15	23	3	1	1	7	11	18	4	2	.326	.335
Bonds, Barry	.277	160	539	116	150	26	5	38	105	138	80	36	8	.555	.424
Cruz, Jacob	.274	68	243	36	67	17	1	5	35	24	38	6	0	.414	.340
Delgado, Wilson	.256	44	147	15	38	8	1	3	18	8	30	2	0	.388	.293
Hamilton, Darryl	.281	132	505	81	142	25	4	6	47	58	59	15	7	.381	.355
Hayes, Charlie	.263	88	314	35	83	15	1	8	48	30	57	3	1	.396	.327
Javier, Stan	.282	120	393	64	111	19	3	7	43	46	64	24	3	.397	.357
Johnson, Brian	.268	121	373	36	100	17	2	13	54	18	56	1	1	.434	.302
Kent, Jeff	.262	153	560	84	147	35	2	24	100	43	118	8	3	.460	.314
Mayne, Brent	.278	79	206	21	57	10	0	4	17	16	29	1	1	.383	.331
Mirabelli, Doug	.228	18	58	7	13	4	0	1	7	9	15	0	0	.373	.330
Mueller, Bill	.295	133	421	56	124	29	3	6	46	51	71	3	3	.421	.371
Powell, Dante	.250	18	65	14	16	4	0	2	6	8	18	3	0	.403	.329
Snow, J.T.	.270	142	502	70	136	27	1	22	84	71	100	4	4	.459	.361

247

PITCHING

PITCHER	W	L	SV	ERA	G	GS	IP	H	HR	BB	SO
Darwin, Danny	6	10	0	4.50	29	22	144	160	23	36	84
Estes, Shawn	17	7	0	3.53	32	32	204	173	12	106	182
Fernandez, Osvaldo	5	8	0	4.71	20	20	109	130	15	34	65
Gardner, Mark	10	8	0	4.37	31	26	165	177	26	55	129
Hershiser, Orel	13	6	0	4.32	27	27	171	179	21	55	99
Johnstone, John	1	0	0	3.52	24	0	33	33	2	17	22
Nen, Robb	6	3	36	3.53	73	0	76	73	5	34	83
Poole, Jim	4	1	0	5.09	60	0	49	58	6	23	32
Reed, Steve	4	4	4	3.00	60	0	63	47	8	20	47
Rodriguez, Rich	4	4	1	3.55	64	0	61	62	6	21	33
Rueter, Kirk	13	8	0	3.70	34	34	194	203	19	52	111
Tavarez, Julian	5	3	0	4.17	63	1	73	79	6	25	38
Ortiz, Russ	3	3	0	3.35	12	12	64	55	5	27	45

FREE AGENT
1998 PROJECTIONS

PLAYER	BA	G	AB	R	H	2B	3B	HR	RBI	BB	SO	SB	CS	SA	OBA
Anthony, Eric	.250	45	92	13	23	4	1	4	10	14	24	1	1	.446	.349
Ashley, Billy	.234	83	158	17	37	6	0	8	25	17	60	0	0	.424	.309
Berblinger, Jeff	.250	33	124	14	31	4	2	2	13	12	28	4	0	.363	.316
Berroa, Geronimo	.279	141	523	83	146	24	1	26	85	60	106	3	3	.478	.353
Berry, Sean	.273	95	300	37	82	24	1	10	52	22	48	4	5	.460	.323
Brito, Tilson	.253	69	186	21	47	8	1	2	16	14	44	1	0	.339	.305
Brumfield, Jacob	.250	41	132	20	33	7	1	3	16	11	25	5	3	.386	.308
Candaele, Casey	.242	26	95	13	23	6	0	2	12	9	15	1	0	.368	.308
Canseco, Jose	.253	98	359	56	91	19	0	22	71	48	98	6	1	.490	.342
Carr, Chuck	.257	78	222	37	57	14	2	3	17	20	44	13	6	.378	.318
Cordero, Wil	.285	140	551	78	157	29	2	15	71	32	111	3	3	.426	.324
Daulton, Darren	.255	127	380	61	97	20	7	12	59	71	68	5	1	.439	.373
Dunston, Shawon	.301	123	452	60	136	22	5	12	53	10	69	23	6	.451	.316
Franco, Julio	.288	102	378	60	109	15	1	10	54	56	86	10	5	.413	.380
Franklin, Micah	.233	51	159	25	37	6	0	6	22	24	44	1	0	.384	.333
Garcia, Carlos	.266	90	320	38	85	18	2	4	31	17	55	11	4	.372	.303
Gilbert, Shawn	.232	33	95	16	22	4	0	3	10	12	26	4	0	.368	.318
Guillen, Ozzie	.272	125	427	56	116	21	6	3	46	17	24	5	4	.370	.300
Gulan, Mike	.241	42	145	17	35	6	2	4	20	9	52	1	0	.393	.286
Hamelin, Bob	.250	114	324	44	81	15	0	16	51	53	75	3	1	.444	.355
Henderson, Rickey	.251	103	342	71	86	14	1	7	29	81	67	33	8	.360	.395
Hill, Glenallen	.267	107	363	48	97	25	3	14	61	23	81	8	4	.468	.311
Howard, Thomas	.272	91	235	28	64	14	3	3	24	19	39	4	3	.396	.327
Incaviglia, Pete	.244	47	135	17	33	4	0	7	17	11	41	0	0	.430	.301
Johnson, Mark	.238	76	210	31	50	11	0	7	28	35	60	3	2	.390	.347
Karkovice, Ron	.222	37	108	13	24	5	0	4	15	10	29	0	0	.380	.288
Kirby, Wayne	.257	36	105	17	27	5	1	3	12	9	17	4	0	.410	.316
Lemke, Mark	.261	95	322	36	84	14	1	3	26	34	41	2	1	.339	.331
Lennon, Pat	.284	71	148	19	42	8	1	1	16	21	45	0	1	.372	.373
Liriano, Nelson	.268	43	71	8	19	5	0	1	10	5	9	0	0	.380	.316
Mashore, Damon	.253	102	289	57	73	12	2	4	21	51	86	6	4	.349	.365
May, Derrick	.258	59	128	12	33	6	1	2	16	11	20	2	1	.367	.317
Merced, Orlando	.278	96	360	49	100	21	2	11	50	43	58	6	3	.439	.355
Meulens, Hensley	.223	56	184	29	41	7	1	9	27	22	64	5	0	.418	.306

248

PLAYER	BA	G	AB	R	H	2B	3B	HR	RBI	BB	SO	SB	CS	SA	OBA
Morgan, Kevin	.245	14	53	6	13	2	0	0	4	6	7	1	0	.283	.322
Mouton, James	.248	70	165	23	41	9	1	2	20	18	31	11	6	.352	.322
Obando, Sherman	.212	41	66	8	14	3	0	3	10	8	19	1	0	.394	.297
Orsulak, Joe	.248	70	121	14	30	8	1	1	10	12	17	0	1	.355	.316
Phillips, Tony	.268	121	459	87	123	25	2	10	49	91	103	11	8	.397	.389
Plantier, Phil	.242	58	157	20	38	7	0	6	23	19	38	1	2	.401	.324
Pose, Scott	.277	59	166	35	46	6	4	1	19	21	25	6	0	.380	.358
Pride, Curtis	.247	76	170	28	42	7	4	4	20	22	45	7	4	.406	.333
Raabe, Brian	.280	49	193	28	54	10	1	4	22	11	10	0	0	.404	.319
Ramos, Ken	.283	39	99	12	28	3	0	0	9	18	7	1	0	.313	.393
Reed, Jody	.246	23	69	7	17	3	0	0	7	8	8	1	1	.290	.325
Rose, Pete	.234	35	128	16	30	7	0	5	20	8	26	0	0	.406	.279
Sagmoen, Marc	.262	36	126	14	33	10	2	2	14	8	36	1	0	.421	.306
Sanchez, Rey	.275	119	338	38	93	19	0	2	24	18	48	5	5	.349	.312
Sanders, Deion	.281	104	420	54	118	14	7	5	26	33	67	45	13	.383	.333
Sheldon, Scott	.231	46	156	23	36	10	2	5	20	15	46	1	0	.417	.298
Shipley, Craig	.282	55	131	19	37	7	0	3	16	5	19	3	1	.405	.309
Sierra, Ruben	.256	33	121	14	31	6	1	3	17	12	23	1	1	.397	.323
Tavarez, Jesus	.267	41	120	24	32	4	2	1	13	14	19	7	0	.358	.343
Thurman, Gary	.259	22	54	8	14	3	0	0	6	9	15	2	0	.315	.365
Tinsley, Lee	.250	47	116	16	29	5	1	1	9	11	34	4	3	.336	.315
Whiten, Mark	.256	68	215	36	55	10	0	8	30	32	56	6	3	.414	.352
Williams, Eddie	.234	58	192	31	45	8	0	12	32	17	43	1	0	.464	.297

249

ABOUT THE AUTHORS

Gary Gillette is a nationally recognized baseball author, analyst, and consultant. He is the Executive Editor of Total Baseball Daily and is the founder of The Baseball Workshop, which is now a part of Total Sports.

Gillette is a contributor to *Total Baseball*, the official encyclopedia of Major League Baseball. His books include *The Scouting Report: 1995* and *1996* and the *Great American Baseball Stat Book 1992-1994*. He has also contributed to many other books and periodicals, including *USA Today, Baseball Weekly, Baseball Weekly Almanac, Baseball Today, Bill Mazeroski's Baseball, Ultimate Sports Baseball,* and *The Baseball Blue Book*.

In addition to his writing, Gillette has provided baseball commentary for several National Public Radio stations for more than ten years and has served as a consultant to prominent player agents as well as an expert witness in baseball-related litigation.

Assisting Gary Gillette in *The Spy* is Total Baseball Daily Managing Editor Stuart Shea. Shea has contributed to many baseball annuals, including the *Baseball Almanac, Ultimate Sports Baseball,* and *The Scouting Report*.

WEB SITE

To stay *au courant* throughout the 1998 baseball season, be sure to check out *The Spy*'s web site (http://BaseballSpy98.TotalSports.net) for news, articles, updated rosters and projections, spring injury information, etc. While visiting *The Spy*'s web site, you can also sign up for Total Baseball Daily, which will deliver a daily dose of baseball news & views to your e-mail address all year long.